Cultural Materialism

UPDATED EDITION

2 5

Cultural Materialism

The Struggle for a Science of Culture

UPDATED EDITION

Marvin Harris

With an Introduction by
Allen Johnson and Orna Johnson

ALTAMIRA
PRESS

A Division of Rowman & Littlefield Publishers, Inc.
Walnut Creek • Lanham • New York • Oxford

Grateful acknowledgment is made to the following for permission to reprint previously published material:

American Folklore Society: Excerpt from *Bella Bella Tales* by Franz Boas, Memoirs of the American Folklore Society, Vol. 25, 1932. Annual Reviews, Inc.: Excerpt from "Adaptation" by Alexander Alland, *Annual Review of Anthropology*, Vol. 4, Copyright © 1975 by Annual Reviews, Inc. Barnard College: Excerpt from "Structuralism and Ecology" by Claude Lévi-Strauss, *Barnard Alumnae Magazine*, Spring 1972. Copyright © 1972, Associate Alumnae of Barnard College. Beacon Press: Excerpt from *The Elementary Structures of Kinship* by Claude Levi-Strauss. Revised edition translated from the French by James Harle Bell, John Richard von Sturmer, and Rodney Needham. Translation Copyright © 1969 by Beacon Press. Reprinted by permission of Beacon Press. George Foster: Excerpt from *Tzintzuntzan: Mexican Peasants in a Changing World* by George Foster. Published by Little, Brown and Company 1967. International Publishers: Excerpt from Eleanor Leacock's Introduction to F. Engels's *Origins of the Family, Private Property and the State*, 1972. *Journal of Asian and African Studies:* Excerpt from "Reflections on the African Revolution: The Point of the Biafran Case" by Stanley Diamond. *Peking Review:* Excerpt from "The Task of Continuing the Revolution Under the Dictatorship of the Proletariat" by Wu Chiang. *Philosophy of Science:* Excerpt from "The Rationality of Scientific Discovery" by Nicholas Maxwell. Karl R. Popper: Excerpt from *The Logic of Scientific Discovery* by Karl R. Popper. London: Hutchinson, 1959, 9th impression 1977; published in New York by Basic Books and Harper & Row. Rand McNally and Company: Diagram by Douglas White, "Mathematical Anthropology," from *Handbook of Social and Cultural Anthropology*, John Honigmann, ed. Copyright © 1973 Rand McNally College Publishing Co. Reprinted by permission. Random House, Inc.: Excerpts from *Reinventing Anthropology*, Dell Hymes, ed. Selection from "Toward a Reflective and Critical Anthroplogy" by Rober Scholte, Copyright © 1972 by Random House, Inc. Selection from "Anthropology in Question" by Stanley Diamond, Copyright © 1971 by Stanley Diamond. Sage Publications, Inc.: Excerpts from "Marxism, Maoism and Social Change: A Ee-Examination of the the 'Voluntarism' in Mao's Strategy and Thought" by Andrew G. Walder. Reprinted from *Modern China*, Vol. 3, No. 2 (April 1977) by permission of the Publisher, Sage Publications, Inc.

ALTAMIRA PRESS
A Division of Rowman & Littlefield
Publishers, Inc.
1630 North Main Street, #367
Walnut Creek, CA 94596
www.altamirapress.com

Rowman & Littlefield Publishers, Inc.
4720 Boston Way
Lanham, MD 20706

12 Hid's Copse Road
Cumnor Hill, Oxford OX2 9JJ, England

British Library Cataloguing in Publication
Information Available

Library of Congress Cataloging-in-Publication Data

Harris, Marvin, 1927–
    Cultural materialism : the struggle for a science of culture / Marvin Harris; with an introduction by Allen Johnson and Orna Johnson.—Updated ed.
    p. cm.
    Includes bibliographical references (p.) and index.
        ISBN 0-7591-0134-5 (cloth : alk. paper) – ISBN 0-7591-0135-3 (pbk. : alk. paper)
    1. Ethnology—Philosophy. 2. Culture. 3. Marxist anthropology. 4. Social evolution. I. Title.
GN357.H37 2001
306—dc21   2001034094

Printed in the United States of America

⊖™ The paper used in this publication meets the minimum requirements of American National Standard for Information Sciences—Permanence of Paper for Printed Library Materials, ANSI/NISO Z39.48–1992.

Contents

Introduction to the Updated Edition

Allen Johnson and Orna Johnson

CULTURAL MATERIALISM (*CM*) was first published in 1979. At that time Marvin Harris was widely regarded as the leading theorist in anthropology. Yet a critical and interpretative move in cultural anthropology was already well underway that was strongly antiscience and dismissive of materialistic explanations of human behavior in particular, and ultimately of any kind of causal explanation. That move so fascinated journalists both within anthropology and in the larger literate community that the steady accumulation of knowledge in support of cultural materialist theory, both in cultural anthropology and archaeology, was largely overlooked. But this development was, as often is the case in intellectual fashion, a pendulum that ultimately swung too far in the other direction, exposing the intrinsically destructive relativism of antiscience (D'Andrade 1995; Harris 1995). The critical, interpretive anthropologists were in danger of becoming like the child in the classroom who goes around kicking over other people's blocks. This is a good time to revisit a research orientation that develops strong theories that are frankly exposed to challenge on logical and empirical grounds and that equally develops specific and direct critiques of competing theories.

Harris's cultural materialism is an effort to develop a scientific theory of culture, "to create a pan-human science of society whose findings can be accepted on logical and evidentiary grounds by the pan-human community" (*CM*:xii). For Harris, science has two great strengths: first, as a communal enterprise in which agreement among a community of scholars is based on evidence that is rigorously tested and challenged; and second, as a source of strong theories, that is, theories that make specific predictions that can be supported (or not supported) with reference to evidence.

Scientists, however, do not always agree on the evidence. On the contrary, they frequently contend vehemently about what constitutes evidence and whether certain evidence is sufficient to make a case. But it is the *process* of contending about evidence that differentiates science from other forms of knowing: Scientists want to know how what is being claimed as evidence was *measured*, and they set standards for what constitutes adequate measurement of what is being explained. In keeping with the scientific method, cultural materialism focuses on entities and events that are observable and quantifiable and uses operations that are capable of being replicated (*CM*:27).

A good example is an early paper, "The Economy Has No Surplus?" (Harris 1959). In this classic essay, Harris took on the argument by Harry Pearson that attempted to debunk the scientific theory that cultural complexity depends on the capacity to produce a surplus above the basic needs of the producer households. Pearson made the cultural relativist argument that surplus only exists in the minds of the members of a particular cultural community: they could either choose to work harder to produce more than they needed, or they could just produce enough to live on and then stop working and enjoy leisure activities. In effect, Pearson argued that an acceptable standard of living is a cultural construct, varying from one culture to another.

Harris responded sensibly by pointing out that a minimum standard of living could be objectively measured. For example, scientists can set reasonable standards for diet, below which people begin to suffer such measurable conditions as protein-calorie malnutrition or scurvy. Cultural relativism in such cases comes up against hard biological realities. Pearson's argument, Harris (1959:188) writes, becomes merely another effort to persuade us "that cultural phenomena are essentially the result of whimsical and capricious processes."

Such reasoning led Harris (1964b) early in his career to write a book that influenced a whole generation of students (Murphy and Margolis 1995; A. Johnson 1996; Dehavenon 1977; O. Johnson 1980). In *The Nature of Cultural Things*, Harris pointed out that anthropological concepts are abstractions that should be judged by the degree that they are related to the ongoing "behavior stream" (Sanjek 1995:46). Here Harris developed the argument that culture was not only the content of people's minds, but actually was constituted of patterns of behavior that could be measured. People in separate cultures differ not only in the way they think, but in how they behave: from how they make a living to the content of their social activities, art, and rituals. This ultimately led him to make one of his major theoretical contributions in elaborating the distinction between *emics* and *etics*.

The distinction originated with the linguist Pike (1967), and some discussion followed about whether Harris and Pike attribute the same meaning to the terms (Headland, Pike, and Harris 1990). But Harris's intent is clear: The concepts and categories applied by members of a cultural community to their own lives and the world in which they live (emics) are to be kept distinct from the categories employed by anthropologists in describing and understanding them (etics). Emics and etics thus represent two perspectives for viewing and interpreting cultural phenomena (Harris and Johnson 2000).

Emic knowledge represents views of thoughts and behavior from the perspective of the participants.	Etic knowledge represents views of thought and behavior from the perspective of the observer/researcher.
Emic descriptions are regarded as meaningful and appropriate by members of the culture being studied.	Etic descriptions are expressed in terms of categories that are regarded as meaningful and appropriate by the community of scientific observers.
Emic knowledge may not be applicable for generating scientific theories.	Etic observations are designed to be applicable for generating theories of cross-cultural differences and similarities.
Emic knowledge achieves the status of "emic" by passing the test of informant consensus.	Etic knowledge is obtained through direct observation or elicitation, or through participants trained to be observers.
Emic descriptions describe what is culturally meaningful, rather than what is theoretically significant.	Etic descriptions do not have to be meaningful or appropriate to members of the culture to be deemed valid.

In a scientific anthropology, the "etic grid" is ideally the shared standards of measurement to be used in describing cultural phenomena. By accepting the etic grid, one puts oneself on the line. For example, in continuing his commitment to measure "surplus," Harris compiled data on the per capita output of individuals at different levels of technological complexity to show a dramatic increase in energy output (Harris and Johnson 2000: 69–70). He may be correct or incorrect, but by specifying that the !Kung foragers and Tsembaga horticulturalists produce about 700 calories per capita while the Chinese peasants of Luts'un produce about 5,400, he exposes himself to criticism. Other scientists now have a target to expand upon or criticize. Has Harris measured production correctly, and do his measures support his argument (derived from Leslie White 1949) that increased energy production correlates with increased social complexity?

For Harris, these are not esoteric scholarly matters. A scientific anthropology holds the promise that we can build knowledge on which to base effective action. Science is the predominant system of knowledge that can claim to build reliable knowledge that accumulates over time. While art and philosophy may change over time, it is always possible to argue that ancient arts and philosophies are as true today as they ever were. Not so with science, which does reliably identify past errors and moves on. The hope that science brings to anthropology inspired one of Harris's most eloquent passages in this book:

Granted that discrepancies between science as an ideal and science as it is practiced substantially reduce the difference between science, religion, and other modes of looking for the truth. But it is precisely as an ideal that the uniqueness of science deserves to be defended. No other way of knowing is based on a set of rules explicitly designed to transcend the prior belief systems of mutually antagonistic tribes, nations, classes, and ethnic and religious communities in order to arrive at knowledge that is equally probable for any rational human mind. Those who doubt that science can do this must be made to show how some other tolerant and ecumenical alternative can do it better. Unless they can show how some other universalistic system of knowing leads to more acceptable criteria of truth, their attempt to subvert the universal credibility of science in the name of cultural relativism, however well-intentioned, is an intellectual crime against humanity. It is a crime against humanity because the real alternative to science is not anarchy but ideology; not peaceful artists, philosophers, and anthropologists, but aggressive fanatics and messiahs eager to annihilate each other and the whole world if need be in order to prove their point. (27–28)

Harris's materialism starts in an ecological understanding of what is primary in human affairs—infrastructure (that which is beneficial to the sustenance and reproduction of human lives). The scope of his view can be appreciated in his explication of the "Universal Pattern" (*CM*:51–54). Although presented as a set of etic categories for describing and analyzing human behavior, the underlying theory is embedded in his "tripartite scheme": Infrastructure, Structure, and Superstructure. As his discussion of Marx (*CM*:55–56) makes clear, Harris's materialism is a commitment to search for the probabilistic causes of human behavior in the infrastructure (the mode of production and the mode of reproduction), a principle he later calls, "priority of infrastructure." It states that "innovations arising in the infrastructural sector are likely to be preserved and propagated if they enhance the efficiency of the productive and reproductive processes that sustain health and well being and satisfy basic biopsychological needs and drives" (1996:278).

The ecological focus of cultural materialism is on how humans make a living and manage to reproduce the next generation. The logic is similar to that of Julian Steward (1955), whose concept of the "cultural core" (aspects of culture "most closely related to subsistence") suggests that what really matters in human affairs, from a theoretical standpoint, is how people solve the problems of survival that face all living beings. Plants and animals require nutriment, defense from predators, and means of reproduction. Humans are no exception, and, in Harris's view, many of their most interesting behaviors can be understood as solutions to the problems of maintaining material existence.

This said, the most dramatic characteristic of humans as distinct from all other animals is the degree to which their solutions to problems are *cultural* (Johnson and Earle 2000:21–22). As early as his dispute with Pearson, Harris (1959) was already arguing that Pearson's mistake, and the mistake of cultural relativists in general, was to assume that some important aspects of cultural behavior were irrelevant to making a living. Where Pearson assumed that the surplus people were capable of producing over and above survival needs was somehow *superfluous*—and hence a matter of choice—Harris argued that the surplus was *necessary*, to pay the artisans, craftspeople, road builders, astronomers, and others on whom their complex economy depended. Peasants must know when the season is right to sow their seeds and must be able to get to market. In this sense they have no choice but to grow crops beyond their families' basic needs so as to be able to afford to pay taxes and buy necessities.

Elements of structure (e.g., political relations to the state) and superstructure (e.g., clergy and astronomers) are intrinsically linked to infrastructural process.

Thereafter, Harris dedicated himself to a series of analyses, many summarized in this book, to fight back against the seemingly inexhaustible supply of cases sought by anthropologists to draw attention to cultural behaviors that seem to make no practical sense. The taboos on pork or sacred cattle (a waste of nutritious food), the rotting of yams left on display for prestige (another waste of good food), and the seemingly senseless practice of tribal warfare or human sacrifice (a waste of human life) are just a few of the behaviors trotted out over the years to somehow prove that human beings irrationally allocate their scarce energies. Evidently humans, possessed of culture and hence no longer like animals, are free to squander energy in useless, foolish, even deadly displays because their beliefs dictate them to do so.

What Harris demonstrates in each case is that the behavior in question does make sense within a cultural materialist perspective. This requires an expanded understanding of the relationship between survival issues (the infrastructure) and the broader world of social relations and ideologies in which all humans live. Pigs carry diseases, sacred cattle are essential draft animals and supply other basic materials, excess yams only rot in abundant years (being security against famine in bad years), and so on. That such behaviors are encouraged and strengthened by belief systems that invoke feelings of loyalty to community and fear of supernatural punishment is the cultural part of the powerful human capacity for adaptation that has permitted our species to colonize virtually every ecosystem on the planet. In Harris's deft hands, these connections become obvious, always supported by carefully accumulated evidence.

A major goal of cultural materialism is to provide causal explanations for similarities and differences in human behavior and thought. The Universal Pattern provides the guidelines for collecting and organizing cultural data—the recurrent components or parts of sociocultural systems. The principle of primacy of infrastructure gives priority to the formulation of hypotheses in which etic behavioral components of infrastructure are treated as independent variables, while etic components of structure and superstructure are treated as dependent variables. The causality is far from absolute; it embraces a determinism that is probabilistic, yet calls for generalizations that make it possible to search for basic laws through careful data collection and hypotheses testing.

In this light, we may understand why Harris takes such umbrage at Eclecticism. Ordinarily, one might think of eclecticism as a harmless, or even a good thing: After all, broad-minded people recognize how complicated the world is and can take a certain enjoyment in diverse perspectives. But for Harris, the business of anthropology is serious. The world is in trouble, and much of the trouble comes from a weak understanding of the causes and consequences of human behavior. Science encourages us to formulate strong theories, capable of making predictions about the world that can be supported or thrown into doubt by gathering evidence. Weak theories are untestable: They produce complicated statements about the world that are comfortably vague, assuring the theorists that, although they may not be saying anything very useful, at least they can never be proven wrong. Also, "by picking and choosing epistemological and theoretical principles to suit the convenience of each puzzle, eclecticism guarantees that its solutions will remain unrelated to each other by any coherent set of principles" (CM:287–288).

A similar point pertains to Harris's critique of Idealism. Strong theories are clear about causality, and for Harris, the causes of human behavior patterns lie ultimately in the infrastructure. To say that humans behave the way they do because of the ideas put in their heads by culture (a process, by the way, that idealists tend to assume rather than analyze and explain) is to locate causality in the unfathomed process by which "cultures" come to be. If some cultures ban pork while others do not, and some people fight wars while others are peaceful, purely because their cultures came to emphasize one or the other, then we have no causal theory to explain human behavior. Such "theories" may seem to use culture as an explanatory principle, but since they offer no theory of how cultures come to be, other than to invoke "history" or "creativity," cultural relativism is no theory at all. It is, rather, an assumption that cultural process is either a random process or an aesthetic that just mysteriously *is*.

In the years since *Cultural Materialism* first appeared, the world has not become a safer and kinder place. If anything, the main problems that confront us in the new century are just those that arise out of a steady set of developments in the infrastructure: population growth; intensification of production leading to deforestation, the collapse of fisheries, pollution, and economic integration leading to greater globalization of the economy and the depersonalization of work. Harris's book, and indeed his life's work, offer us a set of theoretical and methodological tools with which to increase our understanding of, and ultimately our ability to influence the direction of, these changes.

References

D'Andrade, Roy. 1995. "Moral Models in Anthropology." *Current Anthropology* 36, no. 3 (June 1995): 299–408.

Harris, Marvin. 1994. "Cultural Materialism is Alive and Well and Won't Go Away until Something Better Comes Along." In *Assessing Cultural Anthropology*, edited by Robert Borofsky, 62–75; New York: McGraw Hill Inc.

Harris, Marvin. 1995. Anthropology and Postmodernism. In *Science, Materialism, and the Study of Culture*, edited by Martin Murphy and Maxine Margolis, 62–77. Gainesville: University of Florida Press.

Harris, Marvin. 1996 "Cultural Materialism." In *Encyclopedia of Cultural Anthropology*, edited by David Levinson and Melvin Ember, 277–281. New York: Henry Holt and Co.

Harris, Marvin and Orna Johnson. 2000. *Cultural Anthropology*, 5th edition. Boston: Allyn and Bacon.

Headland, Thomas N., Kenneth L. Pike, and Marvin Harris, eds. 1990. *Emics and Etics: The Insider/Outsider Debate*. Newberry Park, Calif.: Sage.

Johnson, Allen. 1996. "Time Allocation." In *Encyclopedia of Cultural Anthropology*, edited by David Levinson and Melvin Ember, 1313–1316. New York: Henry Holt and Co.

Johnson, Allen and Timothy Earle. 2000. *The Evolution of Human Societies: From Foraging Group to Agrarian State*. 2d edition. Stanford: Stanford University Press.

Johnson, Orna. 1980. "The Social Context of Intimacy and Avoidance: A Videotape Study of Machiguenga Meals." *Ethnology* 15 (3): 353–366.

Murphy, Martin F. and Maxine Margolis. 1995. *Science, Materialism, and the Study of Culture*. Gainesville: University of Florida Press.

Insert Pike 1967 ref here.

Sanjek, Roger. 1995. "Politics, Theory, and the Nature of Cultural Things." In *Science, Materialism, and the Study of Culture,* edited by Martin Murphy and Maxine Margolis, 39–61. Gainesville: University of Florida Press.

Steward, Julian. 1955. Theory of Culture Change. Urbana: University of Illinois Press.

White, Leslie. 1949. *The Science of Culture.* New York: Grove Press.

Preface

CULTURAL MATERIALISM is the strategy I have found to be
most effective in my attempt to understand the causes of differences
and similarities among societies and cultures. It is based on the simple premise that human social life is a response to the practical
problems of earthly existence. I hope to show in this book that cultural materialism leads to better scientific theories about the causes
of sociocultural phenomena than any of the rival strategies that are
currently available. I do not claim that it is a perfect strategy but
merely that it is more effective than the alternatives.

In its commitment to the rules of scientific method, cultural materialism opposes strategies that deny the legitimacy or the feasibility
of scientific accounts of human behavior—for example, humanist
claims that there is no determinism in human affairs—and it opposes the currently popular attribution of the malaise of industrial
society to too much rather than too little science. Cultural materialism, with its emphasis upon the encounter between womb and belly
and earth and water, also opposes numerous strategies that set forth
from words, ideas, high moral values, and aesthetic and religious
beliefs to understand the everyday events of ordinary human life.
Aligned in this regard with the teachings of Karl Marx, cultural materialism nonetheless stands apart from the Marx-Engels-Lenin
strategy of dialectical materialism. Condemned by dialectical materialists as "vulgar materialists" or "mechanical materialists," cultural materialists seek to improve Marx's original strategy by drop-
ping the Hegelian notion that all systems evolve through a dialectic
of contradictory negations and by adding reproductive pressure and
ecological variables to the conjunction of material and conditions
studied by Marxist-Leninists.

Although significant numbers of anthropologists have adopted
the cultural materialist strategy, most of my colleagues continue to

prefer one of several available alternatives. The most popular of these denies the need to have a definite strategy at all. This I call the strategy of eclecticism. Eclectics argue that the strategic commitments of cultural materialism or any of the other self-identified strategies such as dialectical materialism or structuralism prematurely close off possible sources of understanding. To be an eclectic is to insist that *all* research strategies may be relevant to the resolution of some puzzles and that it cannot be foretold which strategies will be most productive in any given case. Eclecticism presents itself as the defender of the "open mind." Yet eclecticism represents as much of a closed strategic commitment as any of its rivals. To uphold all options indefinitely is to take a definite strategic position. Moreover, it is not a conspicuously open-minded attitude to insist a priori that better scientific theories will result from the use of more than one strategy per problem. This claim actually happens to be wrong. It is not eclecticism but the clash of strategic options, eclecticism among them, that is the guarantor of an open mind. In arguing for the superiority of cultural materialism, therefore, I have no intention of advocating the annihilation of rival strategies. I insist only that the systematic comparison of alternative strategies be an integral part of the scientific enterprise.

Eclecticism reigns triumphant because it seems no more than common sense that there must be a little bit of truth in each of the rival isms, and that none can contain the whole truth. I disagree, however that it is common sense to abandon the quest for the possibility of larger truths in order to settle for the certainty of smaller ones. I also disagree that it is common sense to suppose that the alternative strategies are equally well endowed with truth and nonsense. No strategy has the whole truth, but the whole truth is not the sum of all strategies.

Although I did not invent "cultural materialism," I am responsible for giving it its name (in *The Rise of Anthropological Theory*). Let me explain why I chose these two words and not some others. By the mid-1960s many colleagues shared my conviction that as long as anthropologists underestimated the importance of Karl Marx, there could be no science of human society. Marx had come closest in the nineteenth century to being the Darwin of the social sciences. Like Darwin, Marx showed that phenomena previously regarded as inscrutable or as a direct emanation of deity could be brought down to earth and understood in terms of lawful scientific principles.

Marx did this by proposing that the production of the material means of subsistence forms "the foundation upon which state institutions, the legal conceptions, the art and even the religious ideas of the people concerned have evolved, and in the light of which these things must therefore be explained instead of *vice versa* as has hitherto been the case" (see p. 141). The "materialism" in "cultural materialism" is therefore intended as an acknowledgement of the debt owed to Marx's formulation of the determining influence of production and other material processes.

Now I am aware that a strategy which calls itself materialism runs a special risk of being dismissed by the general public as well as by the academic professorate. Materialism is a dirty word among the young, who aspire to be idealistic in their thought and behavior. Materialism is what happens to you when you abandon your ideals and sell out. (Never mind that the more money people make, the more likely they are to think of themselves as idealists.) But cultural materialists have idealistic motives just like everyone else. And as for pure, unselfish devotion to humankind, rightly or wrongly, a large segment of world opinion today ranks Marx as the equal or superior of Jesus Christ. Needless to say, the technical distinction between cultural materialism and idealism has nothing to do with such invidious comparisons. It refers exclusively to the problem of how one proposes to account for sociocultural differences and similarities. Despite the negative images the word "materialism" evokes, I would be intellectually dishonest not to use it.

It was also obvious when I began to write *The Rise of Anthropological Theory* in 1965 that a genuine science of society would not develop, Marx or no Marx, as long as Marxist-Leninists (and other social scientists) continued to avoid or ignore the facts and theories of modern anthropology. Marx's strategic assumptions, like Darwin's, are burdened with nineteenth-century philosophical concepts which reduce their plausibility and usefulness for twentieth-century anthropologists. Because Marx's materialism is wedded to Hegel's notion of dialectical contradictions, Engels gave it the name "dialectical materialism." Under Lenin, the dialectical tail was made to wag the materialist dog. Marxism-Leninism came to represent the triumph of dialectics over the objective and empirical aspects of Marx's scientific materialism.

Cultural materialism is a non-Hegelian strategy whose epistemological assumptions are rooted in the philosophical traditions of

David Hume and the British empiricists—assumptions that led to Darwin, Spencer, Tylor, Morgan, Frazer, Boas, and the birth of anthropology as an academic discipline. Yet cultural materialism is not a monistic or mechanical alternative to dialectics. Rather, it is concerned with systemic interactions between thought and behavior, with conflicts as well as harmonies, continuities and discontinuities, gradual and revolutionary change, adaptation and maladaptation, function and dysfunction, positive and negative feedback. To drop the word "dialectical" is not to drop any of these interests—it is simply to insist that they must be pursued under empirical and operation auspices rather than as adjuncts to a political program or as an attempt to express one's persona.

Now for the cultural part of cultural materialism. The word "cultural" comes to the fore because the material causes of sociocultural phenomena differ from those which pertain strictly to inorganic or organic determinisms. Cultural materialism, for example, stands opposed to biological reductionist materialisms such as those embedded in racial, sociobiological, or ethological explanations of cultural differences and similarities. And the term "cultural" conveys more adequately than such alternatives as "historical" or "sociological" the fact that the phenomena to be explained are human, synchronic as well as diachronic, and prehistoric as well as historic. "Cultural" also draws attention to the fact that the strategy in question is a distinctive product of anthropology and its subfields—that it is a synthesis which seeks to transcend disciplinary, ethnic, and national boundaries.

The task of cultural materialism is to create a pan-human science of society whose findings can be accepted on logical and evidentiary grounds by the pan-human community. In view of increasing national, ethnic, and class interests in subordinating science to politics and to short-term sectarian benefits, I must confess that the prospects for a pan-human science of society appear dimmer today than at any time since the eighteenth century. I cannot therefore appeal to the reader to follow my brief for cultural materialism in the name of the jubilant enlightenment. I make no utopian claims. I merely ask all those who fear the onset of a new dark age to join together to strengthen the barriers against mystification and obscurantism in contemporary social science.

Acknowledgments

I WISH TO THANK the following people for helping me to formulate the ideas in this book. They do not necessarily agree with me, but I am grateful for their expertise and their advice.

Ernie Alleva
Allen Berger
Douglas Brintall
Brian Burkhalter
Michael Chibnik
Myron Cohen
Anna Lou DeHavenon
William Divale
Brian Ferguson
Morton Fried
Frederick Gamst
Ashraf Ghani
Ricardo Godoy
Daniel Gross
Michael Harner
Allen Johnson

Orna Johnson
Cherry Lowman
Richard MacNeish
K. N. Nair
David Ostrander
Barbara Price
K. N. Raj
Anna Roosevelt
Eric Ross
Jagna Sharff
Samuel Sherman
Brian Turner
A. Vaidyanathan
Benjamin White
Karl Wittfogel

I am very grateful to the following people for helping to bring this book through the trauma of publication: Virginia Brown, Jason Epstein, Brian Ferguson, Madeline Harris, Nancy Inglis, and Simah Kraus.

Finally, I thank those involved in process of getting this book reissued: Allen Johnson, Orna Johnson, and B. J. Brown.

About the Author

MARVIN HARRIS is one of the world's best-known anthropologists and among its most highly respected theorists. He was a member of the faculty of Columbia University's Department of Anthropology from 1953 to 1980 and chairman there from 1963 to 1966. Since 1980, he has been graduate research professor at the University of Florida. Harris has done fieldwork in Brazil, Mozambique, India, and East Harlem.

Marvin Harris is author of seventeen books including popular introductory textbooks, books for the general public, and important scholarly works. In addition to *Cultural Materialism: The Struggle for a Science of Culture*, he is best known for *Culture, People, Nature* (7 editions between 1971 and 1997); *The Rise of Anthropological Theory: A History of Theories of Culture* (1968, 2001); *Cows, Pigs, Wars, and Witches: Riddles of Culture* (1974, 1991); *Cannibals and Kings* (1977); *Our Kind* (1989); and *Theories of Culture in Postmodern Times* (1998). Harris's books have been translated into sixteen languages.

Harris is past chair of the General Anthropology Division of the American Anthropological Association and the organization's Distinguished Lecturer for 1991.

Part I

Cultural Materialism as a Research Strategy

Introduction to Part I

THERE ARE two parts to the description and evaluation of a research strategy, and hence there are two parts to this book. First there is the task of describing and evaluating the basic features of that strategy. And then there is the task of describing and evaluating the strategic alternatives.

In Part I, therefore, I attempt to set forth the epistemological and theoretical principles underlying the construction of cultural materialist theories. And I also attempt to outline a broad set of interpenetrating theories in order to show the actual or potential scope and degree of coherence of cultural materialism's theoretical corpus.

Part II, on the other hand, deals with alternative strategies. Both parts are necessary because intelligent descriptions and evaluations require us to say not only why we are for something but also why we are against what it is not.

Chapter One

Research Strategies and the Structure of Science

Cultural materialism is or aspires to be a scientific research strategy. This means that cultural materialists must be able to provide general criteria for distinguishing science from other ways of gaining knowledge and for distinguishing one research strategy from another. I want to make these criteria explicit, not only for the sake of defining cultural materialism but also for the sake of comparing cultural materialism with those alternative strategies that likewise claim to be scientific strategies. We need to know the general rules of the scientific method. Then we can go on to define what a research strategy is and to compare one with another in order to see which one best fulfills the requirements for achieving scientific knowledge about human social life. The definition of science and the definition of research strategies therefore are basic ingredients in the epistemology of cultural materialism.

Other Ways of Knowing

BEFORE PROCEEDING to the question of what distinguishes science from other ways of knowing, let me clarify my attitude toward nonscientific research strategies. I believe that science is a superior way for human beings to obtain knowledge about the world in which we live. But I readily admit that there are domains of experience the knowledge of which cannot be achieved by adherence to the rules of the scientific method. I am thinking of the ecstatic knowledge of mystics and saints; the visions and hallucinations of drug users and of schizophrenics; and the aesthetic and moral insights of artists, poets, and musicians.

One does not obtain knowledge of God and flaming cherubim or of the beauty of a Beethoven quartet by applying the rules of the scientific method to sunsets or by studying the sound waves produced by bows drawn over taut strings. Science does not dispute the authenticity of aesthetic knowledge. Moreover, I can readily subscribe to the popular belief that science and religion need not conflict. But one proviso must be kept in mind. Science does not dispute the doctrines of revealed religions as long as they are not used to cast doubt on the authenticity of the knowledge science itself has achieved. For example, there is no conflict between biological and theological versions of the origin of species as long as the Bible is regarded as metaphor. But if fundamentalists insist that the revealed word is more authentic than science as a source of information about evolution, then the lines of a battle are necessarily drawn.

Narrow Inductionism

EARLY IN THE sixteenth century, Francis Bacon proposed that science consisted in the elevation of the authority of experiment and observation over that of reason, intuition, and convention. Bacon thought that as more and more reliable and precise particular facts accumulate, they can be classified and generalized, resulting in an ever-expanding hierarchy of useful "axioms." This is what he meant by "induction." In the *Novum Organum* (New System), Bacon wrote:

But then and then only, may we hope well of the sciences, when in a just scale of ascent, and by successive steps not interrupted or broken, we rise from particulars to lesser axioms; and then to middle axioms, one above the other; and last of all to the most general. . . . (Bacon, 1875:97)

Although many people today continue to regard the collection of facts and their arrangement by induction into theories as the heart of the scientific method, Bacon's conception of what facts and theories are and of the relationship between them was hopelessly unrealistic even in his own time. The most important early scientific discoveries —such as those made by Galileo about the movement of the earth, by Keppler about the elliptical shape of planetary orbits, and later by Newton about the "force" of gravity—could never have been made if Bacon's rules had prevailed.

Determined to avoid all premature speculations, Bacon proposed that data gathering be carried out by illiterate assistants with no interest in whether an experiment turned out one way or another. Plain facts, properly arranged, would automatically lead to certain knowledge of the universe. Nothing could be more misrepresentative of the actual problem-solving techniques of the scientific method. That plain facts do not speak for themselves is evident from Bacon's own acceptance of the errors contained in what appeared to be the plainest of facts. For Bacon, that the earth did not move was a fact because it could be seen not to move; and for Bacon it was a fact that life was being spontaneously generated because maggots always developed in putrid flesh and frogs appeared after every rain.

What is clear is that the great breakthroughs of a Newton, Darwin, or Marx could never have been achieved solely on the basis of Baconian fact gathering. Facts are always unreliable without theories that guide their collection and that distinguish between superficial and significant appearances.

Nonetheless, we should not forget that theories are equally meaningless without facts. Bacon's emphasis upon fact gathering was an important departure in its day. The inductive model of science was intended as a corrective to the subordination of inquiry to Aristotelian intuitions and as a condemnation of those who would test theories by appeal to political-religious dogmas and doctrines. Bacon's was an age in which people argued about the number of angels on the head of a pin and in which learned men could dismiss Galileo's discovery of Jupiter's moons *because* it contradicted established theories and principles. As argued by the astronomer Francesco Sizi: "The satellites [Jupiter's moons] are invisible to the naked eye and therefore can have no influence on the earth and therefore would be useless and therefore do not exist" (quoted in Hempel, 1965:48). Faced with this flight of fancy, who can blame Francis Bacon for warning that knowledge should not be "supplied with wings, but rather hung with weights, to keep it from leaping and flying" (Bacon, 1875:97)?

The Inductive-Deductive Balance

AS A PHILOSOPHICAL theory about scientific knowledge, Baconian inductionism had always been confronted with opposing philosophical theories that assert the priority of imaginative theory over facts, of deduction over induction. René Descartes, for example, with his search for certainty through the deduction "I think, therefore I am," viewed his work as a corrective to Bacon's. Both Bacon and Descartes can be associated with extensive philosophical lineages: the Empiricists and Positivists on the one hand, and the Cartesians and Rationalists on the other.

It is important to separate the work of these philosophers from that of individuals who have faced the task of actually formulating substantive scientific theories. In the actual history of the physical, natural, and social sciences, neither the inductive nor the deductive mode of thought has ever been pursued exclusively. Pure Baconian inductionists have been as rare as Cartesian realists. In the second edition of his *Principia*, Newton, for example, master of mathematical "leaping and flying," declared: *"Hypotheses non fingo"* ("I offer no hypotheses"), while Charles Darwin, exasperated by the failure of twenty years of fact gathering to convince his critics, finally had to admit that "when we descend to details, we can prove that no one species has changed; nor can we prove that the supposed changes are beneficial, which is the groundwork of the theory" (cited in Hull, 1973:32). Science has always consisted of an interplay between induction and deduction, between empiricism and rationalism; any attempt to draw the line on one side or the other conflicts with actual scientific practice. The main function of these alternatives—besides giving jobs to philosophers—has been to provide ammunition for shooting down someone's theories or building up one's own. One's rivals have overindulged themselves with speculative, metaphysical assumptions or they have been obsessed with superficial empirical appearances, depending on which particular moment in the interplay one chooses to emphasize. As Gerald Holton has shown, the young Einstein was an admirer of the positivist-empiricist Ernst Mach, because Mach had objected to the unexamined, metaphysical, theory-laden content of the classical concepts of space, time, and force.

Mach at first approved of relativity theory, and Einstein wrote to him saying that his approval was a source of "enormous pleasure." But Mach denounced Einstein's later work as being too metaphysical, while Einstein attempted to fend off his critics by emphasizing the importance of deductive mathematical reasoning for the development of theory:

> Coming from sceptical empiricism of somewhat the kind of Mach's, I was made, by the problem of gravitation, into a believing rationalist, that is, one who seeks the only trustworthy source of truth in mathematical simplicity. (cited in Holton, 1973:241)

Hume's Empiricism

THE MOST IMPORTANT source of modern-day empiricism and positivism is not Francis Bacon but rather the eighteenth-century British philosopher David Hume. In his *An Enquiry Concerning Human Understanding,* Hume drew a distinction between the knowledge that can be obtained about the relationships between logical propositions and knowledge about the relationships between empirical facts. Logical propositions such as those encountered in mathematics can be shown to be certainly true by the exercise of reason. But mere reason or intuition can never establish the relationships between matters of fact. The reason for this is that *logically,* the contrary of every matter of fact is possible and the mind never encounters any fundamental obstacle in the way of conceiving it to be possible.

> *That the sun will not rise tomorrow* is no less intelligible a proposition, and implies no more contradiction than the affirmation *that it will rise.* We should in vain therefore attempt to demonstrate its falseness. (Hume 1955 [1748]:40)

Observation and experience thus become essential for understanding the relationship between nonmathematical facts. In this regard Hume did not differ from Bacon. All conjunctions of events being equally logical, "In vain, therefore, should we pretend to determine any single event, or infer any cause or effect, without the assistance of observation and experience" (ibid.:44).

But it was in his understanding of the limits of induction that Hume made his most important contribution to the philosophy of science.

Ever since the publication of *A Treatise of Human Nature* (1739), empiricists have recognized that induction cannot lead to generalizations or laws which possess certainty. Hume pointed out that all inductive generalizations about cause and effect are merely based on the observation of a recurrent conjunction between events. This conjunction can never be shown to be necessary in some absolutely certain sense, since it can never be demonstrated that events previously conjoined and interpreted as "cause and effects" must in all future instances be so conjoined.

Hume, I should like to emphasize, advanced this critique of induction not as a point against empiricism but as an argument against the claim that rationalists could achieve certainty on the basis of deductions from a priori principles. Hume argued that if the very idea of causal relationships was merely a human psychological consequence of the conjunction between events, then one had to doubt all deductive a priori notions of "necessity" as well.

Hume's remedy for the lack of certainty in scientific knowledge based on induction was not rationalism (or mysticism) but insistence that empirical verification of constant conjunctions was the best way to acquire knowledge about the world even if the future recurrence of such regularities had to be taken on faith and could never yield certain knowledge. Philosophers belonging to diverse schools quickly seized on Hume's appeal to faith as a compromise fatal to his empiricist program. But Hume never doubted that science was a way of knowing that was superior to the superstitious and dogmatic systems that had previously dominated the human intellect.

Hume's tough anti-metaphysical credo was the direct inspiration for the extreme forms of positivism of the late nineteenth and early twentieth centuries:

If we take in our hand any volume of divinity or school of metaphysics, for instance, let us ask does it contain any abstract reasoning concerning quantity or number? No. Does it contain any experimental reasoning concerning matters of fact and existence? No. Commit it then to the flames for it can contain nothing but sophistry and illusion. (Cited in Ayer, 1959:10)

It should be clear from what I have already said about alternative ways of knowing that I do not endorse the arrogant dismissal of nonscientific knowledge to which Hume seemed to be inclined and of which the twentieth-century logical positivists have been accused

(Suppe, 1977). Nonetheless, as a cultural materialist I do subscribe to Hume's basic intention of separating knowledge gained by the interplay of reason and controlled observation from knowledge gained by undisciplined experience, inspiration, or revelation.

Who Needs Certainty?

ANTI-EMPIRICISTS belonging to diverse schools have treated Hume's critique of induction as if it were the exposed jugular of the empiricist definition of science. Induction can never yield certainty. But certainty is a crucial issue only to people—mainly philosophers—whose minds are enthralled by metaphysical cravings for absolute truths. Hume's critique of induction was never much of an obstacle to the scientists who were responsible for the great theoretical advances of the nineteenth century, and the whole issue became a dead horse as far as practice is concerned when the notion of certainty was replaced by statistical measures of probability.

In the words of Karl Pearson (1937[1892]:83), one of the founders of the discipline of mathematical statistics, the "provable is the probable." "Proof . . . is the demonstration of overwhelming probability."

After Hume, science could no longer be considered a distinctive way of knowing because it alone among ways of knowing can achieve certainty. Rather, it is a distinctive way of knowing because it claims to be able to distinguish between different degrees of uncertainty. In judging scientific theories one does not inquire which theory leads to accurate predictions in all instances, but rather which theories lead to accurate predictions in more instances. Failure to achieve complete predictability does not invalidate a scientific theory; it merely constitutes an invitation to do better.

Positivism Defined

POSITIVISM is the name which the nineteenth-century social philosopher Auguste Comte gave to the scientific way of knowing. Like Hume, Comte wanted science to transcend futile debates about metaphysical concepts such as God, the soul, and eternal essences. He believed that the human mind and its reflection in history had passed through two previous stages of development: the theological and metaphysical. Now the age of science was dawning. It was to be a positivistic age because thought and action would be based only on well-tested, systematized, "positive" knowledge.

Much of the critical abuse to which positivistic approaches in the social sciences are now being subjected arises from the failure to distinguish positivism and empiricism from narrow inductionism. (Claude Lévi-Strauss, for example, uses the word "empiricism" as an epithet—see p. 213) But of the many errors of thought that can be found in the work of Auguste Comte, narrow inductionism is definitely not one. In Comte's words: "No real observation of any kind of phenomena is possible which is not initially guided and finally interpreted by some kind of theory" (1830–42, IV:418).

Who better fulfills the image of a nineteenth-century empirical scientist than Charles Darwin? Yet Darwin no less than Comte understood the futility of doing research in the absence of explicit hypotheses for the systematic identification of relevant and crucial facts. Wrote Darwin, "Observation must be for or against a view if it is to be of any service" (cited in Hull, 1973: 21). And the mere mention of the name Herbert Spencer should suffice to silence the chorus of anti-empiricists who imagine that nineteenth-century social science was blinded by too much induction. Of Spencer, it has aptly been said, "He was a man for whom the definition of tragedy was a beautiful theory killed by an ugly fact."

Among those who today or in the recent past regard themselves as allies of the empiricist, anti-metaphysical tradition, there are few who would defend what Karl Hempel (1965:11) calls "the narrow inductivist conception of scientific inquiry" (although, in conformity with the eclectic strategy, there are many who would defend the need for a strategy-free approach; see Chapter 10). Hence recent attacks on empiricist-positivist models of science distort the history of science when they associate positivism or empiricism with the absence of a hypothetico-deductive phase in the conduct of research.

Moreover, neither Comte nor Hume insisted that the observer ought to maintain a cold, detached, value-free orientation. It is a total distortion of the development of social science during the nineteenth century to depict the minds of such founding figures as Comte, Mill, Spencer, Darwin, Tylor, and Morgan either as hung with Bacon's weights or as advocating a detached value-free approach. Alvin Gouldner's (1970:101–102) characterization of positivism as a nineteenth-century movement that called for a "detached scientific method of studying society" because of "the failure cf middle-class politics to yield a coherent image of the new social order," is such a distortion. The proposal to develop the scientific study of society did not originate in the nineteenth century (although it was Comte who coined the term "positivism"). Positivism was born in the eighteenth century with Hume, not out of despair, but out of hope; not out of a narrow-minded view of the truth, but out of a broad vision of new methods for increasing knowledge; not out of detachment and disinterest in human well-being, but out of a passionate belief in the ultimate perfectibility of social life; not out of Comte's conservative "order and progress" but out of the Enlightenment's search for "liberty, equality, and fraternity."

True, at the end of the nineteenth century the stage was being set for the development of technocratic, micro-focused, allegedly value-free social sciences. In both sociology and anthropology, broad evolutionary syntheses gave way to narrow anti-theoretical studies. But philosophical positivism had nothing to do with this regressive development. Rather, as I show in *The Rise of Anthropological Theory*, the micro-focused viewpoints in the first part of this century, as represented by Franz Boas, were part of the attack against Marxist macro history and the Marxist science of society.

Logical Positivism

HUME'S ANTI-METAPHYSICAL position was elaborated and defended during the first half of the twentieth century by the philosophical movement known as logical positivism. This movement, which arose in Vienna, carried forward the empiricist struggle against metaphysical, absolute, and transcendent entities. It was called "positivist" because of the aggressive anti-metaphysical stance, and "logical" because it employed modern, logical principles in the attempt to identify the meaning of utterances.

Following Hume, the logical positivists divided significant statements into two classes: formal propositions, such as those of logic or pure mathematics, which they held to be definitions or tautologies; and factual propositions, of which it was required that they should be empirically verifiable. These classes were supposed to be exhaustive, so that if a sentence succeeded neither in expressing something that was formally true or false nor in expressing something that could be empirically tested, the view taken was that it did not express any proposition at all. It might have emotive meaning, but it was literally nonsensical. A great deal of philosophical talk was held to fall into this category: talk about the meaning of life, about absolute or transcendent entities and substances such as souls, or about the destiny of man. Such utterances were said to be metaphysical; and the conclusion drawn was that if philosophy was to constitute a genuine branch of knowledge it would have to emancipate itself from metaphysics. The Viennese positivists did not go so far as to say that all metaphysical work deserved to be committed to the flames; they allowed, somewhat perfunctorily, that such writing might have poetic merit or even that it might express an exciting or interesting attitude to life. Their point was that if a statement did not state anything that could be found either true or false, it could contribute nothing to the increase of knowledge. Metaphysical utterances were condemned not for being emotive, which could hardly be considered objectionable in itself, but for pretending to be cognitive, for masquerading as something that they were not (Ayer, 1959:10).

Operationalism

FOR THE LOGICAL positivists of the Vienna school, the significance of a statement was inseparable from an account of the logical and empirical steps one has to take to verify the existence of the events or relationships to which the statement refers. In the version developed by the physicist-philosopher Percy Bridgman (1927), these steps were given the name "operations," and the meaning of any term with an empirical referent was held to be identical with the operations by which the existence of the event could be established by independent observers. Bridgman went so far as to insist that entities or events identified by means of one set of operations could not be considered the "same" entities or events if they were identified by another set of operations.

Now, the need to operationalize concepts employed in scientific statements is universally recognized as a fundamental methodological requirement by all scientists. However, it is also recognized that operationalism in the extreme version propounded by Bridgman would lead to the impoverishment of the scope of scientific theories, if not to a total breakdown of all scientific communication. The very task of specifying the operational steps that should be taken to reach agreement about whether or not a complex structure exists cannot be carried out without relying on at least some terms whose meanings derive from natural language and whose validity is a matter of practical experience within a given scientific community.

Nonetheless, a strong dose of operationalism is desperately needed to unburden the social and behavioral sciences of their overload of ill-defined concepts, such as status, role, superordination and subordination, group, institution, class, caste, tribe, state, religion, community, aggression, exploitation, economy, kinship, family, society, social, culture, cultural, and many others that are part of every social scientist's basic working vocabulary. The continuing failure to agree on the meaning of these concepts is a reflection of their unoperational status and constitutes a great barrier to the development of scientific theories of social and cultural life. True, in psychology and linguistics, the logical positivist influence of the 1930s and 1940s led to the declaration that concepts like mind, intuition, instinct, and meaning were "metaphysical" survivals unworthy of study because they had not been operationalized. Pushed to such counterproductive extremes, operationalism was bound to provoke restorative movements rallying under the banners of humanism and rationalism.

For many social scientists the decisive turning point in the operationalist tide was reached with Noam Chomsky's (1964[1959]) attack on psychologist B. F. Skinner's book *Verbal Behavior*. Chomsky showed that by insisting on operational purity appropriate to the study of rats, Skinner had obscured the most distinctive aspect of human language: our intuited sense of what is grammatical. Chomsky no doubt rendered a valuable service to linguistics. His influence on the social sciences, especially on anthropology however, has been less salutary. Anthropology never had a Skinner. Logical positivism, behaviorism, or operationalism had made absolutely no impression on the most influential cultural anthropologists of the 1940s. Hence, Chomsky's defense of intuited knowledge did not have the effect of restoring a balance between loosely and narrowly operationalized concepts, but rather of further increasing the propensity of anthropologists to smother in a blanket of personalized concepts and idiosyncratic data languages.

Demarcation and Karl Popper

UNDER THE INFLUENCE of logical positivism, the line between science and other forms of knowledge became for many thinkers the formulation of testable hypotheses whose probable truth depended upon operationalized observations or experiments carried out by independent observers. Scientific hypotheses were to be tested by means of the predictions which can be deduced from them (Hempel, 1965:12), such as the existence of new particles or previously unknown species. By testing hypotheses and accepting some as better confirmed than others, science advances toward ever more powerful and accurate theories from which predictions about increasingly wider ranges of phenomena can be made. Most working scientists would probably find this unobjectionable as a minimum definition of how scientific knowledge is acquired, but it has been severely attacked in recent years and must be modified. The most influential figure in the development of new criteria was the English philosopher Karl Popper.

According to Popper, Hume's critique of induction cannot be answered by substituting probabilities for certainties. Logically, science cannot be described as a method for *verifying* hypotheses. All that science can logically lead to is the *falsification* of hypotheses. Popper's argument in support of this contention is that there is a basic logical asymmetry between verification and falsification. Thus the hypothesis "all swans are white" cannot be verified even if a million observations have been made of white swans because on the millionth and first time, a black swan may still be found. (Black swans have in fact been found in Australia and many other places.) On the other hand, if the hypothesis states "not all swans are white," one observation of a black swan suffices to confirm the hypothesis.

Popper's objection to using the concept "probably verified" in the first case, arises from the fact that, logically, repeated observations cannot be regarded as increasing the probable truth of a false statement. If an empirical statement is false, its probability cannot go from zero to a million to one as the number of apparently confirming instances goes from zero to a million. Otherwise, one would be led to attribute the probability 1/2—instead of 0—to a hypothesis that has been tested two thousand times and falsified a thousand times (Popper, 1959:316).

The practical implications of this dilemma can be seen in the conflict between Newton's and Einstein's laws of gravity. Newton's formulas seemed to be verified by over two hundred years of experiment and observation, yet they were proved false when they were applied to subatomic particles and to objects moving near the speed of light relative to each other. From these considerations Popper drew the conclusion that the line between science and other ways of knowing is the systematic exposure of hypotheses to tests of "falsification."

These considerations suggest that not the *verifiability* but the *falsifiability* of a system is to be taken as a criterion of demarcation. . . . I shall not require of a scientific system that it shall be capable of being singled out, once and for all, in a positive sense; but I shall require that its logical form shall be such that it can be singled out, by means of empirical tests, in a negative sense. *It must be possible for an empirical scientific system to be refuted by experience.* (Popper, 1959:40–41)

Of what, then, does scientific knowledge consist? It consists of theories that maximally expose themselves to falsification because they are conjectural, highly concise, simple statements from which a broad range of apparently *improbable* inferences can be made.

But these marvelously imaginative and bold conjectures or "anticipations" of ours are carefully and soberly controlled by systematic tests. Once put forward, none of our "anticipations" are dogmatically upheld. Our method of research is not to defend them, in order to prove how right we were. On the contrary, we try to overthrow them. Using all the weapons of our logical, mathematical, and technical armoury we try to prove that our anticipations were false—in order to put forward, in their stead, new unjustified, and unjustifiable anticipations, new "rash and premature prejudices," as Bacon derisively called them. (Ibid.:279)

Falsifiability versus Verifiability

POPPER'S EMPHASIS upon "falsifiability" and his rejection of probable verification is not quite the drastic challenge to the logical positivist model of science that one might suppose (and that Popper intended). Its implications for working social scientists are in fact trivial, since Popper himself emphasizes the distinction between the *logical* and *practical* consequence of the basic asymmetry between verification and falsification. Popper was well aware of the fact that as a practical matter, one negative instance never falsifies a well-established or fondly held hypothesis. One black swan does not lead to the falsification of the belief that all swans are white but rather to such questions as: Is this black bird with a long neck really a swan? To provide for the practical problems that arise in deciding whether a hypothesis has been falsified, Popper was obliged to develop a calculus of what he called "degree of corroboration," in which all of the positive criteria for establishing verification, including statistical tests of significance, are simply reintroduced in negative form as disconfirming rather than confirming procedures. Competing theories are then still to be judged by the extent to which they account for events, those which have been least falsified but which are most falsifiable and most tested being preferred over all others. According to Popper, "degree of corroboration" differs from "degree of verification" because the sole purpose of the latter is "to establish as firmly as possible the surviving theory [as] the *true* one."

As against this, I do not think that we can ever seriously reduce by elimination, the number of competing theories, since this number remains always infinite. What we do—or should do—is *hold on to the most improbable of the surviving theories* which is the one that can be most severely tested. We tentatively *"accept"* this theory—but only in the sense that we select it as worthy to be subjected to further criticism, and to the severest tests we can design. (Ibid.:419)

That all of this merely adds up to an exquisite psychological or metaphysical emphasis devoid of operational significance in the conduct of research seems to be confirmed by the following: "On the positive side, we may be entitled to add that the surviving theory is the best theory —and the best tested theory—of which we know" (ibid.). The weaknesses of Popper's falsificationist criterion can be seen in his own tendency to present highly improbable theories, such as: "I assert that our own free world is by far the best society that has come into existence during the course of human history" (Popper, 1965:369). Indeed, it is impossible to understand Popper's demarcation proposal or the attention it has received without placing it in the context of his political-economic beliefs and his active opposition to Marxist theory and practice. In his book *The Poverty of Historicism*, Popper attempts to show that to the extent that Marxism is falsifiable, it has been falsified, and therefore should be regarded as refuted, along with all other attempts to apply science to history. Being a faithful Popperian falsificationist does not restrain Brian Magee (1973:89) from declaring: "I do not see how any rational man can have read Popper's critique of Marx and still be a Marxist."

Thomas Kuhn's "Paradigms"

THE OBVIOUS LACK of correspondence between the conduct of research and Popper's view that science consists or should consist of an unremitting attempt to prove one's own beliefs false has helped to stimulate a healthy interest among historians of science concerning the actual psycho-social conditions of scientific discovery. It should come as no surprise that many of the most cherished scientific discoveries were made as a result of following either metaphysical or downright irrational beliefs. Nor should it surprise anyone that once made, many of these same discoveries would have been abandoned had the originators not stubbornly clung to the conviction that they were right, in the teeth of overwhelming evidence to the contrary. Newton's earliest prediction about the orbit of the moon, for example, was incorrect; Darwin had only indirect evidence for natural selection; Galileo's experiments actually proved that the earth is motionless, and the lunar mountains he claimed to have seen through his telescope bear no resemblance to lunar mountains as seen through modern telescopes (Feyerabend, 1975).

Popper's definition of science fails to come to grips with the problem presented by the existence of what Thomas Kuhn once called "paradigms"—i.e., "universally recognized scientific achievements that for a time provide model problems and solutions to a community of practitioners" (1970:viii). These "accepted examples of scientific practice—examples that include law, theory, application, and instrumentation together—provide models from which spring particular coherent traditions of scientific research" (ibid.:10). The existence of a paradigm guarantees that at any given moment a mature science will devote itself to puzzle solving along limited but productive lines. This constitutes what Kuhn calls the period of "normal" science. The greatest scientific discoveries however, are not those made during the period of normal science but rather during periods of paradigmatic revolutions —when, for example, Copernican astronomy replaced Ptolemaic astronomy, or Newtonian dynamics replaced Aristotelian dynamics, or quantum mechanics replaced classical electrodynamics.

Contrary to Popper's falsificationist view, neither normal science nor scientific revolutions are devoted to the falsification of theories. Even verification may be relatively inconsequential for "an apparently arbitrary element compounded out of personal and historical accident, is always a formative ingredient of the beliefs espoused by a given scientific community at a given time." During normal science, research, far from not having verificationist goals, "is predicated on the assumption that the scientific community knows what the world is like." Far from exposing its basic beliefs to falsifying experiments, normal science "often suppresses fundamental novelties because they are necessarily subversive of its basic commitments." But the most serious departure from Popper's model is needed to describe what happens when paradigms clash:

The proponents of competing paradigms are always at least slightly at cross-purposes. Neither side will grant all the non-empirical assumptions that the other needs in order to make its case . . . they are bound partly to talk through each other. Though each may hope to convert the other to his way of seeing his science and its problems, neither may hope to prove his case. The competition between paradigms is not the sort of battle that can be resolved by proofs. (Ibid.: 148)

How, then, are they resolved?

Evaluating Paradigms

FOR KUHN, scientific revolutions occur as a result of "anomalies" encountered by the practitioners of normal science. The practitioners find themselves unable to solve a growing number of problems, which leads to a crisis, which in turn provides the opportunity for the rise of a new paradigm. Kuhn, however, has no theory as to why one paradigm rather than another should triumph at a particular time. Like Popper, Kuhn emphatically denies that the choice of paradigms can be attributed to a selection process favoring paradigms that get closer to the "truth." But he goes beyond Popper and insists that they are not even likely to be selected according to any kind of progressive principle whatsoever. To defend himself against the charge of relativism (I would call it obscurantism), Kuhn did suggest in the second edition of the *Structure of Scientific Revolutions* a series of criteria by which one could distinguish "an earlier from a more recent theory time after time" (205–206). These include accuracy of prediction; more esoteric (less everyday) subject matter; and number of different problems solved.

But these criteria apply to theories within paradigms, not to the paradigms themselves. When paradigms replace each other, different puzzles are solved. Hence, one can never say where a *paradigm*, as distinguished from a theory, fits in the overall history of science. One can never say whether science has really "progressed" or not. Indeed, Kuhn maintains that from a paradigmatic view, "Einstein's general theory of relativity is closer to Aristotle's than either of them is to Newton's" (207).

Paradigms Lost*—Paul Feyerabend

ONLY A SHORT STEP separates Kuhn's disbelief in the inherent progressivism of scientific knowledge from the epistemological anarchism of Paul Feyerabend. And only one step more takes us from Feyerabend to the cults of the California mystics, led by Carlos Castaneda and his flying shamans and hundred-foot gnats (see Chapter 11).

To associate the relativistic doctrines of Paul Feyerabend with the resurgent popularity of witchcraft and shamanism is no hyperbole. Feyerabend is not especially original in urging that in fifteenth- and sixteenth-century Europe, the theory of demonic influences and witchcraft was based on strong empirical evidence and was the best, if not the only, way to account for the observed phenomena (1963:32). But what is novel (at least for a professor of philosophy three hundred years after the great European witch craze) is that he renders this entirely legitimate historical judgment with complete indifference to the question of the truth of witchcraft beliefs. Kuhn's most important contribution, claims Feyerabend, is the recognition that paradigms talk past each other—that they are "incommensurable." Theories can only be refuted when they share the same paradigm; incommensurable theories cannot refute each other:

"Their *content* cannot be compared. Nor is it possible to make a judgment of verisimilitude except within the confines of a particular theory. . . . What remains are subjective judgments, judgments of taste, and our own subjective wishes." (1970:228)

*Apologies to R. M. Keesing (1972).

The similarity between this culminating critique of positivism and the glorious age of hippiedom and California culthood is too close in time, place, content, and form to be ignored. Calling for more, not less, "epistemological anarchy," Feyerabend believes that "Flexibility, even sloppiness in semantical matters is a prerequisite of scientific progress" (1963:33). With Feyerabend we move full circle from probable knowledge of something to no knowledge of anything. The epistemological anarchist, convinced that all knowledge is equally uncertain, faces the ludicrous task of trying to convince others of the certainty (or probability) that all truths are equally false.

The allegation that no two paradigms of sufficient generality ever really disagree is part of the contemporary attack on "objectivity." This attack, as the philosopher Frank Cunningham (1973:22–23) has pointed out, leads to a consequence which even the most ardent epistemological anarchist may find hard to accept. There is no reason to take anything these anti-objectivists say seriously:

If, as I think can be argued, sincerely to believe a theory is to believe that it is objectively true, then the . . . consequence of the anti-objectivist position would be that he would have to admit either that he does not believe his theory or that it is objectively true: neither alternative would be attractive to him. If he does not believe the view, why does he advocate it? If it *is* objectively true, why cannot *other* theories also be objectively true? The burden would lie on the anti-objectivist to show what there is about his endeavor (e.g., its generality, or its specifically philosophical or meta-scientific nature) that allows it and it alone to escape his own anti-objectivist claim (and he would have to show this without himself employing or supposing the conclusions of any theory the objectivity of which he has tried to show impossible).

However, it is not in logical contradictions that one meets the full consequence of Feyerabend's (1970:33) claim that "science as we know it today is not inescapable . . . we may construct a world in which it plays no role whatever (such a world, I venture to suggest, would be more pleasant than the world we live in today)." As long as Feyerabend deals with mountains on the moon or quantum mechanics, his views cannot inflict too much damage. But there are other domains of knowledge in which epistemological relativism poses a grave threat to our survival. Medicine is one such domain, and there are many others in the social sciences. One cannot remain indifferent to whether cancer is caused by witchcraft or some defect in cellular chemistry. Nor can one let unbridled imaginations determine the causes of poverty, or establish the existence or nonexistence of a ruling class in the United States. It cannot be a matter of taste whether you believe or do not believe that pollution is a menace, that the underdeveloped countries are getting poorer, that the multinationals are promoting a nuclear arms race, that war is instinctual, that women and blacks are inferior, or that the green revolution is a hoax. Let Feyerabend stand before the ovens of Dachau or the ditch at Mylai and say that our scientific understanding of sociocultural systems is ultimately nothing but an "aesthetic judgment."

Paradigms Found

FORTUNATELY, Hume's heirs have dug their heels in and refused to be pulled into the grave that the philosophical relativists and anarchists have been digging for them. Acknowledging that there are indeed overarching sets of essentially metaphysical assumptions that take precedence over theories and facts, they see no reason why such assumptions—called "research programs" by Popper's protégé, Imre Lakatos—cannot be compared and evaluated from the perspective of scientific adequacy. Lakatos (who called himself a "sophisticated falsificationist," as opposed to his mentor, the "naive falsificationist"), admitted, with Kuhn and Feyerabend, that no theory ever was or ever should be overturned by a single predictive failure, "for the history of science is the history of research programs rather than of theories" (Lakatos, 1970:133). We may have been comparing the wrong units all along, but that does not mean we should stop our comparisons:

Not an isolated theory but only a *series of theories* can be said to be scientific or unscientific: to apply the term "scientific" to one single theory is a categorical mistake. (Ibid.:119)

The history of science has and should be the history of competing research programs (or if you wish, "paradigms"). (Ibid.:155)

How are research programs to be compared and evaluated? Essentially by showing that theories which originate under the auspices of one paradigm are more effective at solving Kuhn's "puzzles" than their rivals. Although these solutions may be highly tentative, they nonetheless can participate in a "progressive problem shift." The hallmark of a progressive theory is that "novel facts are anticipated" (187), for a "given fact is explained scientifically only if a new fact is also explained with it" (119). This means that the test of falsification cannot be used alone to decide whether a theory is scientific. The falsificationers have another obligation if they wish the results of their skepticism to be regarded as scientific. They themselves must present a theory that explains the facts better—that is, explains new facts as well, in the context of a whole system of theories. "There is no falsification before the emergence of a better theory. [119] . . . Purely negative criticism does not kill a research program [179]."

In other words, scientists are never released from the obligation of being intelligent. One cannot merely mechanically count confirming or disconfirming instances; one must always remain alert to the possibility that tests may not be measuring what they ought to be measuring; and one must accept responsibility for evaluating the consequence of falsification in relation to a network of interrelated theories and be prepared to substitute a new theory which articulates "better" within the same or some other network of theories—"better" in the sense that it can help to explain (predict, account for) more than the rejected theory can.

The Philosophical Justification for This Book

COLLEAGUES OFTEN MISTRUST my attempt to engage in a systematic critique of the basic assumptions and achievements of what used to be called the "schools" of anthropology. Most would prefer to be left alone to do their own work. But the last few years have seen a steadily advancing consensus among philosophers to the effect that scientific progress depends on wide-ranging comparisons of alternative theories, of networks of theories, and of whole paradigms. In the words of the philosopher Larry Laudan (1977:120):

All evaluations of research traditions* and theories must be made *within a comparative* context. What matters is not, in some absolute sense, how effec-

*"A research tradition is a set of general assumptions about the entities and processes in a domain of study, and about the appropriate methods to be used for investigating the problems and constructing the theories in that domain" (ibid.: 81).

tive or progressive a tradition or theory is, but, rather, how its effectiveness or progressiveness compares with its competitors.

Current discussions of the role of paradigms in the development of science are encumbered by the inchoate, partially unconscious, and largely implicit nature of the best-known historical examples. If the history of science is the history of competing paradigms, then the logical next step is to demand that individual scientists be capable of rendering a conscious, coherent account of the paradigm under whose auspices their research is being conducted.

Although for the empiricist the evaluation of competing paradigms must ultimately rest on the productivity and comprehensiveness of testable theories, this does not mean that the *logical* structure of paradigms is any less important. As Nicholas Maxwell (1974a, 1974b) has suggested, if we make one crucial assumption about the purpose of science, then the possibility arises that some paradigms and theories can be evaluated even prior to the examination of their substantive products. This one crucial assumption is that the overall aim of science is to discover the maximum amount of order inherent in the universe or in any field of inquiry. Maxwell calls this "aim-oriented empiricism." Paradigms that aim simply at discovering what's there without any commitment to discovering orderly relationships would then be judged unscientific or at least less scientific than their competitors. This same criterion would be applicable to theories and hypotheses. Writes Maxwell (1974a:152):

Both Lakatos and Kuhn agree that in revolutionary situations in science no rational choice between rival hard cores or paradigms can be made *at the time*, but, at best, only long after the event. According to aim-oriented empiricism, however, such a rational choice *is* possible, since we can assess in an *a priori* fashion the relative simplicity or intelligibility of the rival hard cores or paradigms, the promise which they hold out of realizing the basic metaphysical blueprint . . . of the science.

I agree with Maxwell's evaluation of the importance of coherent aim-oriented paradigms as a criterion of science. As Maxwell says (1974b:294): "Without some kind of agreed aim or blueprint for a science, one hardly has a science at all. It is only when some kind of choice of blueprint has been made that one can have any idea of the kind of theory one is seeking to develop, and the kind of rules that ought to govern the acceptance and rejection of theories." The time is ripe, therefore, to replace the inchoate and unconscious paradigms under whose auspices most anthropologists conduct their research with explicit descriptions of basic objectives, rules, and assumptions. That is why I have written this book.

Science and Research Strategy Defined

RECENT DEVELOPMENTS in the philosophy of science thus leave no doubt as to the importance of paradigmatic presuppositions in the development of effective scientific knowledge. Maxwell's proposal of blueprints and aim orientations is nothing but the recognition that scientific knowledge is enhanced by the conversion of implicit, inchoate, and unconscious presuppositions into alternative sets of explicit, organized, and conscious guidelines. But this is as far as the philosophical study of science can take the practitioners of particular branches of science. The task of specifying precisely what kinds of guidelines ought to be followed falls to the practitioners.

In the presence of disagreement concerning the overlapping relationship of such terms as "paradigm" (Kuhn), "theme" (Holton), "research program" (Lakatos), "research tradition" (Laudan), and "blueprint" (Maxwell), I prefer the term "research strategy" to designate the set of guidelines in question. "Strategy" has the advantage over "paradigm,"* "theme," and "tradition" in that it connotes conscious explicitness, and it is preferable to "program" and "blueprint," which connote rigid adherence to a preestablished series of observations and experiments.

By a scientific research strategy I mean an explicit set of guidelines pertaining to the epistemological status of the variables to be studied, the kinds of lawful relationships or principles that such variables probably exhibit, and the growing corpus of interrelated theories to which the strategy has thus far given rise. The aim of scientific research strategies in general is to account for observable entities and events and their relationships by means of powerful, interrelated parsimonious theories subject to correction and improvement through empirical test-

---

*Kuhn (1977) has responded to the complaint that he used the word "paradigm" in several different senses by suggesting that the terms "disciplinary matrix" and "exemplars" be used instead.

ing. The aim of cultural materialism in particular is to account for the origin, maintenance, and change of the global inventory of sociocultural differences and similarities. Thus cultural materialism shares with other scientific strategies an epistemology which seeks to restrict fields of inquiry to events, entities, and relationships that are knowable by means of explicit, logico-empirical, inductive-deductive, quantifiable public procedures or "operations" subject to replication by independent observers. This restriction necessarily remains an ideal aim rather than a rigidly perfected condition, for I recognize that total operationalization would cripple the ability to state principles, relate theories, and organize empirical tests, and would in effect ignore the existence of research strategies. It is a far cry, however, from the recognition that strategies and unoperationalized, vernacular, and metaphysical terms are necessary for the conduct of scientific inquiry to Feyerabend-like invitations to throw off all operational restraints.

What Is the Alternative?

SCIENCE IS a unique and precious contribution of Western civilization. This is not to deny that many other civilizations have contributed to scientific knowledge by inventing weights and measures, classifying plants and animals, recording astronomical observations, developing mathematical theorems, voyaging to distant lands, experimenting with chemical and physical processes. But it was in western Europe that the distinctive rules of the scientific method were first codified, given conscious expression, and systematically applied to the entire range of inorganic, organic, and cultural phenomena.

It is both foolish and dangerous for intellectuals in any society to minimize the significance of this achievement. We must recognize that there are many ways of knowing, but we must also recognize that it is not mere ethnocentric puffery to assert that science is a way of knowing that has a uniquely transcendent value for all human beings. In the entire course of prehistory and history only one way of knowing has encouraged its own practitioners to doubt their own premises and to systematically expose their own conclusions to the hostile scrutiny of nonbelievers. Granted that discrepancies between science as an ideal and science as it is practiced substantially reduce the difference between science, religion, and other modes of looking for the truth. But it is precisely as an ideal that the uniqueness of science deserves to be defended. No other way of knowing is based on a set of rules explicitly designed to transcend the prior belief systems of mutually antagonistic tribes, nations, classes, and ethnic and religious communities in order to arrive at knowledge that is equally probable for any rational human mind. Those who doubt that science can do this must be made to show how some other tolerant and ecumenical alternative can do it better. Unless they can show how some other universalistic system of knowing leads to more acceptable criteria of truth, their attempt to subvert the universal credibility of science in the name of cultural relativism, however well-intentioned, is an intellectual crime against humanity. It is a crime against humanity because the real alternative to science is not anarchy, but ideology; not peaceful artists, philosophers, and anthropologists, but aggressive fanatics and messiahs eager to annihilate each other and the whole world if need be in order to prove their point.

Chapter Two

The Epistemology
of Cultural Materialism

EMPIRICAL SCIENCE, then, is the foundation of the cultural materialist way of knowing. But merely to propose that our strategy should aim at meeting the criteria for scientific knowledge is to say very little about how scientific knowledge of the sociocultural field of inquiry can be acquired. When human beings are the objects of study, the would-be scientist is soon bedeviled by a unique quandary. Alone among the things and organisms studied by science, the human "object" is also a subject; the "objects" have well-developed thoughts about their own and other people's thoughts and behavior. Moreover, because of the mutual translatability of all human languages, what people think about their thoughts and behavior can be learned through questions and answers. What does a Bathonga call his mother? "Mamani." When does a Maring slaughter his pigs? "When the sacred tree has grown." Why are these Yanomamo men setting out to war? "To take vengeance on those who have stolen our women." Why is this Kwakiutl chief distributing blankets? "To shame his rivals."

No aspect of a research strategy more decisively characterizes it than the way in which it treats the relationship between what people say and think as subjects and what they say and think and do as objects of scientific inquiry.

Epistemological Quandaries of Marx and Engels

IN *The German Ideology,* Marx and Engels proposed to upend the study of sociocultural phenomena by focusing on the material conditions that determine human existence. A basic aim of their strategy was to demystify social life through the destruction of the socially created illusions that warp human consciousness—for example, the illusion that it is buying and selling rather than labor that creates wealth. Picturing social life as continually evolving out of the daily life of ordinary people, they wrote of the need to identify individuals "not as they may appear in their own or other people's imagination, but as they really are . . ."

In direct contrast to German philosophy which descends from heaven to earth, here it is a matter of ascending from earth to heaven. That is to say, not of setting out from what men say, imagine, conceive, nor from men as narrated, thought of, imagined, conceived in order to arrive at men in the flesh; but setting out from real, active men. . . . For the first method of approach, the starting point is consciousness taken as the real living individual; for the second . . . it is the real, living individuals themselves. . . . (Marx and Engels, 1976 [1846]: 36–37)

But what does one mean by "individuals as they *really* are," "*real* active men," and "*real* living individuals"? How does one tell the difference between a real and unreal person? Are all thoughts unreal, or just some? And if the latter, how does one tell them apart?

The epistemological points that Marx and Engels were trying to establish cannot be made by means of the concept of "reality." For scientific materialists, the issue of what is real or unreal is subsumed entirely by the epistemological generalities of the scientific method. If someone claims that shamans can fly, we insist on testable evidence. But our strategy rejects the implication that the thought itself is "unreal." Matter is neither more nor less real than thoughts. The issue of whether ideas or material entities are the basis of reality is not, properly speaking, an epistemological issue. It is an ontological issue—and a sterile one, to boot. Materialists need only insist that material entities exist apart from ideas, that thoughts about things and events are separable from things and events. The central epistemological problem that must be solved then is how one can achieve separate and valid scientific knowledge of the two realms. If materialists wish to solve this problem, I think that they must deal not with "real" and "unreal" but with two different sets of distinctions—first, the distinction between mental and behavioral events, and second, the distinction between emic and etic events. I shall take these up in turn.

Mental and Behavioral Fields

THE SCIENTIFIC STUDY of human social life must concern itself equally with two radically different kinds of phenomena. On the one hand, there are the activities that constitute the human behavior stream—all the body motions and environmental effects produced by such motions, large and small, of all the human beings who have ever lived. On the other hand, there are all the thoughts and feelings that we human beings experience within our minds. The fact that distinctive operations must be used to make scientifically credible statements about each realm guarantees the distinctiveness of each realm. To describe the universe of human mental experiences, one must employ operations capable of discovering what people are thinking about. But to describe body motions and the external effects produced by body motions, one does not have to find out what is going on inside people's heads—at least this is not necessary if one adopts the epistemological stance of cultural materialism.

The distinction between mental and behavioral events moves us only halfway toward the solution of Marx and Engels' quandary. There remains the fact that the thoughts and behavior of the participants can be viewed from two different perspectives: from the perspective of the participants themselves, and from the perspective of the observers. In both instances scientific—that is, objective—accounts of the mental and behavioral fields are possible. But in the first instance, the observers employ concepts and distinctions meaningful and appropriate to the participants; while in the second instance, they employ concepts and distinctions meaningful and appropriate to the observers. If the criteria of empirical replicability and testability are met, either perspective may lead to a knowledge of "real," nonimaginary mental and behavioral events, although the accounts rendered may be divergent.

Emics and Etics

SINCE BOTH the observer's point of view and the participants' point of view can be presented objectively or subjectively, depending on the adequacy of the empirical operations employed by the observer, we cannot use the words "objective" and "subjective" to denote the option in question without creating a great deal of confusion. To avoid this confusion, many anthropologists have begun to use the terms "emic" and "etic," which were first introduced by the anthropological linguist Kenneth Pike in his book *Language in Relation to a Unified Theory of the Structure of Human Behavior.*

Emic operations have as their hallmark the elevation of the native informant to the status of ultimate judge of the adequacy of the observer's descriptions and analyses. The test of the adequacy of emic analyses is their ability to generate statements the native accepts as real, meaningful, or appropriate. In carrying out research in the emic mode, the observer attempts to acquire a knowledge of the categories and rules one must know in order to think and act as a native. One attempts to learn, for example, what rule lies behind the use of the same kin term for mother and mother's sister among the Bathonga; or one attempts to learn when it is appropriate to shame one's guests among the Kwakiutl.

Etic operations have as their hallmark the elevation of observers to the status of ultimate judges of the categories and concepts used in descriptions and analyses. The test of the adequacy of etic accounts is simply their ability to generate scientifically productive theories about the causes of sociocultural differences and similarities. Rather than employ concepts that are necessarily real, meaningful, and appropriate from the native point of view, the observer is free to use alien categories and rules derived from the data language of science. Frequently, etic operations involve the measurement and juxtaposition of activities and events that native informants may find inappropriate or meaningless.

I think the following example demonstrates the consummate importance of the difference between emic and etic knowledge. In the Trivandwan district of the state of Kerala, in southern India, I interviewed farmers about the cause of death of their domestic cattle. Every farmer insisted that he would never deliberately shorten the life of one of his animals, that he would never kill it or starve it to death. Every farmer ardently affirmed the legitimacy of the standard Hindu prohibition against the slaughter of domestic bovines. Yet it soon became obvious from the animal reproductive histories I was collecting that the mortality rate of male calves tended to be almost twice as high as the mortality rate of female calves. In fact, male cattle from zero to one years old are outnumbered by female cattle of the same age group in a ratio of 67 to 100. The farmers themselves are aware that male calves are more likely to die than female calves, but they attribute the difference to the relative "weakness" of the males. "The males get sick more often," they say. When I asked farmers to explain why male calves got sick more often, several suggested that the males ate less than the females. One or two suggested that the male calves ate less because they were not permitted to stay at the mother's teats for more than a few seconds. But no one would say that since there is little demand for traction animals in Kerala, males are culled and females reared.

The emics of the situation are that no one knowingly or willingly would shorten the life of a calf. Again and again I was told that every calf has the right to life regardless of its sex. But the etics of the situation are that cattle sex ratios are systematically adjusted to the needs of the local ecology and economy through preferential male "bovicide." Although the unwanted calves are not slaughtered, they are more or less rapidly starved to death. Emically, the systemic relationship between Kerala's cattle sex ratios and local ecological and economic conditions simply does not exist. Yet the consummate importance of this systemic relationship can be seen from the fact that in other parts of India, where different ecological and economic conditions prevail, preferential etic bovicide is practiced against female rather than male cattle, resulting in an adult cattle sex ratio of over 200 oxen for every 100 cows in the state of Uttar Pradesh.

A while back I mentioned the burden of unoperationalized terms, which prevents social scientists from solving puzzles or even communicating effectively about their research. The first simple step toward operationalizing such concepts as status, role, class, caste, tribe, state, aggression, exploitation, family, kinship, and the rest is to specify whether the knowledge one professes to have about these entities has been gained by means of emic or etic operations. All notions of replicability and testability fly up the chimney when the world as seen by the observed is capriciously muddled with the world as seen by the observer. As I hope to show later on, research strategies that fail to distinguish between mental and behavior stream events and between emic and etic operations cannot develop coherent networks of theories embracing the causes of sociocultural differences and similarities. And a priori, one can say that those research strategies that confine themselves exclusively to emics or exclusively to etics do not meet the general criteria for an aim-oriented social science as effectively as those which embrace both points of view.

Etics, Emics, and Objectivity

KENNETH PIKE formed the words "etic" and "emic" from the suffixes of the words phonetic and phonemic. Phonetic accounts of the sounds of a language are based upon a taxonomy of the body parts active in the production of speech utterances and their characteristic environmental effects in the form of acoustic waves. Linguists discriminate etically between voiced and unvoiced sounds, depending on the activity of the vocal cords; between aspirated and nonaspirated sounds, depending on the activity of the glottis; between labials and dentals, depending on the activity of the tongue and teeth. The native speaker does not make these discriminations. On the other hand, emic accounts of the sounds of a language are based on the implicit or unconscious system of sound contrasts that native speakers have inside their heads and that they employ to identify meaningful utterances in their language.

In structural linguistics, phonemes—the minimal units of contrastive sounds found in a particular language—are distinguished from nonsignificant or nondiscriminatory sounds and from each other by means of a simple operational test. If one sound substituted for another in the same sound context results in a change of meaning from that of one word to another, the two sounds exemplify (belong to the class of) two different phonemes. Thus the spoken p and b of pit and bit exemplify two different English phonemes because native speakers recognize pit and bit (and pat and bat, pull and bull, and so forth) as words that have different meanings. The spoken p and b enjoy the status of phonemes not because they are etically different, but because native speakers perceive them to be in "contrast" when one is substituted for the other in the same context of sounds.

The importance of Pike's distinction is that it leads to a clarification of the meaning of subjectivity and objectivity in the human sciences. To be objective is not to adopt an etic view; nor is it subjective to adopt an emic view. To be objective is to adopt the epistemological criteria discussed in the previous chapter by which science is demarcated from other ways of knowing. It is clearly possible to be objective—i.e., scientific—about either emic or etic phenomena.* Similarly, it is equally possible to be subjective about either emic or etic phenomena. Objectivity is the epistemological status that distinguishes the community of observers from communities that are observed. While it is possible for those who are observed to be objective, this can only mean that they have temporarily or permanently joined the community of observers by relying on an operationalized scientific epistemology. Objectivity is not merely intersubjectivity. It is a special form of intersubjectivity established by the distinctive logical and empirical discipline to which members of the scientific community agree to submit.

Pike's Emic Bias

MUCH CONTROVERSY has arisen concerning the appropriation by cultural materialists of Pike's emic/etic distinction. In large measure this controversy stems from the fact that Pike is a cultural idealist who believes that the aim of social science is to describe and analyze emic systems.

What Pike tried to do was to apply the principles by which linguists discover phonemes and other emic units of language (such as *morphemes*) to the discovery of emic units—which he called "behavioremes"—in the behavior stream. By identifying behavioremes, Pike hoped to extend the research strategy that had proved effective in the analysis of languages to the study of the behavior stream. Pike never considered the possibility of studying the behavior stream etically. He rejected virtually without discussion the possibility that an etic approach to the behavior stream might yield more interesting "structures" than an emic approach. To the extent that one could even talk about the existence of etic units, they were for Pike necessary evils, mere steppingstones to higher emic realms. Observers necessarily begin their analysis of social life with etic categories, but the whole thrust of their analytical task ought to be the replacement of such categories with the emic units that constitute structured systems within the minds of the social actors. In Pike's words (1967:38–39): "etic data provide

*Despite my reiteration of this point, Fisher and Werner (1978) have me equating science and ethics.

access into the system—the starting point of analysis." "The initial etic description gradually is refined, and is ultimately—in principle, but probably never in practice—replaced by one which is totally emic." This position clashes head on with the epistemological assumptions of cultural materialism. In the cultural materialist research strategy, etic analysis is not a steppingstone to the discovery of emic structures, but to the discovery of etic structures. The intent is neither to convert etics to emics nor emics to etics, but rather to describe both and if possible to explain one in terms of the other.

Etics, Emics, and Informants

A COMMON SOURCE of misunderstanding about the emic/etic distinction is the assumption that etic operations preclude collaboration with native informants. But as a matter of practical necessity, observers must frequently rely on native informants to obtain their basic information about who has done what. Recourse to informants for such purposes does not automatically settle the epistemological status of the resultant descriptions.

Depending on whose categories establish the framework of discourse, informants may provide either etic or emic descriptions of the events they have observed or participated in. When the description is responsive to the observer's categories of time, place, weights and measure, actor types, numbers of people present, body motion, and environmental effects, it is etic. Census taking provides the most familiar example. If one merely asks an informant, "Who are the people who live in this house?" the answer will have emic status, since the informant will use the native concept of "lives here" to include and exclude persons present in or absent from the household. Thus in Brazil I had to furnish specific instructions concerning godchildren and servants, who by emic rules could not be considered members of the household in which they were permanent residents. But once my assistant was properly trained in the discriminations that were etically appropriate, the epistemological status of his data was no less etic than my own.

Emics and Consciousness

PIKE AND OTHERS who have used linguistics as the paradigm for emic analysis stress the fact that the immediate products of elicitation do not necessarily furnish the structured models that are the desired end product of emic analysis. For example, in determining whether the two *p*'s in *paper* (the first is aspirated) are phonemically the same or different, one cannot rely on the native's conscious powers of auto-analysis. Native speakers cannot be induced to state their language's phonemic system. Nor can they state the rules of grammar that permit them to generate grammatical statements. It is true, therefore, that many emic descriptions are models of "structures" of which the informant is not conscious. Nonetheless, the validity of such emic models rests on their ability to generate messages that are consciously judged as appropriate and meaningful by the native actor.

Moreover, Pike did provide for what he called *hypostasis*—namely, the elicitation of conscious structural rules, such as "don't use double negatives." When one turns to elicitations concerned with the structure of thought and behavior as distinct from the structure of language, hypostasis is far more common. Questions such as "Why do you do this?" "What is this for?" "Is this the same as that?" and "When or where do you do this?" are no less emic than the question, Does *p'ap'er* (pronounced with two aspirated *p*'s) have the same meaning as *p'aper* (pronounced with one)?

The ethnolinguist Mary Black (1973:524) protests that the "emicist" does not go around "collecting 'verbal statements *about* human action' while an eticist is out there observing human action first hand." Black insists that it is the *structure* of the system of beliefs, including beliefs about action, that is studied in emic research, not the statements about the beliefs themselves: "The idea that ethnoscience is interested in language and linguistics for the purpose of having informants *make statements about their patterns of behavior* is rather simplistic and can be held only by those who have not done ethnosemantic work" (526).

I do not regard it as simplistic to insist that emics are concerned *both* with the conscious content of elicited responses and with the unconscious structures that may be found to underlie surface content. Black cannot maintain that complex emic structures are necessarily unconscious structures which can only be inferred from more superficial elicitations. Many important complex systems of rules are held quite consciously—for example, rules of etiquette, sports, religious rituals, bureaucracies, and governments. Black's notion of what constitutes authentic "ethnosemantic work" would also seem to exclude sociological surveys and opinion polls, whose findings have merely to be tabulated in order to achieve structural significance. Perhaps the fact that most cognitivists (see Chapter 9) have not concerned themselves with manifest hypostatic ideological structures reflects their predilection for dealing with esoteric and politically trivial emic phenomena such as ethnobotanical and kin terminological distinctions.

Mental Etics and Behavioral Emics

IF THE TERMS "emic" and "etic" are not redundant with respect to the terms "mental" and "behavioral," there should be four objective operationally definable domains in the sociocultural field of inquiry*:

	Emic	Etic
Behavioral	I	II
Mental	III	IV

To illustrate with the example of the sacred cow:

I   *Emic/Behavioral:* "No calves are starved to death."
II *Etic/Behavioral:* "Male calves are starved to death."
III *Emic/Mental:* "All calves have the right to life."
IV *Etic/Mental:* "Let the male calves starve to death when feed is scarce."

The epistemological status of domains I and IV creates the thorniest problems. What is the locus of the reality of the emic behavioral statement, "No calves are starved to death"? Does this statement refer to something that is actually in the behavior stream, or is it merely a belief about the behavior stream that exists only inside of the heads of the Indian farmers? Similarly, what is the locus of the reality of the etic mental rule: "Let the male calves starve to death when feed is scarce"? Does this rule exist inside the heads of the farmers, or is it merely

*I am indebted to Brian Ferguson for this clarification.

something that exists inside of the head of the observer? Let me turn first to the problem of the status of emic behavioral descriptions. Descriptions of the behavior stream from the actor's point of view can seldom be dismissed as mere figments of the imagination and relegated to a purely mental domain. First of all, there are many instances where there is a very close correspondence between the actor's and observer's views of what is going on in the world. When Indian farmers discuss the steps they take to transplant rice or to get a reluctant cow to let down its milk, their emic descriptions of behavior stream events are as accurate as any ethnographer's etic description would be. Moreover, even when there are sharp divergences between them, the emic and etic viewpoints are not likely to cancel each other out entirely. Even in the present rather extreme example, note that the farmers do not see the culling of unwanted animals as "bovicide" and that the mode of achieving the death of unwanted animals is sufficiently ambiguous to warrant that interpretation. Clearly the amount of discrepancy between the emic and etic versions of events in the behavior stream is an important measure of the degree to which people are mystified about events taking place around them. Only if people were totally mystified could one claim that their behavioral descriptions referred exclusively to mental phenomena.

The other thorny category, the etics of mental life (IV), has similar implications. People can be mystified about their own thoughts as well as about their behavior. Such mystifications may come about as the result of repressing certain thoughts to an unconscious or at least a nonsalient level of attention. In the example under consideration, the existence of the rule "when feed is scarce, let the male calves starve to death" can be inferred from the recurrently lopsided sex ratios. As I mentioned earlier, something very close to this rule can be elicited from some Kerala farmers when they are confronted with the question of why male calves eat less than female calves. Etic descriptions of mental life, in other words, can serve the function of helping to probe the minds of informants concerning less salient or unconscious beliefs and rules.

The road to etic knowledge of mental life is full of pitfalls and impasses. Extreme caution is called for in making inferences about what is going on inside people's heads even when the thoughts are those of our closest friends and relatives. The hazards increase when the thoughts belong to people in other cultures. For example, I became intrigued by the fact that the children in a small Brazilian town frequently came to school wearing only one shoe. When I asked for an explanation, the children would look embarrassed and say that they had a sore on the unshod foot. However, I never could see anything wrong with the foot in question. This blatant discrepancy between what I could observe and what the children said about the behavioral situation led me to make a false inference about what was actually motivating them. I supposed that, being children, they preferred to go to school barefoot; since that was not permitted, they did the next best thing. But what was really going on in their heads, as I learned by questioning the children and their parents, was something else. Informants said that it was better to wear two shoes. The reason for wearing only one was to enable siblings to share the same pair of shoes, in order to economize.

Psychoanalysts and their patients are familiar with the dangers of making inferences that contradict what the patient says and that rely solely on the analyst's inferences from behavior. Some psychoanalysts find a hidden motive for everything that happens. Thus if the patients arrive for their session early, they are "anxious." If they arrive on time, they are "compulsive." And if they arrive late, they are "hostile." Clearly anthropologists should use the etic approach to mental life sparingly and should not attempt to override every emic explanation with an etic alternative.

Cross-Cultural Emics

I SHALL NOW attempt to clarify the epistemological status of mental phenomena that recur in different cultures. Many anthropologists insist that when mental traits recur cross-culturally, the traits necessarily have an etic status. The focal case concerns the eight key concepts that recurrently figure as components of the world inventory of kin terminological systems.* Following Ward Goodenough (1970) and William Sturtevant (1964), Raoul Naroll (1973:3) identifies these as etic concepts: "These are the eight key etic concepts. . . . The inventory . . . is validated by the fact that every known emic kin-term system can be most parsimoniously defined by using the eight etic concepts." Since, as Naroll says, the eight key concepts are derived

*These are: (1) consanguinity/affinity; (2) generation; (3) sex; (4) collaterality; (5) bifurcation; (6) relative age; (7) decedence; and (8) genealogical distance.

from emic kin-term systems—systems in which the distinctions are real and appropriate from the participant's point of view—it is difficult to see why they should be called etic concepts. The reason cannot be simply that they recur cross-culturally. When a linguist reports that in a certain language voiced and unvoiced bilabial stops form a phonemic contrast, the epistemological status of [b] and [p] does not shift from phonemic to phonetic. Nor does such a shift take place as a consequence of someone reporting that many other languages including English make the same distinction. Or to take another example: suppose that in describing a particular culture, the ethnographer notes that people believe they have a "soul" that leaves the body at death. What difference does it make if a similar belief is found in a thousand additional cultures? As long as the concept is real, meaningful, and appropriate to the members of those cultures, it remains an emic concept with respect to those cultures.

The explanation for the difference of opinion about the status of the key kinship concepts lies in the use of these concepts to make inferences about mental distinctions in cultures that have yet to be studied emically. The fact is that not all eight distinctions are used in all kin-terminological systems (American kin terminology, for example, ignores relative age and decedence—i.e., whether the kinsperson is alive or dead). In analyzing an unknown system, one would naturally infer that it contains at least some of these distinctions, and in that case the operational status of the inferred distinction would be that of the etics of mental life. I can therefore agree with Ward Goodenough (1970:112) when he says that "emic description requires etics, and by trying to do emic descriptions we add to our etic conceptual resources for subsequent description," provided it is understood that mere recurrence is not the hallmark of etics and that "etic . . . resources for subsequent description" refers exclusively to the etics of mental life. I cannot agree, however, that our etic conceptual resources for the study of the behavior stream are dependent upon emic studies. The etic concepts appropriate for the study of the behavior stream are dependent on their status as productive elements in a corpus of scientific theories.

The Epistemological Status
of Speech Acts

MUCH OF THE HUMAN behavior stream consists of verbal messages sent back and forth between relatives, friends and strangers. Does the emic/etic distinction apply to such events? Since language is the primary mode of human communication, and since it is the function of language to convey meanings, one might conclude that the emic mode is the only feasible approach to language as the conveyor of meaning. This is not necessarily true, however; etic as well as emic approaches to speech acts are possible. One does not have to communicate with communicators in order to understand the meaning of communication acts. For example, psychologists, ethologists, and primatologists routinely attempt to identify the meaning of communicative acts among infrahuman species by observing the contexts and consequences of such acts. Among chimpanzees one can say that a "bark" means "danger," a loud whooping means "food," an upturned hand is a "begging" gesture, an upturned rump a sign of "submission." If this approach is possible with respect to primate communication, why should it not also be possible in the case of human communication?

When I first thought about this problem in 1964, I concluded that the meaning of speech acts was accessible only through emic operations. In 1968 (p. 579) I took the same position, stating that "from an etic point of view, the universe of meaning, purposes, goals, motivations, etc., is . . . unapproachable." This was an error. What should be said is that descriptions of mental life based on etic operations do not necessarily uncover the purposes, goals, motivations, and so forth that an emic approach can uncover. For the etic study of speech acts is merely another example of the possibility of an etics of mental life.

The difference between etic meanings and emic meanings of speech acts is the difference between the conventional or "code" meaning of a human utterance and its deeper psychological significance for speaker and hearer respectively. Let me illustrate this distinction with data from a study of speech acts carried out by means of videotape recordings (Dehavenon and Harris, n.d.). The observers intended to measure patterns of superordination and subordination in family life by counting each family member's requests and responses to requests during a week of observation. "Request" is an etic category of speech acts that includes requests for attention ("Mom!"), requests for action ("Take the garbage out"), and requests for information ("What time is it?").

The study was premised on the assumption that the etic meanings which lie on the surface of speech acts correspond in some degree to what is going on inside of the participants' heads. People do not *usually* say "go out" when they mean "come in," or "sit down" when they mean "stand up." But as in other instances of the etics of mental life previously discussed, the inference from what people say etically in the behavior stream to what they mean emically inside their heads can be extremely hazardous. For example, consider the following speech acts involving a mother and her eight-year-old son. At 10:50 A.M. the mother began to request that her son stop playing with the family dog:

Time	Request
10:50	Leave him [the dog] alone.
11:01	Leave him alone.
11:09	Leave him alone.
11:10	Hey, don't do that.
11:10	Please leave him alone.
11:15	Leave him alone.
11:15	Leave him alone.
11:15	Why don't you stop teasing him?
11:16	Leave Rex alone, huh?
11:17	Leave him alone.
11:17	Leave him alone.
11:24	Keep away from him.

During the same scene the mother also repeatedly requested the same child to turn down the volume on the radio in the living room, as follows:

10:40	Keep your hands off that [radio].
10:41	I don't want to hear that.
11:19	Lower that thing [the radio].
11:20	Come on, knock it off.
11:20	Lower that.
11:20	Get your own [radio in another room].
11:20	Keep your hands off this thing [the radio].
11:26	All right, come on. I've got to have that lowered.

Time	Request
11:27	Leave it alone.
11:27	Leave it alone.
11:29	Turn it off right now.
11:29	You're not to touch that radio.
11:29	Keep your hands off that radio.

One cannot assume that the principal emic component in the meanings of the above requests is the intention of the speaker to be taken seriously about turning the radio off or leaving the dog alone. If the mother intends to be taken seriously, why does she repeat the same requests twelve or thirteen times in less than an hour? One cannot argue that repetition is a token of her seriousness (like a prisoner who repeatedly tries to escape from jail) because she has numerous alternatives—she herself can turn the radio off, for example, or she can segregate the child and the dog in different rooms. Her failure to take decisive action may very well indicate that there are other semantic components involved. Perhaps she really intends merely to show disapproval. Or perhaps her main intention is to punish herself by making requests she knows will not be complied with.

The ambiguities are even more marked when we examine the hearer's role. One possibility is that the child rejects the surface meaning of the request, knowing that his mother isn't really serious. Another possibility is that the child thinks that the mother is serious but rejects her authority. Perhaps the child interprets the repetitions to mean that his mother would rather punish herself than punish him. To disambiguate these meanings, one might employ eliciting operations, the hallmarks of emic status. But the etic meanings of the speech acts viewed as a behavior stream event would remain the same.

To be a human observer capable of carrying out scientific operations presumes that one is competent in at least one natural language. Thus, in identifying the etic meaning of speech acts in their own native language, observers are not dependent on eliciting operations and can readily agree that a particular utterance has a specific surface meaning whose locus is in the behavior stream.

This line of reasoning can easily be extended to include foreign speech acts, if we grant the proposition that all human languages are mutually translatable. This means that for every utterance in a foreign language, there is an analogue in one's own. While it is true that successful translation of a foreign speech act is facilitated by the collaboration of a native informant, what the observers intend to find out is which linguistic structures inside their own heads have more or less the same meaning as the utterances in the behavior stream of the foreign actors. Thus the translation amounts to the imposition of the observers' semantic categories on the foreign speech acts. The observers have in effect enlarged their competence to include both languages, and hence they can proceed to identify the surface meanings of foreign speech acts as freely as native speakers of English are able to identify the surface meanings of the English speech acts listed above.

The Emics of the Observer

PARTISANS of idealist strategies seek to subvert the materialist effort by claiming that "all knowledge is ultimately 'emic' " (Fisher and Werner, 1978:198). The allegation is that in the name of demystifying the nature of social life, the observers merely substitute one brand of illusion for another. After all, who are the "observers"? Why should their categories and beliefs be more credible than those of the actors? The answer to these questions is entirely dependent on whether one accepts the scientific way of knowing as having some special advantages over other ways of knowing. To deny the validity of etic descriptions is in effect to deny the possibility of a social science capable of explaining sociocultural similarities and differences. To urge that the etics of scientific observers is merely one among an infinity of other emics— the emics of Americans and Chinese, of women and men, of blacks and Puerto Ricans, of Jews and Hindus, of rich and poor, and of young and old—is to urge the surrender of our intellects to the supreme mystification of total relativism.

True, the practitioners of science do not constitute a community apart from the rest of humanity, and we are filled with prejudices, preconceptions, and hidden agendas. But the way to correct errors resulting from the value-laden nature of our activity is to demand that we struggle against our strategic competitors and critics of all sorts to improve our accounts of social life, to produce better theories, and to achieve higher, not lower, levels of objectivity with respect to both the emics and etics of mental and behavioral phenomena. Once again we must ask: "What is the alternative?"

Chapter Three

Theoretical Principles
of Cultural Materialism

ONE CANNOT PASS directly from a description of the ways of knowing about a field to the principles useful for building networks of interrelated theories. First, I have to say something about what's in the field—its major components or sectors. So far I've referred only to the etics and emics of human thought and behavior. But other components remain to be identified before the strategic principles of cultural materialism can be described.

The limitations of alternative research strategies are very much a consequence of how they conceptualize the nature of human societies and cultures. Idealist strategies approach the definition of social and cultural phenomena exclusively from an emic perspective: society exists to the extent that participants view themselves as members of social groups, sharing common values and purposes; social action is a special kind of behavior identified by the social intentions of the participants; and culture consists exclusively of the shared emics of thought and behavior. In extreme versions, such as those associated with cognitivism (see Chapter 9), even the emics of behavior are dropped and culture is restricted to rules allegedly guiding behavior without any investigation of the behavior itself.

On the other hand, cultural materialists approach the definition of social and cultural phenomena initially but not exclusively from an etic perspective. The social nature of human groups is inferred from the density of interaction among human beings found in a particular spatial and temporal locus. Cultural materialists do not have to know whether the members of a particular human population think of themselves as a "people" or a group in order to identify them as a social group. Nor does the interaction among the members of such a group have to be primarily supportive and cooperative in order for it to be considered social. The starting point of all sociocultural analysis for cultural materialists is simply the existence of an etic human population located in etic time and space. A society for us is a maximal social group consisting of both sexes and all ages and exhibiting a wide range of interactive behavior. Culture, on the other hand, refers to the learned repertory of thoughts and actions exhibited by the members of social groups— repertories transmissible independently of genetic heredity from one generation to the next. (A more extended discussion of the nature of culture will be found in Chapters 5 and 9.) The cultural repertories of particular societies contribute to the continuity of the population and its social life. Hence the need arises for speaking of sociocultural systems, denoting the conjunction of a population, a society, and a culture, and constituting a bounded arrangement of people, thoughts, and activities. The systemic nature of such conjunctions and arrangements is not something to be taken for granted. Rather, it is a strategic assumption that can be justified only by showing how it leads to efficacious and testable theories.

The Universal Pattern

CULTURAL MATERIALIST theoretical principles are concerned with the problem of understanding the relationship among the parts of sociocultural systems and with the evolution of such relationships, parts, and systems. Alternative strategies construe these parts in radically different ways, and many inadequacies of substantive theories are already foreshadowed in general models of the structure of sociocultural systems. Consider, for example, the recurrent cognitive and behavioral components anthropologist Clark Wissler (1926) called the "universal pattern"—components allegedly present in all human societies:

Speech	Knowledge	Property
Material traits	Religion	Government
Art	Society	War

Both epistemological and theoretical problems abound in Wissler's scheme. Note, for example, that the separately listed "material traits" —by which he meant such things as tools, buildings, clothing, and containers—are logically present in at least art, religion, property, government, and war; that "knowledge" must occur in all the other rubrics; that there are such glaring omissions as "economy," "subsistence," "ecology," "demography"; and finally, that it is dubious that "war" and "religion" are universal traits. These defects flow from Wissler's failure to specify the epistemological status of the rubrics in terms of taxonomic principles that would justify the contraction or expansion of the list by reference to systemic structural relationships among its components.

Murdock's Categories

THE RUBRICS under which entries in George Peter Murdock's *World Ethnographic Atlas* (1967) are arranged share the same defects. In the computer punch card version of the atlas, these are the components of sociocultural systems:

Subsistence economy
Mode of marriage
Family organization
Marital residence
Community organization
Patrilineal kin groups and
  exogamy
Matrilineal kin groups and
  exogamy
Cognatic kin groups
Cousin marriage
Kinship terminology for first
  cousins

Type and intensity of
  agriculture
Settlement pattern
Mean size of local communi-
  ties
Jurisdictional hierarchy
High gods
Types of games
Postpartum sex taboos
Male genital mutilations
Segregation of adolescent boys
Metal working
Weaving

Leather working
Pottery
Boat building
House construction
Gathering
Hunting
Fishing
Animal husbandry
Agriculture
Type of animal husbandry
Descent
Class stratification
Caste stratification
Slavery

Succession to office of local
    headman
Inheritance of real property
Inheritance of movable property
Norm of premarital sex behavior
    of girls
Ground plan of dwelling
Floor level
Wall material
Shape of roof
Roofing material
Political integration
Political succession
Environment

Part of the explanation for the peculiar "laundry list" variations in the coverage and focus of these categories (from slavery to shape of roof) is that they reflect the content of ethnographic monographs and are intended to facilitate the tabulation of what is available for tabulation. But that is only part of the story. Note also the neglect of the emic/etic distinction. This neglect adversely affects cross-cultural correlation studies that involve such categories as community organization, mode of marriage, family organization, marital residence, exogamy, jurisdictional hierarchy, clan stratification, and caste stratification—all of which exhibit emphatic emic/etic contrasts. Of course, here, too, the categorizations reflect the fuzzy epistemologies of the anthropologists who have contributed to ethnographic knowledge. But this weakness has been compounded in the coding operations Murdock and his associates employ. For example, the code for postmarital residence refers to "normal residence" without distinguishing between normal in the sense of on-the-ground etic averages or normal in the sense of "normative"—i.e., emically agreed to as the proper or ideal form by a majority of those interviewed.

As we shall see in Chapter 10, it is no accident that cross-cultural survey *theories* also look like open-ended laundry lists. Murdock and his followers have operated under an eclectic research strategy whose characteristic substantive theoretical products are fragmentary, isolated, and mutually opposed generalizations of limited scope. The laundry list of categories out of which such generalizations are constructed both condition and reflect the chaotic nature of the theoretical products of most cross-cultural surveys.

Parsonian Rubrics

IN 1950 A GROUP of five anthropologists and sociologists who subscribed to the research strategy of structural-functionalism associated with the work of Harvard sociologist Talcott Parsons (see p. 279) drew up a list of universal components based on the identification of the "functional prerequisites of a society" (Aberle et al., 1950). The authors specified nine categories as "the generalized conditions necessary for the maintenance of the system":

1. Provision for adequate relationship to the environment and for sexual recruitment
2. Role differentiation and role assignment
3. Communication
4. Shared cognitive orientations
5. Shared articulated set of goals
6. Normative regulation of means
7. Regulation of affective expression
8. Socialization
9. Effective control of disruptive forms of behavior

The logic behind this list is that each item is supposedly necessary to avoid certain conditions which would terminate the existence of any society—namely, the biological extinction or dispersion of its members, the apathy of its members, "the war of all against all," or the absorption of a society by another one. As the proponents of this scheme themselves insisted, their notions about functional prerequisites were integrally linked to their acceptance of Parsons's structural-functionalist research strategy. Structural-functionalism, the most influential strategy in the social sciences in the United States and Great Britain during the period 1940 to 1965, is a variety of cultural idealism, much criticized for its inability to deal with social evolution and political-economic conflict. Its strategic biases are implicit in the preponderance among the alleged functional prerequisites listed above of emic and mental items such as cognitive orientations, shared goals, normative regulation, and affective expressions.

The commitment to the emics of mental life actually extends to the remaining five items as well, however, since in Talcott Parsons's theory of action, every aspect of social life must be approached from the standpoint of the actor's mental goals, thoughts, feelings, and values. The idealist bias here is also painfully evident in the proposal that *shared* cognitive orientations and *shared* articulated sets of goals are functional prerequisites for social survival, when as a matter of fact there is overwhelming evidence to the contrary, not only from complex state societies divided by bitter class, ethnic, and regional conflict, but in very simple societies as well, where sex and age antagonisms bespeak of fundamentally opposed value orientations. Note also the lack of concern with production, reproduction, exchange, and consumption— demographic and economic categories that cannot easily be crammed into "adequate relationship to the environment and sexual recruitment." Production, exchange, and consumption are not merely relationships with the environment; they denote relationships among people as well. Moreover, from retrospective comments made by Parsons (1970), the absence of "economy" in this scheme can only be understood as a visceral rejection of any form of Marxist determinism.

Universal Pattern in Cultural Materialist Strategy

THE UNIVERSAL structure of sociocultural systems posited by cultural materialism rests on the biological and psychological constants of human nature, and on the distinction between thought and behavior and emics and etics. To begin with, each society must cope with the problems of production—behaviorally satisfying minimal requirements for subsistence; hence there must be an *etic behavioral mode of production*. Second, each society must behaviorally cope with the problem of reproduction—avoiding destructive increases or decreases in population size; hence there must be an *etic behavioral mode of reproduction*. Third, each society must cope with the necessity of maintaining secure and orderly behavioral relationships among its constituent groups and with other societies. In conformity with mundane and practical considerations, cultural materialists see the threat of disorder arising primarily from the economic processes which allocate labor and the material products of labor to individuals and groups. Hence, depending on whether the focus of organization is on domestic groups or the internal and external relationships of the whole society, one may infer the universal existence of *etic behavioral domestic economies* and *etic behavioral political economies.* Finally, given the prominence of human speech acts and the importance of symbolic processes for the human psyche, one can infer the universal recurrence of productive behavior that leads to etic, recreational, sportive, and aesthetic products and services. *Behavioral superstructure* is a convenient label for this universally recurrent etic sector.

In sum, the major etic behavioral categories together with some examples of sociocultural phenomena that fall within each domain are:

Mode of Production: The technology and the practices employed for expanding or limiting basic subsistence production, especially the production of food and other forms of energy, given the restrictions and opportunities provided by a specific technology interacting with a specific habitat.

    Technology of subsistence
    Techno-environmental relationships
    Ecosystems
    Work patterns

Mode of Reproduction: The technology and the practices employed for expanding, limiting, and maintaining population size.

    Demography
    Mating patterns
    Fertility, natality, mortality
    Nurturance of infants
    Medical control of demographic patterns
    Contraception, abortion, infanticide

Domestic Economy: The organization of reproduction and basic production, exchange, and consumption within camps, houses, apartments, or other domestic settings.

    Family structure
    Domestic division of labor
    Domestic socialization, enculturation, education
    Age and sex roles
    Domestic discipline, hierarchies, sanctions

Political Economy: The organization of reproduction, production, exchange, and consumption within and between bands, villages, chiefdoms, states, and empires.

Political organization, factions, clubs, associations, corporations
Division of labor, taxation, tribute
Political socialization, enculturation, education
Class, caste, urban, rural hierarchies
Discipline, police/military control
War

Behavioral Superstructure:

Art, music, dance, literature, advertising
Rituals
Sports, games, hobbies
Science

I can simplify the above by lumping the modes of production and reproduction together under the rubric *infrastructure;* and by lumping domestic and political economy under the rubric *structure.* This yields a tripartite scheme:

Infrastructure
Structure
Superstructure

However, these rubrics embrace only the etic behavioral components of sociocultural systems. What about the mental components? Running roughly parallel to the etic behavioral components are a set of mental components whose conventional designations are as follows:

Etic Behavioral Components	*Mental and Emic Components*
Infrastructure	Ethnobotany, ethnozoology, subsistence lore, magic, religion, taboos

Etic Behavioral Components	Mental and Emic Components
Structure	Kinship, political ideology, ethnic and national ideologies, magic, religion, taboos
Etic superstructure	Symbols, myths, aesthetic standards and philosophies, epistemologies, ideologies, magic, religion, taboos

Rather than distinguish the mental and emic components according to the strength of their relationship to specific etic behavioral components, I shall lump them together and designate them in their entirety as the *mental and emic superstructure*, meaning the conscious and unconscious cognitive goals, categories, rules, plans, values, philosophies, and beliefs about behavior elicited from the participants or inferred by the observer. Four major universal components of sociocultural systems are now before us: the etic behavioral infrastructure, structure, and superstructure, and the mental and emic superstructure.

Language Again

ONE CONSPICUOUS omission from the above scheme is the category "language." It should be clear from the discussion of speech acts (p. 42) that studies of etic components usually involve the identification of speech acts and other communication events. For example, the description of domestic hierarchies by means of requests and compliances to requests shows that such hierarchies involve communication components that can be studied by means of etic operations. Since communication acts, especially speech acts, usually occur in human scenes of even moderate duration, all major etic rubrics are to some degree built up out of the observation of communication events.

Communication, including speech, serves a vital instrumental role in coordinating infrastructural, structural, and superstructural activities; hence it cannot be regarded as belonging exclusively to any one of these divisions. Moreover, communication in the form of speech acts is also the very stuff out of which much of the mental and emic superstructure is built. Hence language per se cannot be viewed as an exclusively infrastructural, structural, or superstructural component, nor as an exclusively behavioral or mental phenomenon.

Another important reason for not including language as a separate component in the universal pattern is that cultural materialism makes no claims concerning the functional relationship between infrastructure and the *major* phonemic and grammatical features of particular families of languages. Cultural materialism does not hold, for example, that particular modes of production and reproduction cause people to speak Indo-European rather than Uto-Aztecan languages. (But cultural idealists have proposed the now discredited theory that Indo-European grammatical categories led to the Industrial Revolution—see Whorf, 1956.)

We are now finally in a position to state the theoretical principles of cultural materialism.

The Major Principles of Cultural Materialism

THE KERNEL of the principles that guide the development of interrelated sets of theories in the strategy of cultural materialism was anticipated by Marx (1970 [1859]:21) in the following words: "The mode of production in material life determines the general character of the social, political, and spiritual processes of life. It is not the consciousness of men that determines their existence, but on the contrary, their social existence determines their consciousness." As stated, this principle was a great advance in human knowledge, surely equivalent in its time to the formulation of the principle of natural selection by Alfred Wallace and Charles Darwin. However, in the context of modern anthropological research, the epistemological ambiguities inherent in the phrase "the mode of production," the neglect of "the mode of reproduction," and the failure to distinguish emics from etics and behavioral from mental impose the need for reformulation.

The cultural materialist version of Marx's great principle is as follows: The etic behavioral modes of production and reproduction probabilistically determine the etic behavioral domestic and political economy, which in turn probabilistically determine the behavioral and mental emic superstructures. For brevity's sake, this principle can be referred to as the principle of infrastructural determinism.

The strategic significance of the principle of infrastructural determinism is that it provides a set of priorities for the formulation and testing of theories and hypotheses about the causes of sociocultural phenomena. Cultural materialists give highest priority to the effort to formulate and test theories in which infrastructural variables are the primary causal factors. Failure to identify such factors in the infrastructure warrants the formulation of theories in which structural variables are tested for causal primacy. Cultural materialists give still less priority to exploring the possibility that the solution to sociocultural puzzles lies primarily within the behavioral superstructure; and finally, theories that bestow causal primacy upon the mental and emic superstructure are to be formulated and tested only as an ultimate recourse when no testable etic behavioral theories can be formulated or when all that have been formulated have been decisively discredited. In other words, cultural materialism asserts the strategic priority of etic and behavioral conditions and processes over emic and mental conditions and processes, and of infrastructural over structural and superstructural conditions and processes; but it does not deny the possibility that emic, mental, superstructural, and structural components may achieve a degree of autonomy from the etic behavioral infrastructure. Rather, it merely postpones and delays that possibility in order to guarantee the fullest exploration of the determining influences exerted by the etic behavioral infrastructure.

Why Infrastructure?

THE STRATEGIC priority given to etic and behavioral production and reproduction by cultural materialism represents an attempt to build theories about culture that incorporate lawful regularities occurring in nature. Like all bioforms, human beings must expend energy to obtain energy (and other life-sustaining products). And like all bioforms, our ability to produce children is greater than our ability to obtain energy for them. The strategic priority of the infrastructure rests upon the fact that human beings can never change these laws. We can only seek to strike a balance between reproduction and the production and consumption of energy. True, through technology we have achieved a considerable capacity to raise and lower productive and reproductive rates. But technology in turn confronts a series of physical, chemical, biological, and ecological laws that likewise cannot be altered and that necessarily limit the rate and direction of technological change and hence the degree of control which can be achieved over production and reproduction by technological intervention in a specific environmental context. Moreover, all such interventions are limited by the level of technological evolution—a level that cannot be altered by an instantaneous act of will—and by the capacity of particular habitats to absorb various types and intensities of techno-economies without undergoing irreversible changes.

Infrastructure, in other words, is the principal interface between culture and nature, the boundary across which the ecological, chemical, and physical restraints to which human action is subject interact with the principal sociocultural practices aimed at overcoming or modifying those restraints. The order of cultural materialist priorities from infrastructure to the remaining behavioral components and finally to the mental superstructure reflects the increasing remoteness of these components from the culture/nature interface. Since the aim of cultural materialism, in keeping with the orientation of science in general, is the discovery of the maximum amount of order in its field of inquiry, priority for theory building logically settles upon those sectors under the greatest direct restraints from the givens of nature. To endow the mental superstructure with strategic priority, as the cultural idealists advocate, is a bad bet. Nature is indifferent to whether God is a loving father or a bloodthirsty cannibal. But nature is not indifferent to whether the fallow period in a swidden field is one year or ten. We know that powerful restraints exist on the infrastructural level; hence it is a good bet that these restraints are passed on to the structural and superstructural components.

To be sure, much attention is now being paid to pan-human neuropsychological "structural" restraints that allegedly oblige human beings to think in predetermined patterns. Later on I shall examine these structuralist claims rather carefully. In the meantime, what needs to be said is that if, as Lévi-Strauss claims, the human mind only thinks thoughts that "are good to think," the menu allows for an extraordinary diversity of tastes. No doubt human beings have species-specific patterns of thought—just as we have species-specific patterns of locomotion and body-heat disposal. But how shall we use this fact to account for the tremendous variation in world views, religions, and philosophies, all of which are indisputably equally "good to think"? Structuralists and other varieties of idealists are no more capable of answering this question than they are capable of explaining why human beings, who are naturally terrestrial bipeds, sometimes ride horses and sometimes fly through the air, or why, given a species-specific endowment of sweat glands, some people cool off by sitting in front of air conditioners while others sip hot tea.

The strategic advantage of infrastructural determinism as opposed to structuralism and sociobiology is that the recurrent limiting factors are variables that can be shown to exert their influence in measurably variable ways. This enables cultural materialism to construct theories that account for both differences and similarities. For example, the need to eat is a constant, but the quantities and kinds of foods that can be eaten vary in conformity with technology and habitat. Sex drives are universal, but their reproductive consequences vary in conformity with the technology of contraception, perinatal care, and the treatment of infants.

Unlike ideas, patterns of production and reproduction cannot be made to appear and disappear by a mere act of will. Since they are grounded in nature they can only be changed by altering the balance between culture and nature, and this can only be done by the expenditure of energy. Thought changes nothing outside of the head unless it is accompanied by the movements of the body or its parts. It seems reasonable, therefore, to search for the beginnings of the causal chains affecting sociocultural evolution in the complex of energy-expending body activities that affect the balance between the size of each human population, the amount of energy devoted to production, and the supply of life-sustaining resources. Cultural materialists contend that this balance is so vital to the survival and well-being of the individuals and groups who are its beneficiaries that all other culturally patterned thoughts and activities in which these individuals and groups engage are probably directly or indirectly determined by its specific character. But we do not contend this out of any final conviction that we know what the world is really like; we contend it merely to make the best possible theories about what the world is probably like.

Thought and Behavior

MUCH OF THE resistance to cultural materialism stems from what seems to be the self-evident truth that behavior is governed by thought

—that human social life is rule-governed. I criticize this viewpoint in Chapter 9, but some preliminary clarifications may be appropriate in the present context. What puzzles many people is how it can be maintained that behavior determines thought when their own behavior intuitively appears to be an acting out of mental goals and moral precepts. Take the case of technological change, which is so vital to the evolution of culture. In order for cultures to develop stone tools, bows and arrows, digging sticks, plows, ceramics, and machinery, didn't somebody first have to think about how to make such things?

Cultural materialism does not view inventors or any other human beings as zombielike automata whose activities are never under conscious control. In asserting the primacy of the behavioral infrastructure over the mental and emic superstructure, cultural materialism is not addressing the question of how technological inventions and other kinds of creative innovations originate in individuals but rather how such innovations come to assume a material social existence and how they come to exert an influence on social production and social reproduction. Thoughts in the minds of geniuses like Hero of Alexandria, who invented the steam turbine in the third century, or Leonardo da Vinci, who invented the helicopter in the sixteenth century, cannot assume a material social existence unless appropriate material conditions for their social acceptance and use are also present. Furthermore, the recurrence of such inventions as ceramics and metallurgy independently in different parts of the world under similar infrastructural conditions suggests that not even the most original ideas happen only once. Indeed, from the uncanny way in which the invention of the steamship, telephone, airplane, photography, automobile, and hundreds of other patentable devices have been subjected to conflicting claims of priority by independent individuals and laboratories (cf. Kroeber, 1948), the conclusion seems inescapable that when the infrastructural conditions are ripe, the appropriate thoughts will occur, not once but again and again. Furthermore, there is ample evidence to indicate that some of the greatest inventions ever made—for example, agriculture—were known in thought for thousands of years before they began to play a significant role in the infrastructures of prehistoric societies (see pp. 85ff).

The intuition that thought determines behavior arises from the limited temporal and cultural perspective of ordinary experience. Conscious thoughts in the form of plans and itineraries certainly help individuals and groups to find a path through the daily complexities of social life. But these plans and itineraries merely chart the selection of preexisting behavioral "mazeways." Even in the most permissive societies and the richest in alternative roles, the planned actions—lunch, a lovers' tryst, an evening at the theater—are never conjured up out of thin air but are drawn from the inventory of recurrent scenes characteristic of that particular culture. The issue of behavioral versus mental determinism is not a matter of whether the mind guides action, but whether the mind determines the selection of the inventory of culturally actionable thoughts. As Schopenhauer said, "We want what we will, but we don't will what we want." Thus the human intuition concerning the priority of thought over behavior is worth just about as much as our human intuition that the earth is flat. To insist on the priority of mind in culture is to align one's understanding of sociocultural phenomena with the anthropological equivalent of pre-Darwinian biology or pre-Newtonian physics. It is to believe in what Freud called "the omnipotence of thought." Such a belief is a form of intellectual infantilism that dishonors our species-given powers of thought.

Individual Versus Group Selection

IT IS ESSENTIAL to the task of constructing cultural materialist theories that one be able to establish a link between the behavioral choices made by definite individuals and the aggregate responses of sociocultural systems. One must be able to show why one kind of behavioral option is more likely than another not in terms of abstract pushes, pulls, pressures, and other metaphysical "forces," but in terms of concrete bio-psychological principles pertinent to the behavior of the individuals participating in the system.

Another way to phrase this imperative is to assert that the selection processes responsible for the divergent and convergent evolutionary trajectories of sociocultural systems operate mainly on the individual level; individuals follow one rather than another course of action, and as a result the aggregate pattern changes. But I don't mean to dismiss the possibility that many sociocultural traits are selected for by the differential survival of whole sociocultural systems—that is, by group selection. Because intense intergroup competition was probably present among early human populations, provision must be made for the extinction of systems that were bio-psychologically satisfying to the individuals concerned, but vulnerable to more predatory neighbors, with a consequent loss of certain cultural inventories and the preservation and propagation of others.

However, such group selection is merely a catastrophic consequence of selection operating on or through individuals. Cultural evolution, like biological evolution, has (up to now at least) taken place through opportunistic changes that increase benefits and lower costs to individuals. Just as a species does not "struggle to survive" as a collective entity, but survives or not as a consequence of the adaptive changes of individual organisms, so too do sociocultural systems survive or not as a consequence of the adaptive changes in the thought and activities of individual men and women who respond opportunistically to cost-benefit options. If the sociocultural system survives as a result of patterns of thought and behavior selected for on the individual level, it is not because the group as such was successful but because some or all of the individuals in it were successful. Thus a group that is annihilated in warfare can be said to have been selected for as a group, but if we want to understand why it was annihilated, we must examine the cost-benefit options exercised by its individual members relative to the options exercised by its victorious neighbors. The fact that some people sincerely act in order to help others and to protect the group does not alter this situation. Saints and heroes sacrifice their lives for the "good" of others. But the question of whether the others accept or reject that "good" remains a matter of the balance of individual costs and benefits. Society does not live by saints alone. Altruism, to be successful, must confer adaptive advantages on those who give as well as on those who take.

This is not to say that the direction of cultural change in the short run can be predicted by summing up what is the greatest good for the greatest number of people. Obviously there are many innovations which are bio-psychologically more satisfying to some members of a society than to others. Purdah, the veiling of women in Moslem societies, facilitates domestic and political control by men over women. Presumably the bio-psychological rewards of purdah are greater for men than for women—indeed, one might say that for the women there are severe penalties. But the men have the power to make their own well-being weigh more heavily in the balance of advantages and disadvantages than the well-being of women. The more hierarchical the society with respect to sex, age, class, caste, and ethnic criteria, the greater the degree of exploitation of one group by another and the less likely it is that the trajectory of sociocultural evolution can be calculated from the average bio-psychological utility of traits. This leads to many puzzling situations in which it appears that large sectors of a society are acting in ways that diminish their practical well-being instead of enhancing it. In India, for example, members of impoverished menial castes avidly uphold the rule of caste endogamy and insist that marriages be legitimized by expensive dowries. Abstractly, it would appear that the members of such impoverished castes would be materially better off if they practiced exogamy and stopped insisting on big marriage payments. But the victims of the caste system cannot base their behavior on long-term abstract calculations. Access to such menial jobs as construction worker, toddy-wine maker, coir maker, and so forth depends on caste identity validated by obedience to caste rules. In the lower castes if one fails to maintain membership in good standing one loses the opportunity to obtain work even of the most menial kind, and plunges still further into misery. To throw off the weight of the accumulated privileges of the upper castes lies entirely beyond the practical capacity of those who are at the bottom of the heap; hence, perverse as it may seem, those who benefit least from the system ardently support it in daily life.

Bio-Psychological Constants

THE DANGER IN postulating pan-human bio-psychological drives and predispositions is that one is tempted to reduce all sociocultural similarities to an imaginary genetic "biogram" (see p. 127), whereas most similarities as well as differences are due to sociocultural evolutionary processes. For reasons that I shall spell out during the discussion of biological reductionism in the next chapter, the most important observation that one can make about the human biogram is that it is relatively free from species-specific bio-psychological drives and predispositions. As a species we have been selected for our ability to acquire elaborate repertories of socially learned responses, rather than for species-specific drives and instincts. Nonetheless, without postulating the existence of selective principles operating at the bio-psychological level, one cannot explain how infrastructure mediates between culture and nature.

It is better to begin with a minimal set of human bio-psychological selective principles than with one that tries to render a complete account of what it is to be human. Hence I shall list only four:

1. People need to eat and will generally opt for diets that offer more rather than fewer calories and proteins and other nutrients.
2. People cannot be totally inactive, but when confronted with a given task, they prefer to carry it out by expending less rather than more energy.
3. People are highly sexed and generally find reinforcing pleasure from sexual intercourse—more often from heterosexual intercourse.
4. People need love and affection in order to feel secure and happy, and other things being equal, they will act to increase the love and affection which others give them.

My justification for this list is that its generality is guaranteed by the existence of similar bio-psychological predispositions among most members of the primate order. You may wish to postulate that human beings also naturally seek to create music and art, to dichotomize, to rationalize, to believe in God, to be aggressive, to laugh, to play, to be bored, to be free, and so forth. By succumbing to the temptation to open this list to all nominations, you will rapidly succeed in reducing every recurrent cultural trait to the status of a biological given. But the adequacy of the list must be judged by the adequacy of the theories it helps to generate. The more parsimonious we are about granting the existence of bio-psychological constants, the more powerful and elegant will be the network of theories emanating from sociocultural strategies. Our object is to explain much by little.

Despite the parsimony of my list, everyone can immediately think of antithetical behaviors and thoughts. For the first, there is obesity, voluntary starvation, vegetarianism, and self-inflicted dietary pathology. For the second, there is the intensive expenditure of energy in sports and artistic performance. For the third, there is abstinence, homosexuality, masturbation. And for the fourth, there is infanticide, domestic strife, and exploitation. However, the existence of these apparently contradictory patterns is not necessarily fatal to the scheme as proposed. Nothing in the statement of pan-specific bio-psychological principles indicates that selection acting through the preferences of individuals will in the long term contribute to the maximization of anticipated results. On the contrary, the selection of maximizing traits recurrently leads to ecological depletions. Thus the pursuit of more proteins frequently ends up with people getting fewer proteins; the adoption of labor-saving devices ends up with people working harder; the escalation of male sexual activity leads to a systemic shortage of women; and greater affective bonding transmuted by politics leads to greater exploitation of one class by another. These paradoxes do not invalidate the list of universals nor falsify the principles of cultural materialism; they merely expose the puzzles that cultural materialism proposes to solve more effectively than rival strategies.

Mode of Production and Relations of Production

NO GENERAL AGREEMENT exists as to what Marx meant by infrastructure or the mode of production (Legros, 1979). While he distinguished between the relations and the forces of production, both of these concepts involve fatal ambiguities. As I stressed in the previous chapter, Marx left the problem of objectivity unresolved. Lacking the concepts of emic and etic operations and indiscriminately mixing mental and behavioral phenomena, he bequeathed a heritage of Hegelian dialectical double talk now being pushed to extremes by new-wave Marxists (to be discussed in Chapter 8). I do not believe it is possible to divine what Marx really meant by the mode of production, nor what components he intended to put into it or take out of it.

Rather than argue about what Marx intended, let me simply explain my reasons for the inclusions and omission on p. 52. As a cultural materialist, I hold that infrastructure should consist of those aspects of a sociocultural system which enable one to predict a maximum number of additional components up to the behavior of the entire system if possible. I have therefore removed certain key aspects of what many Marxists mean by "relations of production" from infrastructure to structure and superstructure. The classic Marxist concept of "ownership of the means of production," for example, denotes differential access to the technology employed in subsistence production and hence is an organizational feature of structure rather than a part of infrastructure. The strategic significance of this departure is that I think it is possible to explain the evolution of the ownership of means of production as a dependent variable in relation to the evolution of demography, technology, ecology, and subsistence economy. It would seem futile to object to the removal of ownership from infrastructure until it can be shown that such an explanation cannot be achieved.

Similarly, I view patterns of exchange—e.g., reciprocity, redistribution, trade, markets, employment, money transactions—not as infrastructure but partly as etic structural components—aspects of domestic and political economy—and partly as emic and mental superstructural components. Once again, the justification for this decision lies in the hope that patterns of exchange can be predicted from a conjunction of more basic variables. Clearly, some aspects of ownership and exchange will never be predicted simply from a knowledge of the demographic, technological, economic, and environmental components. There are whole universes of phenomena concerning ownership and exchange in price-market settings, for example, which must be approached by means of the categories and models by which economists describe and predict monetary inputs and outputs, capital investments, wages and prices, and so forth. Let me emphatically renounce any pretension that all economic events and processes can be understood as mere reflexes of the modes of production and reproduction. Remember that cultural materialism asserts the strategic priority of etic and behavioral conditions and processes over emic and mental conditions and processes, and of infrastructural over structural and superstructural conditions and processes, but it does not deny the possibility that emic, superstructural, and structural components may achieve a degree of autonomy from the etic infrastructure. Rather, it merely postpones and delays that possibility in order to guarantee the fullest exploration of the determining influences exerted by the infrastructure. To regard price values, capital, wages, and commodity markets as structure and superstructure rather than infrastructure and to accord them a *degree* of autonomy in determining the evolution of contemporary sociocultural systems is not to reverse or abandon the strategic priorities of cultural materialism. The principles of cultural materialism remain applicable. These principles direct attention to the predominance of the behavioral etics of exchange over the mental emics of exchange, and to the role of the etic behavioral infrastructure in determining the conditions under which price-making markets and money economies have come into existence. Indeed, cultural materialism cannot be reconciled with classical Marxist interpretations of the inner dynamics of capitalism precisely because Marx accorded the essentially emic mental categories of capital and profits a predominant role in the further evolution of modern industrial society, whereas from the cultural materialist perspective the key to the future of capitalism lies in the conjunction of its etic behavioral components and especially in the feedback between political economy and the infrastructure (see pp. 226ff.).

The Modes of Reproduction and Production

CULTURAL MATERIALIST principles also depart radically from classical Marxism in regarding the production of children as part of the infrastructure. I believe that this departure is necessary in order to explain why modes of production undergo changes that result in systemic transformations and divergent and convergent evolution. Marx attempted to explain the change from one mode of production to another by relying on the Hegelian idea that social formations during the course of their existence develop internal contradictions that are at once the cause of their own destruction and the basis for the emergence of new social formations.

According to Marx, modes of production evolve through the development of contradictions between the means of production and the relations of production. "At a certain stage of their development the material forces of production in society come in conflict with the existing relation of production." That is, the relations of production (as, for example, private ownership and the profit motive) hold back the provision of material satisfactions; they become "fetters" on the production process. They are destroyed and replaced by "higher" relations of production (for example, communal ownership) that permit a more ample expression of the potential of the means of production (an economy of abundance instead of scarcity).

In Marx's dialectic of history no less than in Hegel's, each epoch or social formation is urged onward toward its inevitable negation by an uncanny teleological thrust. For Hegel, it was the growth of the idea of freedom; for Marx, the development of the forces of production. In order for Marx's contradiction between forces and relations to provide the motive force of a sociocultural evolution faithful to Hegel's vision of a spiritualized cosmos dialectically negating itself into a heavenly utopia, the mode of production must tend toward maximum realization of its power over nature. As Marx put it: "No social order ever disappears before all the productive forces for which there is room in it have been developed" (1970 [1859]: 21). Why should one expect this to be true?

I believe that demographic factors help to explain the historic expansion of productive forces. Hence, the necessity arises for speaking of a "mode of reproduction" whose effect upon social structures and ideology is no less important than that of the mode of production.

Anthropologists have long recognized that in broadest perspective cultural evolution has had three main characteristics: escalating energy budgets, increased productivity, and accelerating population growth. (1) Over the long haul the amount of energy per capita and per local system has tended to increase. Cultures at the band level of development used less than 100,000 kilocalories per day; cultures at the level of tropical forest slash-and-burn farming villages, used about a million per day; neolithic mixed dry-farming villages, about 2 million per day; the early irrigation states of Mesopotamia, China, India, Peru, and Mesoamerica about 25 billion per day and modern industrial superstates over 50 trillion per day. (2) Production efficiency, measured as energy output per unit of human labor has also increased, rising, for example, from about 10 to 1 among hunters and gatherers to 20 to 1 among swidden farmers to 50 to 1 among irrigation agriculturalists. (3) And human population has increased. There was a global density of less than 1 person per square mile in 10,000 B.C. Today there are over 65 persons per square mile. Settlements grew from 25 to 50 persons per band; 150 to 200 per slash-and-burn village; 500 to 1,500 per neolithic mixed farming village. By 200 B.C. there were more people living in the great preindustrial oriental empires than in all the world ten thousand years earlier.

Why should all three of these factors have increased in unison? Marx never really confronted this question because like Malthus he implicitly assumed that population growth was inevitable. Modern anthropological and archaeological findings, however, don't support this assumption. During as many as two or three million years, hominid populations probably remained stationary or fluctuated within rather narrow limits. Why should population ever have begun to increase? It cannot be argued that it increased as a result of technological progress and rising standards of living. Two additional major evolutionary trends negate such an interpretation. First, despite the increase in technological efficiency, numbers of hours per capita devoted to subsistence increased rather than decreased, reaching a peak with the industrial wage labor system of nineteenth-century capitalism. Second, substantial decrements in quality of life measured in terms of nutritional intake, health, and longevity can be linked to population growth.

In other words, cultures have not generally applied the increments in techno-environmental efficiency brought about by the invention and application of "labor-saving devices" to saving labor but to increasing the energy throughput, which in turn has not been used to improve living standards but to produce additional children. This paradox cannot be explained by the development of class stratification and exploitation, since it was also characteristic of classless societies and was if anything a cause rather than a consequence of the evolution of the state (see pp. 100ff).

The solution to the problem of why new and more efficient modes of production produced people rather than reduced labor and/or increased per capita consumption lies in the methods employed by premodern societies to limit population growth. Malthus correctly perceived that the mode of reproduction throughout the preindustrial epoch was dominated by malign population-regulating techniques involving severe forms of psycho-biological violence and deprivation. It is true that relatively benign techniques were also available, principally homosexuality, coitus interruptus, delayed marriage, postpartum sexual abstinence, masturbation, and prolonged lactation. But these measures alone or in combination in historically or ethnographically ascertainable frequencies cannot account for the remarkably slow (.0007 percent to .0015 percent per annum) rate of increase prior to the neolithic, nor for the less than .056 percent rate between the neolithic and the emergence of the first states (Carneiro and Hilse, 1966; Coale, 1974; Kolata, 1974; Van Ginneken, 1974). Additional means of regulation must be invoked to account for the small size of the human global population prior to 3,000 B.C. in view of the inherent capacity of healthy human populations to double their numbers in less than twenty-five years (Hassan, 1973). I believe that these additional measures involved assault against mother and fetus with whole body-trauma abortifacients, infanticide (especially female infanticide), and systematic selective nutritional neglect of infants, especially of female infants and of preadolescent girls (Divale and Harris, 1976; Polgar et al., 1972; Birdsell, 1968; Devereux, 1967). With mode of production held constant, and an average of only four births per woman, almost 50 percent of the females born must be prevented from reaching reproductive age if a population initially in reasonably good health is not to suffer severe cutbacks in the quality of life in a very short time. This exigency constitutes a great determining force of prehistory.

Before the development of the state, infanticide, body-trauma abortion, and other malign forms of population control predisposed cultures which were in other respects adjusted to their habitats to increase production in order to reduce the wastage of infants, girls, and mothers.

In other words, because prehistoric cultures kept their numbers in line with what they could afford by killing or neglecting their own children, they were vulnerable to the lure of innovations that seemed likely to allow more children to live. Thus Malthus was correct in his surmise that population pressure exerted an enormous influence on the structure of pre-state societies (cf. Dally, 1971).

It has lately been established that pre-state populations generally stop growing when they reach as little as one-third of the maximum carrying capacity of their techno-environmental situation (Lee and Devore, 1968; Casteel, 1972). As we shall see, this has been interpreted by structural Marxists and others as a refutation of the importance of Malthusian forces. Yet no such interpretation is warranted until the nature of the restraints on population growth has been clarified. As I have just said, the evidence indicated that slow rates of population growth were achieved only at great psycho-biological costs through infanticide, abuse, and neglect. This means that even societies with constant or declining populations may be experiencing severe population pressure—or better said, severe reproductive pressure.

The payment of Malthusian costs may account for many specific features of pre-state societies. The most important of these is warfare. Malthus correctly identified warfare as one of the most important checks on population, but he misunderstood the conditions under which paleotechnic warfare occurred and how it functioned to control population growth. He also overestimated the influence of combat deaths upon the rate of growth of modern societies. Pre-state warfare probably does not regulate population through combat deaths but through its effect on the sex ratio, encouraging people to rear maximum numbers of males and minimum numbers of females. Thus pre-state warfare occurs not simply as an aberration caused by the failure of the mode of production to provide adequate subsistence—a view Marx (1973 [1857–58]:607–608) surprisingly enough shared with Malthus. Warfare also occurs as a systemic means of slowing population growth, conserving resources, and maintaining high per capita levels of subsistence. (As for state-level warfare, it is not a check on population but an incentive for rapid population increase and resource depletion [see p. 102].)

The inadequacy of Marx's treatment of what I have called the mode of reproduction resulted from his contemptuous dismissal (1857–58;

1973:606) of the works of the "baboon"* Malthus. Marx's rejection of Malthus was motivated by Malthus's contention that no change in political economy could eliminate poverty (cf. Meek, 1971). But one can recognize the importance of the mode of reproduction in determining the course of sociocultural evolution without endorsing Malthus's reactionary view of history. By rejecting the totality of Malthus's work, Marx cut his followers off from collaborating in the development of a theory of human demography and ecology without which the divergent and convergent transformations of modes of production and their corresponding superstructures cannot be understood. There is no more important aspect of production than reproduction—the production of human beings. While there are structural and superstructural aspects to the modes of population control, the central issue has always been the challenge the biology of sexual reproduction presents to culturally imposed restraints. In this sphere, as in subsistence production, technological advances are of the greatest import, the only difference being that for production it is the means of increase that is decisive, while for reproduction, it is the means of decrease that is decisive. The failure to accord the development of the technology of population control a central role in the evolution of culture does great damage to the credibility of both classical and new-wave Marxist principles and theories.

If it is objected that much of what I have been saying about the relationship between production and reproduction is speculative and in need of further empirical tests, I surely agree. But the fact that an important original and coherent set of testable theories—I shall present more of them in the next chapter—can be formulated by including the mode of reproduction in the infrastructure is a cogent reason for doing so, even though the theories themselves need to be tested by further research.

The Role of Structure and Superstructure

ONE COMMON criticism of cultural materialism is that it reduces structure and superstructure to mechanical epiphenomena that play only a passive role in the determination of history. From this, critics infer that cultural materialism is a doctrine of political and ideological

*Among the other characterizations reserved for Malthus: "plagiarist by profession," "shameless sycophant," "a bought advocate."

apathy and inaction. One might very well wish to question the value of a research strategy which holds that political and ideological struggle are futile because the outcome is determined exclusively by the infrastructure. However, the strategy of cultural materialism is incompatible with any such conclusion. Then what precisely is the role of structure and superstructure in the causal determinations anticipated by cultural materialist strategy?

As I have said in previous sections, infrastructure, structure, and superstructure constitute a sociocultural system. A change in any one of the system's components usually leads to a change in the others. In this regard, cultural materialism is compatible with all those varieties of functionalism employing an organismic analogy to convey an appreciation of the interdependencies among the "cells" and "organs" of the social "body."

The conceptualization of the interrelationships in question can be improved by introducing a distinction between system-maintaining and system-destroying interdependencies. The most likely outcome of any innovation—whether it arises in the infrastructure, structure, or superstructure—is system-maintaining negative feedback, the dampening of deviation resulting either in the extinction of the innovation or in slight compensatory changes in the other sectors, changes which preserve the fundamental characteristics of the whole system. (For example, the introduction of progressive federal income taxes in the United States was followed by a series of privileged exemptions and "shelters" that effectively dampened the movement toward eliminating extremes of wealth and poverty.) However, certain kinds of infrastructural changes (for example, those which increase the energy flow per capita and/or reduce reproductive wastage) are likely to be propagated and amplified, resulting in positive feedback throughout the structural and superstructural sectors, with a consequent alteration of the system's fundamental characteristics. Cultural materialism denies that there is any similar class of structural or superstructural components whose variation leads as regularly to deviation amplification rather than to negative feedback.

The causal priority of infrastructure is a matter of the relative probability that systemic stasis or change will follow upon innovations in the infrastructural, structural or superstructural sectors. Cultural materialism, unlike classical structural-functionalism, holds that changes initiated in the etic and behavioral modes of production and reproduction are more likely to produce deviation amplifications throughout the domestic, political, and ideological sectors than vice versa. Innovations initiated in the etic and behavioral structural sectors are less likely to produce system-destroying changes; and innovations arising in the emic superstructures are still less likely to change the entire system (due to their progressively remote functional relationships with the crucial infrastructural components). To take a familiar example: during the late 1960s many young people believed that industrial capitalism could be destroyed by a "cultural revolution." New modes of singing, praying, dressing, and thinking were introduced in the name of a "counterculture." These innovations predictably had absolutely no effect upon the structure and infrastructure of U.S. capitalism, and even their survival and propagation within the superstructure now seems doubtful except insofar as they enhance the profitability of corporations that sell records and clothes.

Nothing in this formulation of the probabilistic outcome of infrastructural changes warrants the inference that structure or superstructure are insignificant, epiphenomenal reflexes of infrastructural factors. On the contrary, structure and superstructure clearly play vital system-maintaining roles in the negative feedback processes responsible for the conservation of the system. Productive and reproductive processes are functionally dependent on etic domestic and political organization, and the entire etic conjunction is functionally dependent on ideological commitments to values and goals that enhance cooperation and/or minimize the costs of maintaining order and an efficient level of productive and reproductive inputs. It follows from this that ideologies and political movements which lessen the resistance to an infrastructural change increase the likelihood that a new infrastructure will be propagated and amplified instead of dampened and extinguished. Furthermore, the more direct and emphatic the structural and superstructural support of the infrastructural changes, the swifter and the more pervasive the transformation of the whole system.

In other words, although I maintain that the probability is high that certain kinds of changes in the modes of production and reproduction will change the system, I also maintain that functionally related changes initiated simultaneously in all three sectors will increase the probability of systemic change. Indeed, it would be irrational to assert that ideological or political struggle could not enhance or diminish the probability of systemic changes involving all three sectors. But the crucial question that separates cultural materialism from its rivals is this: to what extent can fundamental changes be propagated and amplified by ideologies and political movements when the modes of production and reproduction stand opposed to them? Cultural materialism holds that innovations are unlikely to be propagated and amplified if they are functionally incompatible with the existing modes of production and reproduction—more unlikely than in the reverse situation (that is, when there is an initial political and ideological resistance but none in the modes of production and reproduction). This is what cultural materialists mean when they say that in the long run and in the largest number of cases, etic behavioral infrastructure determines the nature of structure and superstructure.

To illustrate, let us consider the relationship between procreative ideologies, domestic organization, and the mode of production in the United States. When there was an agrarian homesteading, frontier infrastructure, families were large and women's roles as mother and unpaid domestic laborer were emphasized. With urbanization and the increasing cost of reproduction relative to benefits expected from children, women began to "raise their consciousness," demanding entrance to the general employment market on an equal basis with males. Clearly the consciousness-raising process has been an important instrument for liberating women from the role of domestic drudge. But one cannot argue that political-ideological struggle by women was responsible for the vast shifts in technology, production, demand for cheap labor, rise of cities, and increased costs of rearing children, and so forth —all of which provide the functional infrastructural conditions upon which the propagation and amplification of modern feminist political-ideological struggle is premised. In order to grasp the asymmetrical nature of the causal relationships between superstructure and infrastructure, let us suppose that somewhere isolated groups of men are beginning to engage in ideological and political struggle aimed at the revival of nineteenth-century sex roles. Can one assert that the decisive factor in their success or failure will be their commitment to their goal —their degree of political-ideological struggle? Scarcely, because in effect their viewpoint is not likely to be propagated or amplified as long as the present urban industrial infrastructure holds sway.

On the other hand, cultural materialism does not propose that goals will be achieved regardless of whether people struggle consciously to achieve them. Conscious political-ideological struggle is clearly capable of sustaining, accelerating, decelerating, and deflecting the direction and pace of the transformational processes initiated within the infrastructure.

The fear that infrastructural determinism deprives people of the will to engage in conscious struggle is based on an entirely false understanding of the status of politically and ideologically relevant cultural materialist theories. Infrastructure is not some simple, transparent, single-factor "prime mover"; rather, it is a vast conjunction of demographic, technological, economic, and environmental variables. Its description and analysis require enormous amounts of research whose results can only be presented as tentative and probabilistic theories and hypotheses. While some alternative political-ideological courses of action can be dismissed as virtually impossible, several alternative courses of action may appear to be supported by theories and hypotheses to which decisively different degrees of certainty cannot be assigned. Where equally probable alternative cultural materialist theories hold sway—as is often the case—the outcome of political ideological struggle will appear to be decisively influenced by the degree of commitment of the opposing factions and parties. For example, it is difficult to decide whether the productive and reproductive interests of certain low-population-density underdeveloped countries are effectively served by rapid or slow population increase. On the one hand, high rates of population growth intensify the exploitation of the poor; but on the other, slow rates of population growth may lead to labor shortages, underproduction, and the prolongation of economic and political-military subordination to imperialist superpowers. Theoretical ambiguities of this sort can be interpreted in two ways: either the outcome is genuinely open-ended—i.e., not infrastructurally determined but largely dependent upon the respective political-ideological commitments to population growth versus population control; or the outcome is highly determined, but the researchers have failed to provide the amounts or kinds of data necessary for identifying what that determined outcome is likely to be. I contend that from the point of view of the active participants it makes no difference which of these two interpretations one wishes to accept. Unless the theoretical ambiguity can be resolved, the outcome will appear to result from the degree of political-ideological commitment of the opposing factions. (However, the hope always remains that better data collection and better theories will eventually reduce the uncertainties.)

To sum up: cultural materialist theories may invoke different degrees of infrastructural causation ranging from virtual certainty to virtual indeterminacy. Along this entire range, structural and superstructural commitments appear to shape the final outcome through negative and positive feedback processes, in inverse relationship to the ability of existing theories to identify the infrastructural determinants. Some people assert that by upholding the primacy of the infrastructure, cultural materialism contributes to the "dehumanization" of the social sciences. To this I would reply that failure to attempt an objective analysis of the relationship between infrastructure and a particular set of political-ideological goals serves only those who benefit from the wanton waste of other people's lives and possessions. Self-deception and subjectivity are not the measures of being human. I do not accept the moral authority of obscurantists and mystics. They cannot take away the humanity of people who want to understand the world as well as to change it (see Chapter 11).

Dogmatism

THIS IS NO doubt an appropriate moment for me to reaffirm the scientific expectations that underlie these apparently dogmatic assertions. My scientific aim is to formulate interpenetrating sets of theories of broad scope and wide applicability. Such theories can arise only in the context of a definite strategy. It is by requiring every hypothesis worthy of research to implicate etic and behavioral demo-techno-econo-environmental variables that cultural materialism hopes to avoid the proliferating fragmentation of disconnected and mutually contradictory theories.

Against the charge that commitment to cultural materialism is dogmatism (cf. Anderson, 1973:187), there are three rejoinders. First, the credibility of the entire strategy rests upon the empirical status of the interpenetrating theories, and upon their continuous refinement and replacement by more powerful theories. In other words, all of the specific theories that flow from the principle of infrastructural determinism must be the object of continuing critical scrutiny and are held only as tentative approximations. Second, as a matter of existential fact, many competitive research strategies are now actively confronting each other in the social sciences. I do not advocate the elimination of these alternatives; I advocate professional and public evaluations of their respective ability to solve puzzles pertaining to socially significant issues. Elimination of all or most alternative strategies would be a scientific disaster, since the advance of science, as I have said, requires competitive strategies. It is senseless to criticize cultural materialism in terms of a wholly imaginary future state of affairs in which all other strategic alternatives have somehow been eliminated, when under actual conditions, cultural materialism holds a subordinate, minority position within the social science establishment, and is subject to attack from numerous critics on both the left and right of the political spectrum. Third, the charge of dogmatism can easily be flung back at those who make it. If the strategic program advocated here is not acted upon, how can those who reject it pretend to know for certain that cultural materialism is not a more scientifically efficacious way to explain sociocultural differences and similarities than their own? The charge of dogmatism is admissible only on the level of theory; cultural materialists are fully committed to operationalism and to tests of verifiability and falsifiability. To repeat: research strategies cannot be falsified; only theories can be falsified (and only by those who offer better theories!). Nothing corresponds as much to the essence of dogma therefore as the belief that social scientists do not need to choose among research strategies before they embark upon the study of human social life.

Chapter Four

The Scope of Cultural Materialist Theories

THE VALUE of a research strategy does not reside in the profundity of its epistemological viewpoint or the luminosity of its abstract theoretical principles; it lies in the cogency of its substantive theories. Only the capacity of a research strategy's theories to penetrate beneath the surface of phenomena, to reveal new and unsuspected relationships, to tell us why and how things are what they are, can justify its existence. Furthermore, what we want from a strategy is not just a list of disjointed, isolated, and mutually irrelevant or contradictory theories, but an organized set of consistent and concise theories; not the definitive answer to every conceivable question, but tentative answers to important questions over broad and continuously expanding frontiers of knowledge.

A detailed exposition of the total corpus of cultural materialist theories together with the archaeological and ethnological evidence upon which they are based would fill many volumes. Obviously in a single chapter I cannot hope to satisfy the reader's right to know what these theories are about and at the same time provide a satisfactory account of their evidentiary basis.* What I can show, however, is that

---

*Since the issues covered in this chapter correspond to the subject matter of the entire field of social and cultural anthropology, I have refrained from attempting to

the theories generated by cultural materialist principles are of broad scope and wide applicability, that they are highly parsimonious—explaining much with little—and that they form a compact, logically coherent, and interpenetrating set of answers to why human sociocultural systems are both similar and different.

Nomothetic versus Idiographic Theories

AT THE HEART of the cultural materialist theoretical corpus is a set of theories dealing with the origin of the principal varieties of pre-state societies, the origin of sexism, classes, castes, and the state, and the origin of the principal varieties of state level systems. By "origin" I do not mean the unique concatenation of historical events leading to the first appearance of a particular thought or practice in a particular geographical spot, but to the nomothetic process giving rise to a *type* of institution under a set of recurrent conditions. Let me draw this distinction between nomothetic and idiographic events more sharply.

In the extreme instance, the distinction between nomothetic and idiographic explanations poses few difficulties. Nomothetic explanations deal with recurrent types of conditions, general causes, and general effects. For example, warfare, patrilocal residence, astronomical calendars, and ancestor worship, recur under definite but highly general *types* of conditions in different parts of the world. In contrast, the explanation of a particular instance of warfare (say, the Battle of Waterloo) or of the introduction of a particular calendar (say, the one Julius Caesar reformed in 45 B.C.) in terms which make no reference to any general theories of warfare or calendrical record keeping would constitute an idiographic explanation. Such explanations usually stress the unique sequential thoughts and activities of prominent individuals rather than recurrent causal processes.

I do not wish to propose that nomothetic strategies can deal only with events that occur more than once. The origins of Christianity and Buddhism, for example, are unique localized events associated with the

---

provide references for each sentence. References are supplied instead only at critical junctures. I have, however, relied throughout this chapter on the evidence and citations in my textbook, *Culture, People, Nature: An Introduction to General Anthropology*, third edition.

personal lives of two discrete individuals. Yet it is possible to give nomothetic explanations of the origins of Christianity and Buddhism which contrast strongly with common idiographic explanations. The difference is this: in the idiographic explanations, the personalities of Jesus and Gautama impose themselves as unique forces twisting events along unpredictable pathways; in the nomothetic approach, the forces characteristic of the imperial periods in which Jesus and Gautama lived create their personalities. The events unfold along predictable pathways, and the particular individuals involved respond in ways typical of messianic reformers during periods of corruption, exploitation, and widespread misery.

The tension between the unique and the recurrent exists in every field that concerns itself with diachronic processes. Evolution is the record of how out of sameness differences emerge. Although it is always easier to identify the causes of recurrent phenomena, one must recognize that unique happenings result from unique combinations of nomothetic processes. In this regard, cultural materialist theories resemble biological theories that explain the origins of species. Certain recurrent processes account for such recurrent phenomena as DNA replication, photosensitive receptors, and organs of locomotion such as fins, legs, and wings. But the same recurrent processes also account for the uniqueness of each of the millions of species shaped by natural selection.

Hunter-Gatherer Systems

ANTHROPOLOGY's fascination with what Eurocentric historians and philosophers once arrogantly dismissed as "prehistory" confers a distinct advantage in the struggle to create a science of human social life. Ninety percent of all the human beings ever born not only lived during prehistory but lived during that immensely long epoch before the domestication of plants and animals when hunting, fishing, and the collection of wild seeds, nuts, tubers, fruits, and berries was the universal mode of production. The explanation of the principal varieties of hunter-gatherer societies therefore cannot be regarded as a mere footnote to theories that concentrate on more familiar historical periods and on technologically more advanced modes of production. From an aim-oriented view of science, strategies that cannot cope with the similarities and differences found among hunter-gatherer societies suffer greatly by comparison with strategies that can cope with them. Cultural materialism offers a coherent perspective on the social life of hunting and gathering peoples. To begin with, the reliance of hunter-gatherers on dispersed wild flora and fauna explains why hunter-gatherers typically lead a mobile existence. Inability to control the rate of reproduction of the biota, especially of prey species, necessitates a low regional density of human population as well as small, mobile camplike settlements. Hence political organization into bands is a predictable theoretical consequence of the infrastructure of paleolithic peoples and of many surviving groups of recent and modern-day hunter-gatherers. Characteristically, hunter-gatherer bands have between twenty-five and fifty people aggregated at one camp and a regional density of less than one person per square mile; the membership is fluid, however, and band size typically fluctuates with seasonal and other forms of environmentally induced variations in the abundance and distribution of the biotic targets. Since the maintenance of nutritional standards requires seasonal aggregation and disaggregation, as well as daily dispersal and assemblage—as seeds ripen, water holes dry up, animal species appear and disappear—the band benefits from having a labile structure. Throughout the year, small family groups benefit from the freedom to move between campsites, and under duress, to make camps on their own (Lee and Devore, 1968; Bicchieri, 1972; Lee and Devore, 1976). Hence the domestic life of hunter-gatherer bands typically revolves around independent nuclear families related through marriage and descent who maintain separate hearths but share food through reciprocal exchanges. Due to differences in the resource base, to the need for mobility, and to seasonal variations in camp size, one does not expect to find many instances of extended families, lineages, or sibs based on unilocal residence among hunter-gatherers.

Hunter-gatherers achieve their lability on the structural level by intermarriages between neighboring bands. The resultant network of kin ties facilitates visiting throughout the year. Bands reinforce their intergroup solidarity by making joint encampments and by engaging in common ceremonial activities during seasons when resources are abundant. This leads to a theory of incest regulation.

Restrictions on brother-sister, father-daughter, and mother-son sexual intercourse within the nuclear family probably reflect selection against groups who failed to develop inter-band marital alliances and who therefore suffered from a lack of lability and mobility and who consequently had a constricted resource base and lacked trading partners and allies in the event of armed conflict (Y. Cohen, 1978). The investment of the incest taboos with so much guilt, anxiety, and symbolism reflects deep confusion and ambivalence concerning the cost/benefits of incest; hence the need for the imposition of unquestionable "sacred" social rules that cut through that ambivalence and prevent each new generation from repeating the trials and errors of past generations. (The same relationship between the sacred and long-term benefits lies behind many food taboos—see pp. 194ff.)

Political-economic egalitarianism is another theoretically predictable structural consequence of the hunter-gatherer infrastructure. Since settlements are small, membership is labile, and production goes from hand to mouth, therefore daily reciprocal exchanges among campmates cut labor costs. Hunters and collectors can afford to return empty-handed or with half-filled baskets on the expectation that some camp-mates will be luckier. The balance between giver and taker shifts from day to day, thereby ensuring everyone that individual misfortunes will routinely be buffered by the group's collective product. This leads to a theory of economic exchange; reciprocity is the dominant form of hunter-gatherer exchanges, while "big man" redistributive types of exchange systems are correspondingly rare. The infrastructural reason for this is that big-manship is a political-economic instrument for the intensification of production. But intensification, however, poses an immediate threat to hunter-gatherer ecosystems, especially with respect to prey species. Hunters are active no more than one or two days a week; more frequent hunting under the goad of big-man redistributors would rapidly deplete the harvestable animal biomass. Hence hunter-gatherer political-economic ideologies are more likely to insist that the successful hunter be modest and reticent about his productivity (Dentan, 1968). Boasting is bad form when extra effort cannot increase the overall availability of animal protein, but can easily and permanently destroy its availability for everyone (Lee and Devore, 1976).

Egalitarianism is also firmly rooted in the openness of resources, the simplicity of the tools of production, the lack of nontransportable property, and the labile structure of the band. Friction between those who live at a campsite can easily be resolved by the movement of aggrieved parties to new campsites or to the campsites of their relatives. Since there are no standing crops, permanent houses, or heavy equipment, the question of who gets up and moves away and who stays is of little significance. Hence extremes of subordination and superordination are unknown. Headmen, if they are identifiable at all, make suggestions but issue no orders (Fried, 1967). The nature of sex roles and of the relationship between the sexes in band societies is obscured by a lack of information on paleolithic modes of reproduction. One set of cultural materialist theories depicts females as homebodies and specialists in the gathering of plant foods, while males are seen as specialists in big-game hunting. Many believe that this hypothetical division of labor reflects the relative immobility of women because of their frequent pregnancies and their need to nurse children. Men are free of such encumbrances, enjoy a height and weight advantage, have narrower pelvises, and therefore can run faster —all of which combine to make them more efficient hunters. While this theory is supported by the actual division of labor in the surviving hunter-gatherer groups of modern times, I am reluctant to project the modern-day picture of sex roles back upon the entire paleolithic period.

It seems to me not unlikely that women played a more active role in the hunting of big-game animals during Pleistocene times, when such animals were more abundant than they are now. This alternative cultural materialist theory of hunter-gatherer sex roles begins with the hypothesis that prolonged and intensive lactation was an important means of fertility control throughout much of the paleolithic. The effectiveness of the lactation method for spacing births appears to be related to the balance between protein calories and carbohydrate calories in the diet (Frisch and McArthur, 1974; Frisch, 1975; Trussel, 1978; Frisch, 1978). A diet high in protein and low in carbohydrates is optimal for the lactation method because it prevents the accumulation of body fat, the putative signal for the resumption of postnatal ovulation, while sustaining the health of the mother through the strain of producing milk for three or four years at a time. According to this theory, there would be few benefits to be derived from making women into specialist homebodies and plant gatherers. Women are not continuously pregnant, nor are they always nursing helpless infants. There are long intervals between births, and nursing children are big enough to be left at the campsite in the company of older children or other camp-mates. Since the paleolithic hunter-gatherers appear to have hunted big-game herd animals mainly by driving them into pitfalls, over cliffs, and into bogs, women would be important at least as drivers and beaters and would also render valuable service as butchers and bearers once the wounded animals had been dispatched. Nor is there any reason to suppose that women did not carry spears and participate in the actual killing of the trapped animals.

Under optimum ecological conditions, therefore, the relatively slight degree of human sexual dimorphism (slight in comparison with that of the pongids, for example) would not impair the highly egalitarian bent of hunter-gatherer social life. Theoretically, the more abundant the game and the more effective lactation as a means of fertility control, the less common such alternative fertility control measures as abortion and infanticide would be. Abundance of game would also have a dampening effect on intergroup hostility, so warfare would be infrequent; this in turn would dampen any tendency to overvalue males and undervalue females. Women would not be used as the reward for male bravery in combat, sex ratios would be in balance, and serial monogamy for both sexes would prevail (cf. Leacock, 1978).

The advantage of this theory is that it provides a means of predicting the conditions under which patterns associated with ethnographically known hunter-gatherer social life would be innovated and amplified. With less abundant sources of animal protein, lactation would have to be supplemented by higher rates of abortion and infanticide, especially female infanticide. The length of the intervals between births decreases, women get pregnant more often, and their mobility is decreased. At the same time intergroup tensions rise, the frequency of warfare goes up, a premium is placed on rearing combat-ready males, and females are devalued and reared to be the passive rewards for aggressive males. Marriage tends toward polygyny, band territories get defined more sharply, and residence and descent become patrilaterally biased. Thus the cultural materialist strategy previsions the rather complex variations in band level systems of locality and descent that are recorded in the ethnographic literature (Ember, 1978).

Many of these complexities occur among the aboriginal hunter-gatherers of Australia, where the largest game animals were kangaroos and wallabies and desert or semi-desert conditions prevailed throughout much of the interior. Because of their prolonged isolation and the peculiar pattern of resource distribution, Australian bands developed a unique set of formal intergroup marriage alliances based on moieties, sections, and subsections. Under the moiety system, there were two types of bands, A and B, with the marriage rule

$$A = B$$

In the four-section system, there were also two types of bands, but the adjacent and alternating generations were distinguished. The marriage rule was

$$A_1 = B_1$$
$$A_2 = B_2$$

In the eight-section system, the generations continued to be distinguished, but there were four types of bands and the marriage rule was

$$A_1 = B_1 \quad C_1 = D_1$$
$$= A_2 \quad B_2 = C_2 \quad D_2 =$$

These marriage rules have the effect of ensuring that marriage alliances involve appropriately wide networks of bands. Where the simple moiety prevails, only two bands are needed to form a marriage network. With four sections, the marriage network is more likely to involve several type A bands and several type B bands, since one must find a spouse who belongs both to the proper band type and to the proper generation type. In the eight-section system, the obligatory kin network is still larger, since there are four types of bands and a male ego cannot take a spouse from the band type his mother was born in nor from his father's generation type. The infrastructural key to these structural and superstructural features is that the two, four, and eight systems are found in roughly concentric circles from the coast of Australia inward and are correlated with increasing aridity and decreasing population density. The more arid the habitat, the more dispersed the bands, the more vital it becomes to establish multi-band alliance networks (see pp. 231ff.).

An important factor in the evolution of these Australian specialties may have been the relative paucity of large animals, the localization of bands near water holes, and the regularity with which various plant foods became available at known sites. Although ecologically marginal, the interior habitats were homogeneous over vast areas (Callaby, 1971), thus allowing for geographical configurations of bands that remained stable for long periods of time. This stability is attested to by the antiquity of ancestral relics (churingas), which are disinterred from their sacred hiding places during annual ceremonies in order to validate the band's territorial claims. Other hunter-gatherers who have survived into the present in marginal regions exploit different combinations of floral and faunal resources and confront more irregular and unpredictable cycles of scarcity and abundance. The hunter-gatherers of the Kalahari, for example, may lack long-term territorial stability due to shifts in the ranges of their prey species. Marriage classes are also impractical for the Eskimo, who are almost totally dependent upon wide-ranging animal species.

Under conditions of extreme techno-environmental scarcity, hunter-gatherers are organized into small, highly labile, nomadic bilateral camp groups that spend a good part of the year fragmented into nuclear families—as, for example, the Shoshone of the North American Great Basin (Steward, 1938; Thomas, 1972). On the other hand, where biotic resources are especially abundant and resistant to depletions, huntergatherers may develop many of the characteristics of sedentary agriculturalists. The Pacific Northwest provides vivid evidence of the importance of the specific quantitative and qualitative features of the infrastructural conjunction in determining the structural and superstructural features of hunter-gatherer societies. By exploiting rich coastal and riverine resources, groups such as the Haida, Tlingit, Nootka, and Kwakiutl were able to live in large plank houses and permanent villages without possessing domesticated food crops or domesticated animals. Along the coast, dried fish and fish oil played a role analogous to stored plant foods in the creation of asymmetric redistributive systems, incipient classes, intense warfare, and a florescence of woodcrafts and monumental sculpture (Donald and Mitchell, 1975). Post-contact distortions of the infrastructures of these groups—depopulation due to European diseases, trade for guns and bullets, wage labor in Canadian lumber camps and fisheries—also provide the means for comprehending the development of aboriginal redistributive feasts into highly competitive and destructive potlatch ceremonies (Ferguson, n.d.).

The Origin of Neolithic Modes of Production

AS ARCHAEOLOGIST Mark Cohen (1977:5) has stressed, there are two basic questions to be answered about the rise of modes of production based on domesticated plants and animals: "why human populations chose agriculture as a strategy over hunting and gathering and why so many of the world's people chose it during one brief time span . . ." (between 10,000 and 2,000 B.C.).

The strategy of cultural materialism offers parsimonious answers to these questions. Alternative research strategies may cope with either one or the other aspect of the puzzle, but not with both. From an idealist perspective, for example, agriculture and stock raising were great ideas that had to wait upon the appearance of unknown geniuses to unravel the mystery of how to plant seeds and tame wild animals. But how are we to account for the fact that the "idea" for the domestication of plants occurred to so many geniuses all over the world at approximately the same time? Moreover, why were so many different complexes of plants and animals brought into production in differing parts of the world? The proposal that the idea of domestication diffused from some central "hearth" to be readapted in each region in conformity with local ecological possibilities also has relatively little merit. What we are dealing with are complex associations of specialized plants and animals whose overall configurations contrast markedly from region to region (Flannery, 1973). The domestication of gourds, tubers, and pulses took place as early as the domestication of grains (Zohary and Hopf, 1973; MacNeish, 1978). If a genius was needed to initiate the planting of grains in the Near East, he or she was thrice a genius who in South America and Southeast Asia got the idea of planting manioc or yam cuttings from hearing rumors about lands over the horizon where people planted seeds. Idealist theories of agricultural origins are also at odds with the fact that surviving hunter-gatherer groups know about the reproductive functions of plants and under certain conditions engage in activities aimed at increasing the abundance of preferred species. Techniques commonly employed include avoidance of harvesting during the season when wild tubers regenerate (Andaman Islanders); deliberately incomplete harvests of wild grains and scattering of seeds at harvest (Menomini); the use of fire to increase the abundance of plants that are good colonizers of recently burnt land (Western Desert Australian Aborigines); and diversion of melt waters to irrigate favorite fields of wild turnips and carrots (Paiute). Hunter-gatherers are keen observers of the biota upon which they depend, and they cannot fail to note the relationship between seeds, shoots, and mature plants. "Ignorance of this basic principle is almost inconceivable" (Cohen, 1977:23).

To be plausible, agricultural transition theories must be theories of processes, not of singularities. Cultural materialist theories envision these processes as fundamental shifts in the cost-benefits of hunting-gathering as opposed to the cost-benefits of farming and stock raising. These shifts were probably related to the global climatological changes marking the onset of the present interglacial period about 13,000 years ago. The global scale of this event provides an explanation for the simultaneous emergence of agricultural systems. And the diversity of its effects in different ecozones accounts for the diversity of scenarios leading to neolithic types of transitions in different parts of the world. One widespread effect was the depletion or outright extinction of the Pleistocene megafauna that had been the preferred prey species for tens of thousands of years. This must have been a major stimulus for the development of new modes of production regardless of whether the depletions and extinctions resulted primarily from overpredation or from the reduction in suitable grazing and browsing habitats. Hunter-gatherer cost-benefits were also widely affected by eustatic changes, but especially in Southeast Asia, where the post-Pleistocene rise in sea level reduced available land area by half.

In all centers of early agricultural activity, the end of the Pleistocene saw a notable broadening of the subsistence base to include more small mammals, reptiles, birds, mollusks, and insects. Such "broad spectrum" systems were a symptom of hard times. As the labor costs of the hunter-gatherer subsistence systems rose, and as the benefits fell, alternative sedentary modes of production became more attractive. At the same time, lower protein rations may have decreased the effectiveness of the lactation method. More children per female meant higher energy costs for women who had to carry two children at a time over long distances. Or it meant higher rates of abortion and infanticide. Or it meant more disease and hunger, or shorter life spans. All of these costs acted in synchrony but in different proportions in different habitats; the net result, however, was a widely recurrent predisposition for hunter-gatherers to accept modes of production whose start-up costs and cost-benefit ratios had previously been bad bargains.

Mark Cohen's explanation of the transition to agriculture is similar to the above in many respects. However, in accounting for the global synchrony of the development, Cohen attributes little importance to the termination of the last glacial period. Instead, he proposes that the initial period of agricultural investment began simply when hunter-gatherers had occupied every available ecozone and population pressure made the switch to agriculture unavoidable: "The only possible reaction to further growth in population, worldwide, was to begin artificial augmentation of the food supply" (270). I think this theory is somewhat misleading because population pressure is itself a process that can only be described and measured in terms of the relative costs and relative benefits of alternative modes of production and reproduction. It was not the fact that numbers of persons per square mile had reached a particular level that created the pressure for change but rather the fact that under the particular techno-environmental conditions at the end of the last glaciation the harvesting of natural biota could no longer sustain a standard of living higher and less costly than that which agriculture and stock raising could sustain. The massive faunal depletions must be added to the side of the balance weighing against the continuation of the hunting-gathering mode. Although other factors may have been responsible for population pressure, the depletion of resources as a result of the interaction of cultural and natural factors certainly did not improve matters.

In Cohen's view, the recourse to agriculture and stock raising was carried out *in extremis* as if to ward off a total Malthusian collapse. In my view there were many pulls as well as pushes in the transition. The astonishingly rapid florescence of art and architecture at early neolithic sites such as Çatal Huyuk and Jericho suggests that when neolithic economies were based on both agriculture and stock raising they were extremely efficient and that their standard of living quickly (if temporarily) rose beyond that of the terminal hunter-gatherers.

One of the strongest pulls was the intensifiability of agriculture and stock raising through the use of child labor. In many hunter-gatherer groups, children play only a marginal role in the labor force until adolescence. Child labor, however, can be extremely productive in such operations as weeding, harvesting, herding, and retrieving animal droppings. With low population densities in favored habitats during the early phases of the neolithic, four or five children could probably be reared per mother at low cost, yielding a net "advantage" without depleting the essential nonrenewable resources.

Although cultural materialist theories of the origins of neolithic modes of production remain tentative and imperfect, they have an advantage over theories emanating from rival strategies. Structuralism, for example, has virtually nothing to say on the subject, and dialectical materialism suffers as much from its notion of "inner contradictions" as cultural idealism does from its reliance on great ideas. Marx's "fetters on production," the contradiction between forces of production and relations of production, sheds no light on hunter-gatherer transformations. Nature and technology, not the "relations of production," held back the productivity of hunter-gatherers. If there was a dialectic at work, it was a dialectic between population and resources—the rejected dialectic of Malthus, that execrable plagiarist and baboon in parson's clothing.

Varieties of Pre-State Village Societies

THE INFRASTRUCTURES of village societies prior to the evolution of the state acquired specific characteristics in conformity with the adaptive opportunities presented by regional or local ecosystems. Fully sedentary villages based on grain farming and animal husbandry dominated the early phases of the neolithic throughout much of southern Eurasia and North Africa. Sedentism in the Near East, in fact, was already well advanced even before the grains and animals were fully domesticated. New World agricultural villages, however, became fully sedentary at a much slower rate. Because there were no large domesticable herbivores and ruminants in the New World regions where agriculture first developed, New World settlement patterns long continued to be shaped by the quest for animal protein through hunting and fishing. This difference in turn rested on the greater severity of the Pleistocene megafaunal extinctions in the New World, which ultimately may have resulted simply from the lesser land mass of the Americas as compared with Eurasia-Africa and the consequent lack of areas capable of providing refuge for the American megafauna. Whatever its ultimate cause, the extinction of American bovines, equines, domesticable sheep and goats, and pigs played an important role in creating the divergent evolutionary pathways of the New and Old World pre-state agriculturalists. This factor theoretically also helps to explain why agriculture itself was rejected by so many North American hunter-gatherers, especially those in California and the Pacific Northwest: the New World aboriginal neolithic "package" contained few enticements for people who could only obtain animals or fish by continuing a semi-migratory existence.

Beyond the broad differences between the hemispheres in terms of faunal endowment, we come to regional and local differences in basic techno-environmental relationships: species and varieties of domesticates, crop patterns, hydraulic versus rainfall technologies, plows versus hoes and digging sticks, intensive versus extensive regimens, short versus long fallow periods, and so forth. Many major structural and superstructural variations in pre-state agricultural societies are associated with the regimen employed to maintain the nitrogen balance in the soil. In the absence of domesticated herbivores, rainfall agriculture requires frequent fallowing. This leads to various forms of shifting cultivation in which the forest and bush cover are burned and then allowed to regenerate over shorter or longer fallow cycles. Populations dependent on shifting cultivation in tropical rain forests tend to live in surprisingly small villages—under two hundred persons—and to have regional densities not much different from those of hunter-gatherers. Why tropical forest villages remained so small and moved to new sites so often is a much-debated subject. In the Amazon and other rain forest areas, the most important limiting factor was probably the rapid decline in the quantity and quality of game animals available on the peripheries of settlements (Gross, 1975). Villages tended to be much larger and more sedentary along the main branches of the Orinoco and Amazon rivers, where aquatic mammals, turtles, and large fish supplemented the monkeys, birds, and rodents upon which nonriverine peoples had to depend for most of their meat supply.

The occurrence of taboos on the slaughter or consumption of many species of comestible forest animals has long obscured the importance of protein as a limiting factor among shifting cultivators. Cultural idealists, structuralists, and eclectics all invoke these taboos as a challenge to the cultural materialist strategy. But as Eric Ross (1978; 1979) has suggested, many of these taboos are themselves evidence of the need for conservation practices, since they are applied to currently or formerly endangered species. In addition, taboos on species such as sloth, tapir, or deer may also reflect ambiguous cost/benefit situations in which hunters are well advised not to waste their time pursuing hidden animals or solitary specimens that flee into swamps or other remote areas. In this regard cultural materialism offers theories of resource exploitation that have been independently elaborated and tested by animal ecologists concerned with predation and foraging behavior. There is every reason to believe that the major variations in human and animal foraging strategies are governed by similar adaptive principles (Pyke, Pullman, and Charnov, 1977; Winterhalder, 1977; McDonald, 1977).

The widespread occurrence of intense patterns of warfare among low-density shifting cultivators has also raised doubts about the cultural materialist strategy. But a better understanding of the severity of the techno-environmental limits within which shifting cultivators are obliged to live makes their widespread raiding, wife stealing, counter-raiding, trophy taking, and terroristic cannibalism highly intelligible within the cultural materialist framework. Like band-level populations, shifting cultivators lack benign or inexpensive alternatives for regulating population growth. This makes warfare theoretically the least costly of the available alternatives.

Warfare regulates village populations in two ways: first, by promoting female infanticide and the abuse and selective nutritional neglect of young girls (Lindenbaum, 1979; Buchbinder, in press); and second, by promoting the dispersion of enemy villages. (Combat deaths are a less important form of demographic control, since males rather than females are the principal combatants.) Warfare promotes female infanticide and the abuse and selective nutritional neglect of young girls by placing a premium on the rearing of aggressive combat-ready males (Divale and Harris, 1976; Divale, Harris, and Williams, 1978). Because of the decisive advantage of males over females in muscle-powered hand-to-hand combat, the survival of each village depends on rearing maximum numbers of brawny males. As villages increase in size, they deplete their habitats and become less affluent. To protect their living standards, they split and spread apart, opening up no man's lands on the peripheries of their hunting territories. These no man's lands in turn play a vital role in maintaining regional populations at densities compatible with the densities of game animals and other resources. They probably also function as game preserves where endangered species can find refuge from their human predators (Hickerson, 1965).

Warfare in turn initiates and sustains lengthy theoretical causal chains which partially or wholly account for many features of domestic and political economy and the emic superstructure of village peoples. When warfare is carried out in the form of raids and counter-raids between neighboring villages, it tends to strengthen the formation of solidary male fraternal and paternal interest groups. Groups of fathers, brothers, and sons exchange women with other groups of fathers, brothers, and sons in order to obtain and consolidate within-village and between-village military alliances. Males therefore tend to constitute the residential core of households and village; post-nuptial locality tends to be virilocal and patrilocal; and filiation and descent tend to be reckoned in the male line. To encourage male aggressiveness, wives are withheld from junior males and awarded to dominant seniors. This theory accounts for the prevalence of polygyny even in groups that have more men than women in the nubile cohorts. Training for aggression also gives rise to severe male puberty ordeals involving mutilations, scarification, and drug-induced hallucinations. Male aggressiveness engenders strong antagonisms between males in adjacent generations, giving rise to Oedipal motifs in dreams and mythology; at the same time, male dominance gives rise to marked sex antagonism and to myths and rituals involving body paint, masks, bull-roarers, and other paraphernalia whose function it is to mystify and justify male supremacy. Cultural materialism therefore supplies a coherent set of theories linking early farming infrastructures to characteristic features of etic and emic behavioral and mental superstructures, including the entire Freudian approach to culture and personality (see pp. 263ff)

The Rise of Chiefdoms

VILLAGE-LEVEL big men play a central role in cultural materialist theories concerning the origin of advanced forms of inequality. These big men act as the "nodes" of three important institutional complexes: they intensify production; they carry out redistribution of the resultant temporary harvest surpluses and of trade goods; and they use their prestige and material wealth to organize trading expeditions and military engagements against enemy villages. The expansion of the managerial aspects of these functions rapidly leads to permanent and severe forms of hierarchy, which eventually culminates in there being differential access to strategic resources; this in turn lays the basis for the emergence of classes and of the state.

Simple chiefdoms come into being with the first intensifier-redistributor-warrior complexes. The more production is intensified, the more there is to redistribute and to trade, the larger the population, the more intense the warfare, the more complex and powerful the chiefly sector. Other things being equal, all such systems tend to move from symmetric forms of redistribution (in which the primary producers get back everything they produce) to asymmetric forms (in which the redistributors retain more of what is produced for longer and longer periods). Eventually the retained portion of the harvest surplus provides the chief with the material means for coercing his followers into further intensifications. (For example, as in Hawaii, where the chief acquired a permanent military retinue.) Contributions to the redistributive portion of the economy gradually cease to be voluntary; soon they verge on taxation, and at that point, chiefdoms stand poised at the threshold of becoming states.

The extent to which a particular chiefdom will move along this trajectory is largely, if not entirely, a matter of the demo-techno-econo-environmental conditions peculiar to each instance. Various kinds of limiting factors—soils, space (as on islands), water, availability of domesticated plants and animals, such seasonal events as storms and frosts, and disease vectors—will block off further growth in the size and complexity of the redistributive networks and prevent the emergence of marked differences in rank and power.

The advantage of cultural materialism over most of its rival strategies again lies in its ability to account for variations—in this case, to account for the quantitative and qualitative variations in the structural and superstructural features associated with trends leading toward state-level societies. Since the infrastructures of village societies are based on profoundly different combinations of domesticated animals and plants, one expects profoundly different varieties of intensifications, redistributions, trade and military activities, and divergent as well as convergent forms of managerial functions within the chieftain sector.

In order for large, asymmetrical redistribution systems to develop, the redistributors must be able to act as "energy gates," opening and shutting the flow of critical amounts of proteins and calories needed by the primary producers (cf. Odum, 1971). Certain crops can be made to function as energy gates more readily than others. Melanesian yams, for example, are poor energy gates. They are high in calories but low in protein, and cannot be stored for long periods without rotting. As a consequence, in Melanesia, where yams are the staple crop, the managerial functions of island big men seldom involve much more than the building of a few communal men's houses or one or two seagoing canoes. Manioc is another low-protein, high calorie crop. When made into a flour and toasted, manioc has good preservation characteristics. Nonetheless, it is not suited to act as an energy gate. The best way to preserve manioc is to let the mature tubers remain in the ground until they are needed. Since there are no well-defined harvest periods, marked managerial functions cannot develop on the basis of manioc redistributions.

Grains are inherently more valuable than tubers and gourds, since their higher protein content may constitute a vital component in the nutritional balance. Anna Roosevelt (1977) has shown that the introduction of maize along the Orinoco River resulted in a rapid growth of village populations, possibly because of maize's higher protein content as compared with that of manioc. Similarly, the adoption of maize by the archaic Olmec and Maya laid the basis for rapid population growth and the emergence of complex chiefdoms at an early period (Hammond, 1978; Harrison and Turner, 1978; Adams, 1977).

The absence of domesticable ruminants and pigs in the Americas and the absence of storable grains in Oceania influenced the intensification and redistributive complexes of each region in different ways. In the Americas, the lack of ruminants or pigs slowed the rate at which managerial functions were taken over by headmen and chiefs, but it did not ultimately prevent the emergence of huge harvest surpluses of maize. In Oceania many precocious forms of redistributive systems based on yams and pig raising have been identified. But the evolutionary potential of these systems appears not to have been much greater than that of interfluvial Amazonian villages lacking maize (cf. Morren, 1974; Lathrap, 1973).

The shifting cultivators of New Guinea and Melanesia who possess the domesticated pig resemble the interfluvial Amazonians in having many of the features of the military male supremacist complex I described in the last section, even though New Guinea population density is much higher and the people are much more preoccupied with rank differences validated through redistributions. As suggested in the work of Roy Rappaport (1967), such specific features of the superstructure as feasting, dancing, myth-making and animal sacrifice arise from the infrastructural conjunction and may play a regulatory role with respect to the use of forest resources and the alternation of periods of war and peace. But once again, there is considerable variation, as, for example, between highland and lowland New Guinea, and it is cultural materialism that offers the best if not the only hope of providing nomothetic solutions to the many puzzles that remain (cf. Brown, 1978).

The paleotechnic infrastructures most amenable to intensification, redistribution, and the expansion of managerial functions were those based on the grain and ruminant complexes of the Near and Middle East, southern Europe, northern China, and northern India. Unfortunately these were precisely the first redistributive systems to cross the threshold into statehood, and they therefore have never been directly observed by historians or ethnologists. Nonetheless, from the archaeological evidence of storehouses, monumental architecture, temples, high mounds and tells, defensive moats, walls, towers, and the growth of irrigation systems, it is clear that managerial activities similar to those observed among surviving pre-state chiefdoms underwent rapid expansion in these critical regions immediately prior to the appearance of the state. Furthermore, there is abundant evidence from Roman encounters with "barbarians" in northern Europe, from Hebraic and Indian scriptures, and from Norse, Germanic, and Celtic sagas that intensifier-redistributor-warriors and their priestly retainers constituted the nuclei of the first ruling classes in the Old World (Piggott, 1965, 1975; Smith, 1956; Renfrew, 1973).

Similarly, the appearance of the first masonry temple structures in lowland Tabasco, Veracruz, and Yucatán among the early Olmec and Maya correlates with the adoption of maize as the primary source of carbohydrates (Gifford, 1974; Coe, 1968; Sanders, 1972).

Varieties of Pre-State Village Structures and Superstructures

THE INTENSIFIER-redistributor-warrior complexes provide the theoretical key to understanding additional aspects of pre-state village life. As ranking becomes an ever more conspicuous feature of domestic and political economy, competitive relationships within villages are exacerbated. The male-centered kin groups find themselves competing for permanent garden and grazing lands, and they develop valuable patrimonies consisting of animal herds, stored crops, granaries, family shrines, and burial grounds. Hence the question of the transmission or devolution of property can no longer be settled by burning it or burying it, as is the custom among less affluent and less sedentary band and village societies. Thus there arise the classic instances of narrowly restricted kin groups based on patrilineal descent: the patrilineage or the patri-sib.

As Michael Harner (1970) has shown, among pre-state societies, the greater the intensity of agricultural production (measured by decline in dependence upon hunting), the greater the likelihood of unilineal descent groups. Such groups constitute a systemic attempt to reconcile the claims of the close kinsmen of redistributor big men to a share in the permanent forms of property and wealth they have helped to create. While not yet private property—since land is held in common by the kin group—lineage and sib patrimonies nonetheless constitute a definite step toward the development of marked inequalities in access to strategic resources.

By emphasizing the significance of strategic property in the affairs of unilineal descent groups, many puzzling variations and associated features can be brought within a single coherent explanatory framework. For example, as I will show later in my discussion of structuralist theories of "circulating connubia" and asymmetrical cross-cousin marriage, the struggle for material resources, not the fancied "structure" of the mind, accounts for the superordinate status of wife-givers over wife-takers in pre-state situations. Similarly the solution to conundrums such as the occurrence of Crow and Omaha type kinship terminologies (in which descent group identity overrides generational identity) lies in a better understanding of the quantitative and qualitative features of descent group patrimonies and the struggle by descent groups for autonomy and hegemony.

A major puzzle is why a small proportion of unilinear descent groups are matrilineal instead of patrilineal. Here let me point first to the relatively unsatisfactory status of explanations put forth under idealist auspices. Lewis Henry Morgan, for example, proposed that matrilineality was a survival of the period of group marriage when the identity of one's father could not be ascertained. It is now clear that group marriage never existed; that in polyandrous situations such as in Tibet, paternity is easily reckoned by assigning it arbitrarily first to one husband and then to another; and that most matrilineally organized societies are not polyandrous anyway and hence have no difficulty whatsoever in knowing who fathered whom. That leaves us with the ultimate idealist wisdom that matrilineal societies are matrilineal because they want to be matrilineal. Structuralists have little to add other than that since there is patrilineality, its dialectical opposite, matrilineality, should also occur.

Following suggestions by Morgan and Engels, plausible materialist theories of the origins of matrilocality have emphasized the increased significance of women's labor resulting from the shift from hunting-collecting to simple forms of horticulture. Since women work the fields, they gain control over them. This approach, however, has too many factual and logical flaws (Sanday, 1973). Horticultural societies are five times more likely to be patrilineal than matrilineal (Murdock, 1967). Furthermore, even in many hunter-collector societies female labor is more important than male labor. And finally, there is no compelling reason to expect that people who work the land will gain control over its inheritance. Indeed, one could argue that generally the people who work the least have the greatest control over strategic resources.

A more powerful theory of matrilineal phenomena can be constructed by starting from the fact that males continue to control access to strategic property and to dominate the military and political economic functions of matrilineal societies. In other words, matrilineal systems are not matriarchies (Rosaldo and Lamphere, 1974). Under what conditions, then, would it be compatible with a male's interests in the control over the management and devolution of property to permit the focus of domestic organization to shift from himself to his sister, and from his son to his sister's son? The appropriate conditions probably exist when a man is obliged to be absent from his lands, animals, children, and food stores for several weeks or months at a time. Long-distance warfare, long-distance hunting expeditions, and long-distance trading expeditions are the most important reasons for staying away. Under patrilocal or virilocal forms of residence (the proximate causes of patrilineality), prolonged absence of males means that a man's wife—a woman whose alien descent group loyalties override any obligation to her husband—becomes the de facto "boss" of the domestic corporation. With uxorilocality and matrilocality, however, a man in effect puts his sister in charge of their joint patrimony. His sister stays at home where she is joined part of the year by a husband, while her brother goes to live nearby in his own wife's residence also for only part of the year. The rest of the time most of the able-bodied men are away on joint expeditions, relatively secure in the knowledge that the administration of their respective patrimonies is being carried out by someone whose interests correspond to their own and not to those of an alien descent group.

This model fits the archaeological and historical evidence concerning the emergence of matrilineality in eastern North America and elsewhere. For example, with the introduction of maize, Middle Woodlands Iroquois settlements became more sedentary and their average size increased. Local faunal resources, especially deer (needed for clothing as well as for food) were depleted; warfare intensified and trade increased; men remained absent for half the year in long-distance combined hunting, trading, and raiding expeditions; and residence shifted from bilocality or virilocality to matrilocality (Trigger, 1978; Gramby, 1977).

Many apparently anomalous combinations of descent rules and locality practices become theoretically intelligible if we keep in mind the fact that males do not relinquish their political-economic hegemony in matrilineal societies. The so-called strains of matrilineal organizations, for example, reflect the tendency of males to reassert control over their own children as well as over their sister's children (cf. Schneider and Gough, 1961). Moreover, the frequent association of avunculocal residence with matrilineal descent (Murdock, 1967) can be seen either as a step in the direction of returning to male-centered domestic units or as a means of partially overcoming some of the costs which uxorilocality exacts from the male. Polygyny, for example, is difficult to arrange when a man is a temporary sojourner in his wife's household. While avunculocality means that an absent male must entrust his homestead to his wife, various forms of preferential marriage mitigate the penalties. For example, matrilateral cross-cousin marriage occurs often among avunculocal peoples (ibid.). This leads to households in which a man's daughter marries his sister's son. Hence the female resident corps consists of daughters as well as alien wives. Moreover, as we will see later on when I turn to the critique of structuralist explanations of asymmetrical cross-cousin marriage, matrilateral cross-cousin marriage sets up ranked wife-giving and wife-taking relationships between kin groups. These relationships are characteristic of societies in which the struggle between domestic groups for resources and labor has become acute. In the matrilineal avunculocal context, this means that a man's sister's sons join his household as dependents and that they usually must furnish bridewealth or render suitor service to him. Unlike matrilineal matrilocal households, in other words, matrilineal avunculocal households permit aggressive male intensifier-redistributor-warriors to build up large menages consisting of many wives, daughters, and dependent sons-in-law.

Another kind of compromise can be achieved by combining matrilocality with preferential patrilateral cross-cousin marriage (see pp. 181ff). This combination results in setting up domestic groups in which a man's sons and daughters leave his household, while his grandchildren through his sons return to it. In other words, patrilateral cross-cousin marriage in a matrilineal context represents a step toward the restoration of a man's control over his own children without sacrificing control over his sister's children.

William Divale has shown that the practice of external warfare is strongly associated with matrilocality and matrilineal descent. Divale's (1975) explanation for this association is that in order to wage successful large-scale warfare against distant enemies (or in order to defend oneself successfully against enemies who come in force from distant lands), the fraternal-paternal interest groups characteristic of male-centered domestic economies have to be broken up. Matrilocality does this. It promotes the formation of male combat teams whose members are drawn from different lineages and who have learned to live together even though they do not belong to the same descent group. Matrilocality in a sense renders males less parochial and prepares them to cooperate with each other in large-scale military ventures. If true, Divale's theory would provide additional reasons for the development of matrilineality in relation to long-distance hunting, trading and raiding expeditions, since it would give matrilineal groups an edge over patrilineal groups in all three endeavors. I am inclined to doubt this aspect of Divale's theory, however, because patrilineal descent groups are also capable of making between-village alliances and of sending large groups of warriors into combat.

Many East African groups like the Nuer, Masai, Nandi, Turkana, and Dinka effectively rallied small armies on the basis of cooperation between maximal patrilineages. All these groups, however, were semipastoralists preeminently concerned with cattle rather than land as a source of wealth. Among such groups, warfare was waged during the course of the migrations of lineages searching for new grazing lands. Hence the question of who was left at home to care for the warrior's patrimony was not as significant as it was for people whose wealth consisted of land or fishing spots. It is surely no accident that in the so-called matrilineal belt of South Central Africa, groups like the Bemba, Pende, Yao, Lele, Plateau Tonga, and many others, are primarily agriculturalists rather than pastoralists (Murdock, 1959, 1967). The long-distance trading and raiding carried out by the men of these groups probably raised important questions concerning the management of the domestic economy by alien women.

Let me turn now to the relationship between unilineal descent groups and the emergence of stratification and the state. At a certain stage in the development of asymmetrical redistributive functions, the presence of unilineal descent groups inhibits the activities of the emerging ruling class. The interests of increasingly powerful chiefs no longer coincide with the interests of their entire lineages, and it is convenient to set aside the automatic claims which distantly related lineage members put upon the chief's largesse. This sets the stage for the emergence of ramages and other nonunilinear or cognatic descent groups. Ramages, for example, probably represent a systemic response to the elite stratum's need for dismissing kin claims and for achieving greater flexibility in recruiting warriors and workers from among a growing pool of potential followers. The membership of a ramage is determined by the tracing of descent optionally through either male or female ancestors. These nonunilineal groups are known best from Micronesian and Polynesian societies characterized by marked differences in rank and by incipient statehood. Ramages are well adapted to the needs of societies that are no longer interested in maintaining a regulated balance between population and resources and that have embarked upon a career of unrestrained intensification and expansion. A variation of this theory explains the development of ramages among the aboriginal peoples of the Pacific Northwest after contact with Europeans and Americans. The introduction of muskets intensified both warfare and the production of trade goods for obtaining these weapons from the white traders (Ferguson, n.d.). At the same time, because of introduced diseases, population declined precipitously, rendering unilineal descent maladaptive for military and other manpower needs.

The *ayllu* of the Inca and the *calpulli* of the Aztec probably represent a further refinement of the use of nonunilineal descent to localize and organize peasant communities under the auspices of full-blown state bureaucracies. Additional ideologically different but functionally similar structural sequelae to the reign of unilineality developed under the influence of variant stratification processes. I shall do no more than mention the probable functional equivalence between cognatic descent and the double descent systems associated with West African states, the hypertrophy of genealogical manipulation and amnesia characteristic of the Chinese clan, and the general disappearance in Eurasia of unilinear descent groups that linked peasants to rulers. Needless to say, changes in the type of descent group and domestic economy are reflected in changes in kinship terminologies. I shall not attempt to encapsulate the immense literature on this subject, but it has been clear since Murdock's *Social Structure* (1949) that if one can understand why locality and descent change, one is well on the way toward understanding why kin-terminological systems change. My intention here cannot be to show that every puzzling feature of domestic economy has already been satisfactorily explained by cultural materialism, but rather that enough of a formulation exists to warrant the application of the same strategic principles to the remaining puzzles.

The Emergence of the State

ALL THE QUALITATIVE components of the state were already present to some degree among advanced chiefdoms. The asymmetric redistribution of harvest surpluses already amounted to an incipient form of taxation. Under primitive forms of redistribution, the redistributor depended on the generosity of the primary producers; in the advanced chiefdoms, the primary producers were already dependent on the generosity of the redistributors (Sahlins, 1960). Sumptuary privileges of the intensifier-redistributor-warrior elites were also already marked in the advanced chiefdoms. Kin groups were hierarchized, and inequalities between the health and well-being of commoners and those of elites were already quite prominent. To judge from the evidence of the Pacific Northwest Coast, there were even small numbers of slaves (Ruyle, 1973). Moreover, like pristine states, the advanced chiefdoms were thoroughly committed to the relief of reproductive pressures not through the regulation of fertility but through territorial expansion, military plunder, and the continuous intensification of production.

Nonetheless, most advanced chiefdoms probably did not evolve directly into states. The incipient stratification on which they were based gave rise to political instability, factional disputes, insurrections, fissioning, and migrations that recurrently dampened the elite sector's ability to command goods and services and to monopolize police-military functions.

While only a fine line separates advanced chiefdoms from pristine states, the change-over is best described not as a qualitative leap or a flip from one form to another but as the continuation of an exponential process of deviation amplification. This process started with the rudimentary intensifier-redistributor-warrior complexes and continued unimpeded up to the point of the consolidation and stabilization of the distinction between the ruling class and the class of peasant food producers (Fried, 1978b). Once this point is passed, the deviation amplification continues along the same exponential trajectory. What determines whether the changes continue to be amplified or whether they are cut off at the chiefdom level? First, the energy base of pristine states must be big enough to permit the ruling class to underwrite the subsistence needs of a permanent police-military corps of several thousand men. This implies the existence of highly intensifiable modes of production such as irrigation grain agriculture or animal-grain mixed farming rainfall systems. Second, even a highly intensifiable subsistence system will not lead to stable class divisions as long as the emergent peasant producers can escape into less densely occupied areas without suffering a net deterioration in labor efficiency and quality of life. As David Webster (1975) and Malcolm Webb (1975) have suggested, this means that the pristine state can be expected to arise only in regions with sharp ecotones. In such regions, the expansionist policies of ad-

vanced chiefdoms lead sooner or later to the condition Robert Car-
niero (1970) has labeled "impaction": the dissatisfied peasants who
cross the ecotone find themselves in a worse situation than those who
remain behind—even though those who remain must now pay taxes
in labor or kind for the privilege of using their native strategic resources. There is a very good fit between this model of pristine state
formation and the conditions that existed in the regions most likely
on archaeological evidence to have been the centers of formation of
pristine states. Egypt, Mesopotamia, northern India, the Yellow
River Basin, central highland Mexico south to Tehuantepec, and the
Peruvian coastal rivers and Andean highlands are all sharply circumscribed by ecotones that cannot support intensifiable forms of preindustrial agriculture.

The consolidation of class-structured life probably required relatively little direct physical confrontation. Villages pressing against the
ecotone might accept permanently dependent statuses in exchange for
the privilege of continuing to participate in the redistributions of the
more affluent parent villages from which they had fissioned. The relationship would be mediated and facilitated by numerous structural and
superstructural arrangements. There would be junior and senior lineages, ancestor worship, cognatic descent, and wife-giving and wife-
taking alliance groups, with wife-takers expected to render labor service
and bride price. To the extent that elite classes rendered useful services
like organizing the construction of waterworks, defending the masses
against enemy troops, and predicting floods and seasons, they could
expect the peasant masses to make tax contributions without too much
fuss or even with considerable enthusiasm. This explains why the early
pristine states invested so heavily in the construction of monumental
statues, altars, temples, pyramids, and other religious structures. Although these were costly enterprises, they more than paid for themselves by helping to convince the peasants that the elites were benevo-
lently trying to control the supernatural and natural forces upon which
human health and well-being were said to be dependent (Service,
1978:31). It is always cheaper to produce obedience through mystification than through police-military coercion.

Once the state becomes a functional reality, its components reso-
nate within a single gigantic amplifier. The more powerful the ruling
class, the more it can intensify production, increase population, wage
war, expand territory, mystify the peasants, and increase its power still
further. All neighboring chiefdoms must either rapidly pass across the

threshold of state formation, or succumb to the triumphant armies of the new social leviathan.

Varieties of State Systems

THE DEVELOPMENT of the state does not reduce the significance of the ecological components in the infrastructure. The advanced technology and higher productivity of state-level modes of production do not relegate ecological variables to a subordinate role due to some supposed increase in a people's capacity to control their environment. Nor is the culture/nature interface rendered less critical because of the very real distortions exploitative class relations introduce into the ecologically adaptive responses of sociocultural systems. Every attempt to control nature and to expand and intensify production has its distinctive repercussions regardless of the level of technological advance. And every system of class exploitation realizes its evolutionary potential within a definite ecological and demographic context. No purely internal dynamic of classes can account for the major varieties of state systems. It is true that the cost-benefits of intensification are not the same for peasants or workers as for members of the ruling classes. But the specific nature of class relations is very much conditioned by the "external" interactions at the culture/nature interface.

Cultural materialist theories aimed at explaining varieties of states focus on the differential effects of state-level intensifications in different techno-environmental contexts. First, there is the question of the different rate of development and scale of imperial systems in Eurasia and Africa as contrasted with the New World. In this regard, the post-Pleistocene endowments of the two hemispheres with respect to domesticable fauna probably had a decisive influence. The absence of traction animals in the Americas inhibited the development of the wheel, thereby slowing the pace of all mechanical inventions and assuring the eventual subordination of New World populations to European armies when transatlantic contact between the hemispheres was established.

Differential effects of intensification resulting in strategic depletions and shifts in rainfall and drainage patterns account for variations in the size and longevity of different state and imperial systems within the hemispheres. The peculiar trajectory of growth and sudden collapse of the Maya states, for example, seem to be closely related to the

limitations on intensive forms of agriculture associated with the lime-
stone formations of the Yucatán Peninsula, the prolonged dry season,
and the exhaustion of soils due to prolonged overcropping (Harrison
and Turner, 1978; Olson, 1978).

The largest and most enduring ancient imperial systems (if not the
earliest) were those based on irrigation agriculture. Following the logic
of Karl Wittfogel's (1957) theory of oriental despotism, one can render
intelligible phenomena of vast scope and significance throughout the
ancient world (Mitchell, 1973). It seems likely that there was a causal
relationship between the size and importance of irrigation systems and
the degree of centralization of political power (Wittfogel, 1972; Service, 1978:30). Large-scale control of irrigation and drainage in the big
river valleys led to the hypertrophy of agro-managerial functions. Moreover, since control over water amounted to control over the basic
energy supply in the form of food calories, the agro-managerial elites
had the power to annihilate all political dissenters. The hydraulic infrastructure also plausibly accounts for the cyclic nature of dynastic
upheavals and restorations characteristic of the ancient riverine empires: reformatory movements aimed at alleviating peasant discontent
could not avoid the reconstruction or extension of the waterworks and
thus the restoration of the political forms determined by the hydraulic
base.

The theory of oriental despotism is not a theory which aims to
explain only one type of ancient polity. It is aimed at explaining differences as well as similarities, and it lends itself to this broader objective
because it is concerned with measurable variables at the interface
between culture and nature. Following Wittfogel's distinction between
compact and loose hydraulic societies, plausible explanations of the
differences between the ancient empires can be constructed in which
hydrographic features, patterns of rainfall, and other environmental
factors constitute important independent variables. The Nile and the
Yellow River, for example, have very different kinds of channels and
flood periods, and their hinterlands have very different potentials for
rainfall agriculture (cf. Butzer, 1976). One expects a smaller and more
compact form of hydraulic state in Egypt as compared with China
simply because of the narrowness of the Nile's flood plain. Smaller
irrigation systems may in fact not be amenable to state control and can
exist in the midst of feudal or even chiefdom polities (Hunt and Hunt,
1976).

Wittfogel's theory can also be turned around to illuminate the nature of state systems with rainfall agricultural infrastructures. Such states possess evolutionary potentials entirely different from hydraulic systems. Rainfall agriculture leads to dispersed, multicentered forms of production. Hence it is doubtful that any pristine state ever developed on a rainfall base. Most rainfall states were probably secondary formations brought into existence to take advantage of the opportunity for trade and plunder created by the expansion of hydraulic empires (Fried, 1967). Rainfall states during preindustrial times typically possessed loose feudal structures. In Europe, feudal kings remained weak compared with hydraulic emperors, since they could not prevent the rain from falling on friend and foe alike. Political decentralization in turn fostered the rise of independent merchant classes and the growth of private commercial interests, which further pluralized the balance of power. Given the small scale of the ancient Mediterranean city-states, their continuity with egalitarian forms of chiefdoms, and their continued pluralism, the much-mystified roots of Western democracy can be brought within the compass of an intelligible process. We can also begin to understand why the Roman Empire, with its base in rainfall agriculture and control over trade routes, never completely lost its republican institutions; why the Roman hegemony over Europe lasted a mere half a millennium (compared with four millennia for China); and why when it fell apart (due primarily to its growing dependence on cheap labor in the provinces and the depletion of resources at home), no one could manage to put it back together again. A similar line of reasoning leads from the continued importance of decentralized forms of agriculture in the post-Roman period; to the gradual filling up of northern Europe and the depletion of its resources by people and domestic animals; to the shift in political-economic power from agrarian to commercial interests; and on to the abortive attempt to create divine right despotisms in France; until we finally arrive at the peculiar set of conditions that underwrote the rise of the political economy of capitalism with its individualistic creeds, private conscience, and parliamentary politics.

From a slightly different perspective, the same set of factors explains why capitalism and parliamentary democracies did not and could not develop within the hydraulic states. Following Marx, one can say that feudalism was the necessary prerequisite for the emergence of capitalism. But contrary to the Leninist and Stalinist versions of dialectical materialism, it is clear that feudalism was incompatible with large-scale hydraulic systems. Only a decentralized mode of production could have set the stage for the emergence of the pristine forms of capitalism. Feudalism of course has its political economic subtypes qualified by both natural and cultural features: seasonal precipitation patterns; crop inventories and proximity of other state societies, especially of large empires and their associated trade routes. Here the cultural materialist catches a glimpse of the probable causes of the slow rate of growth and special structures and superstructures of the secondary states that developed in Africa south of the Sahara. As Jack Goody (1976) has emphasized, African agriculture was much less productive than European agriculture. Indigenous agricultural modes of production were highly developed in West Africa. But the absence of grazing lands and the presence of the tsetse fly inhibited the husbandry of domestic animals. Hence the Mediterranean tradition of mixed farming and animal husbandry was never replicated in this or any other aboriginal African region south of the Sahara (Grigg, 1974). Horses did achieve importance for the West African cavalry, but neither equines nor bovines could be raised cheaply enough to serve as plow animals. From which we get: the absence of the plow in West Africa; the use of the hoe as the principal agricultural implement; the survival of shifting forest agriculture and bush-following systems; and the relatively restricted energy base of the secondary trade states of Ghana, Mali, and Dahomey. This explains why the feudal polities of Africa were weaker, less centralized, and more egalitarian than their European counterparts, and why it was ultimately the Europeans who developed capitalism and enslaved the Africans rather than vice versa.

The consequence of the absence of the plow ramify in many other directions. As Goody suggests, we can begin to lift the veil on puzzles such as why bride price is the characteristic mode of legitimizing marriages in Africa, whereas across preindustrial Europe and Asia, dowry was and is the predominant form of marital exchange. Given the greater extent of economic differentiation in the plow regions, marriage alliances functioned to consolidate property holdings within classes, estates, castes, and descent groups. As Goody explains, dowry is used to prevent property from passing out of privileged strata into less privileged strata. Bride price, on the other hand, expresses a greater willingness to share privileges compatible with a situation in which population density is relatively low, land is cheap, and the social distance between rulers and commoners is not very great.

But there is more to this than Goody sees for reasons to be discussed in Chapter 10. African elites use the bride price to establish and consolidate alliances. As wife-givers, they receive wealth from, rather than give wealth to, each son-in-law. And they pay out for each son's wife. This system is predicated upon a much greater degree of equality between the sexes than in the dowry system. Dowry is unintelligible unless it is seen as an attempt to compensate husbands for the responsibility of supporting women whose productive and reproductive potentials are held in small esteem. The crucial question is: when will this be the case? A plausible answer: when intensification has proceeded to the point that the fecundity of women and further population increase endanger the standard of living. Dowry, in other words, is a symptom of acute reproductive pressure; while bride price is a symptom of the ability of the infrastructure to absorb more labor. By this route we return to the basic techno-environmental conjunction emphasized by Goody: on the one hand, plow agriculture, with its displacement of human labor by animal labor; and on the other hand, shifting cultivation based on the hoe, in which human labor is more valuable than land.

Many additional features of the Euro-Asian marital pattern can now be brought into focus: monogamy, patrilineal inheritance, primogeniture. Each declares the same thing: there is a shortage of land; more than one wife means too many heirs; inheritance must be restricted; the fecundity of women dissipates wealth and power. The logical culmination of the devaluation of female fecundity among the Euro-Asian elites is the practice of female infanticide. From this we get, as I shall explain in greater detail in the next chapter, secondary hypogamous marriages or concubinage between elite men and subordinate women whose children cannot inherit. Make the shortage of land even more acute as in northern Uttar Pradesh and Tibet, and not only is there female infanticide but polyandry to boot (cf. Goldstein, 1978).

One of the great puzzles of the social sciences is why India developed its immensely complex system of stratified endogamous descent groups. Patterns of intensification in relation to resources again probably furnish the key. One cultural materialist line of inquiry sets forth from the fact that medieval Europe also had a burgeoning system of caste distinctions characterized by endogamous unions among nobility, knights, serfs, merchants, and many smaller occupational groups (Goody, 1976:105). Such pluralities of economic interest groups reflect the decentralized structure of the rainfall agricultural polities characterizing both Europe and most of India. There are relatively few castelike groups in the irrigation states, whose rulers imposed a single set of laws on everybody and, as in China, even encouraged upward mobility for talented people through competitive examinations.

In Europe, the caste system was swamped by the development of entrepreneurial contracts, the bourgeoisie's challenge to hereditary privileges, and the breakthrough to capitalism. The reason for the hypertrophy of caste relations in India must therefore be situated inside a theory explaining why capitalism developed in Europe and not in India.

Part of the answer to this question is that in northern India, especially in the central Gangetic plain, the earliest states had a hydraulic base. From 600 B.C. to the Moslem conquest in 800 A.D., a series of irrigation empires ruled the northern regions but failed to establish permanent hegemony over the smaller southern kingdoms, which had highly productive rainfall farming systems. The feudal character of these southern Indian kingdoms is especially clear along the Malabar Coast, where no significant irrigation works were ever built (Mencher, 1966; Namboodripad, 1967). By the fourteenth century a very vigorous form of mercantile capitalism had in fact begun to take root in Kerala, only to be nipped in the bud by a succession of Arab, Portuguese, and finally British conquests. India thus lay trapped between the internal plunder of hydraulic despotisms and the external plunder of capitalist imperialism. It is in the study of this drawn-out agony of internal and external exploitation that the solution to the puzzle of India's proliferating castes may someday be found.

Many of the structural and superstructural features of state societies can only be understood as reactions to the deepening misery of the lower castes and classes. Cultural materialism sees this misery as a composite result of politico-economic exploitation and Malthusian penalties. Initially pristine states probably enjoyed improved standards of living. But the temptation to use extra calories to feed extra children was irresistible, especially since child labor on irrigated lands could be made energetically profitable when children reached age six. Within a few hundred years, standards of living would begin to fall (Angel, 1975; Armelago and McArdle, 1975; Polgar, 1972; Dumond, 1975), and the peasants could be expected to take measures to slow their rate of growth by all available techniques. But because of the pressures of taxation and because of the state's encouragement of large families, the leveling off of population growth in the great circumscribed river valleys of China, India, Southeast Asia, Mesopotamia, and Egypt probably occurred at a point much closer to carrying capacity than had been characteristic of hunter-collector or early village societies. Therefore, despite the introduction of the plow and improvements in hydraulic engineering, poverty increased. The relentless intensification demanded by the necessity of feeding tens of millions of people where previously only thousands had lived steadily depleted forests, soils, and water resources. One general symptom of deepening misery was the growing scarcity of the flesh of domesticated animals, which had been consumed freely in the chiefdoms and earliest Euro-Asian states. The tabooing of the flesh of the pig in the Near East and India and of the cow in India should be seen in this context. I shall not elaborate on the explanation of these taboos here, since I discuss this matter at some length in the chapters on structural Marxism and structuralism.

The great universalistic religions can also best be understood as products of the misery the Old World imperial systems created in their futile attempt to relieve reproductive pressures by intensification, exploitation, and warfare.

Under Confucianism, the Chinese emperors recognized that the strength of the kingdom lay in the well-being of the peasant masses. Love and mercy were seen for the first time as the source of strength and power. No longer capable of acting out the role of great provider-redistributors, the elites increasingly favored contemplative and ascetic solutions to poverty. Redistribution became spiritualized, and the great redistributors became great believers. Enormous reformatory movements or "revitalizations" swept across Eurasia. In India, where the misery was most intense, Buddhism preached the overthrow of the hereditary priesthoods, declared poverty a virtue, outlawed the slaughter of vital plow animals, and converted the de facto vegetarianism of the semi-starved peasants into a spiritual blessing. Similar reformatory movements interacting with Buddhism arose in China in the form of Taoism and at approximately the same time in Persia in the form of Mithraism. All of these universalistic spiritualizing religions were co-opted by imperial elites and spread by conquest. Christianity was the form in which the spiritualization of the state's redistributive functions expressed itself during the terminal cancer of the Roman Empire. It acquired its specific messianic motif because it originated during a colonial struggle in which the Jews expected to be led to military victory and to the founding of their own empire by a supernatural emissary (Harris, 1974). Islam is another case of revitalization through messianic redemption. Similar movements dominate much of subsequent European history, crop up independently in China, and figure prominently in the history of Euro-American colonialism, as in the Ghost Dance and the cargo cults.

The demystification of the world religions begins with this simple fact: Confucianism, Taoism, Buddhism, Hinduism, Christianity, and Islam prospered because the ruling elites who invented or co-opted them benefited materially from them. By spiritualizing the plight of the poor, these world religions unburdened the ruling class of the obligation of providing material remedies for poverty. By proclaiming the sacredness of human life and the virtue of compassion toward the humble and weak, they lowered the cost of internal law and order. At the same time, by convincing enemy populations that the purpose of the state was to spread civilization and a higher moral code, they substantially lowered the cost of imperial conquests. This is not to deny that at various times and places the underclasses also benefited materially from the revitalizations and reforms that were integral to the pristine initiatives of the founders of each movement. The Buddhist-Hindu sacred cow complex, for example, protected millions of small, marginal farmers from the loss of a vital instrument of production. One can no more say that everything that arose in the name of the universalistic spiritual religions exclusively served the interests of the ruling classes than one can say that everything done in the name of the emperor or the king was inimical to the welfare of the common citizen. But the stratified nature of state-level structures and superstructures means precisely that nothing that significantly benefits the lower strata can endure unless it benefits the upper strata even more.

An important component in the spiritualization of the Old World imperial systems was the development of the taboo on human flesh. With domestic animals available for slaughter and later for milking, Old World prisoners of war were more valuable as a source of manpower than as a source of protein (cf. Gelb, 1972, 1973). We know that human sacrifice was gradually replaced by animal sacrifice. As animals became scarcer, however, the universalistic religions came to ban animal sacrifice as well. In India the caste that had formerly had a monopoly over the slaughter of cattle became the caste that was most devoted to preventing any further consumption of beef (see p. 248ff). And in ancient Israel, after 200 A.D. the temple at Jerusalem literally ran out of animals suitable for ceremonial slaughter. In the New World, the paucity of domesticated animals in Mesoamerica has plausibly been linked to the capture, sacrifice and eating of large numbers of enemy soldiers (Harner, 1977). Harner's critics have failed to see that this theory is a theory of why the Aztec religion did not taboo the consumption of human flesh. Harner's (1978) rejoinder, in addition to correcting the errors in the arguments leveled against him, emphasizes the fact that sources of animal protein available to other state societies were either absent or unusually depleted and degraded among the Aztecs. Hence the failure to develop a taboo on human flesh. This explanation does not, as some critics suppose (Marshall Sahlins, 1978), depend on proving that prisoners of war were cheaper than beans. Rather, it depends on proving that the depletion and degrading of alternative sources of animal protein was more intense in the Aztec case than in the generality of state societies in which human flesh came to be tabooed. In the context of this dispute nothing could be more absurd than to argue that the Aztecs remained cannibals because of "motivational factors, such as religion" (Ortiz de Montellano, 1978:616). I shall return to this case in the final pages of this book.

Recent Evolution of State Systems

THUS FAR I have discussed the corpus of cultural materialist theories about band, village, chiefdom, and archaic state societies. Cultural materialist principles are equally relevant for understanding what has been happening in the world during the past five hundred years, down to the present global crisis of East, West, and third-world power blocks, resource depletion, the struggle for alternative sources of energy, and the politico-economic consequences of new centralized industrial modes of production.

All of these issues demand an understanding of the origins of capitalism. Following Richard Wilkinson's (1973) analysis, the development of capitalism in Europe can be seen largely a response to the depletion of the resources upon which Europe's feudal mode of production had been based. Unfettered by the agro-managerial bureaucracies of the irrigation empires, yet enjoying a highly productive form of mixed farming, Europe was uniquely situated to attempt to solve the crisis of overintensification by the use of labor-saving machinery. But as Wilkinson shows, each new set of inventions imposed damaging demands on the environment which had to be repaired with another set of inventions. I shall not attempt to sketch in all of the ramifications of the capitalist mode of production. Every aspect of society's structure and superstructure from family to sex roles to religion was torn apart, rearranged, and constructed anew as the specific requirements of profit-making enterprises interacted with the labor and resources available at particular times and places all over the globe. The insatiable need for cheap labor, raw materials, and markets, interacting with local material conditions, determined the rise and fall of slavery, peonage, migratory and wage labor, and homesteading settlements in Africa, the Americas, and Oceania (cf. Wallerstein, 1974). As I tried to show in an earlier volume (Harris, 1964), the examination of specific capitalist infrastructures interacting with specific demographic and ecological conditions can lead to plausible theories explaining why slavery was the predominant form of capitalist plantation labor systems; why slaves were taken out of Africa to work on plantations in the New World; why slaves were not used in highland Mexico and the Andes; why the system of fiestas and *cargos* developed in these regions (cf. Wasserstrom, 1978; Rus, 1978); why Brazil did not develop a system of racial identity based on descent; why race antagonisms in the United States emically over-shadow class antagonisms; and why the melting pot failed in North America but succeeded elsewhere (cf. Despres, 1975:113).

Similar attention paid to the specific cost-benefits of different capital and labor systems in the far-flung quarters of the globe yield plausible theories of development and underdevelopment. To protect their own textile industries, for example, the British crushed the industrial revolution in India (Edwardes, 1967:88ff.); the Dutch used Indonesia for plantation crops and destroyed the indigenous merchant classes (Geertz, 1963); and Portugal's "development" investments contributed to the steady underdevelopment of Africa (Harris, 1972). Meanwhile Japan, alone among the advanced feudal societies to escape the thralldom of European economic penetration, achieved an advanced form of industrial capitalism in a mere fifty years (Geertz, 1963).

Infrastructural cost-benefits in the neocolonial regions also provide plausible keys to such phenomena as the population explosion, the demographic transition, .peasant conservatism, and the failure of modernization programs. Capitalism's demand for labor, cash crops, and raw materials upset the demographic balance throughout the world. Although much research remains to be done, it appears likely that the current population explosion is essentially a manifestation of the extraordinary demand for labor unleashed by the expansion of capitalist markets. Population continues to grow despite a general decline in standards of living in high-density areas because large families continue to be relatively profitable, given the present-day mixture of cash farming and wage labor (Mamdani, 1973; White, 1976; Nag, White, and Peet, 1978). Similarly, the failure of modernization programs such as the "green revolution" probably have little to do with peasant ideologies but much to do with differential class-biased access to petrochemical and hydraulic inputs (Franke, 1974; Hewitt de Alcantara, 1976).

Meanwhile the population growth rate in the developed countries is moving steadily downward as the cost to parents for rearing children to adulthood rises beyond $100,000 per child, and the expected long-term economic benefits fall to zero (Minge-Kalman, 1978). In the United States this is happening at the same time that resources are being depleted and domestic capital is flowing overseas at an increasing rate in search of cheap labor, leading to inflation and the necessity for having two wage earners per middle-class family. From this we get quite plausibly the generation gap, the flamboyant redefinition of sex roles, delayed marriages, "shacking up," communes, homosexual couples, and one-person families. And from the general closing down of the American dream, which was founded on the rape of the previously unexploited resources of an entire continent, we get the revival of religious fundamentalism, astrology, and salvation in or from outer space. To this I would add, as a final ideological product of a decaying infrastructure, the growing commitment of the social sciences to research strategies whose function it is to mystify sociocultural phenomena by directing attention away from the etic behavioral infrastructural causes.

An Important Reminder

THE ABOVE SET of macro theories is not intended to show that cultural materialism has found the answer to every conceivable question that one might want to ask about sociocultural phenomena. Nor is it even intended as a display of a representative body of cultural materialist theories.* No doubt other cultural materialists will want to substitute their own theories for many that I have presented

---

*Conspicuously unrepresented, for example, are the theories of cantometrics and choreometrics which link aspects of music, song and dance to the evolution of subsistence (Lomax et al., 1968; Lomax and Arensberg, 1977).

here. Rather, the point is that these theories have broad scope and wide applicability and are logically interconnected and coherently related. The reason for this is that they all implicate the infrastructure, distinguish between etic and emic phenomena, and are diachronic as well as synchronic, pan-global and pan-human.

Part II

The Alternatives

Introduction to Part II

IN TURNING now to the comparison of cultural materialism with its main rivals, I hope to render a responsible account of the basic epistemological and theoretical principles and key thoughts of the main alternative strategies in use today.

I shall consider only the central, active, and currently most influential strategies. Some readers may therefore lament the absence of separate chapters devoted to diffusionism, Boasian historical particularism, and British structural-functionalism. I shall not devote separate chapters to these strategies because they have few active partisans and hence are primarily of historical interest (see Harris, 1968). I shall nonetheless briefly note in the appropriate contexts how they relate to the more active alternatives.

My frank purpose is to expose the shortcomings of cultural materialism's rivals. Although I shall make every effort to be accurate, it would be hypocritical for me to claim that I offer a fair and comprehensive treatment of each strategy. Only the respective partisans of these alternatives can be relied on to present the best case for each. Yet my analysis would be less subject to distortion if I could draw upon summaries of the main epistemological and theoretical points prepared by the active proponents of each research program. I shall do this wherever possible. But it is characteristic of several of the alternative strategies that they are not sufficiently explicit about their basic epistemological and theoretical assumptions. My hope is that the advocates of such strategies will be moved by the possible biases of my interpretations and that they will seek to clarify, if not to change, their positions.

Chapter Five

Sociobiology and Biological Reductionism

SOCIOBIOLOGY is a research strategy that seeks to explain human social life by means of the theoretical principles of Darwinian and neo-Darwinian evolutionary biology. Its aim is to reduce puzzles pertaining to the level of sociocultural phenomena to puzzles that can be solved on the biological level of phenomena. Biologists find sociobiology plausible and attractive because of its forthright commitment to the general epistemological principles of science. In this respect, cultural materialism and sociobiology are natural allies. In every other respect however, the two strategies are far apart. Cultural materialists of course accept neo-Darwinist principles when applied to the explanation of the social life of infrahuman species, but we insist that the same principles are capable of explaining only an insignificant proportion of human sociocultural differences and similarities. None of the puzzles reviewed in the previous chapter can be solved effectively by means of the reductionist principles of sociobiology.

Basic Theoretical Principles of Sociobiology

IN THE NEO-DARWINIST evolutionary synthesis, the social behavior of different species of animals evolves as an outcome of differential reproductive success among individuals. Since the instructions for reproductive success are carried in the genes, one can view the entire course of biological evolution, including the evolution of patterns of animal social life, as the outcome of the preservation and propagation of the chemical organization of DNA.

Even among the simplest forms of organisms, however, behavior is not exclusively genetically determined. The actual observed response repertories of individual organisms result from the interaction of genetic instructions on the one hand, and the environment in which each organism is situated, on the other. Thus each organism has a behavioral *genotype*—the ensemble of its hereditary instructions affecting behavior; and each organism has a behavioral *phenotype*, the genetically orchestrated product of its behavioral experiences in particular living sites. This is as true of human beings as of any other species as far as it goes.

Before the development of sociobiology, social behavior had presented a special challenge to classical Darwinian selection theory, because social life frequently involves reproductive costs that result in the lowering of individual "fitness" (i.e., the number of adult offspring in the next generation attributable to an individual's reproductive behavior). The sterile worker castes of insect societies are the extreme instance of such "altruism." According to classical evolutionary theory every organism is a means and a consequence of reproductive competition among individuals, so how could there have evolved behavior benefiting another individual at reproductive cost to the performer? (Eberhard, 1975). The puzzle of "altruism" was solved for infrahuman species with W. D. Hamilton's (1964) development of the concept of "inclusive fitness." Inclusive fitness explains genetically costly social acts in terms of the joint effect of such acts upon the fitness of individuals and their genetically related social partners. The closer the genetic resemblance between the altruistic individual and the benefited social partners, the greater the probability that altruistic behavior results in the preservation of the altruistic individual's genotype. Thus the development of the concept of inclusive fitness made it possible to explain the evolution of all genetically controlled variations in infrahuman animal behavior in conformity with the principle of natural selection.

It is understandable, therefore, why sociobiologists find the temptation to apply the same principle to the explanation of human social behavior well-nigh irresistible. Natural selection, however, has repeatedly been shown to be a principle under whose auspices it is impossible to develop parsimonious and powerful theories about variations in human social life (cf. Harris, 1968:80ff). The extension of natural selection to altruistic behavior in infrahuman social species in no way alters or diminishes the objections raised against other forms of biological reductionism, such as racism and instinctualism.

The Emergence of Culture

THE WEAKNESS of human sociobiology and all other varieties of biological reductionism arises initially from the fact that genotypes never account for all the variations in behavioral phenotypes. Even in extremely simple organisms, adult behavior repertories vary in conformity with each individual's learning history. Hence the behavior repertory of conspecific social groups necessarily includes learned responses, and the prominence of such responses necessarily increases with the complexity of the neural circuitry of the species in question. These learned responses play an important role in the evolution of infrahuman social life, since they constitute a strategic part of each organism's behavioral phenotype. Selection acts on the behavioral phenotype, increasing the fitness of organisms with advantageous innovations in their response repertories. For example, a caterpillar accidentally captured by a wasp with an instinct for eating flies might be the first step toward the evolution of wasps equipped with an instinct for eating caterpillars. In classical evolutionary theory, therefore, behavior and genes form a positive feedback loop: innovative behavior is preserved and propagated by its contribution to the organism's fitness and is thus converted from an accidental byproduct of learning to a highly determined expression of the genotype.

Given sufficiently advanced forms of learning circuits, socially assisted learning is another and radically different process by which learned responses that have been found useful by one organism can be preserved and propagated within a social group. The social response repertories acquired by means of socially assisted learning constitute a group's tradition or culture. In principle, cultural repertories can change and evolve entirely independently of feedbacks involving natural selection—that is, entirely independently of the reproductive success of the individuals responsible for innovating and propagating them. For example, Thomas Alva Edison's invention of the phonograph would have spread around the world even if Edison and all his close kinspeople had been entirely childless.

Infra-Human Culture

THERE IS NOTHING hypothetical or mysterious about culture. It did not come into existence through some sudden abrupt reorganization of the human mind; rather, it emerged as a byproduct of the evolution of complex neural circuitry, and it exists in rudimentary form among many vertebrate species. But as in all evolutionary analysis, a balance must be struck between the continuities and discontinuities of emergent forms and processes. Sociobiologists underestimate by several orders of magnitude the extent to which human cultures represent an emergent novelty. They must therefore accept responsibility for disseminating a biased picture of the evolutionary processes affecting human societies. For human culture has doubtless fulfilled the theoretical potential of cultural evolution to a point that is absolutely unique among all organisms.

Examples of infrahuman culture are the dialects and call variations of birds and mammals; bird and vertebrate flyways, trails, display grounds, and nesting sites; and primate tool-using, feeding, and line-of-march specialties. The best-studied cases involve controlled colonies of Japanese macaques who responded to novel ways of provisioning by inventing novel ways of food processing. One troop developed the tradition of washing sweet potatoes in sea water and then went on to washing all its food in a similar manner. When wheat was thrown on the beach, members of the same troop discovered how to separate it from the sand by casting fistfuls of the mixture into the water and letting the grit sink to the bottom while scooping up the edible grains which floated on the surface. No genetic changes were required for these behavioral innovations to spread from individual to individual (Itani and Nishimura, 1973).

Under normal conditions, however, behavioral innovations among infrahuman species are almost always brought back into the genetic feedback loop. If innovations persist at all, it is because they are valuable, and if they are valuable, they will affect reproductive success. For example, Wilson (1975:17) mentions an island-dwelling species of lizard *(Uta palermi)* which alone in its desert-adapted genus forages in the island's intertidal zones. The origin of this adaptation may have been purely behavioral, as in the case of the Japanese macaque innovations. But the lizards were soon genetically selected for their ability to forage at the seashore, and this innovative behavior became part of a genetically controlled species-specific behavioral repertory. In the Galapagos there are species of iguanas that swim and dive for their food, presumably as a consequence of a similar series of behavior-gene feedbacks.

The same kind of feedback probably accounts for many of the species-specific attributes of *Homo sapiens*. Among the primordial hominids of the Pliocene and Pleistocene periods, cultural innovations in tool use would undoubtedly have amplified trends leading toward the greater precision and power of the human thumb, and this in turn would have placed a selective premium on the neural circuitry needed for the intelligent use of hand-held tools. There is also little doubt that the development of *Homo sapiens'* unique language facility proceeded in a similar fashion, with selection favoring individuals able to transmit, receive, and store ever-more-complex messages. In the human case, however, these selection processes had a paradoxical outcome. In effect, by enhancing the capacity and efficiency of human learning functions, natural selection itself greatly reduced the significance of genetic feedback for the preservation and propagation of behavioral innovations. By progressively severing hominid cultural repertories from genetic coding, natural selection conferred an enormous adaptive advantage on *Homo sapiens*—namely, the advantage of being able to acquire and modify a vast range of useful behavior far more rapidly than is possible when genes maintain or regain control over each behavioral innovation.

The Evidence for Gene-Free Culture

HOW DO WE KNOW that *Homo sapiens* has been selected for the capacity to acquire and modify cultural repertories independently of genetic feedback? The evidence for this viewpoint consists of the uniquely large amount of variation in the social response repertories of different human populations. Even the simplest of human societies exhibit tens of thousands of patterned responses not found in other human groups. As I indicated in Chapter 3, George Peter Murdock's *World Ethnographic Atlas* contains forty-six columns of variable cultural traits. Over a thousand variable components per society can be identified by using the alternative codes listed under these columns. No two societies in the sample of 1,179 have the same combination of components. By adding more categories and by making finer distinctions, additional thousands of distinctive traits can be identified in the infrastructural sectors alone. In fact, lists employed by anthropologists interested in studying the phenomenon of diffusion include as many as six thousand traits (cf. Kroeber and Driver, 1932). The amphibious truck company of which I was a member during World War II had a supply manual with over one million items listed in its pages. A complete inventory of the material culture of U.S. society would certainly exceed a trillion items.

How do we know that these items are not part of a behavior-gene feedback loop? Because they can be acquired or wiped out within the space of a single generation, without any reproductive episodes taking place. For example, human infants reared apart from their parents in another breeding population invariably acquire the cultural repertory of the people among whom they are reared. Children of English-speaking American whites reared by Chinese parents grow up speaking perfect Chinese. They handle their chopsticks with flawless precision and experience no sudden inexplicable urge to eat McDonald's hamburgers. Children of Chinese parents reared in white U.S. households speak the standard English dialect of their foster parents, are inept at using chopsticks, and experience no uncontrollable yearning for bird's-nest soup or Peking duck.

Social groups and individuals drawn from a vast variety of populations have repeatedly demonstrated their ability to acquire every conceivable aspect of the world cultural inventory. American Indians brought up in Brazil incorporate complex African rhythms into their religious dances; American blacks who attend the proper conservatories readily acquire the distinctly non-African requisites for a career in classical European opera. Jews brought up in Germany acquire a preference for German cooking; Jews brought up in Yemen prefer Middle Eastern dishes. Under the influence of fundamentalist Christian missionaries, the sexually uninhibited peoples of Polynesia began to dress their women in dowdy Mother Hubbards and to follow rules of strict premarital chastity. Native Australians reared in Sydney show no inclination to hunt kangaroo, create circulating connubia, or mutilate their genitals; they do not experience uncontrollable urges to sing about witchetty grubs and the emu ancestors. The Mohawk of New York State came to specialize in construction trades and helped erect the steel frames of many skyscrapers. Walking across narrow beams eighty stories above street level, they were not troubled by an urge to build wigwams rather than office buildings. The rapid diffusion of such traits as sewing machines, power saws, transistor radios, and thousands of other industrial products points to the same conclusion. Acculturation and diffusion between every continent and every major race and micro breeding population prove beyond dispute that the overwhelming bulk of the response repertory of any human population can be acquired by any other human population through learning processes and without the slightest exchange or mutation of genes.

Among human beings, in other words, cultural life is not some sort of peripheral oddity. Each instance of a genuine cultural performance by a macaque or a chimpanzee is worth a journal article. But all the journals in all the libraries of the world would not suffice to render a running account of human cultural activities. Cultural evolution is thus responsible for creating an amount of intra-specific behavioral variation in the human species that does not exist in any other species. Moreover, this immense quantity of variation involves functional specialties whose analogues are associated with great phylogenetic distances in the evolution of other bioforms. The contrast between a paleotechnic foraging band and an industrial superpower is surely not inferior to the contrast between whole phyla—if not kingdoms—in the Linnaean taxonomy. It took billions of years for natural selection to create specialized adaptations for fishing, hunting, agriculture; for aquatic, terrestrial, and aerial locomotion; and for predatory and defensive weaponry, such as teeth, claws, and armor. Equivalent specialties were developed by cultural evolution in less than ten thousand years. The main focus of human sociobiology ought therefore to be the explanation of why other species have such minuscule and insignificant cultural repertories and why humans alone have such gigantic and important ones. But sociobiologists conceive their task to be something else—namely, the identification of the genetic components in human cultural traits. This represents a fundamental misdirection for human social science and a diversion of resources from the more urgent task of explaining the vast majority of cultural traits that do not have a definite genetic component.

The Scope of Sociobiological Theories

POPULAR REPRESENTATIONS of sociobiology have created a false impression of how sociobiologists relate human social behavior to its genetic substrate. Sociobiologists do not deny that most human social responses are socially learned and therefore not directly under genetic control. Wilson (1977:133) has made this point without equivocation: "The evidence is strong that almost but probably not quite all differences among cultures are based on learning and socialization rather than on genes." Richard Alexander (1976:6) has made the same pronouncement: "I hypothesize that the vast bulk of cultural variations among peoples alive today will eventually be shown to have virtually nothing to do with their genetic differences." Thus few if any sociobiologists are interested in linking variations in human social behavior to the variable frequencies with which genes occur in different human populations. The principles by which sociobiologists propose to implicate natural selection and reproductive success in the explanation of sociocultural phenomena are less provocative but also a good deal less precise and far less interesting.

Two such principles provide the auspices for most sociobiological theories concerned with human social life. The first of these seeks to explain the recurrence of certain universal or near universal traits as the consequence of a genetically programmed human nature; the second seeks to explain cultural variations as a consequence of a genetically programmed "scale" of alternatives which are allegedly turned on and off by environmental "switches."

Regarding the first principle, under the best of circumstances the search for human nature can yield only an understanding of the similarities in sociocultural systems and not of the vast repertory of differences. I shall demonstrate, moreover, that sociobiology is strategically biased in favor of exaggerating the number of pan-human traits that are part of human nature. This bias acts as a definite barrier to an adequate exploration of the causes of widely recurrent traits.

As for the second principle, I shall demonstrate that the sociobiological commitment to "behavior scaling"—the genetically predetermined traits turned on and off by environmental switches—introduces a superfluous set of variables into the solution of sociocultural puzzles. These puzzles are solved as soon as the environmental switches are adequately described in terms of the demo-techno-econo-environmental conjunction of the modes of production and reproduction. This aspect of sociobiology therefore emerges as simply a prolegomenon to cultural materialism.

Human Nature

MUCH CONFUSION arises from the fact that sociobiologists present the concept of a genetically controlled "biogram," or human nature, as if there is a significant body of informed opinion asserting that human beings are not genetically programmed to be predisposed toward certain behavioral specialties. In principle there can be no disagreement that *Homo sapiens* has a nature. One does not have to be a sociobiologist to hold such a view. As every science fiction fan knows, a culture-bearing social species whose physiology was based on silicon instead of carbon and that had three sexes instead of two, weighed a thousand pounds per specimen, and preferred to eat sand rather than meat would acquire certain habits unlikely to be encountered in any *Homo sapiens* society. As proposed in Chapter 3, the theoretical principles of cultural materialism hinge on the existence of certain genetically defined pan-human psychobiological drives that mediate between infrastructure and nature and that tend to make the selection of certain patterns of behavior more probable than others. Nothing I have said about the gene-free status of most cultural variations is opposed to the view that there is a human nature shared by all human beings. Hence the disagreement about the human biogram is entirely a matter of substance rather than of principle—that is, precise identification of the content of the biogram.

The disagreement between sociobiologists and cultural materialists on the issue of human nature is a matter of the contraction versus the expansion of the postulated substance of human nature. Cultural materialists pursue a strategy that seeks to reduce the list of hypothetical drives, instincts, and genetically determined response alternatives to the smallest possible number of items compatible with the construction of an effective corpus of sociocultural theory. Sociobiologists, on the other hand, show far less restraint and actively seek to expand the list of genetically determined traits whenever a plausible opportunity to do so presents itself. From the cultural materialist perspective, the proliferation of hypothetical genes for human behavioral specialties is empirically as well as strategically unsound, as I shall show in the next section.

Hypothetical Genes

ACCORDING TO WILSON (1977:132), we share a number of gene-controlled behavior traits with the Old World primates, while other traits are uniquely human. Among the more general primate traits Wilson mentions the following: (1) "size of intimate social groups on the order of 10–100"; (2) polygyny; (3) "a long period of socialization in the young"; (4) "[a] shift in focus from mother to age- and sex peer groups"; and (5) "social play with emphasis on role practice, mock aggression, and exploration." Among the features restricted to hominids, Wilson mentions: (6) facial expressions; (7) elaborate kinship rules; (8) incest avoidance; (9) "semantic symbol language that develops in the young through a relatively strict time table"; (10) close sexual bonding; (11) parent/offspring bonding; (12) male bonding; (13) territoriality. Wilson claims that "to socialize a human being out of such species-specific traits would be very difficult if not impossible, and almost certainly destructive to mental development" (ibid.).

But it is clear that most of these traits are not, on the ethnographic record, actually universal; and that socializing people out of them is no more difficult than socializing human beings out of thousands of other cultural traits.

1. Human relationships are at their most intimate in domestic groups. But the size of such groups varies over a far larger span than Wilson acknowledges. Needless to say, hundreds of millions of people in the world today live in domestic groups smaller than ten persons. While domestic groups larger than a hundred are less common, they do exist. For example, elite Chinese family compounds containing seven hundred persons are reported for the Sung dynasty (cited in Myron Cohen, 1975:227). But intimate relationships are not necessarily limited to co-residential domestic groups. Relationships within such nonlocalized kinship groups as lineages and kindreds may also satisfy definitions of "intimacy." Such groups commonly contain several hundred persons. In Brazil studies of elite families have demonstrated that the *parentella* or bilateral kindred may contain as many as five hundred living relatives who keep track of one another's birthdays, attend marriages and funerals together, and help one another in business and

professional life (Wagley, 1963:199). The size of such human groups as families, lineages, kindreds, villages, and "communities" varies in conformity with known infrastructural conditions and nowhere exhibits significant uniformities that render the existence of even minimal genetic restraint plausible.

2. True, polygyny is a common form of human mating, but the human species is not polygynistic. Human sexual behavior is etically so diverse as to defy any species-specific characterization. The heterosexual range runs from promiscuity through monogamy, with each type practiced by tens of millions of people. Human females in general may not have plural mates as often as males, but there are millions of women who entertain a plurality of sexual partners as often as, if not more often than, the most active men in other societies. This is particularly evident in the de facto forms of polyandry or rapid mate changes prevalent among the matrifocal households of the Caribbean and Northeast Brazil (Rodman, 1971; Lewis, 1966b). Moreover, polyandry is an emic as well as an etic commonplace in Southwest India and Tibet. The idea that males naturally desire a plurality of sexual experiences while women are satisfied by one mate at a time is entirely a product of the political-economic domination males have exerted over women as part of the culturally created, warfare-related male supremacy complex. Sexually adventurous women are severely punished in male-dominated cultures. Wherever women have enjoyed independent wealth and power, however, they have sought to fulfill themselves sexually with multiple mates with no less vigor than males in comparable situations. I cannot imagine a weaker instance of genetic programming than the polygyny of *Homo sapiens*. Sexuality is something people can be socialized out of only at great cost. But people can be socialized into and out of promiscuity, polygyny, polyandry, and monogamy with conspicuous ease, once the appropriate infrastructural conditions are present.

3. Human socialization does take a long time, and this indeed is part of *Homo sapiens'* primate heritage. But this feature of the biogram is closely related to the development of elaborate socially learned response patterns that constitute "traditions" or cultures. The trait of prolonged socialization merely points up the fact that human infants have a lot of traditions to learn and that *Homo sapiens'* most characteristic genetic heritage is the expanded capacity for cultural behavior. However, it does not point to any particular content for pan-human social life other than the existence of an extended training period for infants and children. What infants and children are trained to do is another story.

4. The alleged genetically controlled shift in focus from mother to age and sex peer groups is much more likely to be one of the things that *Homo sapiens* needs to be trained to do and that people can be socialized out of doing with little difficulty. Indeed, there is a very extensive anthropological and psychological literature suggesting that once strong dependency relationships are established between children and parents, costly training techniques are necessary to pry children loose and send them out into the world on their own. *Homo sapiens* is the only primate species that needs puberty rituals to shock and cajole the junior generation into accepting adult responsibilities (Harrington and Whiting, 1972). Moreover, it is a caricature of human socialization processes to represent them primarily in terms of mother-child relationships, since human fathers often play as important a role in socialization as mothers do. And both human parents frequently continue to dominate the activities of their offspring well into adulthood. If Wilson's notion of primate genetic control over human role socialization were correct, the system of financing higher education through twenty years or more of heavy parental investment would never have been invented.

5. *Homo sapiens* does share with other primates a genetically programmed tendency toward exploratory social play in connection with role practice. However, this feature is redundant with respect to item 3—the prolonged nature of human socialization—and merely points once again to the importance of socially acquired response repertories rather than to the importance of genetic control over definite response categories. On the other hand, Wilson's specification of "mock aggression" as a genetically controlled feature of childhood social play lacks credibility. Children explore the social roles and behavior patterns their cultures encourage them to explore. As formalized in sports and games, the balance between aggressive and nonaggressive childhood behavior patterns varies widely from culture to culture. Competitive team sports for males, for example, are correlated with training for warfare (Sipes, 1973). In societies lacking warfare patterns, such as the Semai of Malaysia, children's play is quite free of conspicuous aggressive displays (Dentan, 1968; Montague, 1976:98–103). Obviously human beings have the genetically controlled capacity to act aggressively, but the conditions under which aggressive behavior actually manifests itself is not defined by a narrow set of genetic instructions.

6. Facial expressions probably constitute one of the best cases for definite genetically controlled response patterns. There is a universal tendency for *Homo sapiens* to laugh and smile in order to communi-

cate pleasure, to frown and stare when communicating anger, and to grimace and cry when communicating pain and sorrow. Even in this case, however, the genetic programming cannot be very strong, since many cultures override the species-specific meanings and use the same facial expression to denote something quite different. All over the world people are socialized to hide their feelings and to laugh when they are sad, look forlorn when they are happy, and smile when they are angry. It is customary in many Amazonian Indian societies to weep profusely in honor of arriving guests. Elsewhere, as in the Middle East and India, the rich pay professional mourners to weep at funerals. Wherever it is important not to show true feelings—as in the game of poker or during job interviews—people learn to master their facial muscles just as readily as they learn bladder and sphincter control and with much less threat to their mental and physical well-being. In most societies it is dangerous to rely on facial expressions in order to predict what people are getting ready to do.

7. True enough, complex kinship rules are not found in any other species, but the varieties of kinship terminologies, family organization, and prescribed behavior for kinspeople is far too great to be accounted for by genetic controls. These rules are "elaborate" precisely because they are not under genetic control. What kind of gene would it be that could lead some societies to distinguish cross- from parallel cousins or mother's brother from father's brother? Or that would give the members of Australian aboriginal groups in the eight-section zones an uncontrollable urge to marry their mother's mother's brother's daughter's daughter (as per the marriage rules diagrammed on p. 84)? Moreover, despite their universality in one form or another, kinship rules need not be regarded as permanent features of the universal pattern. The entire history of state society is one convergent thrust toward the replacement of kin-organized groups by those based on the division of labor, class, and other achieved statuses (see p. 100).

8. That the widespread prohibition on mother-son, father-daughter, and brother-sister mating is genetically programmed I find dubious. Brother-sister mating was practiced by the Egyptian pharaohs, the ruling elites of Hawaii, the Inca, and the early Chinese emperors as a routine means of consolidating power at the apex of the social pyramid. On the other hand, there are excellent infrastructural reasons why brother-sister marriage was prohibited virtually everywhere else, since all alliances and exchanges between commoner domestic groups are based on brothers not taking their sisters for themselves (see p. 80).

One expects father-daughter marriages to be rare for the same reason. However, sexual relations between father and daughter take place on a rather frequent basis, sometimes in overt ritual contexts. If incest avoidance is part of the human biogram, why are there, conservatively estimated, several hundred thousand cases of father-daughter incest in the United States each year (Armstrong, 1978:9)?

The rarest form of nuclear-family incest is the mother-son relationship. The problem here is to disentangle an instinctual repugnance from the generally subordinate status of women and the rules against adultery. Does fear of father and husband or fear of incest per se keep sons and mothers apart? If psychoanalytic evidence is admissible, then it is clear that in childhood and adolescence sons do have a rather powerful sexual interest in their mothers. That interest, however, has to be blocked if sons are to develop in the image of their aggressive masculine fathers. Because of the prevalence of male supremacy women are usually awarded to men for achievement and not as a birthright. Hence virtually all societies currently have an interest in preventing mother-son incest as part of the process of training males into their masculine role. Very probably, as the premium on training males for aggressive masculine roles diminishes, less effort will be expended on discouraging sons from fulfilling their Oedipal fantasies, and the incidence of mother-son incest may increase. As long as the infrastructural and structural conditions sustaining the nuclear-family incest taboos remain in force, the conclusion that the taboos are instinctual remains unconvincing (cf. Y. Cohen, 1978). Only if the taboos persist after the sustaining infrastructural and structural conditions disappear will there be convincing evidence of their genetic base. Moreover, no argument using the antiquity of the incest taboos as evidence of their instinctual status is admissible. The hunter-collector mode of production lasted a million years or more, yet it was swept away in a mere handful of generations when changed infrastructural conditions altered the balance of costs and benefits.

9. The human capacity to communicate by means of a "semantic symbol language" does involve a genetically programmed predisposition to acquire such a language, and it is definitely known that no other species on earth shares the same predisposition. But the inclusion of this one momentous instance of genetic specialization in a list of dubious or untrue features of the human biogram reveals the weakness of the sociobiological strategy. For the behavioral implication of the unique language facility of human beings is that *Homo sapiens* has a unique, genetically based capacity to override genetic determinism by

acquiring, storing, and transmitting gene-free repertories of social responses. I shall return to this point in a moment.

10. Close sexual bonding? How can one assert this as a species-specific feature when under appropriate infrastructural and structural conditions, the sexual bond extends no further than rape, prostitution, and slave-forms of concubinage?

11. Parent/offspring bonding? But as I pointed out in Chapter 3, sex ratio studies indicate that infanticide, especially female infanticide, and neglect of young girls were routine means of regulating human population growth throughout history as well as prehistory.

12. Male bonding? To be sure, cross-culturally, solidary male groups outnumber solidary female groups. But that merely reflects once again the cultural tendency of males to keep females subordinate by preventing them from forming aggressively solidary coalitions. To suggest that women cannot form strong solidary bonds among themselves because they are "catty" and preoccupied with what men think of them (cf. Tiger, 1970) has little merit. There is enough ethnographic evidence to indicate that women can and do form effective solidary political groups, as in the Bundu of Sierra Leone (Hoffer, 1975) as well as in the more recent burgeoning of feminist associations. Female sodalities will undoubtedly become more common as women achieve political and economic parity with men.

13. Territoriality? As I said in Chapter 4, recent studies of hunter-gatherers support the theory that the primordial units of human social life were open camp groups whose membership fluctuated from season to season and whose territories were not sharply defined. Strong territorial interests probably became widespread only after the development of sedentary village modes of production and the rise in reproductive pressure. Moreover, the ownership of territory by groups or individuals is certainly not something that it is difficult to socialize people out of, nor is the lack of territorial interests "destructive of mental development." (Indeed, one might argue more cogently that the territorial interests of modern states are destructive not only of mental development but of physical existence as well.)

Sociobiological Misrepresentation of Human Nature

SOCIOBIOLOGISTS ARGUE quite persuasively that *"Homo sapiens is distinct from other primate species in ways that can be explained only as a result of a unique human genotype" (Wilson, 1977:132). Yet when it comes down to the details of characterizing that genotype, sociobiologists overlook or minimize the genetic trait that by their own criteria ought to be emphasized above all others. That trait is language. Only human language has semantic universality—the ability to communicate about infinite classes of events regardless of when and where they occur. This trait and the neural circuitry that makes it possible account for the astonishing fact—agreed to by most sociobiologists—that the enormous within-species variations in human social response repertories are not genetically controlled.

The attempt by sociobiologists to add what are at best dubious and hypothetical genes to the human behavioral genotype leads to the misrepresentation of human nature based on an erroneous construal of the course of hominid evolution. According to the latest paleontological evidence, the phyletic lines of the ancestral hominids and their closest pongid relatives have been separated for at least 5 million years. During all that time, natural selection favored a behavioral genotype in which the programming acquired through learning progressively dominated the programming acquired through genetic change. Every discussion of human nature must begin and end with this aspect of the human biogram, for its importance overrides every other conceivable species-specific trait of *Homo sapiens.* Indeed, the emergence of semantic universality constitutes an evolutionary novelty whose significance is at least as great as the appearance of the first strands of DNA. As I have said, culture appears in rudimentary form among the lower organisms, but it remains rudimentary; it does not expand and accumulate; it does not evolve. Hominid culture, however, has evolved at an ever-increasing rate, filling the earth with human societies, artifacts, and countless divergent, convergent, and parallel instances of behavioral novelties. Even if the dubious hypothetical genetic predispositions of sociobiological human nature actually do exist, knowledge of their existence can lead only to an understanding of the outer "envelope" (to use a metaphor proposed by Wilson—Harris and Wilson, 1978) within which cultural evolution has thus far been constrained. It could not lead to an understanding of the differences and similarities within sociocultural evolution. The poverty of this strategy can best be grasped by imagining what evolutionary biology would be like if it confined itself only to the similarities of life forms and not to their differences.

Darwin's contribution would then amount to nothing more than the assertion that all species are constrained by their common carbon chemistry and by the laws of thermodynamics. The question of why whales are different from elephants or why birds are different from reptiles could not be asked. Or at least it wouldn't pay to ask it, since the answer would be: "They are not really different: they are all constrained within the envelope of carbon chemistry and thermodynamics."

The Principle of Behavior Scaling

IN ORDER to overcome the apparent irrelevance of genetic controls for the explanation of sociocultural differences, sociobiologists turn to the concept of "behavioral scale" (Wilson, 1975:20–21). "Scaling . . . refers to those cases in which the genetic code programs not for invariant phenotypic response, but for variant, but predictable responses to varying environmental conditions . . ." (Dickeman, 1979:1). The most familiar examples of behavioral scaling involve responses dependent on changes in population density. For example, aggressive encounters among adult hippopotami are rare where populations are low to moderate, but at high densities, males begin to fight viciously, sometimes to the death. Normally, snowy owls do not engage in territorial defense, but under crowded conditions, they defend their territories with characteristic displays. Availability of food also triggers different parts of the behavior scale. Well-fed honeybees let intruding workers from neighboring hives penetrate the nest and take away supplies without opposition. But when the same colonies have been without food for several days, they attack every intruder. "Thus the entire scale, not isolated points on it, is the genetically based trait that has been fixed by natural selection" (Wilson, 1975:20).

Applied to human social response repertories, the principle of behavior scaling is meant to provide an explanation for why some human populations are polygynous while others are polyandrous, or why some human populations are cannibals while others are vegetarians, and so forth. These alternative behaviors constitute a genetically programmed "range of possible behavioral responses" evoked by particular ecological contexts.

The Scope of Behavioral Scaling

THE PREMISE that cultural innovations are preprogrammed along a species-specific scale suffers from the strategic liabilities associated with the notion of human nature. Since selection in the main has acted against genetically imposed limitations on human cultural repertories, the principle of scaling leads to an evolutionarily unsound strategy in the human case. Once again the problem is that the diversity of human responses is far too great to be accounted for by a genetic program. Unlike hippopotami, human beings do not merely change from being placid to being aggressive and back again under the variable stress of environment. Instead, humankind has evolved an enormous series of institutions such as lineages, polygyny, polyandry, redistribution, slavery, sacrifice of prisoners of war, infanticide, vegetarianism, and all the other infrastructural, structural, and superstructural traits which I have discussed in the previous chapter. Clearly the concept of behavior scaling cannot be applied to this entire series of innovations. To do so would in effect reduce all cultural evolution to a predetermined set of genetic instructions, a conclusion at odds with the agreed-upon fact that most human behavior is not under direct genetic control. For example, consider the evolutionary series: bands, village, chiefdom, state. Surely no one would want to suggest that these alternative forms of political economy are merely preprogrammed points on a genetically controlled behavior scale. That would be the equivalent of saying selection already favored the state even before there were chiefdoms or villages and when only bands existed. Behavior scaling, in other words, still leaves the explanation of the origin of most of the diversity of human social life beyond the pale of sociobiological theory, and hence does not alter the relative lack of scope and power built into the sociobiological approach to human social life.

The Superfluous Gene

TO AN IMPORTANT but limited extent, the principle of behavior scaling resembles the cultural materialist principle of infrastructural determinism. What the two principles share in common is the specification of an ecological context and the assumption that variations in social response repertories are in some sense "adaptive" to that context.

In the cultural materialist strategy the ecological conditions embodied in the infrastructure raise or lower the bio-psychological costs and benefits of innovative responses, none of which are necessarily genetically preprogrammed to occur under the given conditions. Certain innovative behaviors rather than others are retained and propagated not because they maximize reproductive success but because they maximize bio-psychological benefits and minimize bio-psychological costs. In contrast, the fundamental premise of the principle of scaling is that the innovative behavior is genetically preprogrammed to occur under the given conditions because under the given conditions it maximizes reproductive success.

I contend that the principle of behavior scaling leads at best to unparsimonious theories concerning the manner in which innovations come to take their place in the human behavioral repertory. The lack of parsimony results from the need to rely on hypothetical genes in order to fulfill the genetic cost-benefit optimizing or mini-max logic of the sociobiological strategy. The logic of the cultural materialist optimizing mini-max, cost-benefit analysis, on the other hand, is fulfilled in a more direct fashion and is to be preferred on that account. Indeed, from the cultural materialist perspective, the invocation of genetic factors in behavior scaling explanations constitutes a redundant and gratuitous addition to an adequate ecological and psycho-biological cost-benefit analysis.

The Case of Elite Female Infanticide

AS AN EXAMPLE of the lack of parsimony and the redundancy involved in the behavior scaling version of sociobiological theory, let us examine the explanation anthropologist Mildred Dickeman (1979) has proposed for the occurrence of female infanticide among elite castes and classes of late medieval Europe, India, and China. To explain this important and empirically valid phenomenon, Dickeman relies on a sociobiological model developed by Richard Alexander (1974), which predicts that female preferential infanticide is more likely among women married to high-ranking men and less likely among women married to low-ranking men. The logic behind Alexander's model is this: when male infants can be reared with confidence, their fitness (i.e., number of offspring) will tend to exceed that of females, since men can have many more reproductive episodes than women. Hence in elite castes and classes, where males have an excellent chance of surviving because living conditions are good, the maximization of reproductive success of both male and female parents will be achieved by investing in sons rather than daughters. On the other hand, in the low-ranking castes and classes, where male survival is very risky, reproductive success will be maximized by investing in daughters, who are likely to have at least some reproductive episodes rather than none at all. To complete the model, elite men can be expected to marry beneath their station, while lowly women can be expected to marry up if their parents can provide them with a dowry to compensate the groom's family.

The cultural materialist explanation for the occurrence of female infanticide in elite groups dispenses with the need to suppose that this pattern has been selected for genetically and that it is part of a genetic program that automatically manifests itself under conditions of extreme poverty and wealth. We begin with the fact that daughters were less valuable than sons for the Eurasian elites because men dominated the political, military, commercial, and agricultural sources of wealth and power. (As I explained in the chapter preceding this one—p. 91 —male politico-economic domination itself is also a product of cultural rather than genetic selection.) Sons have the opportunity to protect and enhance the elite family's patrimony and political-economic status. But daughters, who have access to significant sources of wealth and power only through men, are an absolute or relative liability. They can only be married off by paying dowry. Therefore, preferential female infanticide is practiced by the elite groups to avoid the expense of dowry and to consolidate the family's wealth and power. Among the subordinate ranks, female infanticide is not practiced as frequently as among the elites because peasant and artisan girls can readily pay their own way by working in the fields or in cottage industries.

The genesis of this system lies in the struggle to maintain and enhance differential political-economic power and wealth, not in the struggle to achieve reproductive success. The proof of this lies in the outcome of the hypogynous marriages (marrying down) of the elite males. Such marriages generally take the form of concubinage and do not bestow the right of inheritance upon the offspring, be they male or female. The elites, in other words, systematically decrease their inclusive fitness by failing to provide life-support systems for their own children. Indeed, I would argue that the entire complex of infanticide and hypergamy boils down to a systemic attempt to prevent the elites from having too much reproductive success in order to maintain the privileged position of a small number of wealthy and powerful families at the top of the social pyramid.

Who Needs Behavior Scaling?

SOCIOBIOLOGISTS PROPOSE that human beings are preprogrammed to switch from infanticide to mother love; from cannibalism to vegetarianism; from polyandry to polygyny; from matrilineality to patrilineality; and from war to peace whenever the appropriate environmental conditions are present. Cultural materialists also maintain that these changes take place whenever certain infrastructural conditions are present. Since both cultural materialists and sociobiologists take the position that the enormous diversity represented in the alleged genetic scaling of human responses is at least genetically possible—within the "envelope"—the need for the scaling concept itself seems gratuitous. The focus in both strategies has to be on the question of what kinds of environmental or infrastructural conditions are powerful enough to change human behavior from war to peace, polygyny to polyandry, cannibalism to vegetarianism, and so forth. To the extent that sociobiologists sincerely pursue this issue, they will inevitably find themselves carrying out cost-benefit analyses that are subsumed by the infrastructural cost-benefit analyses of cultural materialism.

True, sociobiological models based on reproductive success and inclusive fitness can yield predictions about sociocultural differences that enjoy a degree of empirical validity, as in the above case of infanticide and female hypergyny. But the reason for this predictability is that most of the factors which might promote reproductive success do so through the intermediation of bio-psychological benefits that enhance the economic, political, and sexual power and well-being of individuals and groups of individuals. The exploitation of lower-ranking women by higher-ranking men, for example, is the kind of stuff out of which theories of reproductive success can easily be spun. But exploitation confers much more immediate and tangible benefits than genetic immortality on those who can get away with it. Because of the bias toward reproductive success, the principle of behavior scaling leads away from the most certain and powerful interest served by infrastructure toward the most remote and hypothetical interests served by having genetic survivors. Thus sociobiology contributes to the obfuscation of the nature of human social life by its commitment to the explorations of the least probable causal relationships at the expense of the most probable ones. However, it is not the sociobiologists who are primarily to blame for this situation.

Who Is to Blame for Sociobiology?

THE DECISIVE consideration concerning the appropriateness of genetic models for human behavioral repertories must be whether or not there are cultural, nongenetic theories that account better for the observed phenomena. Sociobiological theories are welcome only in the absence of plausible sociocultural theories, because the latter derive from principles capable of explaining both rapid and slow changes and both similarities and differences, whereas the former derive from a principle—natural selection—capable of explaining only slow changes and few if any of the differences as well as the similarities. Anthropologists who operate with synchronic, idealist, structuralist and eclectic research strategies incapable of producing interpenetrating sets of theories about the divergent and convergent trajectories of sociocultural evolution have only themselves to blame if sociobiologists step in to what appears to be an intellectual disaster area. Sociobiology has achieved instant popularity in part because the better-known social science research strategies cannot provide scientific causal solutions for the perennial puzzles surrounding such phenomena as warfare, sexism, stratification, and cultural life-styles. Sociobiologists have been accused of being racists and sexists and have been verbally abused at scientific meetings by academics who are committed to obscurantist and explicitly antiscientific strategies. This abuse at the hands of people who have made no contribution of their own to the explanation of sociocultural phenomena can only serve to strengthen the conviction of the sociobiologists that they are being martyred for their devotion to the scientific method and that the study of the most momentous issues in human life has been monopolized by those least competent to carry it out. The answer to sociobiology does not lie in still more abuse; it lies in the development of a corpus of coherent sociocultural theory that is more parsimonious and that has greater scope and applicability than the corpus of theories produced under the auspices of sociobiological principles. To repeat the words of Imre Lakatos (see p. 24): "Purely negative criticism does not kill a research program."

Chapter Six

Dialectical Materialism

CULTURAL MATERIALISM and sociobiology have similar epistemologies but radically different theoretical principles; whereas cultural materialism and dialectical materialism have similar theoretical principles but radically different epistemologies.

I have already described the great debt the principle of infrastructural determinism owes to Marx. Cultural and dialectical materialists disagree about the content of infrastructure, but they share common ground when it comes to the predominating influence of the material conditions of social life. When Engels eulogized Marx at the graveside, he chose to emphasize Marx's discovery of the dependence of structure and superstructure on the immediate material means of subsistence:

Just as Darwin discovered the law of evolution in organic nature, so Marx discovered the law of evolution in human history: he discovered the simple fact, hitherto concealed by an overgrowth of ideology, that mankind must first eat and drink, have shelter and clothing before it can pursue politics, science, religion, art, etc., and therefore the production of the immediate material means of subsistence and consequently the degree of economic development attained by a given people or during a given epoch, form the foundation upon which the state institutions, the legal conceptions, the art and even the religious ideas of the people concerned have evolved, and in the light of which these things must therefore be explained instead of *vice versa* as has hitherto been the case. (Engels, in Selsam and Martel, 1963:189)

It is this aspect of Marx's work that cultural materialists regard as his greatest contribution.

On the epistemological level, however, cultural materialists and dialectical materialists are as far apart as cultural materialists and sociobiologists are on the theoretical level. The nub of this disagreement is to be found in the Marxist advocacy of Hegel's dialectical conception of history. Hegel stands to dialectical materialism as the empiricist David Hume stands to cultural materialism. Marx himself recognized a great debt to both the Scottish and the British empiricists such as Adam Smith and David Ricardo, and he himself never engaged in a campaign to substitute dialectical science for empiricist science. Instead, it was Lenin who first argued that empiricism and Marxist materialism were based on irreconcilable epistemologies. Cultural materialists reject Lenin's disdain of the empiricist tradition. By pitting dialectics against empiricism, Lenin opened the door to the mystification of the communist state, and especially the mystification of the communist ruling class. In order to complete the demystification of the social world, materialism must be joined with the quest for objective knowledge. I do not reject the Hegelian ingredient in Marx in order to repudiate the Hegel-Marx struggle for freedom and economic equality, but in order to insist that there can be no freedom and economic equality without objective knowledge.

What Hegel Hath Wrought

LIKE OTHER idealists, Hegel believed that things are expressions of ideas. But Hegel insisted that ideas are not only what they are but also what they are not. Moreover, ideas are continuously changing from what they are into what they are not. What exists today is not merely destined to change, as many philosophers had previously insisted, but is destined to change into its opposite, or its "negation." Everything that exists can therefore be said to contain the "seeds of its own destruction." These seeds of destruction can be identified by analysis aimed at exposing "contradictions." The core of Hegel's contribution to Marx is the recognition that change, movement, and vitality arise out of "contradictions." As Hegel put it in his book on logic:

It has been a fundamental prejudice of hitherto existing logic and of ordinary imagination that Contradiction is a determination having less essence and immanence than Identity; but indeed, if there were any question of rank, and the two determinations had to be fixed as separate, Contradiction would have to be taken as the profounder and more fully essential. For as opposed to it Identity is only the determination of the simple immediate, or of dead Being, while Contradiction is the root of all movement and life, and it is only in so far as it contains a Contradiction that anything moves and has impulse and activity. (Hegel, in Selsam and Martel, 1963:332)

According to Hegel, the movement in ideas that arises from inner contradictions does not merely result in an oscillation from one idea to the other; rather, it results in a continuous world process of progressive change. The negation of the negation does not result in the restoration of the original situation because there is an overall direction to the world historical process—a direction which Hegel described as the growth of freedom through the growth of rational consciousness.

Hegel saw the negations of earlier by later ideas as part of a grand process of spiritual contradictions leading to the ultimate union of human thought with the logic of the "world spirit." Marx turned this analysis "right side up" and saw the grand process of history as the record of successive modes of production, each containing its internal contradictions, moving by successive negations toward a classless communist utopia.

Hegel in Marx

IT IS IN the analysis of the contradictions specific to capitalism that Hegel's dialectic served most importantly both to validate and to inspire Marx's scientific and political goals. According to Marx, the fundamental "contradiction" of capitalism is that in order for capitalists to make a profit, they must exploit labor. Marx believed that this contradiction would force capitalism into a series of deepening crises. To stay in business against their competitors, capitalist entrepreneurs attempt to substitute machines for laborers, but in doing so they unwittingly cause their rate of profit to decline, since profits come from the exploitation of people, not from the exploitation of machines. To restore profitability, capitalists intensify the exploitation of labor, leading to falling purchasing power among the laborers, growing concentration of wealth among the capitalists, and glutted markets. Thus the seeds of destruction are present in the deepening misery of the class of industrial workers—the proletariat. Capitalism creates the proletariat, and in doing so, seals its own doom. The more it exploits the proletariat, the more the proletariat organizes itself into a revolutionary force capable of expropriating the expropriators, "negating its negation."

In Marx's words:

Along with the constantly diminishing number of the magnates of capital . . . grows the mass of misery, oppression, slavery, degradation, exploitation; but with this too grows the revolt of the working class, a class always increasing in numbers, and disciplined, united, organized by the very mechanism of the process of capital production itself. The monopoly of capital becomes a fetter upon the mode of production, which has sprung up and flourished along with, and under it. Centralisation of the means of production and socialisation at last reach a point where they become incompatible with their capitalist integument. This integument is burst asunder. The knell of capitalist private property sounds. The expropriators are expropriated. (Marx, 1975 [1867]:763)

Although Marx carried out only an in-depth study of the contradiction between classes in the transformations of feudalism and capitalism in Europe, he generalized class antagonism as the basis of the evolution of all state societies: "The history of all hitherto existing society is the history of class struggles" (Marx and Engels, 1959 [1848]:7). Here again the debt to Hegel is clear, since "struggle" is merely an active form of contradiction and negation.

Finally, as we saw in Chapter 3, Marx's ultimate dialectical generalization relates the form of class antagonism to the component parts of the mode of production. Here, too, contradiction and the shifting of things into their opposites reveal the Hegelian heritage:

At a certain stage of development, the material productive forces of society come into conflict with the existing relations of production, or—this merely expresses the same thing in legal terms—with the property relations within the framework of which they have operated hitherto. From forms of development of the productive forces, these relations turn into their fetters. Then begins an era of social revolution. . . ." (Marx, 1970 [1859]:21)

The Hegelian Monkey

ALTHOUGH HEGEL himself did not make any sustained contribution to the analysis of capitalism, the study of Hegel's ideas about dialectics undoubtedly helped Marx develop his specific theory of capitalism. One cannot dispute that fact, nor minimize its historical significance. It does not follow, however, that to build upon Marx's unique contribution to social science, one must accept Marx's evaluation of the importance of Hegel's dialectic. Hegel is not the giant on whose shoulders Marx thought he had to stand, but a monkey clinging to Marx's back. That Marx never finally and decisively shook Hegel off into merited oblivion is a measure of the cultural limitation on Marx's genius.

The central weakness of dialectical epistemology is the lack of operational instructions for identifying causally decisive "negations." If every event has a negation, then every component in that event also has a negation. However, every event contains an indefinite number of components; therefore every event contains an indefinite number of negations. Which negation is the crucial "contradiction"? For example, patrilineality contains two notions: descent, and descent exclusively through males. Is its negation nondescent or descent not exclusively through males? If it is nondescent, is its negation marriage or some other form of nondescent relationship? And if it is through nonmales, is its negation descent through females alqne (matriliny) or through both males and females (bilaterality)?

Since there are no instructions for identifying the properties or components that are the crucial negations, dialectical relationships can never be falsified. In the next chapter discussing the use of dialectics by the French structuralists, I shall show in detail how dialectics lead to theories which are fundamentally untestable and hence nonscientific. In the hands of dialectical Marxists, however, definitions of the phases of the dialectical process have often been used to rationalize politico-economic repression and the liquidation of individuals, classes, and ethnic groups. Because dialectics offers no instructions concerning how much of a difference constitutes a negation, dialectical Marxism has turned into a great breeding ground of fanatical revelations, grand finalities, and impenetrable metaphors.

Engels's Defense of Dialectics

ENGELS TRIED to answer some of these objections in his book *Anti-Dühring*. He argued that dialectical contradictions can be identified because they do not merely negate a static situation but set the stage for further development: "Each class of things . . . has its appropriate form of being negated in such a way that it gives rise to a development . . ." (1972 [1878]:155). When applied to the process of sociocultural evolution—or to any other evolutionary sequence—Engels's "development" results in a tautology. For the name cultural materialists give to the process in which there is both discontinuity and continuity—in which a thing is both changed and not changed, is negated but affirmed, is destroyed but preserved—is evolution. To call such changes "dialectical" adds no additional information about evolutionary processes unless one is prepared to state some general principles by which dialectical negations can always be distinguished from other evolutionary "negations" (i.e., "transformations"). No one has ever succeeded in stating these principles. Indeed, from Engels on, many dialectical materialists have explicitly denied that there is any kind of general formula according to which the crucial dialectical ingredients in any particular situation can be identified. Thus, in berating Dühring, Engels states that Marx himself did not identify the dialectical negations as a first or even last step in his attempt to discover the laws governing the origin, transformation, and extinction of capitalism. According to Engels, only when it was all over, when Marx looked back on what he had done, did he see fit to draw attention to the fact that the laws governing the development of capitalism were dialectical laws.

Marx merely shows from history . . . that just as the former petty industry, necessarily, through its own development, created the conditions of its annihilation, i.e., of the expropriation of the small proprietors, so now the capitalist mode of production has likewise itself created the material conditions which will annihilate it. The process is a historical one, and if it is at the same time a dialectical process, this is not Marx's fault, however annoying it may be for Herr Dühring.

It is only at this point, after Marx has completed his proof on the basis of historical and economic facts, that he proceeds: "The capitalist mode of appropriation, the result of the capitalist mode of production, produces capitalist private property. This is the first negation of individual private property as founded on the labors of the proprietor. But capitalist production begets, with the inexorability of a law of nature, its own negation. It is the negation of the negation. [See Marx, 1975 (1867):763]

In characterizing the process as the negation of the negation, therefore, Marx does not dream of attempting to prove by this that the process was historically necessary. On the contrary; after he has proved from history that in fact the process has partially already occurred, and partially must occur in the future, he then also characterizes it as a process which develops in accordance with a definite dialectical law. (Engels, 1972 [1878]:147)

From Engels's own argument it seems clear that dialectical principles do not constitute a distinct mode of inquiry; that a knowledge of dialectical logic neither promotes the discovery of lawful relations nor contributes to the testing of specific hypotheses.

The Negative Attitude: Not Dialectics

IT IS IMPORTANT to draw a distinction between dialectics as a rigorous means of obtaining knowledge—as an epistemological principle—and dialectics as a general attitude or stance toward knowledge. Marx lost his technical interest in Hegelian philosophy as he moved away from the German university scene and as he became immersed in the critique of capitalism. But Marx never ceased to be inspired by Hegel's advocacy of dialectics (Seigel, 1978:390ff). Marx pointed out that by making contradiction and change the focus of knowledge, Hegel served notice on the bourgeoisie that all seemingly eternal laws and imperishable institutions contained the seeds of their own destruction. In the afterword to the second German edition of *Capital* (1975 [1867]:20). Marx wrote that dialectics

is a scandal and abomination to bourgeoisdom and its doctrinaire professors because it includes in its comprehension and affirmative recognition of the existing state of things, at the same time also, the recognition of the negation of that state, of its inevitable breaking up; because it regards every historically developed social form as in fluid movement, and therefore takes into account its transient nature not less than its momentary existence; because it lets nothing impose upon it, and is in its essence critical and revolutionary.

Dialectics viewed as an epistemology of skepticism, transience, ephemerality, and novelty has much to commend it. In the hands of some advocates, dialectics is virtually synonymous with the intelligent, skeptical, and creative search for probable knowledge. Robert Murphy, for example, has presented this view of dialectics as the "negative attitude":

The dialectical exercise is simple in the extreme, for it requires only that the analyst of society question everything that he sees and hears, examine phenomena fully and from every angle, seek and evaluate the contradiction of any proposition, and consider every category from the viewpoint of its noncontents as well as its positive attributes. It requires us to also look for paradox as much as complementarity, for opposition as much as accommodation. It portrays a universe of dissonance underlying apparent order and seeks deeper order beyond the dissonance. It urges the critical examination, in the light of ongoing social activity, of those common-sense guidelines to behavior and common-sense interpretations of reality that lie at the core of our cultural systems. It enjoins us to query the obvious and given truths of both our culture and our science. (Murphy, 1971:117)

If this is dialectics, then cultural materialism is as "dialectical" as "dialectical materialism." Point by point, cultural materialism fits Murphy's requirement for a dialectical approach to social life. Cultural materialism seeks to: "question everything" (by demanding operationalized empirical tests); "examine phenomena fully and from every angle" (by locating them as parts of systems and in sets of interpenetrating diachronic and synchronic theories); "evaluate the contradiction of any proposition" and "noncontents as well as . . . positive attributes" (by examining null hypotheses and rival theories, and by attempts at falsification); "look for paradox" and "for opposition" (by emphasizing both positive and negative feedback; continuity and change; solidarity and conflict; adaptation and maladaptation). It "portrays a universe of dissonance underlying apparent order and . . . deeper order beyond the dissonance" (idem); urges the critical examination of "common-sense guidelines" (by distinguishing between emics and etics); and "enjoins us to query the obvious" (by implicating the etic infrastructure in theories about superstructure; by showing the complexity of demo-techno-econo-environmental relationships; by demanding empirical data as the basis for all substantive generalizations).

But there is much more to the dialectical attitude than Murphy's description allows. The missing ingredient is Lenin's uncompromising hostility to the empiricist-positivist position.

Lenin and the Dungheap

BY EXCORIATING positivism, Lenin totally misrepresented the source of the reactionary tendencies in twentieth-century bourgeois social science. As I see it, scientists like Karl Pearson and Ernst Mach were reactionary not because they were followers of Hume but because they were eclectics who failed to grasp the role of infrastructure in cultural evolution.

By misrepresenting positivism as an inherently bourgeois philosophy, Lenin succeeded in setting up positivism harnessed to an evolutionary materialist paradigm as the antithesis of dialectical materialism. Hence Lenin's assertion that dialectical idealism was closer to "intelligent materialism" than "undeveloped, dead, crude, rigid" materialism, and his dismissal of nondialectical materialists as "farmyard cocks" who spurned Hegel's "jewels."

Marx and Engels . . . did not worry about the elementary truths of materialism, which had been cried by the hucksters in dozens of books, but devoted all of their attention to ensuring that these elementary truths should not be vulgarized . . . should not lead . . . to forgetfulness of the *valuable* fruit of the idealist system, Hegelian dialectics—that pearl which those farmyard cocks, the Büchners, the Dührings and Co. (as well as Leclair, Mach, Avenarius and so forth) could not pick out of the dungheap of absolute idealism. (1972 [1909]: 248)

Lenin failed to show, however—indeed, never really considered— why Hume's opposition to metaphysical pearls had to be considered inherently reactionary. All that he showed was that positivism linked with eclectic, idealist, or synchronic paradigms was implicated in reactionary political positions. But to view all of positivism, even positivism in the service of a materialist paradigm, as a bourgeois ploy has deadly consequences for the meaning of science, for the possibility of a science of society, and for the role of a science of society in the conduct of political life.

True, Marx was scornful of Auguste Comte, who regarded himself as the Pope of Positivism (Diamond, Scholte, and Wolfe, 1975:872). But it is irresponsible to incorporate the work of Auguste Comte within the tradition connecting Hume to logical positivism and logical positivism to cultural materialism. Comte's grandiose scheme for a secular religion was a wholly metaphysical and operationally morbid creation (see p. 11). As a metaphysician, Comte even surpassed Hegel. Moreover, he was an incorrigible idealist (cf. Harris, 1968:59–66). If by positivism one means Hume's instructions about what was worth saving in philosophy (see p. 10), not a page written by Comte could survive Hume's bonfire. Dialectical materialists cannot flay modern positivists for allegedly advocating "value-free science" and at the same time crucify them on behalf of Comte's advocacy of bourgeois "order and progress."

The real reason for Lenin's attack on empiricism had little to do with the scientific failings of empirical social science, but rather with the need to validate and strengthen revolutionary activity aimed at destroying capitalism and building socialism. Marx may not have used the dialectic to identify the central contradictions of capitalism, but once they were laid bare he and Engels insisted that capitalism would develop according to a definite "dialectical law" (see above). Capitalism brings the proletariat into existence; the proletariat expropriates the expropriators; a new classless social formation results. The revolutionaries had to be victorious; history was on their side; the negation of the negation had to occur. The dialectic thus provided Lenin and his followers with a "scientific" means of predicting the future. Like oracular prophecies based on astrology or the cracks in shoulder blades, the dialectic rallied the proletariat under a leadership to whom the cosmos itself guaranteed ultimate victory. Small wonder, then, that the metaphysics of Hegel's idealism should be preferred to the empiricism of Darwin and of "bourgeois" science.

Cultural materialism is more of an anathema than cultural idealism because, as we shall see, it presents a far greater threat to the mystifications of revolutionary praxis. Cultural materialists can accompany the Marxist analysis of capitalism step by step from the exploitation of labor to the declining rate of profit and still at the last great divide refuse to take the leap of faith demanded by the dialectic. Capitalist systems are full of internal and external stresses, but the resolution of these stresses will not necessarily lie in the emergence of utopian classless and stateless societies. It takes a highly mystified consciousness to believe that the Soviet Union is now or ever will be the dialectical negation of capitalism and of class society and the state. Clearly, there are many different varieties of socialism and capitalism, each with its particular infrastructure shaped by distinctive evolutionary and historical experiences. No one knows which forms will ultimately predominate. For long-term predictions about sociocultural transformations, cultural materialists find Hegel's crystal ball to be worth just about as much as a pair of shoulder blades. In rejecting dialectics, cultural materialists do not embrace mechanical materialism; rather, they merely reaffirm their belief that an objective science of society is worth fighting for and that it cannot be reared apart from a relentless struggle against all forms of religious and political mysticism.

Do We Need Dialectics?

ANTHROPOLOGIST Eleanor Leacock (1972:62–63) has made four points in defense of the Marxist-Leninist dialectic as a scientific concept. First, she says that dialectics are essential to the understanding of "change as an inherent attribute in all matter." Any phenomenon is a "unity of opposites" because it is always in the process of becoming something else. Any phenomenon is thus "an expression of 'struggle,' involving 'contradiction' or 'negation' . . . such terminology is essential to deal conceptually with the reality of constant change."

Here I would concede only that contradiction and negation have useful connotations in restricted spheres of change, as in the struggle between nations and classes. But to say that these metaphors are essential for conceptualizing all transformation is not correct. Indeed, in many evolutionary processes, "contradiction" is not only merely metaphorical but superfluous and misleading. I fail to see, for example, how a description of the transformation of radium into lead is not encumbered by picturing the nuclear processes as the struggle of opposites (neutrons and protons do not "contradict" each other, and lead is not the "opposite" of radium). I also fail to see how such metaphors serve any useful function in relation to bioevolutionary processes. To view birds as the negation of fish would tell us very little about how they are related; to define *Homo sapiens* as the negation of *Homo erectus* is to set human paleontology back over a hundred years. Turning specifically to sociocultural transformations, it is again not correct that dialectical metaphors are essential for dealing with the reality of change. The theories about convergent, divergent, and emergent trajectories of sociocultural evolutions in Chapter 4 would in no way be improved by the addition of Hegelian imagery. As discussed in Chapter 4, the transformation of hunter-collectors to horticulturalists proceeded by slow steps in which infrastructural variables underwent complex continuous synergetically related changes. Or to take another example, also discussed in Chapter 4, under conditions which promote prolonged absence of men from households, patrilocal, patrilineal organizations have repeatedly evolved into matrilineal, matrilocal organizations. In no case, however, is it possible to argue that patrilocality and matrilocality are dialectical opposites, since intervening stages such as bilocality, neolocality, avunculocality, and virilocality present continuous statistical departures from patrilocality or matrilocality (which at any rate seldom occur in 100 percent of all households). Similarly, the transitions to class society and the state were not processes in which there was only a simple contradictory alternative—namely, egalitarian or stratified redistributors. Rather, there were and still are significant degrees of egalitarian sharing, as well as significant degrees of exploitation associated with different infrastructural conditions.

The second point Leacock makes is that the dialectic teaches us how to obtain a correct view of interrelationships among phenomena.

Without the concept of contradictions . . . change is by implication external to any given phenomenon, a result of the interaction between it and other phenomena that are conceived in somewhat static terms. [Since] matter as a process, is integrated in a marvelously complex series of successively more inclusive levels . . . that which can be studied by the scientist as the external "interactions" between two phenomena at one level are in fact internal "contradictions" at the more inclusive level where the two interacting phenomena form a more complex system. This is the understanding of reality that Harris is brushing aside when he decries Marx's Hegelian infatuation with "contradictions." (Ibid.)

But the concept of things as events or processes (see p. 14) is at least as highly developed within Darwinism and positivism as within dialectical materialism, and therefore cultural materialism does not brush aside this understanding of reality. On the other hand, the question of whether the causes of transformational processes are internal or external to a particular event is an empirical issue. Both occur. Cultural materialism through concepts such as intensification, functional stress, conflict, exploitation, and environmental depletion is capable of dealing with both internal and external causal processes and with their interrelations. "Other phenomena" will be "conceived in somewhat static terms" not by those who lack familiarity with Hegelian hocus-pocus but by Rip Van Winkles who have managed to remain isolated from the intellectual influences emanating from evolutionary biology, evolutionary astronomy, all modern physics and chemistry, genetics, cybernetics, and systems theory.

The third point made by Leacock is that the Hegelian dialectic is necessary in order to identify the emergence of a qualitatively new transformation. In *The Rise of Anthropological Theory* I criticized dialectical evolutionism by pointing out that Darwinian and cybernetic models of evolution are perfectly capable of dealing with slowly accumulating strains that lead to a "violent collapse of the whole system" as well as with "evolution through the slow accumulation of minor changes wrought by minor adjustments to minor stresses" (1968:236).

Leacock rejoins that "it is not just collapse of the old but *replacement* by the new that is essential to the process of evolution that has been called 'negation.' " By this she presumably means that prediction of an emergent feature is enhanced by knowledge that the old system already contained its negation even before it collapsed. But as I just showed a moment ago, even Marx and Engels were adamant in their rejection of the idea that the dialectic itself could be used to identify the contradictions of a particular system. The problem for dialectical analysis, as much as for any causal explanatory strategy, is not merely to identify any contradictions (or stresses, malfunctions, deviations, amplifications, etc.) but to identify those which decisively determine the system's future state. It is useless to be told as a generality that some components are more important than others. One needs to know which ones they are, and dialectics will not tell us which ones they are. Dialectics, for example, will not tell us whether infanticide has been a decisive factor in the evolution of modes of production. It will not resolve the question of whether males exploit females in pre-state societies; whether egalitarian redistributors were the structural base for the development of a ruling class; or whether irrigation agriculture promoted the evolution of oriental despotisms in the Middle East and China. As I shall show in a moment, when dialectical materialists have to confront the task of providing answers to particular puzzles, they do not necessarily excel in comparison with nondialectical materialists.

Finally, Leacock implies that dialectics are in some sense confirmed by the need to distinguish qualitative from quantitative changes: "Since Harris agrees that evolution is transformation, there is presumably a point at which the accumulation of minor strains results in transformation or qualitative change in accordance with the principles of Marxist-Hegelian dialectic" (ibid.:63). But Hegelian epistemology muddles the distinction between quantity and quality. From an operationalist point of view, the identification of an emergent transformation is a taxonomic decision. All taxonomic decisions contain an arbitrary component in the sense that there are no natural units or taxonomic categories. All classifications are the product of the intersection of human logical and empirical labor with natural features varying along an infinity of quantitative axes. All taxonomic decisions must first of all reflect scientifically measurable dimensions as accurately as possible; beyond this they can only be judged heuristically. Scientific strategies demand that qualitative emergents be identified in ways that maximize the ability of scientists to construct empirically testable theories of broad scope and wide applicability.

The dialectical interpretation of the relationship between quantity and quality is surprisingly nondialectical. It more closely resembles Platonic archetypical modes of thought than a doctrine emphasizing impermanence and unending contrariety. It confuses species-given capacities and predilections for taxonomic distinctions that have proved useful for biological adaptations with the deeper structure of reality (cf. Betalanffy, 1955; Campbell, 1974; Harris, 1964b). Science must reject many phylogenetically adaptive qualitative discriminations if it is to develop theories of broad scope and wide applicability. For example, we naturally discriminate between infrared radiation, which we experience as heat, and higher electromagnetic frequencies, which we experience as light. Physics has shown, however, that the qualitative distinction between radiant heat and light has no contribution to make to the theory of electromagnetic spectra. This does not mean that the distinction between the infrared and humanly visible radiation is unreal, but merely that for scientific purposes it is best to refer to such differences in terms of precise wavelengths rather than in terms of anthropocentric qualitative contrasts.

The danger inherent in the dialectical approach to the difference between quantitative and qualitative transformation is that preconceptions concerning the qualitative characteristics of particular systems may be permitted to dominate the analysis of such systems. If one insists, for example, that the distinction between socialism and capitalism is qualitative, little room is left for an empirical analysis of such hybrid systems as Sweden and Yugoslavia have. Furthermore, the dialectic is implicated in many stupefying conceptual rigidities—such as, for example, that socialist democracies cannot have ruling classes, exploitation, or slave labor.

The Trees-in-the-Forest Problem

ON THE OTHER HAND, there is an opposite danger—namely, the failure to locate quantitative observations in a proper holistic qualitative context. But once again, this is the error of narrow inductionism and eclecticism, not of positivism (Willer and Willer, 1973). True enough, endless studies of the welfare and working poor in the United States are carried out as if the fact that the United States has a capitalist economy is a mere peripheral contingency. But these studies suffer from eclecticism, idealism, and obscurantism—not from too much science, but too little! One does not have to be a *dialectical* materialist to see the forest as well as the trees, to grasp the absurdity of "accounts of 'cultures' abstracted from the contexts of capitalism and imperialism, racism and domination, war and revolution" (Diamond, Scholte, and Wolf, 1975:873).

Dialecticians are right to argue that the whole must be grasped before the parts can be analyzed. But there is no royal road to grasping the whole. Instead, there has to be a continuous interplay between the qualitative and quantitative implications of theory. The whole is never to be grasped at the expense of the parts, nor are the parts to be grasped at the expense of the whole. Dialectical genuflections in themselves are no guarantee that the most intelligent balance will be achieved. Dialecticians may be less prone than positivists to mistake the part for the whole, but they are more prone than positivists to get a wrong idea of the whole and to distort every part in the defense of that wrong idea.

The Dialectic and the Unity of Theory and Practice

MARXISM HAS ALWAYS been more than a strategy for understanding the world, more than a set of theories about the evolution of society and culture. Dialectical materialism is fundamentally a political strategy dedicated to the destruction of capitalism and the birth of communism. For the participants in this struggle, dialectics functions as a political-ideological theme, a nexus of symbols and metaphors, which validates the belief that the desired transformations will occur only as a result of revolutionary opposition to the capitalist class. To understand why Lenin despised the positivists even more than he despised the Hegelian idealists, we must turn to the doctrine known as the unity of theory and practice. This doctrine seeks to overcome the political hesitation that might arise from a purely scientific critique of the revolutionary process. It makes the dialectic analysis of capitalism self-fulfilling by linking the testing of sound revolutionary theory to the practice of effective revolutionary politics. As Marx put it: "the question whether objective truth can be attributed to human thinking is not a question of theory but is a practical question. In practice man must prove the truth of his thinking" (2nd Thesis on Fuerbach). Or as Engels (Selsam and Martel, 1963:142) expressed it: "the proof of the pudding is in the eating." The proof of dialectical predictions about the end of capitalism is made more likely by belief in the dialectical inevitability of the outcome. Any diminution of faith subverts the process. Therefore positivist skepticism is viewed as a reactionary political doctrine, as well as an erroneous scientific strategy.

Identification with the Oppressed

I HAVE PREVIOUSLY characterized dialectical materialism as "explicitly bound to a political program" in conformity with the principle of the unity of theory and practice. According to Leacock (1972:63), however, "the Marxist commitment is not to a program as such; instead, the principle underlying the necessary unity of theory and action is that active identification with the presently oppressed but emergent class involves a commitment to the future direction of social change that is basic for full understanding." Leacock's rejoinder seems to me to confirm the potential for subordinating science to politics inherent in dialectical epistemology. By linking "full understanding" to a "commitment to the future direction of social change," she is saying that traditional Marxists possess knowledge of the determined future by means of dialectical revelation and that only by confirming that revelation can science function in a progressive manner. This accounts for Leacock's peculiar notion that "mechanical materialism" can interpret the past but not the present or future: "By hindsight, mechanical materialism seems to work. The objective conditions—technological, economic, environmental—that preceded—hence 'caused'—later developments can necessarily and inevitably be located" (p. 66). To interpret the present and future, however, one needs to know the "internal stresses, alternative choices, and revolutionary versus conservative ideologies." All that this can mean is that our predictions about the future are more risky because our knowledge of future infrastructures is less complete than our knowledge of past infrastructures. This is inevitable because evolution involves emergent phenomena with no precedent in the past. I fail to see how paying attention to "internal stresses, alternative choices and revolutionary versus conservative ideologies" will compensate for this lack of knowledge. If the future, like the past, depends on "objective conditions," these are the conditions we must know to make predictions. I suspect that what Leacock is arguing for is an act of faith in the name of the unity of theory and practice.

An example of how dialectics leads to conceptual rigidities is Eugene Ruyle's (1975:19) reaction to the emergence of capitalist societies which solve their inner contradictions by multiple compromises rather than by the "negation of the negation." For Ruyle, this is to be explained by the fact that the "ruling class has intervened in the revolutionary process in order to keep the struggle of the working class within acceptable limits." This seems a perfectly reasonable way to express the situation as far as I am concerned. But Ruyle immediately follows with what I consider to be the indigestible essence of Hegelian metaphysics: "This may have prolonged the struggle, but cannot change its outcome." In other words, no matter how many disconfirming cases accumulate, one is not obliged to regard the theory that fails to predict them as being in need of change. A classless society *must* emerge out of capitalism. For my part, I hope so; but I do not see any evidence that would make its appearance a matter of certainty.

Obviously, mere identification with the currently oppressed classes can lead to false theories as easily as it can lead to true ones. Idealists and eclectics readily identify in active ways with the suffering of exploited classes. Their explanation of why that exploitation occurs, and their political intelligence, however, cannot be judged merely from their sentiments or their well-intentioned actions.

Cultural Materialism, Theory, and Politics

LIKE DIALECTICAL materialism, cultural materialism accepts and affirms the interdependence of science and politics. It also vigorously rejects the myth of value-free science. It insists that there is a determined relationship between dominant research strategies and political-economic structures and infrastructures (cf. Blackburn, 1973; Willer and Willer, 1973). Even though cultural materialists do not share a political line about how capitalism and state socialism will be transformed, nor a line about what they will be transformed into, pursuit of the cultural materialist strategy inevitably contributes to a radical critique of the status quo.

Ruling groups throughout history and prehistory have always promoted the mystification of social life as their first line of defense against actual or potential enemies. In the contemporary political context, idealism and eclecticism serve to obscure the very existence of ruling classes, thus shifting the blame for poverty, exploitation, and environmental degradation from the exploiters to the exploited. Cultural materialism opposes cultural idealism and eclecticism because these strategies, through their distorted and ineffectual analyses, prevent people from understanding the causes of war, poverty, and exploitation. Cultural materialism opposes dialectical materialism for the very same political and scientific reasons. As a political ideology, Marxist-Leninist dialectical materialism attempts to advance the struggle against exploitation by promoting a scientifically unjustifiable sense of certainty about the future. But the same sense of certainty gives additional opportunities for the perpetuation of exploitation by new ruling classes, providing these new classes with an elaborate ideology for justifying the self-serving obfuscation of the exploitative aspects of the state systems they control. Disparagement of positivist epistemologies can lead to the dialectical inevitability of even the most misguided analysis. Cultural materialism holds that the elimination of exploitation will never be achieved in a society which subverts the empirical and operational integrity of social science for reasons of political expediency. Because without the maintenance of an empiricist and operationalist critique, we shall never know if what some call democracy is a new form of freedom or a new form of slavery.

Mechanical Materialism

AS AFFIRMED and reaffirmed by Engels and countless Marxists, Marx's materialism was not based on a one-to-one or one-way relationship between infrastructure, structure, and superstructure. Bridget O'Laughlin, a recent participant in this chorus, correctly states that

Marx never claimed that history merely expresses productive relations; such economism is antithetical to his understanding of the dialectical relationship between base and superstructure. . . . In positing the determinance of the base, Marx was not, therefore, reducing all social relations to relations of production; religion, politics, and chivalry are not primarily economic institutions. Quite to the contrary, he wished to show that the relations of the social system were of different qualities, with those of the base ultimately determining the structure of the whole. (1975:349)

In *The Rise of Anthropological Theory* I also took reasonably adequate precautions against the predictable charge that acceptance of Marx's historical materialist principles committed cultural materialists to narrow "simplistic, monistic determinism." I quoted extensively from Engels's 1890 letter to Joseph Bloch, in which Engels wrote:

According to the materialist conception of history the determining element in history is *ultimately* the production and reproduction in real life. More than this neither Marx nor I have ever asserted. If therefore somebody twists this into the statement that the economic element is the *only* determining one, he transforms it into a meaningless, abstract and absurd phrase. (1959 [1890]:-397–398)

And I accompanied this with my own interpretation of the relationship between base and superstructure and of what was meant by *ultimately:*

Far from propounding "simplistic" explanations in terms of a single factor, Marx and Engels repeatedly emphasized the need for considering the interaction between base and superstructure in accounting for any particular historical situation. They made it perfectly clear that the determinism which they saw extending from base to superstructure was not an absolute one-to-one effect. Engels used the term "ultimately" to qualify the selective influence of the mode of production on ideology, much as we would today seek to qualify any deterministic statement in probabilistic terms, *given a sufficient number of cases* and in the long run. (1968:244)

My warning proved futile. Elman Service (1969) immediately denounced cultural materialism as "simplistic, monistic determinism," disregarding the statement of cultural materialist principles and the actual exemplification of those principles in attempted solutions of such specific substantive puzzles as the contrast between race relations in Brazil and the United States, and the taboo on cow slaughter in India.

Despite all the published evidence to the contrary, dialectical materialists continue to attack cultural materialism as a strategy that is unaccountably uninterested in the feedback between infrastructure and ideology. O'Laughlin even misrepresents cultural materialism as epistemologically committed exclusively to etic data: "Positivist approaches that take their categories from the concrete itself are of two types in anthropology: cultural materialist (etic) strategies that observe and measure fact in the material world; and ethnoscientific (emic) methods designed to discover the cognitive categories inside of peoples' heads. . . ." (1975:343)

Cultural materialists do not deny that there is an interactive exchange among the components of sociocultural systems. The point at issue is not whether such interactions occur, but how to characterize and study them in relation to general and specific transformations. As I have said in Chapter 3, the clearest way to explicate the relationship is to employ the concept of feedback. Infrastructure, structure, and superstructure exhibit negative feedback, or system-maintaining relationships. But they also exhibit positive feedback, or system-changing relationships. Cultural materialism holds that the transformation of social systems is usually (probabilistically) initiated by deviation amplifications within the infrastructure; that these usually then induce additional deviations and amplifications both within and between the other parts of the system. Cultural materialism holds that it is not likely that deviation amplifications initially confined only to the structural level will produce fundamental transformations, and even less likely that those initially confined to the superstructure will produce such changes. But it does not deny the importance of the feedback that takes place among superstructure, structure, and infrastructure in sustaining, accelerating, decelerating, or deflecting the direction and pace of transformational processes initiated within the infrastructure (see p. 72).

The Degradation of the Materialist Strategy

THE DEVELOPMENT of the strategy of dialectical materialism was historically rooted in and nourished by a Eurocentric concern with the problems of industrialism and capitalism. Despite the extraordinary range of Marx's interests, the initial formulation of dialectic materialist strategy lacked the global, pan-human diachronic and synchronic perspective of modern cultural materialism. The original limited scope of dialectical theories is apparent in the *Communist Manifesto* when Marx and Engels declare: "The history of all past society has consisted in the development of class antagonisms, antagonisms that assumed different forms in different epochs." Engels later corrected this absurd equation—the equation of the history of "all past society" with the history of society since the evolution of the state. In a footnote to a later edition of the *Manifesto,* he noted that the phrase applied only to historical, not prehistorical, epochs. As Lawrence Krader (1972, 1973a) has shown, Marx attempted to broaden the scope of dialectical materialist theories by reading early European history and everything that was available by way of ethnographic sources. It was not until Marx encountered Lewis Henry Morgan's *Ancient Society,* however, that he began to reckon seriously with the complexity of pre-state systems and with the challenge they presented to both dialectical and materialist principles. Marx died not long after reading Morgan's book, and Engels was left alone to reinterpret Morgan's work on the basis of Marx's extensive notes. Engels then wrote *The Origin of the Family, Private Property and the State,* which remained the anthropological centerpiece of Marxism until the end of World War II. Although Marx thought that he could detect in Morgan's work the independent corroboration of the materialist conception of history, *Ancient Society* actually was based on a confused medley of principles imputing causality as much to "original germ ideas" and natural selection as to infrastructural determinants. Engels could not transcend the limitations of Morgan's eclecticism, and *The Origin of the Family, Private Property and the State* emerged as a flawed work that at crucial junctures is neither materialist nor dialectical. For example, neither Engels nor Morgan could provide an infrastructural explanation for the development of the clan and other exogamous descent groups lying at the heart of village and chiefdom social structure. Engels followed Morgan in believing that the key to primitive kinship phenomena lay in the mental progress made possible by broadening proscriptions on endogamous mating:

In this ever-widening exclusion of blood relatives from the bond of marriage, natural selection continues to work. In Morgan's words [marriage between non-consanguinous gentes], 'tended to create a more vigorous stock physically and mentally. . . . When two advancing tribes . . . are blended into one people

. . . the new skull and brain would widen and lengthen to the sum of the capabilities of both.' (Engels, 1972 [1884]:111)

When it came to explaining why primitive sexual communism (an imaginary stage in Morgan's evolutionary scheme) gave way to monogamous pairing, Engels could only suppose that women must have longed "for the right of chastity, of temporary or permanent marriage with one man only, as a way of release" (ibid., 117). Elsewhere Engels (in Krader, 1973b:244n.) frankly admitted that he was baffled by the apparent lack of correlation between specific structural and infrastructural features of band and village societies. The fact is that dialectical materialism was originally formulated to deal with the internal laws of capitalism, so it left Marx and Engels singularly ill-prepared to cope with the great bulk of non-European and precapitalist history and prehistory. No strategy that emphasizes inner contradictions at the expense of the external relations of subsistence, population, and environment can begin to make sense out of the specific varieties of institutions characteristic of bands, villages, and chiefdoms. As I pointed out in Chapter 3, Marx's failure to develop a general theory of population growth leaves the central question of the replacement of successive modes of production dangling in midair. As a consequence, dialectical materialism lacks a coherent theory of the origin of the state; and the absence of interest in the ecological context of state formation further deprives dialectical materialism of a coherent corpus of theory accounting for varieties of state systems other than capitalism, such as European and African feudalism and the hydraulic empires.

At one phase in his career Marx did verge on developing a systematic interest in the "geographical factor." This happened when he confronted the problem of an Asiatic mode of production distinct from that of feudalism and capitalism. Marx even went so far as to identify control over waterworks as the core feature of these historically "stationary" Asiatic agro-managerial despotisms. But as Karl Wittfogel has shown, the implications of the Asiatic mode of production for dialectical principles and for the entire program of world communism were so devastating that Marx and Engels found it expedient simply to cover up the whole question. And so in Marx's later work and in *The Origin of the Family, Private Property and the State,* there occurs what Wittfogel calls "the sin against science": the omission of any discussion of the Asiatic mode of production, and the downplaying of the role of bureaucratic management in intensification and redistribution and in the origin of class exploitation. The first ruling class is pictured as a class that owns slaves as private property, while exploitation by state managers under the Asiatic mode of production goes unnoticed.

> Obviously the concept of Oriental despotism contained elements that paralyzed his [Marx's] search for truth. As a member of a group that intended to establish a total managerial and dictatorial state . . . Marx could scarcely help recognizing some disturbing similarities between Oriental despotism and the state of his program. (Wittfogel, 1957:387)

Dialectical materialism was paralyzed by the ancient hydraulic agro-managerial despotisms in another sense. As Marx realized in his analysis of India (and indeed, as Hegel himself had earlier perceived), the great civilizations of the Orient were class-structured but structurally "un-progressive"—that is, Marx believed that if they were left to their own devices, they would not advance from feudalism to capitalism to socialism in conformity with the dialectical necessities of antagonistic interests. Instead, ancient China, Mesopotamia, and Egypt underwent recurrent upheavals ending in the restoration of the hydraulic infrastructure and its agro-managerial structure and superstructure.

After World War II, dialectical materialism could no longer be insulated against the critique of Western bourgeois social science. The discrepancy between Morgan's view of sociocultural evolution and the findings of archaeologists and modern ethnographic fieldworkers ceased to be covered over in the name of party discipline. At the same time, the divergent interpretations of Marxism adapted to the specific politico-economic requirements of countries in various stages of agrarian and industrial evolution began to make their influence felt in world politics. Increasingly at a loss to cope with the proliferating anomalies of the empirical situation, dialectical materialism itself soon underwent a remarkable series of transformations leading to the degradation of the materialist and scientific components in Marx's great principle of infrastructural causality.

By stressing the feedback effect of structure and superstructure upon infrastructure in the name of the dialectic, Marxist materialism rapidly dissolved itself back into its bourgeois origins, passing from dialectical materialism to structuralism, from structuralism to eclecticism, from eclecticism to idealism, and from idealism to obscurantism. Much of what calls itself Marxism in the world today is nothing but idealism, eclecticism, and obscurantism papered over with revolutionary rhetoric. I am not interested in pursuing the question of whether these idealist, eclectic, and obscurantist strategies really deserve to be called Marxism. If Marx at bottom was not a scientist but a dialectician, a historian who practiced no particular discipline, a realistic socialist rather than a scientific one (Diamond, Scholte, and Wolf, 1975: 872), so much the worse for Marx and the Marxists who have fashioned themselves in that image. If Marxism is best epitomized as a "theory of social, hence, political constraints on material possibilities" (Diamond, 1972:416), rather than as a research strategy emphasizing material constraints on social and political possibilities, then so much the worse for Marx that he failed to warn future generations of Marxists not to cast him in such a mold. But regardless of how one epitomizes Marxism, the principle that structure or superstructure determines infrastructure does not solve the problem of what determines structure and superstructure. And if Marx really did not propose that infrastructure determines structure and superstructure, so much the worse for those who in the name of Marx divert our attention from the causes of sociocultural life, including the causes of poverty and exploitation.

Chapter Seven

Structuralism

FRENCH STRUCTURALISM is the most influential anthropological strategy in contemporary Western Europe. It is antipositivist, dialectical, idealist and ahistorical. Its founder-genius, Claude Lévi-Strauss, avows a disinterest in testable theories and ignores causality, origins, and historical processes. And yet this is the anthropological strategy that hundreds of trained academic minds in Europe and the Americas have found most worthy of lifelong study.

Structuralism as Cultural Idealism

THE SUCCESS of structuralism remains incomprehensible until one grasps that it is the most important surviving European representative of the cultural idealist tradition. For the "structure" in structuralism, despite its evocation of contrasts with superstructure, refers exclusively to the mental superstructure. To be sure, structuralists insist that they are not idealists or mentalists because they "accept the primacy of the infrastructure" (Rossi, 1974a:98). To be sure, Lévi-Strauss himself speaks of the "undoubted primacy of the infrastructure." But these declarations are hollow because structuralism does not concern itself with the etic and behavioral infrastructure. Thus, according to Lévi-Strauss, ethnology is the study of the psychological superstructure of sociocultural systems; other disciplines study the infrastructure—disciplines with which Lévi-Strauss does not identify:

It is to this theory of superstructures, scarcely touched on by Marx, that I hope to make a contribution. The development of the study of infrastructures proper is a task which must be left to history—with the aid of demography, technology, historical geography and ethnography. It is not principally the ethnologist's concern, for ethnology is first of all psychology. (1966:130–131)

Nothing could be more baldly evident—structuralism is a set of principles for studying the mental superstructure. These principles deliberately avoid implicating etic behavioral infrastructure (except in lip service or as dependent variable) and therefore cannot be part of a materialist strategy. Ino Rossi (1974a:98) claims that structuralism is not "idealistic" because it does not hold that "social phenomena are just mere ideas or products of mind." This claim rests on the ontological meaning of idealism and the hoary, moribund, scientifically irrelevant dispute about whether the essence of being is mind or matter. But as soon as structuralists specify their epistemological and theoretical research principles (as distinct from their ontology), idealism and mentalism are rampant. Rossi (1974b:108), for example, agrees that to Lévi-Strauss, social phenomena "are nothing but objectivated systems of ideas," that "mind has to be their ultimate explanation" (1974:115), that "structuralism is a kind of 'psycho-logic' " and that "structuralism is aimed at discovering basic mental processes and structures" (1974a:100:n.5). "Ethnology is first of all psychology" only for ethnologists who are first of all mentalists and cultural idealists.

The Nature of Structuralist Structures

THE IDEALIST tradition behind structuralism includes the peculiar notion of the French sociologist and moralist Emile Durkheim that human society has (or is) a *conscience collective*. This collective consciousness or collective conscience (the words are the same in French) is a set of ideas exterior to any given individual but endowed with coercive force over individual thought and behavior.

The collective consciousness is the highest form of the psychic life, since it is the consciousness of the consciousness. Being placed outside of and above individual and local contingencies, it sees things only in their permanent and essential aspects, which it crystallizes into communicable ideas . . . it alone can furnish the mind with the molds which are applicable to the totality of things and which make it possible to think of them. (Durkheim, 1915:444)

Structuralists follow Durkheim in believing that the mind has "molds" that make it possible to think of the totality of things. These molds are the structuralists' structures. In their most elementary form they are present in all human minds and are ultimately part of the neurophysiology of the human brain. However, each culture fills the "molds" with its own distinctive content—its own ideas. It is the task of structural analysis to show how the surface content in its distinctive way actually expresses or conforms to the underlying universal structures. As we shall see, knowledge of structures is achieved by an indiscriminate mixture of inferences from behavior stream events such as rituals and myth-tellings, and elicited rules and categories such as marriage rules and kinship terminologies. Since structuralists reject the emic/etic distinction as well as the mental/behavioral distinction and the entire positivist tradition, the epistemological status of structuralist structures remains unoperationalized. As we shall see, this means that there is a distinct possibility that structuralist structures exist only in the imaginations of the structuralists themselves.

The Basic Theoretical Principles of Structuralism

STRUCTURALISM represents an attempt to explain the *conscience collective* in terms of a pan-human, neurologically based unconscious mental dialectic. As I have said, this dialectic allegedly sets limits to what can be thought—determines what is "good to think." Hence underneath apparently disparate thoughts are similar meanings. These hidden meanings are always reducible to two ideas, one of which is the opposite of the other. Pairs of opposed ideas—or binary oppositions—therefore constitute the "structures" of structuralism. A structuralist explanation consists essentially in finding the binary oppositions in the collective social mind. Some commonly identified oppositions are

me : other
life : death
culture : nature

Whether these oppositions are reducible to each other, or whether there are fundamental oppositions which remain to be discovered, is not yet known. Additional "understandings" are achieved as in Hegelian dialectics by regarding the paired oppositions as contradictions which tend to produce third elements as "mediators," or resolutions. Unlike Hegelian dialectics, however, this mediation is not viewed as part of a general cosmic process of development. The same binary oppositions appear and reappear with the same mediators in all epochs and in all cultures. Hence for the structuralists, the more things change, the more they remain the same. One could therefore argue that structuralism is a synchronic form of Hegelian idealism, a stationary dialectic—a dialectic lacking movement in time and space, if such a thing is conceivable.

Will the Real Oppositions Please Stand Up

ALTHOUGH Lévi-Strauss (1963) has insisted that there is a method for finding the correct oppositions and mediations of which surface phenomena are transformations, the method is not very methodical, and is heir to all the ambiguities of Hegelian and Marxist dialectics discussed in the previous chapter. For the most part it consists of trying out progressively more remote and arcane analogies, based either on contrasts or similarities. The fact that one can get to underlying oppositions through concepts that have dissimilar meanings ("inversions"), and the fact that the final output can consist of anything that vaguely resembles an "opposition," make it virtually certain that structuralists will find "structures." But little scientific value can be assigned to the discovery of such "structures." The only means by which a structuralist statement can be tested is by finding similar (or dissimilar!) "structures" in the same or some other culture, and it is a foregone conclusion that with a modicum of ingenuity, corroborating analyses can be carried out in great profusion.

Part of the appeal of structuralism is precisely that it permits armchair anthropologists to work with collections of myths or kinship terminologies in libraries far removed from the live context in which the data were originally collected. "To discover hidden meanings is what structural analysis aims at" (Maquett, 1974:123). What can be more delightful than to discover hidden meanings that no one can dispute?

"What Does This Matter?"

I SHALL PROCEED in a moment to examine examples of structuralist theories drawn from the major lines of structuralist inquiry. Before doing so, let me consider the general objections structuralists have raised concerning the canons of empirical testability. Lévi-Strauss has repeatedly avowed a profound disdain for anthropologists who insist that structuralist models be tested for their relative ability to predict or retrodict empirical phenomena. On occasion he has even been moved to deny that structuralist models have any empirical significance: "Social structure . . . has nothing to do with the empirical reality but with models built up after it" (Lévi-Strauss, 1963:279). This indifference to empirical testing derives from a long-standing distinction in continental philosophy between the natural and human sciences. According to this tradition, human phenomena are not amenable to the kinds of lawful generalizations that are the goal of physics or chemistry. The collective conscience is to be explained by grasping its meanings, not by quantifying its relationship with other phenomena. Thus structuralism is not concerned with empirical proof but with "understanding." In the human sciences "no work can be scientific in the traditional sense." The charge that structuralism cannot be falsified by empirical procedures is dismissed as "completely senseless," because when one is dealing with culture, "nothing is falsifiable" (Lévi-Strauss, quoted in Rossi, 1974b:93).

If on occasion Lévi-Strauss avers a "slavish respect for concrete data" and claims that "anthropology is first of all an empirical science" (ibid.), on other occasions he proposes that empirical data are of small consequence, since his own thoughts are themselves evidence of the dialectic process, which constrains what other people think:

Let me say again that all the solutions put forward are not presented as being of equal value, since I myself have made a point of emphasizing the uncertainty of some of them; however, it would be hypocritical not to carry my thought to its logical conclusion. I therefore say in advance to possible critics: *what does this matter?* For if the final aim of anthropology is to contribute to a better knowledge of objectified thought and its mechanisms, it is in the last resort immaterial whether in this book the thought processes of the South American Indians take shape through the medium of my thoughts, or whether mine take place through the medium of theirs. What matters is that the human mind, regardless of the identity of those who happen to be giving it expression, should display an increasingly intelligible structure as a result of the doubly reflexive thought movement of two thought processes acting one upon the other, either of which can in turn provide the spark or tinder whose conjunction will shed light on both. (1969a:13; italics added)

Does it matter that "this book on myths is itself a kind of myth" (ibid.:6)? Does it matter that only those who practice structuralist thought know, "through intimate experience, that impression of plenitude its exercise brings, through which the mind feels it is truly communicating with the body" (Lévi-Strauss, 1971:619)?

Cultural materialists say that it does matter. For the "final aim of anthropology" is not what Lévi-Strauss says it is—not just the achievement of "a better knowledge of objectified thought and its mechanisms." Rather, it is the achievement of a scientific knowledge of the causes of the divergent and convergent evolutionary trajectories of sociocultural systems, which consist of behavior and the products of behavior as well as thoughts. As I pointed out in the discussion of Paul Feyerabend's brief for epistemological anarchy, the nature of one's understanding of sociocultural reality is a very serious matter. It is not something that ought to be lightly surrendered to the thought processes of those who equate their own imaginations with the thoughts, feelings, and activities of the rest of us. History shows that to treat as heroes people who abominate empirical reality is to risk destruction. "What does this matter?" If you do not wish to be held accountable for what you do in someone else's nightmares, you know what it matters (see pp. 22 and 324).

Elementary Structures of Kinship

LÉVI-STRAUSS first attracted the attention of the international anthropological community with his theories about varieties of kinship systems and modes of marriage. His book *The Elementary Structures of Kinship* remains an essential starting point for comparative studies of kinship systems. It organizes and minutely analyzes a vast range of phenomena. Nonetheless, it already exhibits in full bloom the shortcomings of the developed structuralist strategy. Although it claims to be "an introduction to a general theory of kinship systems" (xxiv), it does not offer an interpenetrating set of explanations of the divergent and convergent evolution of marriage or locality rules or kinship terminologies. While Lévi-Strauss sees some kinship systems as evolutionary emergents, he pays no attention to the nomothetic conditions under which the various structural types can be expected to evolve. At best, we are told why a system might evolve in one direction rather than another, but never why some did evolve in the structurally possible manner while others did not.

The grand theme of *The Elementary Structures of Kinship* is that all varieties of kinship and marriage systems are best understood as manifestations of the binary opposition between mine and yours, or "us" and "them." The mediator of this opposition is a gift, and the best mediator is the gift of women. All such gift giving is exchange, which requires a gift in return. All forms of marriage and kinship are therefore merely different expressions of exchange, in which groups of men bestow women as gifts upon other groups of men who reciprocate. Once a particular system has been shown to be logically assimilable to one or another variety of exchange, the author conducts us to another system, which in turn is shown to be still another minor or major variant of a rule for transferring women from one group to another.

Thus it is always the system of exchange that we find at the origin of rules of marriage. . . . Sometimes exchange appears as direct (as in the case of marriage with the bilateral cousin), sometimes as indirect. . . . Sometimes it functions within a total system . . . and at others it instigates the formation of an unlimited number of special systems and short cycles. . . . Sometimes exchange appears as a cash or short-term transaction . . . and at other times as a long-term transaction. Sometimes the exchange is explicit and at other times it is implicit. . . . Sometimes the exchange is closed, while sometimes it is open. . . . But no matter what form it takes, whether direct or indirect, general or special, immediate or deferred, explicit or implicit, closed or open, concrete or symbolic, it is exchange, always exchange, that emerges as the fundamental and common basis of all modalities of the institution of marriage. (478–479)

The kind of enlightenment that one achieves from realizing that it is "exchange, always exchange" typifies the structuralist sense of "understanding." Exchange is the "hidden meaning" of the surface forms of marital and kinship systems. One understands a kinship system when it is reduced to a particular type of exchange; and one understands exchange when it is reduced to a binary opposition striving for resolution: the opposition "mine: yours."

The emergence of symbolic thought must have required that women, like words, should be things that were exchanged . . . This was the only means of overcoming the contradiction by which the same woman was seen under two incompatible aspects: on the one hand, as the object of personal desire, thus exciting sexual and proprietal instincts; and, on the other, as the subject of the desire of others, and as seen as such, i.e., as the means of binding others through alliances with them. (496)

"Exchange, Always Exchange"?

NOTE THAT Lévi-Strauss simply assumes that women were always seen as the sex to be given away and received as gifts. This is tantamount to accepting male supremacy as a universal given. But male supremacy, as I pointed out in Chapter 4 is not universal, having arisen under definite conditions involving reproductive pressure and warfare. While Lévi-Strauss is correct in emphasizing the fact that women are exchanged far more often than men (virilocality is far more common than uxorilocality), we do not know that women are always seen in this light. Many paleotechnic hunter-gatherers have bilateral, ambilineal, and ambilocal organizations in which group membership is too fluid for the notion of exchange to apply. As was discussed in Chapter 4, strong unilocality is associated with advanced agriculturalists or pastoralists. Where there is frequent residence of married couples among both wife's relatives and husband's relatives, I doubt that marriage is seen as a gift of women from one group to another. In any event, Lévi-Strauss presents no evidence concerning what male and female participants actually "see."

A second point to be noted, even if one grants the general importance of marital exchange, is that incest taboos, exogamy, and reciprocity are not the *only* means of overcoming the "contradiction" between individual sexual desires and the sexual desires of others. Men and women can very easily think about resolving this "contradiction" by means of complete sexual communism. The fact that sexual communism rarely occurs is not proof that something in the structure of our *minds* prevents us from carrying it out. Rather, it suggests that certain adverse biological and infrastructural consequences flow from narrow endogamy, and certain positive consequences from marriage and exogamy under particular demographic and ecological conditions. But I do not wish to dwell on Lévi-Strauss's theory of incest because it is not the central preoccupation of *Elementary Structures of Kinship*. I wish to turn now to his peculiar notion that the principle of reciprocity underlies all systems of marriage, descent, and kinship nomenclature, for that is the central theme of his book. According to Lévi-Strauss, beneath all the contingencies and idiosyncrasies of social life, there is "exchange, always exchange." This "principle" is a creative, instrumental, active force, one immune to the vicissitudes of history. It is "always at work and always oriented in the same direction," using the matter which history places at its disposal to express itself:

The contrast, the apparent contradiction . . . between the functional permanence of systems of reciprocity, and the contingency of the institutional matter placed at their disposal by history, and moreover ceaselessly reshaped by it, is supplementary proof of the instrumentality of these systems. Whatever the changes, the same force [i.e., reciprocity] is always at work, and it is always to the same effect that it organizes the elements offered or abandoned to it. (1969b:76)

Although structuralists may claim it doesn't matter whether this theory can be tested or not, that doesn't mean cultural materialists should refrain from testing it. I contend not only that this is a testable theory but that it is clearly false and readily replaceable by a better theory, to wit: "systems of reciprocity" are the basis of marriage systems only in egalitarian societies. To the degree that a society is stratified into political and economically superordinate and subordinate groups, marriage systems function to prevent reciprocal exchange. Hence either the alleged principle of reciprocal exchange is nonuniversal, or it lacks the necessary strength to "reshape" or "organize the elements offered or abandoned to it" by a large proportion of the world's societies. That is, in conformity with the entire set of interpenetrating theories developed under the auspices of cultural materialism, marriage rules are determined by the conjunction of infrastructural variables, not by unconscious ideas about reciprocity or by the need to think of giving gifts in order to think about receiving them.

Restricted and Generalized Exchange

ACCORDING TO Lévi-Strauss, there are two basic forms of marriage exchange, both of which are equally supposed to reflect the operation of the principle of reciprocal exchange. First, there are systems of *restricted* exchange, in which if an A man marries a B woman, then a B man must be able to marry A's sister. And second, there are systems of *generalized* exchange, in which if an A man marries a B woman, a B man cannot marry A's sister, but must marry a woman from a third group, C. The Australian eight-section system discussed in Chapter 4 is an example of the A ⇄ B or restricted exchange type. I have no quarrel with the idea that this system can be represented as an attempt to reciprocate the transfer of women between groups. However, note that Lévi-Strauss's explanation as to why the Aranda (and other groups) have a restricted exchange system is counterfactual. His explanation rests on the notion that all groups with restricted exchange have "disharmonic regimes"—that is, they have either patrilocal residence and matrilineal descent or matrilocal residence and patrilineal descent. But as Francis Korn (1973:17–35) has shown in great detail, there is not the slightest evidence that the Aranda had the matrilineal moieties Lévi-Strauss attributes to them. Furthermore, Lévi-Strauss never states the conditions under which such "disharmonic regimes" occur. But I shall not dwell on these problems either, because as I have said, restricted exchange does conform to Lévi-Strauss's notion that all marriage systems are at bottom expressions of the principle of reciprocity. The remainder of this discussion deals only with generalized exchange.

The Problem of Generalized Exchange

IN THE NOTION that generalized exchange expresses the principle of reciprocity we meet the central weakness of Lévi-Strauss's analysis. On the surface at least, generalized exchange seems not to be a system of reciprocal exchange at all. Naturally, Lévi-Strauss claims that this is a mistaken impression, and that the principle of reciprocal exchange is always at work just as much here as in restricted exchange. This claim is based on the alleged existence of cycles which balance the exchange from A → B → C by a return flow.

Now not only does Lévi-Strauss claim that this return flow always takes place, but he further insists that it takes two forms, a *long* cycle and a *short* cycle. In the *long cycle*, A → B → C → A, an A man marries a B woman whose brother marries a C woman whose brother marries an A woman (the cycle can be expanded to include D, E, F, and so forth before it closes back upon A). In the *short cycle*, an A man marries

a B woman whose brother marries a C woman whose brother marries
an A woman in one generation; and then in the next generation, a C
man marries a B woman whose brother marries an A woman whose
brother marries a C woman: $C \leftarrow A \leftarrow B \leftarrow C$; $A \rightarrow B \rightarrow C \rightarrow A$.

Lévi-Strauss points out that the difference between restricted exchange and the long and short cycles of generalized exchange embodies
the logical implications of marriage with different kinds of cross-cousins.

In restricted exchange, a man can marry his mother's brother's
daughter or his father's sister's daughter. This is the *symmetrical* form
of cross-cousin marriage.

In generalized exchange, cross-cousin marriage is *asymmetrical*—
i.e., restricted to one or the other of the cross-cousins for both the long
and short cycle. In the long cycle, mother's brother's daughter is preferred. This is called *preferential matrilateral cross-cousin marriage*. In
the short cycle, father's sister's daughter is preferred. This is called
preferential patrilateral cross-cousin marriage. The relationship between the long and short cycles and their asymmetrical marriage rule
is shown below:

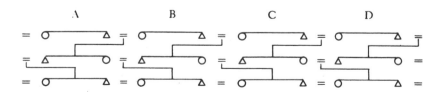

Long cycle, matrilateral (mother's brother's daughter) marriage.

Short cycle, patrilateral (father's sister's daughter) marriage.

Cycles in the Sky

ALTHOUGH BOTH forms of asymmetrical marriage are relatively uncommon, the matrilateral variety occurs much more frequently than the patrilateral variety. Why should this be so? Lévi-Strauss tries to use the notion of exchange to explain the difference. The long cycle is "better" than the short cycle because it represents "continuous exchange" while the other represents "discontinuous exchange":

> What is meant by this? Instead of constituting an overall system . . . marriage with the father's sister's daugther is incapable of attaining a form other than that of a multitude of small closed systems, juxtaposed one to the other, without ever being able to realize an overall structure. (1969b:445)

> If, then, in the final analysis, marriage with the father's sister's daughter is less frequent than that with the mother's brother's daughter, it is because the latter not only permits but favors a better integration of the group. . . . (Ibid.:448–449)

Before showing that these claims remain either without empirical evidence or in overt conflict with such evidence as does exist, let me comment in a preliminary way on the assumption that what is good for the integration of the group governs the form of marriage. This assumption makes sense only in an imaginary dematerialized world of Platonic structures. It does not make sense in relation to the material conditions underlying the development of sharply defined descent groups. As I explained in Chapter 4, the greater the intensity of agricultural production, the greater the likelihood of unilineality. Sibs and lineages reflect a growing concern with claims for and counterclaims against permanent forms of property and wealth. It is a travesty of the evolutionary process leading to social stratification and the state to picture unilinear descent groups as functioning to enhance solidarity when in fact they are the tangible expression of a growing lack of solidarity caused by the struggle over increasingly scarce resources.

As for the empirical basis of the structuralist model, no societies have been found in which matrilateral marriage can be said to "realize an overall structure." Although cycles like A → B → C → A do occur, they rarely involve every member of the community. Instead, there are several such cycles, as in the following diagram:

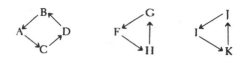

This situation certainly cannot be described as an "overall structure" even if women are always given away in the same direction. But to make matters worse, the best empirical examples of long cycles—those found among the Purum of eastern Manipur—frequently give and take women in direct exchange.

Charles Ackerman (1964, 1965) was the first to point out that there were numerous violations of the matrilateral rule among the Purum.

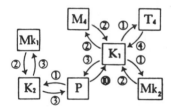

Purum patrilineages involved in direct exchange (D. White, 1973:405). Numbers in circles refer to number of marriages, and arrows show the direction in which women moved.

Although Ackerman has been criticized for exaggerating the discrepancy between the asymmetric rule and the actual practice of marriage (Geoghegan and Kay, 1964; Wilder, 1971), the crux of the issue is not whether practice and the rule show a relatively high degree of conformity, but rather whether the degree of conformity is sufficient to support the contention that matrilateral asymmetric alliances are more solidary than patrilateral alliances. Rodney Needham (1971:lxxix) urged those who "with their insidious talk . . . have presented a sorry and deteriorating exhibition from a subject that is supposed to be a learned discipline" to "seriously apply themselves to the comprehension of the ethnographic evidence—work before talk" (ibid.:lxxx). The proper assignment, however, is to think before one works. No amount of counting and recounting of

Purum marriages can disguise the fact that the Purum do not have a system in which women are etically exchanged by descent groups in only one direction. The ethnographic data refer to the existence of twelve subsibs or lineages. Seven of these engage in two-way exchanges (see the figure on page 177). In reckoning the numerical significance of this departure from Lévi-Strauss's model, I reject statistical manipulations that would count only the number of women in these seven groups who have been transferred in the "wrong" direction. Once two groups, A and B, are observed to practice direct exchange A $\rightleftarrows$ B, the "right" direction of the exchange cannot be read off automatically from the balance of the exchange at the moment of observation. Thus even if the balance stands at 10 to 3 (K1 $\frac{3}{10}$ P), we have no right to assume that three marriages are in the "wrong" direction and ten are in the "right" direction. Unless there is some independent way of ascertaining the "right" direction, the conclusion that the larger number represents the "right" direction is tautological —an item of faith already included in the theory. As soon as one marriage takes place in both directions, both groups will contain mother's brother's daughters (actual and classified); hence it becomes possible for members of either group to conform with the rule of matrilateral prescription by marrying in either direction.

One way to decide which marriages are right and which are wrong is to elicit that information from the participants. Needham, however, is mired in the general structuralist conviction that mental structures have a locus outside of the individual minds of the actors. So he was never in much danger of doing anything so drastic, even if the original Purum informants had not passed away by the time he had begun to work on his scheme. We are therefore left with no choice but to regard each marriage that occurs in pairs of groups that engage in two-way exchanges of women as a bit of evidence disconfirming Lévi-Strauss's concept of a long cycle. Thus we can say that from the point of view of the total number of descent groups, 58 percent make both restricted and generalized alliances; and from the point of view of the total number of marriage acts (each marriage involving a choice by a man and a woman), 66 out of 252 do not conform to the asymmetric model for reasons already stated. Notice should also be taken of two additional anomalies: lineage K_2 gave three women to lineage K_1 (not diagrammed). This has usually been counted as disconfirming evidence on the grounds that it involves an exchange within the same class (K), but I don't regard it as such because it is the subsib which must be treated as the descent groups required by Lévi-Strauss's model. However, eight marriage acts must be removed from the total, because the subsib in question, M_3, received 4 wives from T_1 but gave no wives to anyone (also not diagrammed). Therefore we are not entitled to conclude that M_3 is or is not part of a circulating connubium. Thus 66 out of 274, or 24 percent of the marriages, cannot be reconciled with Lévi-Strauss's model. Now although 24 percent two-way marriages may not seem like an unreasonable departure from the one-way marriages predicted by the matrilateral cross-cousin preference rule (what it does to Needham's insistence that he is dealing with absolute prescription rather than mere preference is another matter) but it is certainly fatal to the idea that the Purum are a good example of a society held together by asymmetrical, "long-cycle" exchanges. True enough, there are cycles of the type predicted in the model among the Purum; but these cycles do not constitute a system that "realizes an overall structure" of descent groups in the A → B → C → A manner called for by Lévi-Strauss's model. Moreover, these cycles exist side by side with a form of direct exchange in more than half of the subsibs.

In all of this we must separate out Rodney Needham's interest in the Purum from the larger issue of Lévi-Strauss's explanation of the greater frequency of matrilateral preference. Needham seems to think that he has to defend the concept of matrilateral prescriptions from an attack launched by anthropologists denying any empirical validity to the kinship structures based on the matrilateral rule. He seems genuinely puzzled by the objections "lodged against the idea that societies also exist in which the category of spouse is unilaterally prescribed" (ibid.:lxxx). I for my part have never doubted that such rules exist, nor that they are related in some way to etic phenomena. What I object to is Lévi-Strauss's explanation of matrilateral preference in terms of the superior solidarity of the long cycle. (I have also disparaged Needham's attempt to distinguish prescription from preference—but since Lévi-Strauss [1969b: xxxi ff] himself thinks this distinction is useless, it obviously has nothing to do with the thrust of my argument against the main point of *Elementary Structures;* viz, the importance of reciprocal exchange for all marriage systems.)

Needham's student William Wilder has attempted to restore the Purum to their status as a prime case of the long cycle by a stratagem that inadvertently further subverts Lévi-Strauss's explanation of the matrilateral preference. According to Wilder, the subsibs are not necessarily the minimal groups actually establishing alliances through marriage. He suggests that when a wrong marriage takes place it is not wrong at all; rather, it may simply mean that there are additional subdivisions that have broken away from their subsib (localized perhaps in different villages) and have embarked upon a new circulating connubium whose women move in what was the wrong direction before the split. Thus Wilder estimates that there are actually about twenty village-localized segments in three Purum villages, and that there are no real exceptions to the matrilateral rule. While this saves Needham's distinction between prescriptive and preferential systems, it leaves the structuralist theory of matrilateral marriage in dire straits. Wilder's model calls for a very high rate of fissioning among the Purum descent groups—fissioning objectified in the reversed circulations of sib, subsib, and sublineage and in the drastically unequal populations of the several units (K, for example, has 55 married members, whereas M_3 has only 4). If, as Wilder says, "Needham and Leach have both shown in practice alliance groups are constantly forming through lineage segmentation and 'deviant' marriages" (quoted in Needham, 1971: lxxi), then what is left of the contention that this system of exchange establishes solidary relationships and that reciprocal exchange lies behind all marriage systems? Why should a mere 300 people split themselves up into twenty or more different marital exchange and alliance groups if matrilateral cycles are such a boon for solidarity?

Thus the notion that reciprocity underlies matrilateral cross-cousin marriage systems must be abandoned. This will become forcefully evident in a moment when I take up the relationship between matrilateral marriage and the superordination and subordination of descent groups and offer an alternative theory that specifies the material conditions under which matrilateral systems arise. But first let me turn to another fact that cannot be adequately explained by Lévi-Strauss's imaginary long and short cycles.

Descent and Asymmetrical Cousin Marriage

IT HAS BEEN known for many years that most of the societies practicing the patrilateral form of cousin marriage have matrilineal descent; while most of the societies which practice the matrilateral form have patrilineal descent. Although originally ignored by Lévi-

MARRIAGE

		Patrilateral	Matrilateral
DESCENT	Patrilineal	2	22
	Matrilineal	4	5

The relationship between descent and asymmetrical marriage (cross-cousin preference).

Strauss, this correlation is explained in the second edition of *The Elementary Structures of Kinship* in the following manner:

> . . . matrilateral and patrilateral marriage are both consistent with the two modes of descent, although patrilateral marriage is more likely in a regime with matrilineal descent (because of its structural instability which makes it prefer short cycles), and matrilateral marriage more likely in a patrilineal regime (which more easily allows the cycles to be lengthened) . . . (1969b:241)

The idea behind this is that since matrilineal systems tend to be unstable, they cannot invest in the long cycle as a means of achieving marital reciprocity (it's too risky), whereas being more stable, patrilineal societies can invest in the long cycle. This argument is specious. If the formal structures of reciprocity, consciously or unconsciously apprehended by the human mind, "constitute the indestructible basis of marriage institutions" (ibid.:440), and if reciprocity ceaselessly reshapes the materials of history (see above), one would expect matrilineal societies to jump over backwards in their haste to institute long cycle marriages and thus enjoy the benefits of the "better integration of the group"!

Why Patrilateral Marriage?

AN ATTRACTIVE alternative awaits if one abandons the 'fixation that reciprocity lies at the heart of every marriage system and begins instead to think about the fact that males and females often seek special benefits and privileges objectified in power differences and unequal access to resources at one another's expense. The association of patrilateral cross-cousin preferences (which should be seen as a bias against matrilateral unions) with matrilineal descent follows directly from the fact that such a preference amounts to a cryptic form of patrilineal descent insinuated into a matrilineal pattern. A glance at the diagram in the figure below will clarify what I mean. Here we see Lévi-Strauss's short cycle embellished, with black marks indicating membership in a unilineal group based on descent exclusively through females:

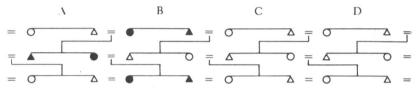

Matrilineal Descent, Patrilateral Marriage

Observe that after the second generation of patrilateral cross-cousin marriage, grandfather's grandchildren through his son are members of grandfather's own matrigroup, even though descent is based exclusively on females. Here then is a simple reassertion of father's control over male descendants in a matrilineal system. In other words, what Lévi-Strauss calls short cycles may not be cycles at all —not manifestations of exchange, but manifestations of the struggle between men and women to control labor and resources. Whenever patrilateral marriage occurs between matrilineal descent groups, a patrilineal bias has been successfully expressed in a matrilineal system. No cycles are needed to explain why this should be a recurrent pattern (just as no marriage cycles are needed to explain why avunculocality occurs more frequently than matrilocality in matrilineal systems—see p. 98).

The cogency of this alternative can be demonstrated by examining the reverse situation. What does patrilateral cross-cousin marriage accomplish in a system which is already thoroughly patrilineal? Does it strengthen or protect male interests? No, on the contrary, it would amount to a strengthening of the capacity of women to control labor and resources through their female descendants, for it would place a woman's daughter's children in the woman's own patrigroup, despite descent based exclusively on males.

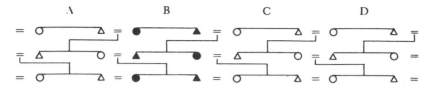

Patrilineal Descent, Patrilateral Marriage

This arrangement thus amounts to a dilution or subversion of the continuity of control through males. And I do not mean some abstract contradiction between emic notions of matrilineal or patrilineal descent, but rather the etic management of land, labor, property, and other tangible assets. Hence patrilateral marriage seldom occurs in patrilineal systems for essentially the same reason that patrilineality is more common than matrilineality; that polygynists outnumber polyandrists; that men exchange women in marriage; and that males in pre-state societies dominate war and politics (see pp. 90ff).

Why Matrilateral Marriage?

ALTHOUGH MATRILATERAL cross-cousin marriage represents for Lévi-Strauss the quintessence of generalized exchange and hence is intelligible as a form of reciprocity, he never supplies any explanation for why some societies but not others should have this particular form of reciprocity. The notion that reciprocity lies behind all marriage systems is a definite handicap in the attempt to explain the origin of matrilateral asymmetry. It is much more consistent with the ethnographic facts to view the matrilateral preference as a manifestation of the struggle between lineages (as distinct from the struggle between males and females in the patrilateral case) for control over land, labor, and resources. Matrilateral marriage, far from promoting solidarity, reflects a breakdown in reciprocity, and a movement toward differential control over production and reproduction by hierarchized descent groups. Unlike patrilateral or symmetrical marriage, matrilateral marriage divides a community up into descent groups that stand to each other as wife-givers to wife-takers. To be compensated for the "gift" of their sisters and daughters, the wife-givers do not wait upon the completion of the cycle A → B → C → A. Rather, they almost always demand immediate compensation in the form of bride price or bride service or a combination of both. This means that any group managing to raise and marry off more daughters than another group is in a position to concentrate wealth and labor power to a greater extent than other groups. On the average, the larger the descent group, the larger the number of daughters. The more daughters, the greater the concentration of dependent labor power and wealth in the form of sons-in-law and bride price. Large prosperous groups have no difficulty in meeting their obligations both as wife-givers and wife-takers. Smaller and less prosperous groups, however, soon become in effect dependents of the larger ones, and as their fortunes decline, their married men may even take up residence among the dominant wife-givers (reside uxorilocally) as permanent second-class citizens (cf. Fried, 1967:206). Additional stresses develop within the less prosperous groups as senior and junior sons compete for the limited number of wives who can be obtained through bride price. The dependent subgroups will therefore tend to fission and to enter into new alliances that release them from the threat of permanent subordination and bondage (accounting for the frequent violation of the direction of marriage and high rate of fission among the Purum, as discussed above).

This complex process has nothing to do with a deep structure (collective consciousness) forcing history into a particular mold; rather, it reflects the emergence of advanced big man/chieftain hierarchies under definite conditions of production and reproduction. The rule of asymmetrical matrilateral cross-cousin marriage is not the cause of this emergent phenomenon; rather, asymmetrical marriage is merely a mechanism for facilitating the concentration of productive and reproductive forces in the hands of certain groups at the expense of others.

Lévi-Strauss is well aware of the fact that the matrilateral system of "reciprocity" appears to be connected with incipient stratification. Indeed, like Edmund Leach, he recognizes that among the Kachin of Burma: "matrilateral cross-cousin marriage is . . . a correlate of a system of patrilineal lineages rigged into a class hierarchy" (Leach, quoted in Lévi-Strauss, 1969b:240). However, Lévi-Strauss attributes the correlation of matrilateral marriage with class hierarchy to the influence of the imaginary "formal structure," the marriage cycle. He claims that the structure of the long cycle is the cause of the tendency toward stratification! "This dichotomy [between wife-givers and wife-takers] is not the result of a political system. Rather it is the cause . . . " (ibid.). Lévi-Strauss goes on to imply that the marriage rules are also in some sense the cause of the evolution from relatively "unstable" feudal relationships to the more "stable" relationships of full-blown caste systems. What, then, is the cause of the dichotomy between wife-givers and wife-takers, or rather of the role of matrilateral cross-cousin marriage that lies behind this dichotomy? According to Lévi-Strauss, the establishment of the matrilateral rule represents an attempt on the part of patrilineal groups to resolve "a state of tension between paternal and maternal lineages" (241). Matrilateral asymmetrical marriage "characterizes lineages which seek, in alliance (i.e., in recognition of cognates), a means of affirming their position as agnates." In other words, the marrying-down of women among the Kachin is a result of a "state of tension" not between a superordinate group seeking to control labor and resources and a subordinate group threatened with the specter of exploitation at the hands of an incipient ruling class, but between the structural principles of paternal and maternal descent. The world is created by the struggle of principles, not the struggle of people. This too is the legacy of Hegel.

Hypogyny, Hypergyny, and Political Economy

LÉVI-STRAUSS's emphasis upon "structures" systematically blocks off the path to an explanation of why in weakly stratified societies such as the Kachin and Purum the superordinate lineages give women to subordinate lineages, while in more highly stratified societies such as those in India and feudal Europe, the elite castes take women from below. This problem was discussed in Chapters 4 and 5. When a superordinate group gives its women in marriage to subordinate groups (hypogyny), it does so not because it has an asymmetrical rule of marriage but because it is using marital alliances to consolidate or increase its control over its subordinates. The asymmetrical rule of marriage is an instrument of political economy. Thus in the case of the Kachin, as Lévi-Strauss himself notes, the chiefly lineages give women to their subordinates and receive free labor and cattle in return as bride price (ibid.:238).

The universal tendency in all stratified systems, however, is for superordinates to dispense with wife-giving to subordinates (hypergyny)* whenever the overall police-military situation permits them to extract surpluses and conscript labor by means of purely political ma-

---

*That is to say, marrying up from the woman's husband's point of view—marriage with a "higher" woman.

chinery. The emergence of asymmetrical woman-taking (hypogyny) by superordinate strata expresses the developed capacity for exploitation, not the triumph of one "structural principle" over another. As explained in the discussion of infanticide in Chapter 5, with hypogyny, the superordinate group continues to receive payment in the form of dowry, but now it also gets the "gift" of lower-ranking women, who are used as secondary wives or concubines (cf. Pillai, 1975; Dickeman, 1975a, 1975b). In unstratified systems, the superordinate lineages gain control over subordinate males by giving them women; in stratified systems, the superordinate lineages control subordinate males firmly enough to exploit their labor *and* their women without giving anything in return. Actually "hypergyny" and "hypogyny" are sterile formalisms that must be interpreted in the context of inheritance. For the crux of the matter is not whether men marry up or down, but whether their children are able to share in the wealth and politico-economic machinery of the superordinate group they marry into or out of. In the Kachin case, the children of hypergynous marriages between lineages are disenfranchised, because inheritance is unilineal, through men not women, just as the children of hypogynous marriages between full-blown Indian castes are disenfranchised.

What the structural analysis of these phenomena leaves wholly unexamined—indeed, deliberately blocks off—is the fact that the marriage systems of advanced stratified societies are not primarily systems of exchange at all, but systems of no exchange—that is, primarily endogamous systems that function to concentrate wealth and consolidate and maximize politico-economic control. Wretched legions of poor and exploited castes cry out against the structuralist sophistry which would have us believe that the reciprocal exchange of women lies at the basis of stratified marriage systems. In fully developed state societies, when the highest-ranking superordinates enter into alliances, it is always with groups, families, or individuals who are themselves superordinates to most of the population. While one can speak of the royal houses of Europe making alliances through the exchange of women (and men!), to lose sight of the fact that royalty married royalty is to miss the basic significance of these marriages. Endogamy continues to be the dominant marriage form among ethnic, racial, and religious groupings within modern state societies. How can "exchange, always exchange" explain the marriage system of endogamous groups whose marriage rule, as in the case of Europeans and Africans in South Africa, or Moslems and Christians in Lebanon, is "don't exchange"?

Elementary versus Complex Systems

LÉVI-STRAUSS claims that he has thus far only concerned himself with "elementary structures"—i.e., marriage systems that have both negative and positive kinship stipulations (rules specifying not only which relatives cannot be married but also which genealogically defined relatives should or must be married). A promised work dealing with complex systems—those which have only negative rules—never appeared. But it is becoming increasingly evident that the complex/elementary distinction is an obstacle to the development of even idealist theories of marriage. The notion of an "elementary" system is based on the stereotype that band and village peoples decide whom they will marry exclusively on the basis of kinship relationships. As Alice Kasakoff (1974) has shown, in small societies it's hard to separate out preferences based on kinship from preferences based on rules relating to other dimensions of social life, such as residence, status, transmission of property, and politics. Because these factors are also operative in any etic behavioral context, Lévi-Strauss's "elementary" models are virtually worthless for predicting actual marriages.

In fact, like the conscious models from which they were derived, his structures serve to mask the realities of kinship. The structures that do characterize actual marriage systems will therefore have to contain concepts that are the opposite of Lévi-Strauss's: endogamy, not exogamy; bilaterality not unilineality; wealth and status to be gained, not exchanges which come out even. (Ibid: 164)

To this I would add that the realities of "complex" marriage systems cannot be understood if we fail to realize that modern societies continue to have both negative and positive marriage rules based on "kinship." Membership in minorities, ethnic groups, castes, and "races" is wholly or partially dependent upon culturally defined descent, and these groups usually prefer endogamous unions. Both of these criticisms simply help to reinforce the conclusion that the structuralist approach to marriage and kinship lacks an interpenetrating set of nomothetic theories relating kinship and marriage to domestic, political, and infrastructural variables. Although the cultural materialist alternatives remain highly tentative, they have the advantage of parsimony, clarity, and logical coherence. They offer in prospect at least the possibility of explaining in causal terms why particular societies have their specific types of domestic ideologies. In structuralism, however, the search for historical causality is never confronted squarely, is deliberately held in abeyance, while the search for dubious mental commonalities in divergent cultures is given free reign.

The Raw, the Cooked, and the Half-Baked

LEAVING THE FIELD of kinship, I turn now to other aspects of the corpus of structuralist theory. One intriguing application of structuralist principles concerns the mental components of digestion. Lévi-Strauss is struck by the idea that meals have a structure. Can it be that gastronomic patterns reflect thoughts rather than appetites? Can it be that our meals consist of certain foods not so much because they are good to eat but because they are good to think? Yes, says Lévi-Strauss. People select foods for the messages they convey rather than for the calories and proteins they contain. All cultures unconsciously send out messages coded in the medium of foods and in the modes of preparation of foods.

The basic contrasts in this culinary language are those between cooked, raw, and rotted foods. Within the category of cooked foods, the main structural components communicate messages about whether the product is on the side of nature or on the side of culture. Boiled food, Lévi-Strauss argues, is on the cultural side, because boiling requires a container and a barrier of water between the food and the fire, whereas roasted food is on the side of nature, because roasting brings food and flame into direct contact. Hence the formula:

roasted : boiled :: nature : culture

With this formula on hand, Lévi-Strauss purports to explain why roasted food is served to guests, while boiled foods are served to close kinsmen. Guests are strangers and hence are associated with nature, but close kin are at the center of cultural life.

The boiled can most often be ascribed to what might be called an "endo-cuisine," prepared for domestic use, destined to a small closed group, while the roasted belongs to "exo-cuisine," that which one offers to guests. Formerly in France, boiled chicken was for the family meal, whole roasted meat was for the banquet. . . . (1966:589)

Not satisfied with reducing the complex question of how guests are entertained in different etic infrastructural and structural contexts to a universal mental formula, Lévi-Strauss goes on to make a seemingly brilliant prediction about cannibalism. Sometimes cannibalism involves eating enemy strangers, and at other times it involves eating one's own relatives. Kin are associated with culture, so they should be boiled; strangers are associated with nature, so they should be roasted. (Note that this dialectical logic could just as easily have led to the opposite conclusion!)

While still an undergraduate at Harvard, Paul Shankman tested these predictions. What Shankman found was that in a sample of sixty cannibal societies, seventeen boiled while twenty roasted. Six both boiled and roasted. Of the sixty societies, twenty-nine were exo-cannibals, twenty-six were endo-cannibals, and five were both exo- and endo-cannibals. Did the exo-cannibals do more roasting? No. About 34 percent of both groups were roasters. Did the endo-cannibals do more boiling? No. On the contrary. Over half of the exos were boilers while only two of the endos were boilers. But Shankman made an even more damaging discovery: of the societies using only one method of cooking, neither roasting nor boiling was the most common preference. Instead, they used a different method, not considered at all by Lévi-Strauss—namely, baking. Finally, a third of the societies prepare one kind of person—relative or enemy—in more than one kind of way. And different groups within the same culture prepare the same kind of person in different ways. "The most obvious finding of this study is that Lévi-Strauss' exclusive focus on the roasted and the boiled has been spoiled by the natives who have discovered a veritable smorgasbord of ways of preparing people" (Shankman, 1969:61).

In setting forth a defense of the raw, the cooked, and the rotted, Edmund Leach (1970:28) admits that some readers "might begin to suspect that the whole argument was an elaborate joke." But the theory that foods are selected primarily because they are good to think rather than because they are good to eat is not funny. It mocks the hungry living and dead by transforming the struggle for subsistence into a game of mental imagery. The idea that cooking is primarily a language is food for thought only among those who have never had to worry about having enough to eat.

Anthropologists concerned with the question of why people eat certain foods cannot reasonably ignore the infrastructural constraints that determine the costs and benefits of particular diets. Beyond that, given a set of comestible substances, modes of preparing foods primarily reflect the availability of containers, ovens, fuels, and cooking utensils. For example, the Asiatic tradition of rapid frying of small chopped morsels developed in relationship to fuel shortages in heavily populated deforested regions. Where large animals are to be prepared for communal feasts, roasting the animal whole over an open fire does away with the need for cutting portions out of raw meat and for the construction of large ovens or vats (provided there is enough wood available). What people eat and how they prepare it is also clearly influenced by domestic routines. For example, cow dung is a preferred fuel in India because it provides a cool, long-lasting flame that enables peasant women to work in the fields while the food cooks itself. To explain food habits, priority must be given to material conditions, to messages in the stomach and intestines of hungry human beings, rather than to cute thoughts in the heads of well-fed idealists.

Structuralism and the Pig

THE IDEA that meals are messages has been an inspiration to many anthropologists. One case in particular has become well-known. It is Mary Douglas's attempt to explain why the book of Leviticus prohibits the consumption of pork and other animals. The pig was tabooed, claims Douglas, because it had an anomalous status in the zoological taxonomy of the ancient Hebrews. Animals with such a status are dirty because universally, anything that defies classification or is out of place in an ordered view of the world evokes feelings of defilement or pollution. "Dirt is matter out of place" (Douglas, 1966: 35). Therefore animals that were out of place in the Hebrew zoological taxonomy were dirty. Why was the pig out of place? The pig was out of place because the Israelites defined proper livestock as animals with cloven feet who chewed the cud. Since the pig has cloven feet but doesn't chew the cud, it is dirty. "I suggest that originally the sole reason for its [the pig's] being counted as unclean is its failure as a wild boar to get into the antelope class, and that in this it is on the same footing [sic] as the camel or hyrax" (ibid.:55). In other words, the explanation for the pig taboo is to be found in the structuralist formula:

pig : livestock :: disorder : order :: dirty : clean :: nature : culture

Let us accept the idea that the pig is unclean because it can't be placed in the category of livestock. What accounts for the fact that livestock are defined in such a way as to exclude the pig (cf. Bulmer, 1967:21)? Douglas (1972) tried to answer this question by expanding her discussion of the inner logic of the biblical proscriptions. Two new components of cleanliness were added: animals and birds that hunt or eat carrion are unclean (because God commands Israel not to shed blood); and if those who belong to an endogamous group avoid others as unclean in marriage and sex, they will regard the animals others keep as unsuitable for eating:

On mature reflection . . . I can now see that the pig . . . carries the odium of multiple pollution. First it pollutes because it defies the classification of ungulates. Second it pollutes because it eats carrion. Third it pollutes because it is reared (and presumably as prime pork) by non-Israelites. (Douglas, 1972: 79)

This adjustment merely trebles the logical and empirical difficulties of the first explanation. Even if one accepts the chain of analogies leading from the uncleanliness of human beings who shed blood to the uncleanliness of animals that shed blood, and thence to those that eat carrion, nothing about the pig makes it more likely to eat corpses than dogs (which do not pollute upon touch)—or than goats, for that matter, which when given a chance will eat anything. Furthermore, among the pig lovers of New Guinea, the pollution acquired by shedding human blood, far from rendering the pig unclean, could only be removed by slaughtering and eating pigs! (Rappaport, 1967:205–207). And what are we to make of the Egyptian and Sumerian restrictions on the pig, which arise presumably in conjunction with a markedly different structure of mythic and ritual components long before the Israelites formulated their own religion? More difficulties assault us as we ponder the third principle. If the pig pollutes because it is raised and eaten by foreigners and enemies, then why weren't cows, sheep, and goats regarded as unclean? Didn't any of Israel's enemies raise cows, sheep, and goats? (Of course, they all did.) Worse still, many of these foreigners also regarded the pig as unclean! Douglas says that in tabooing the pig the Israelites were safeguarding themselves from marrying foreigners: "An Israelite who betrothed a foreigner might have been liable to be offered a feast of pork" (Douglas, 1972:79). But the Israelites were frequently the neighbors of people who were as unlikely to eat pork as they were.

Cultural Materialist Alternatives

THE STRUCTURALIST approach to animal taboos is unable to escape the constrictive embrace of a tautology: the pig is anomalous because it is anomalous in a taxonomic and ideological system in which it is anomalous. (Just as the Aztecs ate their prisoners for "religious motives"—see Chapter 11.) What we want to know is why the taxonomic system is set up in such a way as to render the pig anomalous, since there obviously is no universal reason why pigs are not good to think as well as to eat. The only way out of this tautology is to relate the ideological elements to variable infrastructures at the etic behavioral culture/nature interface.

It is true that the pig had an anomalous emic status for the ancient Israelites (as well as for many other ancient and modern peoples of the Near and Middle East). But the source of this anomalous status is not the binary code of an arcane mental calculus; rather, it is the practical and mundane cost-benefit of raising pigs under marginal or inappropriate infrastructural conditions.

Unlike most of the creatures whose flesh is forbidden in Leviticus, the pig is a domesticated beast. Hence it brings with it the presumption of great utility. But unlike the other interdicted domestic species, it was domesticated exclusively as a source of meat. The pig's utility resides primarily in its flesh. It can't be milked, it doesn't catch mice, it can't herd other animals, it can't be ridden, it can't pull a plow, and it can't carry a cargo. On the other hand, as a supplier of meat the pig is unrivaled; it is one of the most efficient converters of carbohydrates to protein and fat in the animal kingdom. For example, the pig is almost twice as efficient as cattle in this regard (NRC, 1975:116). Moreover, the Middle East was one of the earliest—if not the earliest—centers of domestication of the pig. There is even some evidence that the pig was used for sacrifice in the Levant prior to the appearance of the Israelites. The pig continued to be eaten during the Bronze Age (c. 2100 B.C.), and on into biblical times. According to the New Testament, Jesus cast out devils into swine kept by certain villagers. Even today some pigs are raised in the forested areas of northern Galilee and Lebanon (Epstein, 1971, vol. II:349–350; Ducos, 1968, 1969).

The pig was originally a creature of forests, river banks, and the edges of swamps. It is physiologically maladapted to high temperatures and direct sunlight because it is unable to regulate its body temperature without external sources of moisture (it can't sweat) (Mount, 1968). It cannot subsist on grass (unlike the ruminants). Its original domestication therefore took place during a period when extensive forests covered the hilly flanks of the Taurus and Zagros mountains. From 7,000 B.C. onward, however, the spread and intensification of neolithic mixed farming and herding economies converted millions of acres of forests to grasslands and grasslands to deserts. R. O. Whyte (1961:76) estimates that the forests of Anatolia were reduced from 70 percent to 13 percent of the total surface area between 5,000 B.C. and the recent past. Only a fourth of the Caspian shorefront forest remains, a half of the mountain humid forest; a fifth to a sixth of the oak and juniper forests of the Zagros; only one-twentieth of the juniper forests of the Elburz and Khorassan ranges. The regions that suffered most were precisely those that were taken over by pastoralists. Throughout the history of this region agriculture contracted as the desert expanded. In northern Syria and Iraq prehistoric settlements outnumber historic settlements by five to one; population declined between 2500 B.C. and the onset of intensive irrigation about five hundred years later. "The bald mountains and foothills of the Mediterranean littoral, the Anatolian plateau, and Iran stand as stark witnesses of millennia of uncontrolled utilization" (ibid)

Areas suitable for raising pigs on natural forage therefore became more and more restricted. Increasingly, pigs would have to be fed grains as supplements, rendering them directly competitive with human beings; their costs would increase due to the need to provide artificial shade and moisture. And yet they would continue to be a tempting source of protein and fat.

Pastoral nomads never rear pigs because pigs cannot be herded over long distances in arid grasslands: pigs can't live on grass and can't swim across rivers. Seminomadic groups, who in more humid zones *can* rear pigs, would be especially likely to develop strong explicit sacred prohibitions against both eating and handling pigs, as would settled farmers in regions that had undergone deforestation, erosion, and desiccation. Both kinds of groups would find it tempting to rear the pig for short-time benefits, but the practice would become extremely costly and maladaptive as it intensified. Total interdiction by appeal to sacred sanctions is a predictable outcome in situations where the immediate temptations are great, but the ultimate costs are high, and where the calculation of cost-benefits by individuals may lead to ambiguous conclusions (see p. 81).

This theory takes precedent over Mary Douglas's because it explains why one particular valuable animal gained an anomalous ideological status not only among the Israelites but among the Babylonians, Egyptians, and pre-Islamic Arabs,* whereas it was not given an anomalous status in forested areas such as Europe and pre-Islamic Southeast Asia, Indonesia, and Oceania, nor in temperate-zone China. (See Harris [1977a] for a discussion of the Chinese pig complex.)

Alland's Critique

ALEXANDER ALLAND (1975:67) has defended Mary Douglas and challenged my explanation on the ground that "taboos for nonuse" are ecologically superfluous, meaning that if pigs were an impractical source of meat, there would be no need for tabooing them.

Simplicity demands the hypothesis that experience within a particular environment will lead to conscious or unconscious adaptive choices that do not require taboo. The only requirement is that there be a stated (or even unstated) rule in the culture that a resource not be used. To require a taboo on an animal which is ecologically destructive is cultural overkill. Why use pigs if they are not useful in a stated context?

In rebuttal, first let me say that the distinction between "taboo for use and taboo for nonuse" is meaningless. In an ecological systems context, any taboo for nonuse is in some sense a taboo for use. In prohibiting one species, the taboo encourages the use of another. Thus proscription of the pig was prescription of the cow, sheep, and goat. What must be considered are the direct and indirect cost-benefits of the interdicted species in the total system of production.

Second, Alland's "simplicity demand" runs counter to the basic principles of scientific ecology. It would be reasonable only if ecosystems were static and if adaptation was an on/off binary decision. But adaptation is an evolutionary process in which many major and minor changes take place simultaneously. Just as individuals are ambivalent and ambiguous about their own thoughts and emotions, so whole

---

*Diener and Robkin (1978) dispute the importance of ecological conditions in the explanation of the Islamic pig taboo. They emphasize the importance of the cattle-grain complex to the Islamic ruling class on the mistaken notion that their explanation is antithetical to cultural materialist principles.

populations are ambivalent and ambiguous about aspects of the adaptive processes in which they are participating. (Think of the pros and cons of offshore oil drilling and the debate about the taboos on abortion). It is not cultural overkill for divine laws to prohibit pork any more than it is cultural overkill to have divine laws prohibit homicide or bank robberies.

Alland also seeks to deny the need for divine sanctions in the case of the pig by denying that its meat constitutes a materially tempting source of animal protein. He alleges that in trying to account for the attractiveness of the pig, I fall back on the ethnocentric idea that the pig tastes good, which he describes as an "idealist principle that runs counter to 'techno-environmentalism and anti-idealism' ":

Harris . . . tells us that pig meat is inherently delicious; that people want to eat it. . . . A strong desire is frustrated by a religious sanction. But what makes pig meat more delicious than beef, or horse for that matter? (Ibid.:67)

The point is not that pig meat is *more* delicious than other meat (this is a misconstrual of my contention that pork is a succulent treat), but rather that the pig is inherently no less delicious than beef. (As for the horse, Alland overlooks the fact that it too was forbidden by the Israelite scriptures.) I fall back on no idealist principle when I claim that an animal that can't be bled, milked, ridden, herded, mounted, or plowed with, and which is the product of five thousand years of selective breeding under human control, is a potentially valuable source of edible animal proteins and fats. For five thousand years the neolithic peoples of the Middle East thought that pigs were good to eat. Why did they change their minds? The answer surely has something to do with the fact that the entire ecosystem changed, and with it, the cultural and natural system of production and the role of the pig in that system.

The Structure of Dirt

WHETHER OR NOT the anomalous pig reflects a static sense of dirt or an ongoing process of infrastructural change, there remains the question whether dirt can adequately be defined as "matter out of place." I should like to comment on this aspect of Mary Douglas's theory as well, because it is rooted in the tendency of structuralists to impose their own ethnocentric and even egocentric thought processes on the psyches of the entire human species. Douglas has given us an account of how she came to the discovery that "dirt is matter out of place." The idea came to her while she was in a bathroom in an old house:

> I am personally rather tolerant of disorder. But I always remember how unrelaxed I felt in a particular bathroom which was kept spotlessly clean in so far as the removal of grime and grease were concerned. (Douglas, 1966:2)

The trouble (the "unrelaxment") derived from the fact that the bathroom had been created by putting doors at both ends of a back corridor between two staircases.

The decor remained unchanged: the engraved portrait of Vinogradoff, the books, the gardening tools, the row of gumboots. It all made good sense as the scene of a back corridor but as a bathroom—the impression destroyed repose. (Ibid.)

From this experience she realized that cleanliness is a virtue in her milieu not because dirt is a threat to health but because it was a threat to her idea of order. The bathroom was simply out of place. "In chasing dirt, in papering, decorating, tidying we are not governed by anxiety to escape disease, but are positively re-ordering our environment to conform to an idea" (ibid.). Note how this personal impression somehow acquired the status of a collective experience—"I" becomes "we"—as if others had taken turns seeking the particular variety of repose she had sought in the misplaced bathroom and had found repose unattainable for the same reason. Since we are told only that the grime and grease were removed from the premises, Douglas conceivably was in error concerning the reason why she felt the bathroom wasn't really clean. Some of the empirical issues here cannot be resolved by the intuitive knowledge of one's own culture and personality. How does Douglas know that we share her "structure" of dirt?

Shoes are not dirty in themselves, but it is dirty to place them on the dining table; food is not dirty in itself but it is dirty to leave cooking utensils in the bedroom, or food bespattered on clothing; similarly bathroom equipment in the drawing room; clothing lying on chairs; out-door things indoors; upstairs things downstairs; under-clothing appearing where over-clothing should be, and so on. (Ibid.:36)

It would seem that before one proceeded to attribute the notion that dirt equals disorder to the entire human species, the ethnosemantics of these examples should be based on something more than one trip to the bathroom (see Chapter 9). Even Douglas might not be willing to accept disorder as the sole or principal component of dirt if she was obliged to tidy up a lawn strewn with gold watches and diamond rings. Are some things never considered dirty no matter where they are found? And are some things *always* considered dirty no matter where they are found? It is irresponsible for anthropologists to pretend to know the answer to such questions merely by contemplating the lint in their own belly buttons.

In defense of Lévi-Strauss, Mary Douglas (1967:50) has written: "I do not think it is fair to such an ebullient writer to take him literally." For my part, I do not think it is fair for such writers to expect to be taken seriously.

On the Road with Edmund Leach

PERHAPS THE BEST way for me to demonstrate the need for more skepticism with respect to arcane structuralist interpretations of esoteric elements in the superstructure of remote or extinct societies is to show how unreliable even an apparently simple structuralist "opposition" can be when it is set up on the basis of what appears to be a familiar aspect of Euro-American cultures. A splendid example of this genre has been produced by Edmund Leach. To prove that our minds do in fact function in terms of binary codes, that these codes impose the need for dialectic resolutions, and that social behavior is a transformation of the codes and their resolution, Leach chooses the example of traffic signals on railroads and highways. He asserts that traffic signals are culturally segmented into a tripartite system:

yellow

red   green

How did this happen? According to Leach, the human brain first sought out the extremes of the spectrum, red and green, and assigned them the meaning "stop" and "go." Yellow, which lies midway between red and green, was then selected as the mediator, "caution," which is neither "stop" nor "go":

> With traffic lights on both railways and roads, green means go and red means stop . . . if we want to devise a further signal with an intermediate meaning we choose the color yellow. We do this because, in the spectrum, it lies midway between green and red . . . the color system and the signal system have the same structure; the one is a transformation of the other. (Leach, 1970:17)

It is not essential for Leach's argument that red means "stop" and green means "go," rather than vice versa. The structuralist point is simply that the mind will dichotomize the spectrum—make a binary opposition out of a continuum—and that it will use the extremes to build that opposition and the logical center to mediate those extremes. Thus in order for us to believe that the railroad and road signal system is a "transformation," a universal mental color code—an expression of the structure of the mind—the following propositions must be true:

1. In any given signal system, red and green mean either "stop" or "go."
2. No colors other than red or green mean "stop" or "go."
3. Yellow always means "caution."
4. No other color means "caution."

As Frederick Gamst (1975) has shown, Leach's simple example is full of surprises. None of the above propositions is true of the system of railways and road traffic signals. But unlike the usual types of examples dealt with by structuralists, traffic signals have a short and exquisitely well-documented history. No expensive journeys into remote jungle regions are needed to check up on the structuralist's metaphors and metonyms. The meanings of traffic signals are hidden only from those who do not take the trouble to investigate the relevant documents. Even looking out the window of a railway car would be useful.

All traffic signal systems have a common point of origin in early-nineteenth-century England. The first freight railway signal was a black semaphore arm on a mast. A black flag was used to stop trains during the day on the first passenger line (1830, Liverpool and Manchester), but at night, the stationmaster swung a white light. Rear cars displayed red lights while the train was in motion; blue lights when it stopped. "Thus the ubiquitous blue (stop/danger) light of railroading and other industries was present from the beginning." By 1839 the Liverpool and Manchester used both red and blue flags to mean stop. Black was the preferred color for "caution," but for obvious reasons black couldn't be used at night. So at night a green light meant caution. Between 1840 and 1900, the preferred system for railroad traffic control was the semaphore arm. At ninety degrees the arm meant stop or caution; at zero degrees it meant go. *"No matter which of its aspects were displayed, the arm's color was, of course, always red"* (Gamst, 1975:281). At night semaphores came to be equipped with a red light that could be seen when the arm was in both stop and caution positions. Violet lights, however, replaced red lights on many railroads, particularly on branch lines. Yellow did not become common as a cautionary color until after 1900. But a flashing green and a lunate white light also meant caution. In case you are thinking that "the mind" finally did have its way, forget it. In the system that is still in use throughout the English-speaking world red does not always indicate "stop." "Today in some railroad districts an engineer might run his train for hours [through red lights] without being required to stop even once, in the same way that pioneer British engineers followed the red signal at the rear of a moving train" (ibid: 285). Blue, not red, is the color that means "stop" under all circumstances.

Automobile traffic signals have a slightly less complex history. But no simple triangular set of distinctions is applicable. Detroit and Houston used red and green from the beginning, in combination with railroad-type semaphores. But in New York in 1919, amber meant go for Fifth Avenue traffic and stop for 42nd Street traffic. Green meant go for 42nd Street and stop for Fifth Avenue. White is still used to mean go in pedestrian walk signs in New York City, while in Washington, D.C., a walk signal may be either white or red. Throughout the United States, emergency vehicles are now equipped with flashing blue lights instead of red lights to warn of danger and emergencies.

What is most damaging to the structuralist position is the fact that the modern system of railroad and traffic signals evolved in conjunction with a series of technical achievements which clearly dominated the choice of colors during any given period. Gamst concludes that Leach's system is

not a result of any underlying structural process but among other things of: the balancing of practical and rational considerations; experimentation in the material world; scientific advances in color technology, glass and electric illumination; traffic demands of an evolving industrial civilization; and the advent of large-scale illumination with white lights of streets and houses. (Ibid.: 284)

To propose that this complex process merely expresses the binary propensities of the human mind is to endow mental life with an omnipotence in which only infantile or disturbed minds have hitherto believed.

The Case of the Tricky Coyote

LET US RETURN to the work of the master himself. According to Lévi-Strauss, "Mythical thought always progresses from the awareness of opposites towards their resolution" (Lévi-Strauss, 1963:224). These mediators or resolutions are then likely to be transformed into new binary dialectical contrasts, which in turn produce new mediators. To explain why North American Indian myths personify the supernatural trickster as a coyote or a raven, Lévi-Strauss (1963:224) sets up an opposition between agriculture and warfare as an analogy of the opposition between life and death (agriculture sustains life, war leads to death):

$$agriculture \ : \ warfare \ :: \ life \ : \ death$$

The mediator of *agriculture : warfare* is said to be *hunting* (because hunting is life-sustaining war against animals). Agriculture is associated with plant-eating animals, and hunting is associated with beasts of prey. This leads to a new opposition: *herbivores : beasts of prey*. The mediator of this opposition is a scavenger-type animal that does not kill what it eats—viz, a coyote or a raven. Thus raven and coyote mediate life and death, do good and evil at the same time, and hence are sometimes cunning but at other times the victims of circumstances.

Does this explanation constitute a plausible or parsimonious approach to why coyotes are tricksters? Scarcely. In fact coyotes are not primarily scavengers but are wily predators who hunt rabbits, rats, mice, birds, porcupines, fawns, and many other small animals. Carrion count for only a quarter of their diet (Cahalane, 1947:250; Hall, 1946:240; Bekoff, 1978:118). The salient etic fact about the coyote is not that it is a scavenger but that it is an opportunist. Non-Indian as well as Indian observers agree that the coyote is an extremely cunning carnivore who has to compensate for being small by being smart. Coyotes, widely regarded as a menace by Western sheep ranchers, have proved much more difficult to eradicate than wolves—"due to their cleverness and adaptability" (Cahalane, 1947:253). It is "one of the most difficult animals in Nevada to catch on a trap" and "by reason of its . . . adaptability and cunning, will persist in spite of efforts to exterminate it" (Hall, 1946:243). Under attack by Western ranchers, the coyote is moving into the suburbs, with increased sightings reported from major metropolitan areas.

Coyotes frequently follow along behind larger carnivores, waiting for a chance to steal a portion of the catch. After a bear has caught an animal, they dart in, nip the bear in the leg, and then dart off with the prey when the startled bear lets it fall. Cahalane (1947:249) comments that "after watching many coyotes, I really believe they have a sense of humor at times." The tricky nature of the coyote has even been given a place in biological nomenclature: the subspecies designations are (Hall, and Kelson, 1959:834):

Canis latrans frustrior	=	Tricky coyote
Canis latrans cagottis	=	Cagey coyote
Canis latrans clepticus	=	Thieving coyote
Canis latrans impavidus	=	Undauntable coyote
Canis latrans vigilis	=	Alert coyote

Unless there is some reason why the American Indians were less capable than Euro-American naturalists of recognizing a "tricky" type animal, Lévi-Strauss's explanation of why North American Indians made the coyote their trickster must be dismissed as an intricate device whose sole function is to misdirect attention from the obvious and probable to the obscure and improbable. (Similar conclusions are clearly warranted with respect to the raven—also a notoriously "tricky" creature.)

An Open and Shut Case

FOR MY FINAL example of the corpus of structuralist theories, I have chosen the case of Lévi-Strauss and the clam. According to Lévi-Strauss (1972), certain myths found among the Bella Bella* cannot be explained unless they are seen as the transformed opposites of certain myths found among the Chilcotin. The Bella Bella live along the coast of British Columbia, and the Chilcotin are their distant inland neighbors. Lévi-Strauss calls the Chilcotin myths the "normal" version, and in his words it goes like this:

An infant boy who cried too much was kidnapped by an Owl. . . . This powerful sorcerer treated him well and made him quite happy. So, when the friends and parents of the now grown-up boy discovered him, he was at first unwilling to follow them. When he was finally persuaded to escape, the Owl gave chase to the flying [sic] party, and the boy succeeded in frightening him by putting mountain-goat horns on his fingers which he brandished like claws. He had taken with him all the dentalia shells . . . of which the Owl was the sole owner, and it is since that time that the Indians have dentalia shells which they value as their most precious possession. (Ibid.:8)

This myth is supposed to have influenced the Bella Bella and in the process to have undergone a series of dialectical transformations. The Bella Bella myth goes as follows, again in Lévi-Strauss's words:

A girl or a boy who cried too much is kidnapped by a cannibalistic supernatural being, generally female, named Kāwaka. . . . In order to free himself or herself from the ogress, the girl or the boy is instructed by a supernatural helper to collect the siphons (the correct zoological term, I think, is "siphuncle"†) of the clams dug by the Kāwaka—that is, the part of the molluscs she does not eat and that she discards. When the hero or heroine places these siphons on the tips of his or her fingers and moves them toward the ogress, she becomes so frightened that she falls down a steep mountain and kills herself. . . .
    . . . The youth's father thus obtains all the property which the ogress

---

*I have been advised by John Rath that the people of Bella Bella speak Heiltsuk, which is a North Wakashan language. Since Heiltsuk is spoken by people at settlements other than Bella Bella, the people of Bella Bella should be referred to as the Bella Bella Heiltsuks.
    †"Siphon" is the correct term; "siphuncle" refers to structures found in cephalopods.

previously owned. He distributes it around. Thus is explained the origin of the potlatch.

Lévi-Strauss stresses the fact that the cannibal ogress in the Bella Bella tale is frightened to death by something harmless and insignificant—namely, the clam siphons. For Lévi-Strauss these siphons constitute a paradox not present in the Chilcotin tale. Anyone can understand why the owl-shaman is frightened by the horns of mountain goats. Horns are hard, sharp, and pointed like claws. But only a structuralist can explain why something as inoffensive as a clam siphon can terrorize an ogress. Drawing upon observations of clam anatomy made not among the Bella Bella but during a previous sojourn in New York City, he poses the basic paradox of the Bella Bella myth as follows:

Why a powerful ogress, twice as big as an ordinary human being, should be frightened by something as harmless and insignificant as clam siphons— these soft, trunklike skinny funnels for admitting and expelling water which are conspicuous in some species of clams (and by the way, quite handy to hold the steamed shellfish and dip it in drawn butter, a delicious treat which one could get in a place near Times Square when I was living in New York many years ago)—this is something that the Bella Bella myths do not explain. (Ibid.:8)

Question: Why should a powerful ogress be frightened when her intended victim waggles a few skinny clam siphons in her face? Answer: The clam siphons are not really clam siphons, but the dialectical opposite of mountain-goat horns!

Whenever in a given version of a myth, a detail appears which seems "off-pattern" in respect to the other versions, it is most likely that the deviant version is trying to say the opposite of a normal version which exists elsewhere and usually not far from the other one. . . . In the present case the normal version is easily located. It belongs to the Chilcotin. . . .

According to Lévi-Strauss, the lawful transformations myths undergo result from neighboring people's hearing each other's tales and transforming them dialectically.

Listeners hearing tellers from a neighboring tribe . . . will borrow the myth while consciously or unconsciously deforming it along pre-ordained paths.

They appropriate it not to appear unequal to their neighbors, and they remodel it at the same time so as to make it their own. (Ibid.:9)

So soft, harmless, skinny siphons among the Bella Bella result when the Bella Bella storyteller "tries to think of the opposite" of hard, harmful, sharp mountain-goat horns; and goat horns endure when the Chilcotin storyteller "tries to think of the opposite" of soft, harmless, skinny siphons.

According to Lévi-Strauss, if one part of a myth gets transformed in its telling by one culture to another, all the other parts must undergo a similar coherent set of structural changes. The set of opposites of which horn and siphon are components are to be found, he suggests, by decomposing the Chilcotin and the Bella Bella myths into their respective "means" and "ends." Horns and siphons are respectively the means to the ends of ownership of Owl's dentalia shells and Kāwaka's treasure. Here another set of alleged opposites is invoked: horns come from the land; horns get shells that come from the sea; clam siphons come from the sea; clam siphons get treasure that comes from the land.

Now, all the mythological and ritual data which we have concerning this K āwaka, or Dzōnokwa as the Kwakiutl call her, point to the fact that her treasures come from the landside, as they consist of copper plates, furs, dressed skins and dried meat.

Note that there are seaside and landside elements in both the Chilcotin and Bella Bella versions, and that these elements also get inverted from ends to means and from means to ends. To take the seaside elements first: dentalia for the Chilcotin and clam siphons for the Bella Bella are seaside ends versus seaside means. Lévi-Strauss claims that the logic of this inversion depends upon the fact that clam siphons are worthless and inedible, while dentalia are precious, since the Chilcotin use them as shell money. "Dentalia shells are by far the most valuable objects coming out of the sea while clam siphons are worthless even as food: the myth carefully points out that the ogress does not eat them."

Next, the landside elements: horns among the Chilcotin, treasure among the Bella Bella, land means opposed to land ends. The logic of this opposition is that worthless horns which come from the land become part of the ogress's treasure, just as a worthless sea product—the siphons—reappear in the Owl's treasure as valuable dentalia. The only hitch is that, as quoted above, the Bella Bella's itemized list of the ogress's treasure consists of "copper plates, furs, dressed skins and dried meat." There is no mention of mountain-goat horns. Undaunted, Lévi-Strauss adds the horns to the treasure, arguing that potlatch treasure must also have contained some of those beautiful and valuable spoons that the Northwest Coast peoples carved out of mountain-goat horns and that we see in museums. Once the horns, in the form of valuable spoons, are inserted into the ogress's treasure, we can understand why horns and siphons are the particular items that stand in opposition as the means in the two myths:

Goat horns are unfit for alimentary consumption, but they can be shaped and carved into those magnificent ceremonial ladles and spoons that we see in museums. In the latter capacity they may be made part of a treasure and if not edible, they nevertheless provide, like the clam siphons, a convenient means (cultural instead of natural) to carry the food to the mouth of the eater. (Ibid.:9)

Similarly, we can well understand why clam siphons and dentalia, the sea elements respectively in the Bella Bella and Chilcotin versions, are opposed as means in the first story and an end in the other.

Dentalia shells as a treasure are the *convex, hard outside* of a mollusc unfit for alimentary purpose (there is practically no meat in them) while the *hollow* siphons are a part of the *soft inside* of another mollusc which has a prominent place in the coast people's diet. However, the siphons themselves have no food-value whatsoever and they stand out as a paradoxical appendage, conspicuous but useless. Thus, they can easily be "mythologized" for a reason opposite to but correlated with the position of dentalia shells among inland people who value them but don't have them, while coast people have the clams but do not value their siphons.

I shall now show that these oppositions exist entirely in Lévi-Strauss's head. Although it is true that an ogress in one Bella Bella myth does not eat the siphons of clams, it is false that the siphons she discards in that myth are harmless, insignificant, and soft; it is also false that they are "quite handy to hold the steamed shellfish and dip it in drawn butter, a delicious treat which one could get in a place near Times Square." It is also false that the siphons of the clams the ogress discards "have no food-value whatsoever"; and it is false that the Bella Bella do not value the siphons of these or other clams. Furthermore, there is no known Bella Bella myth in which the contents of the ogress's treasure is said to include mountain-goat horns or spoons made from mountain-goat horns, or only landside treasures.

The main source of Bella Bella myths is the collection published by Franz Boas (1932) under the title *Bella Bella Tales*. This collection contains five myths under the subheading "K!áwag!a Tales." The first and longest has nothing to do with a crying boy, clams, the killing of the ogress, or the origins of the first potlatch. Rather, it has to do with a chief who saves the life of the Kāwaka's son and who is rewarded by the grateful giantess with the specific treasures mentioned above— "coppers, dressed skins, and dried meat of mountain goats and of bears" (plus whistles and cedar-bark ornaments). The story ends with the chief becoming the first cannibal dancer. This is the only one of the five Bella Bella tales that specifies the contents of the ogress's treasure—a point to which I shall return in a moment.

Of the remaining myths, the second, third, and fourth alone mention siphons as a means of killing an ogress. But in the third, the ogress's death leads to an incident that explains not the origin of potlatch but the origin of frogs. In the fourth tale, the death of the ogress doesn't lead to anything, and the fifth (which, as I have indicated, is like the first in not having the clam-siphon incident) also merely ends with her death. In the third and fourth, no mention is made of whether the ogress discards the clam siphons. That leaves the second, which alone among the five Bella Bella Kāwaka tales in this collection has the conjunction of siphons discarded by the ogress and used to frighten her, plus the mention of a potlatch treasure. This second tale is the one that Levi-Strauss identifies as "the more developed Bella Bella version" and which by Levi-Strauss's own designation should therefore contain the best evidence of the alleged dialectical transformations. I reproduce it here in its entirety:

A Kʻ!ā'waq!a Dies of Fright. Story of the Awī'L!īdExᵘ
(Told by Ō'dzē stalis to George Hunt)

L!ā'qwag ilaōgwa was living at Xunē's. She had a young daughter. One night the child began to cry and her mother could not stop her. Late at night, when her mother was asleep, the girl went out of the house intending to go to her grandmother. While she was going along she met an old woman who called her. She thought it was her grandmother, but the strange woman picked her up and threw her into a large basket which she was carrying on her back. It was a Kʻ!ā 'waq!a who had taken her. The Kʻ!ā 'waq!a went up a mountain into her house where she took the girl out of the basket and let her walk about in the house. Suddenly the girl heard someone calling her and she found a woman sitting on the floor. The upper part of her body was like ours, but the lower part was stone. She was called *LōxulīlEmga* (Woman rolling about in the house). She said, "Take care, do not eat the Viburnum berries which she will give you, for they are the eyes of animals and of men. If you eat them you will also become half stone. She will also give you mountain goat fat. This you may cat, it will not hurt you. Every morning *K˙ ¡ā 'waq¡a* will go down to the beach to dig clams and when she comes home she eats everything except the syphons which she will throw away. Pick these up and put them on your fingers and when she comes up the steep trail, hold up one of your fingers with the syphon on it and when you see that she is afraid show all the other fingers and see what will happen. Hang this little bag under your chin and let the Viburnum berries drop into it." The girl did as she was advised and the next day when the *K˙ ¡ā 'waq¡a* was coming up the mountain with her great basket full of horse clams, the girl showed her one finger. The *K˙ ¡ā 'waq¡a* was so badly frightened that she staggered backward. Then the girl put up all her fingers. The *K˙ ¡ā 'waq¡a* rolled down the mountain and was killed. Then the woman who was half stone advised the young woman to put a little of all the stores in the house into a small box and to take it home. "Then tell your father *Mā 'q¡uns* to come with his people and to take everything home." She went to the place where the people used to draw water and before long her younger sister came with her bucket. She asked her to tell her mother that she was sitting down at the spring. When the girl said that she had seen her lost sister, her mother struck her with the fire tongs and said, "I did not expect you to make fun of my dead daughter." The girl asked her to go with her and to see that she had spoken the truth. Then they found the lost daughter who told her all that had happened and her father went with his tribe to get all the property out of the house of the *K˙ ¡ā 'waq¡a*. They even carried the woman who was half stone down the mountain but when they were half way, they left her there. Then her father gave a great potlatch with the property he had obtained. (Boas, 1932:95–96)

Note that this myth says that the ogress digs clams every morning, puts them into a basket, and climbs up the steep trail. On the morning of her demise, the contents of her basket are specified to be "horse clams." What are horse clams?

Horse clams (also called horse necks) are not the soft-shell steamers belonging to the family Myacidae that Lévi-Strauss once enjoyed in Times Square. They are hard-shell clams *(Tresus capax Gould)* that easily measure eight inches across and weigh up to four pounds (Morris, 1952). Here is what one popular writer has to say about the horse neck and its siphon:

Of course it can never retract its huge siphon completely within its shell. . . . The siphon is protected by a tough, brown skin and has at its tip two horny valves that can be used to close the openings. . . . The rough grey shell is covered in life by a brownish periostracum that is often rubbed off in spots, giving the creature a moth-eaten appearance. The bulging body, usually muddy, protrudes from the gaping siphonal end of the ugly shell, and from this part of the body comes the overgrown compound siphon, rough and brown, usually flecked with mud, and with a horny tip. (Gibbons, 1964:186)

According to Johnson and Snook (1967), the horse-clam siphon is capable of squirting water to a height of three feet above the sand. The above clearly refutes the claim that the siphons in the Bella Bella myth are insignificant and soft (they have a horny tip).

Now what about the claim that siphons have no food value whatsoever? The edibility of horse-clam siphons is widely attested to by both Indian and non-Indian connoisseurs. While there are some people who like to eat horse clams and others who detest them (just as many New Yorkers won't touch Lévi-Strauss's "delectable" steamers), all horse-clam eaters agree that the siphon is edible (except for the horny tip), and some say it is the best part.

Most of the edible part is contained in the long muscular siphon which is the only part eaten by present-day clam diggers (Greengo, 1952:67).

Remove but do not discard the big ugly siphon, for many consider this the finest meat in the Horse Clam. Some people prize these clams only for their siphons and throw the rest of the clam away, but I consider this a criminal waste of some very good food. (Gibbons, 1964:187)

Now what about the claim that the Bella Bella themselves do not value the siphons of horse clams? This claim can be checked by asking the Bella Bella themselves. In response to my inquiries, John Rath and Ms. Jennifer Gould, linguist and research coordinator respectively of the Heiltsuk Cultural Educational Center, wrote: "According to five informants still well-versed in our traditional Heiltsuk ways, horse-clams and their siphons are edible" (personal communication). I have also had the opportunity, arranged through Mr. Rath and Ms. Gould, personally to confirm this conclusion by talking with Bella Bella informants.

Once we know the dimensions of the siphons used to frighten the ogress, it is clear that the Bella Bella storyteller has no need, conscious or unconscious, to make siphons the opposite of mountain-goat horns in order to render them effective. An entirely self-sufficient explanation of their lethal efficacy is suggested by the resemblance this large organ bears to a phallus. There can be little doubt that when neo-Americans in Canada and the United States refer to *Tresus capax* as horse *necks*, they are employing a euphemism for a large penis. But in the case of Heiltsuk, the phallic involvement is explicit. I am indebted to John Rath for confirming this rather obvious hypothesis. "Horse clam siphons can be referred to with the one word / ?nik' /. . . . As it happens, among the people of Bella Bella, Klemtu, and Rivers Inlet, / ?nik' / is the word for 'penis' indeed."

It might seem that since Lévi-Strauss himself has designated the version in question as the "developed version," there would be no need to offer additional evidence that the siphons in question were neither insignificant nor of no food value whatsoever. In preparing my rebuttal of Lévi-Strauss, I proceeded nonetheless to take extra precautions, knowing that he would object that the other two versions which mention the word "clam" do not specify what kind of clam. Therefore, I looked for Bella Bella myths about Kāwakas in sources other than Boas's *Bella Bella Tales*. I located two more Bella Bella myths, not used by Lévi-Strauss, that mention clams and ogresses. One of them, collected by Ronald Olson, upholds the view that a very large clam is involved:

One morning Cannibal Woman went out with her basket. When she returned that evening, she had her basket full of geoduck clams. She cooked them, gave the old woman some, and ate some herself. Those she gave to the girl, the girl did not eat but dropped them into her basket. The next day the same things happened but the old lady told the girl, "Put the necks of the clams on your fingers when you see her coming. When she comes in, move your fingers to scare her." The girl met the giantess at the door and waggled her fingers at her. The cannibal was so frightened that in trying to run away she fell, rolled down the cliff, and was killed. (Olson, 1955:339)

The geoduck *(Panope generosa)* to which Olson's version refers is even bigger than the horse clam, and with its four-foot-long siphon is possibly the largest intertidal bivalve in the world.

The next version I located again refers to horse clams. Here is the central incident in this version, as told by Mrs. Mabel Humchitt, a bilingual Bella Bella Heiltsuk speaker:

And she [the old woman] told the child to peel the tips off the horse clams and scare the monster next time it comes home from digging clams. So the child turned them inside out and chanted a short song. . . . So the monster fell back down after trying to beg her not to do that. "I'm afraid of them." So finally she was discovered and the monster was dead. (Storie and Gould, 1973:43–44)

Mrs. Humchitt's version adds two new details: only the "tips" of the siphons are put on the fingers and they are turned inside out. Interviews with Mrs. Humchitt and her husband carried out by J. Rath and J. Gould (in one of which I participated) produced the explanation that the tip of the siphon was torn off and turned inside out because at certain seasons the interior of the tip is colored red. This coloration is caused by the presence of the microorganism responsible for the toxic oceanic bloom known as the red tide. Hence, the imagery involved in Mrs. Humchitt's tale refers directly to a set of blood-red poisoned tipped claws, which rather decisively falsifies, I should think, Lévi-Strauss's dialectical opposition between "harmful" mountain-goat horns and "harmless" clam siphons.

Admittedly, the "developed version" in the *Bella Bella Tales* contains no reference to turning poisonous tips inside out. But this omission could easily have been an artifact of the way in which Boas obtained his collection of Bella Bella myths, which as we shall see was scarcely the result of carefully controlled inquiry. Even if Mrs. Humchitt's version should prove to be idiosyncratic, however, it indicates the proneness of Bella Bella Heiltsuk informants to endow horse-clam siphons with lethal powers quite independently of hypothetical contrasts with mountain-goat horns. If hypotheses about ogresses are appropriate, one can say with considerable confidence that the ogress fell down dead not because she was attacked with the skinny little harmless substitutes for mountain-goat horns, but because she was attacked with horny three-foot-long bloody penises.

Is Structuralism Good to Think?

THE ARGUMENT I have been presenting up to this point was published in *L'Homme* (Harris, 1976), together with a reply by Lévi-Strauss (1976). The reply provides an opportunity for observing the logic of structuralism under controlled conditions. Although Lévi-Strauss used the occasion to investigate another set of far-ranging oppositions, I shall concentrate only on his response to the question of whether or not clam siphons are the dialectical opposite of mountain-goat horns and whether the Bella Bella ogress's treasure consists exclusively of landside elements.

What kind of defense did Lévi-Strauss make against a demonstration that the "developed version" refers to horse-clam siphons and that therefore his attempt to explain the paradox of harmless siphons killing an ogress was all in vain? It is a defense that raises questions about the integrity of structuralist methods.

He begins by counting up the number of times the word clam occurs in the Bella Bella tales collected by Boas. In the three relevant tales, he notes, only the "developed version" specifies "horse clam." This cannot be an oversight resulting from a failure of Boas and his Kwakiutl assistant George Hunt to get the facts straight, he argues, because "Boas and Hunt were scrupulous translators" (1976:24). Therefore in the other two versions the ogress was not killed by horse clams.

However, it is simply false that either Boas or Hunt could have been scrupulous translators of any Bella Bella myth. Hunt spoke Kwakiutl but not Bella Bella. As Boas wrote in the Preface to *Bella Bella Tales:* "the dialect difference [between Kwakiutl and Bella Bella] turned out to be so great that he [George Hunt] gained only a partial understanding of the language, although his services in obtaining comparative data on the vocabulary and grammar were of great value" (Boas, 1932:vi). The reason for Hunt's problem was that Bella Bella is not a dialect of Kwakiutl, as Boas believed, but an entirely separate language. (John Rath, personal communication)

Lévi-Strauss seeks comfort in the knowledge that the first and second Kāwaka tales were obtained by Hunt from a Bella Bella informant named Ō'dzē stalis, who "lived for years at Fort Rupert and who spoke Kwakiutl fluently" (1976:24). This also is incorrect. Ō'dzē stalis is remembered by the Bella Bella Heiltsuk; he was not one of them. He was a Kwakiutl married to a Bella Bella woman. Therefore his ability to render scrupulously authentic accounts of Bella Bella myths is seriously in doubt.

Bella Bella Tales is a sorry basis on which to rear theories about the mental life of the Bella Bella, since we lack the text of the myths as they were told in their original language. That not much faith can be invested in the authenticity of each word in the *Bella Bella Tales* is shown precisely by the carelessness with which the distinction between "clam" and "horse clam" is made. As Lévi-Strauss gleefully points out, in the "developed version" the myth does not say that the ogress digs horse clams every day but only that she digs clams. Yet in context it is perfectly clear that the ogress brings "her great basket full of horse clams" up from the beach every morning. Instead of acknowledging that the *Bella Bella Tales* are a shaky basis for any firm conclusion about anything, Lévi-Strauss tries to turn the ambiguity about clams in the developed version to his own advantage. No matter that the ogress's basket was full of horse clams on the day she died. All the myth says about other clam-digging episodes is that she digs clams. Therefore it's just clam siphons, not horse clam siphons, that the heroine uses, since she picked them off the floor from a previous day's repast! In other words, the day the myth specifies what is in the ogress's basket is to be regarded as an exception. Somehow Lévi-Strauss knows that on all the other days the basket did not contain horse clams!

But what about the Olson and Humchitt versions? Lévi-Strauss disallows Olson's 1955 mention of geoducks because "the entire culture of the Bella Bella had disappeared" by 1923, which was long before Olson did his fieldwork. This can scarcely be true with respect to the recall of myths, however, since Mrs. Humchitt was telling hers in the 1970s. Indeed, Mrs. Humchitt is the only bona-fide bilingual Bella Bella informant whose authenticity as a teller of Bella Bella ogress tales is beyond dispute. Yet Lévi-Strauss thinks he knows better than Mrs. Humchitt what the Bella Bella should make their heroine do to kill the ogress, even though all Lévi-Strauss has to go on is Hunt's translation from Kwakiutl, whereas Mrs. Humchitt, whose family claims possession of the right to tell this tale, has had it handed down to her from her parents and grandparents. Lévi-Strauss declares that Mrs. Humchitt's version is aberrant and that "it belongs to the group, but cannot represent it"!

Forthwith, Lévi-Strauss produces yet another Bella Bella Kāwaka myth Boas had collected in Rivers Inlet and published in German in 1895. In this myth, the hero frightens the ogress by putting the beards of mussels—the byssus—on his fingers. Since the myths sometimes mention horse clams, sometimes just clams, shellfish, or even mussels, it is a capital error to say that the ogress was killed by a definite kind of clam. Only a blighted mind afflicted with the rampant "empiricism that is the servile malady of neo-Marxism" would want to argue about whether it is a particular organ or even a particular family of animal that is involved in these myths.

Contrary to what Harris believes, the myths are as far removed as possible from the empiricism that is the servile malady of neo-Marxism; they do not have their content fixed once and for all, determining in a rigid fashion one particular organ of a unique genus of bivalve. They play upon a theme from which issue diverse empirical examples of a single organ, as well as, moreover, other organs which differ among themselves, and which even belong to distinct families of animals. (Ibid.:28)

If this is so, then perhaps only a mind tottering on the brink of ultimate decay would dare to remind Lévi-Strauss that it was he who made the question of the Chilcotin–Bella Bella transformation a question of clam siphons versus mountain-goat horns. Obviously if the father of structuralism had set out to prove that an unspecifiable set of organs and creatures constituted the dialectical transformation of another unspecifiable set of organs and creatures, neither I nor anyone else would have wished to waste our time refuting such wonderful nonsense.

The question now before us is whether it is necessary to find structuralist structures in order to understand any or all of the different modes of killing ogresses in Bella Bella myths. As soon as the specificity of the organ is changed from clam siphons to some open-ended series, the need for finding arcane oppositions and secret transformations can no longer be upheld. A simple fact emerges: the ogress is frightened to death by appendages the storyteller thinks are likely to be frightening. The whole structuralist game is given away when the ogress sees the mussel beards and cries out.

"What have you got there? I have never seen anything like it and I'm afraid of it." Evidently the ogress is frightened by strange things —small or large, soft or hard. Yes, of course, myths "play on a theme." That is exactly the point. The Bella Bella storytellers have enough ingenuity of their own to keep inventing new and entertaining ways of frightening an ogress with strange things. They don't need any assistance from the imaginary little structuralists Lévi-Strauss sees sitting inside their heads.

If the problem is not specifically "why clam siphons?" but "why sea creatures?" it is too banal to deserve attention. People like the Bella Bella who live on the seacoast frighten their ogresses with strange things from the sea; people like the Chilcotin, who are not so familiar with the anatomy of mussels or clams, frighten their monsters with the parts of animals the Chilcotin are familiar with. Neither one nor the other is "off-pattern." Neither one nor the other is a "paradox." The whole problem as well as its imaginary solution exists in Lévi-Strauss's mind and nowhere outside of it.

There remains the question of the potlatch treasure, and the evidence that Lévi-Strauss can adduce to support his contention that it consists exclusively of land treasures, including spoons made out of mountain-goat horns. We now have a grand total of six Bella Bella Kāwaka stories before us. To the extent that any of them even mentions treasure as the outcome of killing the ogress, none specifies only land treasures or mountain-goat-horn spoons. How does Lévi-Strauss get out of this one? He notes that in his original presentation he had included a phrase "this Kāwaka, or Dzōnoqwa as the Kwakiutl call her" (ibid.:30) in the section devoted to explaining what was in the Bella Bella ogress's treasure (see above, p. 204). This phrase should have made it clear to me that our knowledge of the content of the Bella Bella treasure had to be based on the Kwakiutl myths about Dzōnoqwa rather than on the Bellā Bella myths of Kāwaka! In other words, here we have the clear admission that since there is no mention of what Lévi-Strauss wants to find in the Bella Bella myths, he has taken the liberty of finding it in the Kwakiutl myths.

It is known that the Bella Bella texts published by Boas come above all from Fort Rupert and Rivers inlet, which are Kwakiutl territories or regions where Kwakiutl influence predominates. . . . From which it results that in order to interpret the texts correctly, it is the Kwakiutl myths that one ought to consider, rather than those of more northerly origin [i.e., the Bella Bella]. (Ibid.:30)

Lévi-Strauss next coolly proceeds to show that in the Kwakiutl myths the Dzōnokwa's treasures are indeed depicted as exclusively landside treasures. And I never had any intention of denying that to be the case. But, as Lévi-Strauss points out, I deliberately deleted the phrase "this Kāwaka, or Dzōnoqwa as the Kwakiutl call her" when I quoted his line that "All the mythological and ritual data which we have concerning this Kāwaka . . . points to the fact that her treasures all come from the landside . . ." and so forth. I did this because the paragraph in which this phrase occurs starts off with the words: "Limiting ourselves to the Bella Bella and the Chilcotin myths . . ." It was and remains my understanding that the issue before us is the explanation of a Bella Bella myth, not a Kwakiutl myth! If Lévi-Strauss had intended to demonstrate the structuralist method by analyzing a Kwakiutl myth, I presumed that he would not say that he was going to analyze a Bella Bella myth. But why, one might wonder, did he not follow his own advice and consider the Kwakiutl myths from the outset. Why bother with the Bella Bella at all? The answer to this question is that there is no Kwakiutl myth in which the ogress is killed by clam siphons!

So, lacking the necessary Kwakiutl myth combining ogress, potlatch treasure, and death by clam siphon, Lévi-Strauss in effect created just such a myth by combining elements of the Kwakiutl stories with elements of the Bella Bella stories. This is clearly not a case of the analysis of myths worthy of anthropological science, but a pure and unadulterated case of myth-making in order to con us into believing that we need structuralism in order to understand how people think, when in fact structuralism may only teach us how structuralists think (cf. Thomas, Kronenfeld, and Kronenfeld, 1976).

All of this is not to deny that human beings may have a genetically determined propensity to organize thoughts dialectically. This constant propensity, however, can never explain the complex convergences and divergences of thought and behavior characteristic of sociocultural evolution. Like the aspects of human nature stressed by sociobiology, "binarism" could at best only explain the similarities. In terms of Maxwell's "aim orientation" criterion, therefore, structuralism is a priori a relatively stunted strategy. But there is more to say. To hold that the more things change, the more they are the same not only demeans our hope of understanding the world but dishonors our struggle to change it.

Chapter Eight
Structural Marxism

STRUCTURAL MARXISM is a research strategy combining aspects of structuralism with aspects of dialectical and historical materialism. Structural Marxists heap scorn on cultural materialists as "mechanical," "vulgar," and "so-called Marxists." Yet they represent structuralism with its blatant disregard of evolutionary movement and of infrastructural causality as a genuinely Marxist approach to superstructure.

Epistemologically, what Lévi-Strauss and the structural Marxists share is an aggressive antipositivism. This makes them allies against "empiricists" who allegedly accept surface phenomena as reality, in contrast to their own penetrations into the "real" structure. Some French structural Marxists, like the structuralists, merely pay lip service to the ultimate determination of superstructure by infrastructure. For others, the infrastructure in question is radically different from the cultural materialist infrastructure and contains such mental emic structural and superstructural components as kinship ideologies, rules of marriage, rules of ownership, and rules of inheritance. In fact, as we shall see, structural Marxism makes it possible for anything at all to be packed into infrastructure. Hence in its most depleted form, structural Marxism dissolves into an eclectic strategy notable for its convenient genuflections before the altars of left-wing politics, its cabalistic vocabulary, and its irritating intellectual snobbery. On the other hand, whenever structural Marxists have made a serious attempt to implicate the etic infrastructure, their analyses are compatible with or even similar to cultural materialist theories. I for one hope that structural Marxists will back off from their ritual denunciations of cultural materialists and recognize that there could be more common ground under structural Marxism and cultural materialism than under structural Marxism and French structuralism.

Malthus versus Marx

THE HOSTILITY displayed by structural Marxists and dialectical materialists toward cultural materialism is in many ways a prolongation of the attack launched by Marx and Engels against Malthus. For many Marxists, a commitment to the causal priority of the cultural materialist infrastructure seems to be a commitment to the proposition that inequality and poverty in the modern world are the unavoidable consequences of demographic and ecological pressures. This may explain in part why structural Marxists and dialectical materialists are willing to pitch their tents closer to such right-wing liberals as George Dalton (see below) and such obscurantists as Lévi-Strauss than to the tents of the cultural materialists. But as I have repeatedly pointed out, the recognition that the mode of reproduction plays an independent role in the evolution of sociocultural systems in no way necessarily leads to the conclusion that poverty under capitalism is primarily a matter of population pressure or that it is ineradicable (see p. 70). Once capitalist political economy is in place, its far-flung effects on all domains of social life cannot be overstated, much less denied. But cultural materialists regard it as a great strategic blunder not to see that capitalist, socialist, and all other political economies are products of millennial evolutionary processes which can only be comprehended in totality by specifying the infrastructural conditions that give rise to one form rather than another. And we regard it as an equally grave blunder not to see that even after a particular political economy is in place, its destiny lies in the infrastructural consequences of its politico-economic activities. Capitalism as we know it today cannot be the same thing as capitalism will be after the depletion of its fossil-fuel energy base.

Marx, Lévi-Strauss, and Structural Marxism

THE STRUCTURAL Marxists claim that there is a significant degree of continuity between Marxism and structuralism. Marx and Lévi-Strauss discovered the existence of hidden structures that obey internal dialectical laws of change. Yet both also stressed the irreducibility of one structure to another. Thus, according to Maurice Godelier (1977: 46), structuralism rests on these propositions:

A. all structure is a determined ensemble of relations all connected according to internal laws of change which have yet to be discovered.
B. all structure combines specific elements, which are its proper components and that for this reason it is useless to insist on "reducing" one structure to another.
C. among different structures belonging to the same system, there is a relationship of compatibility whose laws must be discovered, but this compatibility should not be regarded as the effect of essential selection mechanisms for the success of a biological process of environmental adaptation.

Godelier considers Marx's discovery of the true source of capitalist profit in unpaid labor as the paradigmatic example of the discovery of hidden structures.

The final pattern of economic relations as seen on the surface, in their real existence and consequently in the conceptions by which the bearers and agents of these relations seek to understand them, is very much different from, and indeed quite the reverse of, their inner but concealed essential pattern and the conception corresponding to it. (Marx, quoted in Godelier, 1977:46)

This corresponds to Lévi-Strauss's insistence that beneath the surface of myth there is a process of binary oppositions which reverses the apparent reality.

Some structural Marxists freely admit that Lévi-Strauss has only paid lip service to the ultimate priority of infrastructure, but this does not disturb them because they see Marx as sharing with Lévi-Strauss an even more important principle—namely, as I have already indicated, the principle that structures (and superstructures) are not "reducible" to infrastructure. Hence in reformulating the basic Marxist proposal that infrastructure determines superstructure, Maurice Godelier adds an emphasis that other Marxists might not deny, but would scarcely put forward as a salient aspect of historical materialism. Marx, writes Godelier (1977:46),

was the first to formulate a hypothesis about the presence of essential relations of correspondence and structural compatibility between the forces of production and relations of production, as also between the mode of production and superstructures, *without any intention of reducing the former to being merely epiphenomena of the latter.* (italics added)

Does the notion that structuralism "merges" with Marxism because it seeks to penetrate beneath the surface of phenomena have any value? I think not. All research strategies (including cultural materialism) seek in one way or another to get away from surface appearances and to find the inner "secret" of phenomena. For example, the division of the cultural materialist field of inquiry into emic behavior, etic behavior, and emic and etic mental events reflects a strategic intention to find a reality different from the ordinary state of mystified consciousness. The serious question is not whether one seeks "hidden structures" but under what epistemological and theoretical auspices the search will be conducted. On the epistemological level, Godelier's acceptance of Lévi-Strauss's "structures" as paradigmatic examples of what is to be found speaks for a commitment to unoperationalized entities, some of which will enjoy a wholly imaginary or at least untestable existence (as demonstrated in the previous chapter).

On the level of theoretical principles, the alleged agreement between Marx and Lévi-Strauss on the issue of the nonepiphenomenal status of structure and superstructure speaks for a commitment to historical indeterminacy. Godelier's concept of an irreducible structure inevitably aligns structural Marxism with historical particularism and other forms of eclecticism, as well as with structuralism. I shall prove this point in the following sections.

Social Relations of Production

AS DISCUSSED in Chapter 3, Marx's formulation of the principle of infrastructural determinism refers to the mode of production as consisting of forces of production and relations of production. The concept of forces of production seems fairly unambiguous and corresponds to etic behavioral techno-environmental interactions; relations of production, however, pose a serious definitional problem, since they are concerned with the emic and etic arrangements by which access to resources, control over labor inputs, and distribution of output are regulated. This means that social relations of production for Marx included items ordinarily discussed under such rubrics as ownership, class and caste stratification, employment, and even the ideological aspects of these components.

I think a strong case can be made that Marx imputed causal priority to the productive forces over the relations of production when he stated that as the forces of production develop, the relations of production act as a fetter upon them (see p. 144). Nonetheless, Marx did include both forces and relations within the mode of production.

It seems to me for reasons spelled out earlier (pp. 64–70) that a more coherent and parsimonious model of sociocultural causality can be obtained if we separate the emic and etic aspects of social relations of production and if we assign the etic aspects to the level of domestic and political economy. The nub of the difference between cultural materialists and structural Marxists is that the latter embrace the ambiguity in Marx's formulation not as a liability but as an asset; deny the need for distinguishing between emic and etic relations of production (or emic and etic of anything else); and reject the possibility of explaining the relations of production in terms of the forces of production. Since the structural Marxist relations of production by definition contains both etic and emic "structures," it becomes plain why structural Marxists go on to insist that other aspects of structure and superstructure must not be treated as epiphenomena and "reduced" to the mode of production.

According to Jonathan Friedman (1975:162), the social relations of production constitute "the set of social (i.e., non-technical) relations which determine the internal rationality of the economy, the specific use to be made of the means of production and the distribution of total social labor time and product." For pre-state societies, the relations of production consist in the pattern of access to land and other resources as allocated among or by such groups as sections, lineages, or big men and their followers. For capitalist societies, the relations of production consist in the ownership of the means of production by one class, who thereby exploits another:

To oversimplify, it could be said that capitalism is characterized by a social relation between classes which allows one class, the one which "possesses" capital, to exploit a second class. Capital is then itself a social relation of production. This social relation contains a tendency towards a development of the forces of production, a result of the inherent need to expand the rate of exploitation. (Kahn, 1975:147)

Structural Marxists share with dialectical materialists the faith that Marx discovered the secret inner laws of the capitalist mode of production. Their aim is to discover the inner laws of other modes of production, especially those of precapitalist societies, and they hope to find the secret of these yet-to-be-discovered laws of development in the hidden contradictions of the relations of production, or in other more or less autonomous sectors of sociocultural systems:

Unlike a number of materialists, we do not suppose that the different levels of a social formation emerge one from another. On the contrary, the variation and development of the subsystems depend directly on their internal structures and their intrasystemic contradictions. (Friedman, 1975:163)

The question arises, however, as to whether Marx did indeed discover a valid intrasystemic law of capitalist development. Is there a single dynamic of the capitalist mode of production that unfolds independently of external influences—i.e., independently of the demographic, technological, economic, and environmental conditions in the cultural materialist infrastructure? The failure of Marxism to predict the conditions under which the crucial "socialist" revolutions have taken place (in industrially backward Russia and peasant China rather than industrially advanced Germany or Japan) and its failure to predict the considerable extent of socialization achieved by Sweden, Denmark, Holland and Norway *without* revolution do not inspire confidence in the Hegelian-Marxist-Leninist understanding of sociocultural causality. As Raymond Firth (1975:52) recently reminded the proponents of dialectical inner laws:

the working class is not increasing in misery; wages are not being forced down to a minimum; a managerial bureaucracy has often succeeded the capitalist entrepreneur; the Western working class does not unite with the masses of these less-developed countries but connives in the widening gap between them; the revolutionary societies have their own power struggles, if anything more bitter in accusation, nore brutal in treatment of the defeated than in the capitalist world. (Firth, 1975:52)

One wonders, therefore, how the structural Marxists can be so confident that their brand of Marxism is superior to that of the "vulgar" and "mechanical" materialists. Could it be that the predictive failure portrayed by Firth is due to the error of supposing that relations of production have an autonomous role to play in history? Could it be that these predictive failures have something to do with the flouting of operationalism and empiricism? As Jerrold Seigel (1978:351ff) has shown, Marx himself was not sure about the answer to the first question.

Dominance, Constraint, and Double Talk

TO SAVE the doctrine of the independence or irreducibility of structures from full-blown indeterminacy, the structural Marxists invoke a distinction between "dominance" and "constraint." According to Friedman, constraint is a "negative determination": it determines what things can't be, not what they must be. Dominance determines what things must be; it determines their specificities. The cultural materialist infrastructure merely exercises *constraint* on the relations of production; on the other hand, the relations of production *dominate* the entire system:

From the ecosystem up is a hierarchy of constraints which determine the limits of functional compatibility between levels, hence of their internal variation. This is essentially a negative determination, since it determines what cannot occur but not what must occur. . . . Working in the opposite direction, the relations of production dominate the entire functioning of the larger system, defining the specificity of the mode of production and its developmental tendencies. (Friedman, 1975:163–164)

Not only is the distinction between a negative and a positive determination meaningless in an operational sense (not to be confused with negative and positive feedback), but the distinction runs entirely counter to the kernel of truth in Hegelian logic. Ecological constraints do not merely determine what something must not be. The ecology of the Arctic, for example, does more than constrain the Eskimos from hunting in the nude; it determines that they must put something warm on. The ecology of the San does more than merely constrain them from planting crops in the desert; it determines that they will obtain their calorie ration as hunter-collectors. In a moment I shall use the example of food taboos to disprove the allegation that ecological constraints cannot define the specificity of cultural practices. In Hegelian terms, things are not only what they are, but what they are not. Or in positivist terms, any constraint is a determination; any determination is a constraint.

There is a simple way to express what Friedman is getting at. In an operational probability context, the distinction between negative and positive determination means that some factors account for more of the observed variance than others. That is, some factors account for more of the specific features of a sociocultural system because they are more powerful determinants. Thus what Friedman means is that the relations of production in general account for more of the features of sociocultural systems than the cultural materialist infrastructure. But how can one reconcile this proposition with the assertion that it is the "negative" determinations of infrastructure that "determine the limits of functional compatibility"? For if the relations of production operate within limits set by the cultural materialist infrastructure, then that infrastructure must be linked in a series of probabilistic causal chains to any and all of the specific features allegedly dominated by the autonomous dynamic of irreducible "structures."

The question of whether infrastructure merely "constrains" while other sectors "dominate" is a question of the relative parsimony, scope, and applicability of infrastructural versus structural and superstructural theories. Cultural materialists hold that infrastructure both constrains and dominates. But only by comparing the corpus of theories produced under the auspices of the two strategies can this issue be resolved. I shall turn to that comparison in a moment.

The Fetishization of Historical Materialism

I HAVE YET to comment on the antimaterialist implications of the doctrine of the independence or nonreducibility of "structures." When structuralists—Marxists as well as pure Lévi-Straussians—refer to "structure," they intend not to make any distinction between emic and etic, or mental and behavioral, components. Thus what Friedman is proposing as the dominant determinism impinging upon sociocultural systems consists of elements that in the cultural materialist strategy are not only structural rather than infrastructural, but superstructural, mental, and emic rather than structural, behavioral, and etic.

Friedman recognizes that there are numerous summary statements in the writings of Marx and Engels in which the distorted spiritualized images people have of their society's productive processes are unambiguously treated as the consequence and not the cause of those processes. Two of the most famous passages (see p. 30 and p. 55) occur in *The German Ideology* and *The Contribution to the Critique of Political Economy.* However, Friedman proposes to disregard these passages:

We shall disregard, here, *The German Ideology* and *The Contribution to the Critique of Political Economy,* which have in a handful of epigrammatic pronouncements served as an excuse for the most vulgar kind of materialism and move on to the *Grundrisse* and *Capital,* especially the latter, certainly the most scientific exercise of Marx's career. (Friedman, 1974b:30)

Friedman admits that these epigrammatic pronouncements "might, in fact, easily be interpreted in the most vulgar fashion" (ibid.:61, n. 2). (One wonders what kind of effect this constant use of "vulgar" as an epithet would have had on the members of the first French Marxist party founded by Marx's son-in-law, Paul Lafargue, which called itself the "belly party.") But let us suppose that the two works in question can be "disregarded." Everyone knows that there are similar "pronouncements" contained in many other writings by Marx. For example, in the *Communist Manifesto:* "What else does the history of ideas prove, than that intellectual production changes its character in proportion as material production is changed?" (Marx and Engels, 1959 [1848]:26). In *The Poverty of Philosophy:* "In acquiring new productive forces men change their mode of production; and in changing their mode of production, in changing the way of earning their living, they change all their social relations. . . . The same men who establish their social relations in conformity with their material productivity, produce also principles, ideas and categories in conformity with their social relations" (Marx, 1971 [1847]:109). In the eighth thesis on Fuererbach: "Social life is essentially *practical.* All mysteries which mislead theory to mysticism find their rational solution in human practice and in the comprehension of this practice" (Marx 1976[1848]:5). In the letter to P. V. Annenkov: "The economic forms in which men produce, consume, and exchange, are transitory and historical. With the acquisition of new productive facilities, men change their mode of production, and with the mode of production all the economic relations which are merely the necessary relations of this particular mode of production" (Marx 1971[1846]:182). And finally, in *Capital* itself: "technology discloses man's mode of dealing with nature, the process of production by which he sustains his life, and thereby also lays bare the mode of formation of his social relations, and of the mental conceptions that flow from them" (1975 [1867]:372, fn. 3). Not to mention the numerous similar pronouncements by Engels, as for example in the graveside speech already quoted (p. 141); and in *Anti-Dühring:* "All religion . . . is nothing but the phantastic reflection in men's minds of those external forces which control their daily life . . ." (Engels 1972 [1878]:344).

But I do not wish to enlarge this quest for the holy grail. The fact is that neither *Grundrisse* nor *Capital* provide scriptural authorization for the fetishization of historical materialism. What we encounter in these works as in the entire corpus of dialectical materialist theory is the inevitable ambiguity associated with any view of sociocultural causality that fails to distinguish between the mental and behavioral and the emic and etic components of sociocultural systems. Thus for Marx many aspects of capitalist societies other than the distinct religious superstructure were "imaginary," "unreal," or "fantastic." Commodities are "fetishes" because they misrepresent or disguise their origins in labor processes. Money itself is a "fetishized" form of labor. The social relations of production assume in the eyes of the participants "the fantastic form of relation between things." Capital itself is nothing but a mystified form of labor that has the capacity for illusory expansion. It has the "occult quality of being able to add value to itself." Wages, rent, and profits are a mere phenomenal mystification of the mode of production, which renders "the actual relations invisible and indeed shows the direct opposite of that relation, [and] forms the basis of all the juridical notions of both labour and capitalist, of all the mystifications of the capitalist mode of production" (Marx, quoted in Friedman, 1974b:34).

Friedman correctly points out that Marx assigns a determinative role to these "fictions." Thus, the entire inner dynamic that is supposed to bring about the falling rate of profit and the deepening crises of the business cycle is after all predicated on the very elements of capitalism which Marx calls fetishes and which if Marx is to be taken literally are "unreal" and "illusions." But this equating of unreal and illusion is precisely the basis on which it becomes necessary to establish the distinction between mental, behavioral, and emic and etic operations, as discussed in Chapter 2. The categories of capitalist thought are not unreal; they are simply the mental and emic aspects of the processes of production and distribution under capitalist modes of production. Friedman's exegeses of *Capital* prove that Marx lacked the epistemological instruments that would have made it possible to avoid the ambiguity Friedman correctly attributes to him. The task before us is to remove that ambiguity by revising Marxist-Leninist epistemology, since the predictive failures of Marxism mentioned by Firth are directly linked to an overemphasis on the inner dynamic of the mental and emic aspects of capitalist systems.

The structural Marxists, however, are both structuralists and dialectical Marxists precisely because they reject operational empiricist clarifications of the nature of sociocultural phenomena. Friedman therefore views Marx's confusion about mental and behavioral, objective and subjective, and so forth as a dispensation for abandoning the principle of infrastructural determination. He is willing to grant that such "illusions" as profit, rent, and interest are epiphenomena, "truly secondary categories," but he is unwilling to regard money itself as the "mere mystified image of something more real." Money, despite its being a fetish,

is the operator of the system, determining the particular social form of exploitation as well as its misrepresentation. Thus it is a social relationship which is itself a fetish, determining the fact of exploitation as well as its appearance. (Ibid.:35)

Some fetishes are "opaque" in the sense that they disguise the "real" processes of production, but they are not illusory, because they determine the real processes of production: "money capital is not an illusion based on real production, it is the social precondition for it" (ibid.:56).

It is true that Marx's theory of capitalism rests in part upon an inner dynamic corresponding to the logical consequences of a set of emic mental rules governing money exchange and money value (the paper is etic, but its value is emic). But Marx's theory of capitalism does not rest exclusively or even primarily on the inevitability of the falling rate of profit and the deepening crises of the business cycle. Marx placed equal if not greater emphasis on the material (etic) processes of exploitation—the extraction (etic) of quantities of labor from the proletariat for the benefit of the ruling class by means of the ruling class's control over the means of production, an extraction in turn more or less directly contingent on the ruling class's control over the physical (etic) means of coercion, as embodied in the state's police-military apparatus. Without that control, the rules governing money exchange and money value, contracts, wages, interest, rents, profits—the whole emic and mental structure of capitalist enterprise—would disappear overnight. Like all mistaken ideas, the emic and mental categories of capitalism enjoy a power guaranteed not by the frailty of the human intellect but by the frailty of the human body.

The structural Marxist dematerialization of capitalism corresponds closely to Lévi-Strauss's dematerialization of marriage, exchange, asymmetrical alliances, and the origin of stratification. Cycles in the sky on the one hand; capital in the sky on the other.

The Bourbonic Plague

CONVINCED THAT the dominant structure of capitalism consists of the money fetish, Friedman proposes to find comparably "opaque" but nonillusory dominant structures in precapitalist societies. The role of ancestor worship in the evolution of the Asiatic state provides a convenient example. Initially the lineage heads represent the community to the ancestors, and the ancestors are seen as controlling the community. But some lineages then claim to control the ancestors and thus gain a monopoly over wealth-giving spirits. This permits them to exploit their fellows:

If the chief has special privileges, if he receives corvée or tribute, this is only because *he is thought,* as head of the senior lineage, to be the necessary mediator between the community as a whole and the supernatural. . . . It is *because* the process of production is represented upside down that certain lineages can, *by controlling the supernatural,* come to dominate the community. . . . Monopoly over the "wealth-giving" spirits is of the same order as monopoly over money-capital. *The control of both fictitious items ensures the domination over material reproduction and the exploitation of the labor of the society.* (Friedman, 1974b:58–59 [italics added])

Control over production is permanently ceded to a ruling class because the members of the exploited class mistakenly think that the ruling class is entitled to exploit them; and the ruling class persists because it too is dominated by the imaginary "fetishized" relationships: "The chiefly or royal class is entitled to its surplus on no other basis than that it occupies an instrumental place in the imaginary conditions of reproduction of the society" (ibid.:59). As Allen Berger (1976) has pointed out, this analysis fails to provide any theory accounting for the specific religious form of the "fetishization" of the relations of production, or for its necessity. To this I would add that Friedman's model of the evolution of the state stands in opposition to the fundamental premise of all genuinely materialist approaches to social stratification —namely, that the mystification of what goes on in the infrastructure is the consequence, not the cause, of exploitation. All states are based on a monopoly of the material instruments of coercion in the hands of a ruling class. Exploitation is more than the inner dynamics of our fantasies. The executive of the ruling class is not to be mistaken for actors in a Disneyland. Monopolies—over ancestors or capital—rest on the control of material forces, not on ideological illusions. Ruling classes do more than control illusions: they control etic and behavioral phenomena known as policemen and armies, who are capable of doing some very vulgar things to human bodies.

Thus by substituting the monopoly of control over spirit for the monopoly of control over force, structural Marxism unerringly returns Marxism to its bourgeois Hegelian origins. Eric Wolf has suggested that during the 1930s and 1940s anthropologists contributed to the obfuscation of political economy by describing cultures as organic entities that were "all ideology and morality, and neither power nor economy" (1972:257). Structural Marxism is also at bottom indistinguishable from the effete innocence of Wolf's "liberal babes in the darkling woods" who "spoke of patterns, themes, world view, ethos, and values, but not of power" (Wolf, 1972:256–257).

The Structuralist Infrastructure

CULTURAL MATERIALISM acknowledges the importance of such emic and mental creations as ancestors, lineages, interest, rent, and profits in explaining specific events in history. That is what is meant by the existence of feedback between infrastructure and superstructure. But the structuralist Marxists have something else in view. For them, it is not a matter of feedback but of a lack of explicit criteria for what constitutes infrastructure, and therefore of the option of popping any part of the social system in and out of infrastructure to suit their convenience. In Godelier's words:

> When Marx distinguished between infra- and superstructure and proposed that the deep logic of evolution and history depends in the last analysis on the properties of their infra-structure, he did no more than point out . . . that there is a hierarchy of functions and structural causalities, without in any way prejudging the type of social relations which take on these functions nor the number of functions that any structure can assume. (Godelier, 1975:15)

To quote Friedman again (1975:198): "a formerly superstructural element will become part of the relation of production." And to quote Maurice Bloch on Madagascar social organization in the same volume: "for the Merina the kinship system is part of the superstructure, for the Zafimaniry it is part of the infrastructure" (Bloch, 1975:222). The principle enunciated here is the basic theoretical principle of eclecticism (whose theoretical consequences I shall elaborate in Chapter 10). Eclecticism propounded in the name of Karl Marx is still eclecticism. Every empirically valid grounding of structural and superstructural variables in the infrastructure, however tentative or incomplete, is an improvement over the permanent state of mystified ignorance inherent in the acceptance of any aspect of the relations of production or of religion as independent irreducible givens. By grounding religions of love and mercy, pig worship, pig hate, cow love, witchcraft, messianism, human sacrifice, big-manship, descent, polygyny, and so forth in the infrastructure (Harris, 1974, 1977a and Chapter 4), cultural materialists do not suppose that all of the particularities of these phenomena as they occur in specific societies have been exhaustively explained. But these preliminary and tentative clarifications (whose value when compared with total obscurity seems indisputable) strongly suggest that the structural Marxists have made an opaque fetish out of the transparent limitations of their own epistemological and theoretical principles.

Soft-Core Marxism

TO THE EXTENT that structural Marxists emphasize the importance of political economy in state-level societies, their analyses usually parallel cultural materialist analyses but are less complete in not offering an explanation of the origin of the political-economic structures in terms of infrastructural processes.

For example, in attempting to define what he calls "the exact nature of the diversity and unity of the economic and social relations" of the succession of Andean cultures, Maurice Godelier shows that similar religious ideologies and rituals fulfilled different functions in relation to different political systems. Thus in pre-Inca times, religious ideas and practices associated with chiefdoms enhanced the voluntary cooperation of egalitarian producers. After the Inca conquest, the same rituals and ideas were harnessed to a pattern of centrally administered exploitation and used as the basis of recruiting corvée labor. Finally, after the Spanish conquest, new rituals and beliefs—the fiesta and cargo systems —were introduced in order to adjust the pattern of exploitation in a form consistent with Catholic ideology. "The economy of prestige and the competition for *cargos* took root and was tolerated by the dominant Spanish because it was already justified by their own political and Catholic ideology" (Godelier, 1974:71).

None of these conclusions are incompatible with, and several are prefigured in, my own analysis of the fiesta and cargo system (Harris, 1964a). Godelier's explanation is more restricted, however, for it fails to explain why the cargo-fiesta system was not a universal feature of the exploitation of manpower in other parts of the New World, such as Brazil and the Caribbean, where Catholicism was no less the ideology of the dominant classes. Understanding of the different patterns of race relations and class exploitation in the New World begins with the association between African slave systems in the tropical and semitropical lowlands and hacienda serfdom in the highlands. This difference relates to the specific demographic, technological, economic, and environmental features of lowland and highland infrastructures at the time of contact. Ecological factors account for the different levels of sociopolitical development in Brazil and the Andes; from this we get the different size and quality of the indigenous labor forces in Peru and Brazil and hence the importation of African slaves to work on cash crops in one case, and the use of corvée and hacienda peonage involving Amerindian workers on the other (see p. 112 for the general place of such theories in the cultural materialist corpus). Thus Godelier's (1974:67) conclusion that the "mechanisms of competition and redistribution took a form corresponding to the Catholic ideology of the dominant classes and were expressed in a manner tolerated by them" appears to be cogent only because it avoids the question of why the dominant Andean classes were restricted to a particular mode of exploitation—namely, the hacienda system. Godelier thus ends up emphasizing a causal relationship that is merely a feedback loop in a larger adaptive process whose very existence is obscured by the doctrine of the irreducibility of structure to infrastructure. Structural Marxists recurrently present narrow and "unreduced" versions of wider and infrastructurally grounded cultural materialist theories. Moreover, structural Marxists actually mimic the cultural materialist strategy, despite all antagonist pronouncements, whenever they get down to the question of the ultimate causes of different modes of production. Indeed, except for the rhetoric and opacity of the structuralist style, many structural Marxists reveal themselves as cultural materialist in spite of themselves. For example, Godelier's approach to the explanation of the Australian eight-section system (see p. 84) does not stop with the less than earth-shaking discovery that kinship can function as "relations of production." Godelier asks instead: "Under what conditions and for what reasons do certain social relations take on the function of relations of production and thereby control the reproduction of these relations, as well as the reproduction of all social relations?" (1975: 14). In plainer English, what Godelier really wants to know is simply this: what are the causes of the specific features of Australian domestic and political organization known as the section system? But that question is one that has already been asked and tentatively answered by cultural materialists.

As I suggested in Chapter 4, a likely key to understanding Australian descent and marriage rules is to model them as on-the-ground marital exchanges between exemplars of two or four types of exogamous bands. The more arid the habitat, the more dispersed the bands, the more vital it becomes to establish multi-band networks.

The advantages of crisscrossing the desert with all these life lines of descent and affinity should be apparent from our earlier discussion of band ecology. In fact, the section system seems to have been so highly adaptive for the Australians that some of them, especially in the most arid and most sparsely settled areas, went ahead to double the number of types of clans from two to four and the number of sections from four to eight. (Harris, 1971b:340)

What are we to make, therefore, of Godelier's breathless discovery?

Given the level of productive forces and the nature of the techniques of production in the widest sense of the term, the more arid the ecological environment, the more the local groups, the hordes, consisting of several related nuclear families, must move over an ever wider area, leaving the individuals separated one from another by ever greater distances for ever longer periods of time. . . . (1975:9)

Godelier (1977:52ff) also is a latecomer in analyzing the functional fit between Mbuti domestic economy and their forest-adapted hunter-gatherer infrastructure. He sees three "internal constraints" on the Mbuti mode of production:

1. a "dispersion constraint" controlling the spacing and size of bands.
2. a "cooperation constraint" controlling the age-sex composition of the hunting groups using nets.
3. a "fluidity constraint" preventing the formation of lineages and requiring fluid band membership.

Godelier has discovered that these principles can be used to explain the idea of distinct territories, the nonexistence of exclusive rights of bands to their territory; the emphasis in the kin terminology on generation and sex differences, certain ritual performances, and other structural and superstructural features. This discovery, however, merely paraphrases the modern consensus of cultural materialists and cultural ecologists concerning the most characteristic form of the domestic and political arrangements among hunter-gatherer bands (see Chapter 4). One reads with astonishment Godelier's boast that

this method of carrying out a structural analysis within a Marxist framework, as distinct from ordinary cultural materialism [ordinaire = vulgar] or some people's so-called Marxism, does not reduce the various instances of society to economics nor does it represent economics as the only true reality, whereby all other features reflect differing and phantasmic effects. (Ibid.:55–56)

In seeking an infrastructural explanation for the structural "constraints" falsely identified by Godelier as distinctive products of his own analysis, cultural materialists have no intention of representing "economics as the only true reality"! Rather, the intention is to get beyond the more general similarities of hunter-gatherer social life to the specificities of particular hunter-gatherer adaptations. For example, once one has sketched in a plausible functional relationship between Mbuti band organization and the structured "constraints," there remains the problem, completely overlooked by Godelier, that the Mbuti have two very different forms of social organization—one associated with the net hunters, which he analyzes, and the other associated with bow-and-arrow hunting, which he does not mention. Large cooperative bands characterize the net hunters only, while the archers are characterized by independent nuclear families. William Abruzzi (1979) surely does not make "economics the only true reality" when he shows that the variant forms reflect different population densities, which are in turn expressions of differential exposures to the encroachment of sedentary horticulturalists, who are symbiotically related to the archers but not to the net hunters during part of the year.

Nor do I represent economics as the only "true reality" when, going beyond Godelier, I insist on asking why the Australian aborigines alone among band-level hunter-gatherers elaborated their system of marital exchanges, or at least the ideology of such exchanges, into the specific form of sections and subsections. In conformity with the strategy of cultural materialism, I hold that it is reasonable to believe that a higher degree of causal specificity will eventually be uncovered through a more sophisticated diachronic analysis of the demographic, technological, economic, and environmental components of Australian native societies. Perhaps such a solution will start with the observation that warfare in native Australia seems to have been unusually intense for bands of hunter-collectors. Why was this the case? Perhaps, as I have suggested in Chapter 4, it has something to do with the continent-wide absence of large placental mammals. Or perhaps the solution lies in some as-yet-unknown aspect of the other biotic specialties in which Australia abounds. I cannot believe that to be a Marxist one must terminate the study of the causal contribution of these additional aspects of the cultural materialist infrastructure on a priori grounds. Yet as Marx himself once said, "if that is Marxism, then I am not a Marxist."

Sahlins and the Substantivist-Formalist Debate

IN HIS BOOK *Stone Age Economics,* Marshall Sahlins (now of the University of Chicago) thanks Claude Lévi-Strauss for providing him with an office during the period from 1967 to 1969 at the Collège de France in Paris, and notes that he would find it difficult to reciprocate the courtesy and generosity that went with it. Lévi-Strauss must surely also find it difficult to reciprocate a different aspect of the exchange. For in partially converting Sahlins to structuralism, Lévi-Strauss gained a formidable American spokesman whose early work provided a model for much cultural materialist research.

Sahlins's interest in structuralism and his affinity with structural Marxism took shape during what has come to be known as the "substantivist-formalist debate" (Cook, 1974). This debate concerns the legitimacy of applying classical economic concepts derived from the observation of capitalist economic systems to the analysis of pre-state ("primitive") societies. For Sahlins and other substantivist followers of Karl Polanyi (1944), economy means "the process by which society is materially provisioned" (Sahlins, 1973:284), whereas for the formalists, the economy is a system for utilizing scarce means to maximize the satisfaction of wants: "once choice as to the utilization of scarce means is exercised, those wants which are deemed most satisfying or as having the highest marginal utility will be satisfied" (Cook, 1966:335). Substantivists, like structural Marxists, insist that primitive economies are embedded in the social relations of kinship, while capitalist economics are embedded in a wholly different set of social relations. In capitalist societies, concepts such as economizing (allocation of scarce resources for maximum personal gain), capital, profit, rent, interest, wages, and so forth are appropriate analytic categories. But such concepts cannot be applied to societies in which the production, distribution, and consumption of goods are not embedded in social relations of private property and capitalist political economy. The penalty for doing so, according to Sahlins, is the making over of the world in the false, ethnocentric image of bourgeois businessmen.

Broadly speaking, it is a choice between the perspective of Business, for the formalist method must consider the primitive economies as under-developed versions of our own, and a culturalist [i.e. substantivist] study that as a matter of principle does honor to different societies for what they are. (1972:xii)

From a cultural materialist perspective, both the substantivists and the formalists are stuck in a single metaphysical tar pit. To assert that for substantivists the economy is "the process by which society is materially provisioned" (Sahlins, 1973:284) is meaningless unless one states how the categories of the process are to be identified in relation to mental and behavioral events and the native actor's or observer's point of view.

Similarly for the formalists, the central epistemological question is (ought to be) not whether economizing in terms of the maximizing of value can be used to explain noncapitalist behavior but whether economizing and "value" are judged by emic or etic standards. Thus Cook's definition of economy is no less operationally vague than Sahlins's definition. It is meaningless to urge the study of how wants whose satisfaction is "deemed most satisfying" are satisfied by "scarce means." "Wants"—whose wants? "Deemed satisfying"—deemed satisfying by whom? "Scarce"—scarce according to whose criteria of scarcity?

The Economy Has No Surplus

THE BASIC substantivist position that economy is the process of material provisioning would make perfectly good sense if it were the etic and behavioral process of provisioning that one had in view. Unfortunately, the substantivists with whom Sahlins pitched his tent were idealists, relativists, and indeterminists. While it is true that they were interested in "honoring" cultural differences, they seemed to have an even greater interest in dishonoring the attempt to achieve a science of society. Their substantivism consisted of embedding economic process exclusively in the emic domains of social life.

The devastation to which such a commitment inevitably would lead was evident in the substantive treatment of the concept of surplus. In defiance of the quintessential Marxist proposition that the expropriation of a surplus above subsistence constituted the basis for the evolution of social stratification, the substantivist Harry Pearson declared that "the economy has no surplus." By this he meant that surplus, like all economic processes, had no empirical existence apart from the social system in which it was instituted. But since in Pearsons' view, "social systems involve Parsonian-Weberian concepts of social action," the instituted entity—the surplus above subsistence—either existed in the minds of the actors, or it did not exist at all: "Man, living in society, does not produce a surplus unless he names it such, and then its effect is given by the manner in which it is institutionalized" (Pearson, 1957:325–326).

In an article intended to rebut Pearson, I pointed out that "surplus" had to be measurable independently of whether the native participants thought that they had less than enough or thought they had more than enough, because there could be no cross-cultural science of society without an independent measure of production.

His [Pearson's] denial of the chronological and functional primacy of biological needs and of techno-environmental adaptation for the fulfillment of these needs is tantamount to a renunciation of the search for order among cross-cultural phenomena. This is so not merely because his criticism of the surplus theory cannot be sustained, but because the manner in which he has chosen to refute it inevitably leads to the conclusion that cultural phenomena are essentially the result of whimsical and capricious processes. (Harris, 1959:188)

Pearson claimed that society had the "power" to "employ physical resources in ways which may be regarded as even more important than a given level of subsistence." This "power," I wrote, was "the power of choice, elevated to astonishing levels, capable of limitless selection and boundless creation under unknowable conditions locked within the secret confines of the collective or individual will" (Harris, 1959:188). Obviously, Pearson's argument can be applied to any sector of culture. Therefore an effective response to relativism and idealism (with their obfuscation of the material basis of exploitation) requires a reformulation of the entire set of epistemological assumptions, including those employed in the name of materialism (like Leslie White's insistence that culture is a realm of symbols). Hence, while others, notably G. Dalton (1960, 1963), S. Cook (1966), M. Nash (1967), and M. Sahlins (1973) battled on about the possibility of applying classical economic categories to primitive societies, I tried to show that all problems of this sort could only be resolved by adopting an operational approach to sociocultural definitions and by separating emic from etic operations (Harris, 1964).

Exploitation and Substantivism

SAHLINS'S SUBSTANTIVISM, consistently adhered to, leads to a sterile impasse of subjectivity in which the emics of mental and behavioral events dominate the etics of infrastructure. All the basic assertions of Marxism about the nature of objective historical processes are thereby rendered null and void. Consider, for example, what happens to the pivotal notion of class conflict and exploitation when the substantivist George Dalton decides to honor the idea of feudal rents and capitalist taxation. By following the line of reasoning about the nonexistence of an objective economic surplus, Dalton quickly reaches the conclusion that neither classes nor the exploitation of one class by another has any objective existence apart from what people think, say, or imagine about the qualities of human relationships in their subjective experience:

Marxists call the material transactions between lord and peasant "exploitation." . . . But it is impossible to make such a judgment objectively. . . . Are present-day Americans (and Russians) "exploited" by definition because we are forced under threat of legal penalty to pay one-third of our income to federal, state, and local governments? I suggest that whether or not "exploitation" exists in such situations should be made to depend on the tax or tribute payers' subjective reactions. . . . (Dalton, 1972:407)

How can structural Marxists admit that they are "incurably relativist" (Sahlins, 1973:280) and not accept Dalton's argument? And if they accept Dalton's argument that class exploitation has no objective existence outside the minds of people who think they are being exploited, how can they ever again lay claim to being Marxists (G. Frank, 1970)?

Of course there are precedents for relativism in Marxism. Lenin (Selsam and Martel, 1963:158–160) and Engels (as quoted by Sahlins, 1973:280) postulate the existence of different laws of development for different cultural systems. This kind of relativism is rooted in Marx's critique of the classical economists' assertion that bourgeois economic behavior was inevitable—that the propensity to "truck and barter," the "maximization of private profits," "the law of supply and demand," the distinction between rich and poor, "the iron law of wages," "the ineradicability of poverty," and so forth were part of human nature and therefore unmodifiable by culture. Hence, concluded Marx, each social formation operates according to different "laws."

In equating human nature with capitalism, classical economic theory was of course intolerably ethnocentric. One does not have to be a structural Marxist to recognize that fact. Indeed, the entire history of American anthropology in the first half of this century was dominated by the relativist mission of the Boasian historical particularists, for whom there were no such things as universal sociocultural laws or human nature (see pp. 308ff). What, then, is the way out of subjectivism and relativism?

Only by recognizing the difference between emic and etic definitions of such concepts as exploitation and surplus can a demystified substantivist strategy avoid the sterile relativism of the Boasian program. Dalton's (1974:559) accusation that "exploitation and surplus are prejudicial words used by some social scientists (perhaps unintentionally) to condemn only those systems of social stratification they dislike and disapprove of" certainly cannot be answered by accusing him of creating theories "to justify the advance of the enlightened at the expense of the wretched of the earth" (Eric Wolf in Dalton, 1972:411). Dalton has challenged Marxists to come up with a cross-culturally valid definition of exploitation and surplus. They have failed utterly to comply. Neither dialectical materialists nor structural Marxists will ever be able to provide such definitions as long as they hold that "Marx abolished the false dichotomy between ideal and material" (O'Laughlin, 1975:343) and that structuralism transcends the need for the emic/etic distinction (Lévi-Strauss, 1972). Dalton asked a reasonable question: "What is exploitation?" He received in return a political threat: ". . . if people like Dalton cannot decide what exploitation is or whether it exists or not, then it may very well be that it is theoreticians like Che Guevera and Mao Tse-tung who will have the last word in the debate" (Newcomer and Rubenstein, 1975:338). If Marxists can only respond to the question "What is exploitation?" in this manner, then their Marxism isn't much of an answer to anything worth asking.*

Structural "Specifications"

SAHLINS HAS SET himself the task of proving that in the band, village, and "tribal" societies studied by anthropologists, the etic behavioral infrastructure is determined by sociopolitical and ideological factors, rather than the other way around. Structure and superstructure specify what takes place in the infrastructure. I shall consider the structural specifications first. According to Sahlins, the intensity of production is such a specification:

---

*Newcomer (1977) subsequently set forth a more serious but no less unsuccessful definition of exploitation.

Quite generally among the tribal cultivators, the intensity of land use seems a specification of the social-political organization. (1972:48)

In any given cultural formation, "pressure on land" is not in the first instance a function of technology and resources, but rather of the producers' *access* to *sufficient* means of livelihood. The latter is clearly a specification of the cultural system—relations of production and property, rules of land tenure, relations between local groups, and so forth. (Ibid.:49)

That is to say, the society's economic destiny is played out in its relations of production, especially the political pressures that can be mounted on the household economy. (Ibid.:82)

Cultural materialists *insist* no less than structural Marxists that such specifications exist. But it is not part of the cultural materialist strategy to treat structural specifications—even etic structural specifications—as givens. We demand to know how they arise, and we expect to find the answers in the etic and behavioral infrastructure. Sahlins, like other structural Marxists, does not make such demands. Moreover, despite his inability to replace cultural materialist theories with better theories covering the same phenomena, he rejects the possibility that any kind of infrastructural causality will ever explain specific features of social relations of production.

The Underproduction Fallacy

TO PROVE his point that structure "specifies" or dominates infra-structure, Sahlins argues that there is no other way to explain the fact that "primitive" economies are chronically underproductive:

The main run of them, agricultural as well as preagricultural, seem not to realize their own economic capacities. Labor power is underused, technological means are not fully engaged, natural resources are left untapped. (1972:41)

This chronic underproduction is allegedly a function of the propensity of primitive peoples to adjust their labor intensity to the level of bare subsistence and their population to the level of minimum density and maximum dispersion. They have no propensity to increase their population, aggregate into larger groups, and increase their production. Thus one cannot really speak of economizing or of maximizing benefits over costs in the context of band and village societies.

What kind of evidence does Sahlins have for proving that band and village societies are chronically underpopulated and underproductive? The evidence consists of estimates of the extent to which such societies fail to grow up to the limit set by the "carrying capacities" of their habitats. Sahlins cites figures that seem to show that the range of approach to carrying capacity varies from 7 percent among the Kuikuru of Amazonia to about 75 percent for among the Lala of Zambia. It would be interesting to go over each estimate in order to guarantee that they are based on similar assumptions and procedures. In the case of the Kuikuru, for example, the figure of 7 percent does not take into account the limited extent to which animal protein resources can be exploited in tropical forest habitats (cf. Gross, 1975; Ross, 1978). Other limiting factors, such as water, periodic drought, storms, epidemics, and so forth may also have been overlooked. Furthermore, in the "primitive" African societies in Sahlins's sample, restraints on production were byproducts of colonial taxation and labor migration politics, and restraints on population were associated with the legacy of slave-raiding and colonial wars.

But I do not intend to carry out a case-by-case examination of the evidence for underproduction in relation to carrying capacity. Rather, I simply want to deny that the cultural materialist strategy involves an assumption that human populations normally rise to any particular percentage of the absolute carrying capacity of their habitat. Sahlins is quite correct in insisting that carrying capacity for human populations can only be defined in terms of the conjunction of culture and nature. Carrying capacity for human populations is modifiable by the intensification of a given mode of production and by a shift from one mode of production to another. What cultural materialism asserts is this: the intensification of any given mode of production will eventually reach a point of diminishing returns—i.e., the producers will get less for the same or greater effort. Exceeding the point of diminishing returns inevitably leads to lowered life expectancy and standards of well being and to irreversible resource depletions. Band and village societies ordinarily adjust their numbers and hence their demands on the production system below the point of diminishing returns. The situation in stratified societies, where political economic compulsion and exploitation are used to intensify production, is more complicated. However, state societies also cannot continue to intensify production in the face of diminishing returns, even if population is held constant, without increasing the risk of political chaos and military conquest by external enemies.

In the perspective of cultural materialism, "underproduction" cannot be said to exist merely because a population is stabilized below carrying capacity. *Underproduction can be said to exist only when intensification has not yet reached the point of diminishing returns.* Sahlins offers no evidence that any of the groups which he describes as underproductive could increase production without suffering diminishing returns.

The Underpopulation Fallacy

ACCORDING TO SAHLINS (1972:131), "each political organization harbors a coefficient of population density." Cultural materialism holds that each mode of production and reproduction as a conjunction harbors a coefficient of population density *and* a domestic as well as a political organization. Cultural materialism seeks to explain more with less. But there are also logical and substantive discrepancies.

If structure "specifies" population density, how does it do it? According to Sahlins, structure limits population density through the social relations of the domestic mode of production. These social relations characteristically underuse labor, neglect resources, and fail to apply existing technology. But what has this to do with population density? Does the underuse of labor mean that coitus is restricted? Does the domestic mode of production involve a particular level of copulatory intensity? There is no evidence for such restraints, or at least no evidence that they are responsible for restricting population. Indeed, band and village women are physiologically capable of producing astronomical densities within a few generations (see p. 68). Clearly, the production of children has to be controlled by practices that are not predictable from the social relations of production. The structure of Australian aboriginal bands cannot explain their high rates of infanticide. Necessity in such matters arises not from the structure but from the Malthusian situation in which all life forms participate. The necessity to limit population is a necessity imposed by nature on infrastructure. It is not a whimsical invention of social relations. The regulation of population under paleotechnic conditions entails severe penalties. Social structure does not create these penalties; rather, social structure is an emanation of the systemic attempt to limit these penalties within the capacity of the processes of production. Hence the conjunction of these penalties and processes—the cultural materialist infrastructure—

determines the domestic and political structure, and not the other way around. Sahlins himself unwittingly contradicts the contention that structure is the decisive factor controlling population. He agrees that the nonsedentary patterns of hunter-collectors are determined by the "diminishing returns" that a local group confronts if it stays in one place too long: "Thus the first and decisive contingency of hunting-gathering: it requires movement to maintain production on advantageous terms" (1972:33). He also admits that the same avoidance of diminishing returns "causes" (his word) the low density of population through the practice of "infanticide, senilicide, sexual continence for the duration of the nursing period, etc.—practices for which many food-collecting peoples are well known." Indeed, his cultural materialist reasoning is exemplary:

These tactics of demographic restraint again form part of a larger policy for counteracting diminishing returns in subsistence. . . . Insofar as the people would keep the advantage in local production and maintain a certain physical and social stability, their Malthusian practices are just cruelly consistent. Modern hunters and gatherers, working their notably inferior environments, pass most of the year in very small groups widely spaced out. *But rather than the sign of underproduction, the wages of poverty, this demographic pattern is better understood as the cost of living well.* (1972:34; italics added)

And yet a scant eight pages further on in the same book, Sahlins announces that primitive economies are "underproductive": "The main run of them, agricultural as well as preagricultural, seem not to realize their own economic capacities" (1972:41).

But why should they strive to reach their "economic capacities" if as Sahlins admits, they must live less well in order to do so? What kind of "economic capacity" is that?

The Case of the Sacred Cow

CULTURAL RESTRICTIONS on eating domesticated animals constitute an important testing ground of rival research strategies. Using the Hindu taboo on the slaughter of cattle and the Israelite taboo on pork, I have attempted to show that such restrictions usually originate as adaptive responses to infrastructural conditions and that they enhance the material well-being of the populations practicing them (Harris, 1966, 1971a, 1974a, 1974b, 1977b; Azzi, 1974; Bennet, 1967; Dandekar, 1969; Heston, 1971; Raj, 1969, 1971; Rao, 1970).

Structural Marxists have objected that these explanations are nothing more than trite functionalist "just so stories" based on the fact that the observant populations did not become extinct. Like all cultural materialist explanations, the explanations in question are alleged to be vague concerning the specificities of cultural beliefs and practices. I have shown why it is *possible* to taboo beef or pork, but not why it is *necessary* to do so. In the words of Marshall Sahlins (1973:287):

proof that a certain trait or cultural arrangement has positive economic value is not an adequate explanation of its existence or even of its presence. The *problematique* of adaptive advantage does not specify a uniquely correct answer. As principle of causality in general and economic performance in particular, "adaptive advantage" is indeterminate: stipulating grossly what is impossible but rendering suitable anything that is possible. To say that a certain cultural trait is "adaptive" in the light of its economic virtues is only a weak kind of functionalism, accounting not for its existence but merely for its feasibility—and then not necessarily, as materially disadvantageous traits may also be feasible.

This is echoed by Jonathan Friedman (1974a:538):

It is dangerous to take as given the entire system within which the element "cattle" operates. Once one has described the actual state of affairs, it is tautological to say that a particular variable is adaptive simply because it has a necessary function in the total system.

And reechoed by Alexander Alland (1975:67):

While it is useful to employ explanations of this type, they are limited by all the restrictions noted for classical functional analysis. They provide good arguments for neither cause nor necessity.

I shall now take up the theory of the origin of the Hindu taboos in some detail to refute these objections. I shall show that cultural materialism generates testable theories which not only supply negative "constraints" but positive determinants as well, specifying what had to be along with what could not be in a manner beyond the means of structural Marxist principles. In doing so, however, I do not propose to capitulate to the proposal that infrastructural explanations must conform to the standards of nineteenth-century concepts of causality —that is, I do not intend to meet the structuralist Marxist request for "uniquely correct answers." Since uniquely correct answers cannot be attained even in the physical sciences, I see no reason why social science strategies must strive after such will-o'-the-wisps. Cultural materialism does not deal with unique specifications but with probabilistic causes. As I explained in Chapter 3, probabilistic causality exists whenever there is the expectation that theories can never be verified in 100 percent of all tests. Probabilistic theories are not falsified by negative instances as long as positive instances occur with greater-than-random frequencies. A probably correct answer as distinguished from a uniquely correct answer is an answer given by a theory of broader scope, wider applicability, and greater statistical validity than any of its rivals.

Historical Context of the Controversy

WHEN I SET OUT in 1964 to show that the prevention of the development of a beef-slaughter industry in India was vital to the best interest of millions of peasant families, a solid core of professionals held on the contrary that the cow-slaughter ban was a primary cause of India's poverty and underdevelopment. The literature on the subject was filled with emphatic pronouncements: the slaughter ban and beef taboo compelled people to utilize other, scarcer foods of less value; gave rise to a cattle population, as many as one-half of which were "surplus in relation to feed supply," "useless from birth to death," "superfluous," "detrimental to the nation," "more a liability than an asset," "a great burden," "plainly contrary to economic interest," and in competition with the human population for a "scarce existence" (all sources cited in Harris, 1966).

I agree with Friedman that "once one has described the actual state of affairs it is tautological to say that a particular variable is adaptive simply because it has a necessary function." But one does not describe the actual state of affairs by waving a magic wand. Because of the predominance of idealist and eclectic strategies among Indianists, the actual state of affairs was and still is seriously misrepresented. I did not support my theories by invoking tautologies about adaptation but by citing empirical data on milk, meat, and dung production; on the importance of bullock traction to rainfall farmers on hard-packed soils;

on the geographical distribution of cattle sex ratios, of urban milk specialties, of types of fodder, and of methods for culling herds; on the numbers of animals owned per farm unit; on the use of carrion and hides by untouchable castes; and on other material costs and benefits. When these factors are analyzed in an ecosystem context, most, if not all, of the allegedly useless and superfluous cows cease to exist. Many of my findings were coroborated by bioenergetic field research conducted by Stuart Odend'hal in Singur, West Bengal:

The Singur cattle population appears to be efficient in supplying products of value based on the needs and priorities of the society involved. It is doubtful whether any substantial improvement in cattle productivity is possible without considerable sustained outside energetic inputs into the system. (1972:20)

Subsequently my own field studies indicate that within the overall restrictions of Hinduism, Indian farmers cull, select, and manage their bovine stock in a way that is highly responsive to such factors as human population density, size of holdings, rainfall and cropping patterns, soil quality, amount of irrigation, cost of fodder, and other etic conditions (Harris, 1977b). This kind of analysis is essential for an understanding of the possibilities for change in present-day rural India.

The strategic importance of showing that in the present system relatively few of the cattle are actually useless lies in its relevance to the question of causality. If the ideological restrictions on the management of cattle are the cause of massive nutritional and energetic deficits, then it becomes rather ridiculous to suppose that the religious restrictions arose from practical, mundane, and adaptive processes. On the other hand, by demonstrating that the supposedly excess and underutilized cattle are in fact essential, useful, and adapted to local ecological conditions, one enhances the credibility of a materialist strategy. But such a demonstration was never intended to serve as the explanation of all features of the observed pattern of cattle use, nor was it intended to serve as a test of the prediction that the Hindu restrictions on cattle arose *because* they enhanced the energetic and nutritional well-being of the people who put them into practice. It is a cardinal principle of cultural materialism that such explanations cannot be given in a purely synchronic frame.

The effort to show that the pig in Melanesia regulates population growth, warfare, and forest fallow intervals (Vayda, Leeds, and Smith, 1961; Rappaport, 1967; Harris, 1974) must be seen in the same context. In these cases religiously inspired patterns of pig production and pig consumption lead to periodic slaughter of excess animals in large-scale, apparently wasteful intervillage feasts. The synchronic ecological approach to these feasts showed that they are not merely extravaganzas compounded out of childlike whims, cravings, and superstitions (cf. Luzbetak, 1954) but valuable components in an intricate system by which the production and reproduction of animals, people, and plants are regulated (although not necessarily optimally controlled). Again, this demonstration merely removes obstacles that previously impeded the development of a nomothetic explanation of the Melanesian pig complex in terms of practical, mundane, and adaptive processes. But no one associated with the ecological interpretation of pig feasting in New Guinea has ever proposed that the origin of the system was determined by ecological relationships *observed in the present.* Cultural materialists insist upon the indispensability of diachronic processes for the explanation of existing systems. It is an infelicitous misrepresentation,* therefore, for structural Marxists to declare the synchronic cultural materialist approach to dietary taboos null and void because it "provides a good argument for neither cause nor necessity," and because only the feasibility and not the necessity has been demonstrated.

Political Economy and the Cow

ACCORDING TO Friedman, cultural materialists fail to see that even while keeping technology constant, a "radical reorganization of the social structure" in India (Friedman, 1974a:458) could lead to more and better protein, including beef, for most people. Yet I have made it seem as if the improvement of protein supplies depends entirely on the ecology.

In sum, although one might want to argue that the man/cattle relation in India is adaptive given the constraints of the socio-economic system (not discussed by Harris who makes it all sound like a problem of ecology) of which it is a part, it is potentially disastrous not to talk about the system as a whole. (Ibid.:458)

*This phrase does not do justice to the misrepresentations in the work of Diener and Robkin (1978).

Rebuking "vulgar materialism," Friedman suggests that if the "cattle were . . . freely (in the economic sense) mobile among individual plots, then there would be no need for the great numbers implied by holding such factors constant" (467:fn. 17). But I did not ignore the possibility of improving the standard of protein consumption by means of political-economic restructuring; in fact, I made the very suggestions Friedman represents as his own:

Sharing of draught animals on a cooperative basis might reduce the need for additional animals. . . . The "big" farmer manages to cultivate with a pair of bullock a much larger area than the small cultivators. (Harris, 1966:53)

But the point of my analysis was not to show how improvements might be made, but simply to show that the negative effects of the Hindu religion on the management of the bovine stock had been grossly exaggerated. Hence I went on to observe that "the failure to develop cooperative forms of plowing can scarcely be traced to *ahimsa*" —that is, to the Hindu doctrine of the sacredness of life:

If anything, emphasis upon independent, family-sized farm units follows intensification of individual land tenure patterns and other property innovations deliberately encouraged by the British. Under existing property arrangements there is a perfectly good economic explanation of why bullocks are not shared among adjacent households. (Harris, 1966:53)

The point of my original article was that the role played by Hindu ideology was subordinate to the constraints imposed by ecological, political, economic, and other behavioral and etic conditions. The point was not to show that it was all a "problem of ecology." I plainly indicated that there were etic politico-economic factors that had to be considered; but I did not attempt to weigh the politico-economic against the ecological factors, because to the best of my knowledge no one had ever claimed that the Hindu taboo on the consumption of beef had caused the development of private property in India. Moreover, while it is true that very substantial changes in the productivity and equity of Indian agriculture can be brought about by political-economic restructuring, it is equally true that the existing fund of technology, depleted state of natural resources, and enormous population density must be taken into consideration no matter what kind of scheme for politico-economic restructuring is finally adopted.

The Origin of the Sacred Cow

LET US TURN now to the question of why religions that rejected or restricted the consumption of animal flesh developed in India, and why cattle and not some other species came to stand at the center of these proscriptions. Alexander Alland has criticized the cultural materialist explanation of the beef taboo with arguments similar to his objections to the explanation of the pig taboo:

Harris' "etic" explanations, which come from the imposition of an outside grid upon collected field data, tell us much about the adaptive nature of specific traits in terms of what our own science has taught us, but they tell us nothing about the culture in question *as a culture*. The method can be used to answer certain questions which fall into the realm of natural history, particularly whether or not a particular trait is adaptive, but it cannot provide us with a processual theory of human adaptation. (1974:68)

Alland's confidence concerning the inability of cultural materialism to provide a processual theory of specific Indian Hindu cultural adaptations is based on his belief that the essential features of cow love were already present in ancient times under ecological conditions completely different from those which make the present-day restrictions adaptive:

. . . if one examines the situation historically, it will be seen that cow love is an ancient trait, linked to other ancient traits which developed under ecological and demographic conditions vastly different from those found in the present day. Cow love entered Indian culture when the Indian ecology was richer and less degraded than it is today. (Ibid.)

But Alland did not examine the situation historically. True, cow love developed at a time when demographic conditions were vastly different from conditions today. But so were the specific features of cow love. The treatment of cattle was very different in Vedic times; it was not until the infrastructural conditions had changed to approximate those of modern times that the taboo on the slaughter of cattle and the consumption of beef began to be established. As in the Middle East, the intensification and succession of new modes of production altered the ecosystem, and with it, the entire structure of society. And the religions of India, like those of the Middle East and Europe, adapted to these changed conditions in precisely the manner predicted by cultural materialist principles. The facts are as follows. Cattle were already present in India in pre-Vedic times (4000 B.C. to 2000 B.C.). They are found along with sheep and goats in the earliest known neolithic sites in the Indus Valley. In Harappan times (2500 B.C.), bulls are prominent in artwork and seals (Allchin and Allchin, 1968:114, 259). We know that the Harappans ate beef from the fact that charred cattle bones as well as half-burnt remnants of pigs and sheep have been found in and around the houses (Marshall, 1931, vol. 1:37). For the Vedic period (2000 B.C. to 800 B.C.), however, there is the direct testimony of the Rig-Veda and other texts. At this time oxen appeared to have been eaten freely. Even in late Vedic times, it was still customary to kill a big ox to feed a distinguished guest (Prakash, 1961:16). Cows were also eaten, but how often and under what circumstances remains to be clarified. The Rig-Veda distinguishes between the sacrifice of barren or sterile cows and fertile ones, and the Atithigva implies that cows were slain for guests (Prakash, 1961:16). The Tattiriya Brahmana "recommends 180 domestic animals to be sacrificed including horse, bulls, cows, goats . . ." (Mitra, 1881:9). Minutely detailed descriptions of what kind of cattle is to be used for what kinds of sacrifice and how it is to be killed and divided up parallel similar prescriptions in the Old Testament's Leviticus. "The Gopatha Brahmana of the Arthava Veda gives in detail the names of different individuals who are to receive shares of the meat for the parts they take in the ceremony" (ibid.:22).

The slaughter of cattle and the eating of meat in general became increasingly ritualized. A marked resemblance therefore exists between early Brahmanical meat-eating practices and the ethnographically known redistributive rituals of such African cattle keepers as the Kamilaroi (Dyson-Hudson and Dyson-Hudson, 1969) and the Paquot (Schneider, 1957), who restrict the slaughter of animals to ritual occasions. The latter occur, however, with a frequency that corresponds to the maximum harvestability of the herds. According to the Sutras, the Brahmins were in charge of sacrificing animals. Their role was thus analogous to that of the Druids in Europe and the Levites in Israel. Sacrifices were frequent and the animals were eaten, no doubt in redistributive feasts: making gifts and receiving gifts were the special duties of the Brahmin. On the basis of passages in the Vasistha Dharma Sutra, Vishnu Dharma Sutra, and the Sankhayana Grhya Sutra, Prakash (1961:40) makes the following comment about the period immediately preceding the florescence of Buddhism and Jainism (800 B.C. to 300 B.C.): "The general feeling of the time about meat eating seems to be that it should be used in extending hospitality to guests, as offering to gods and manes, but animals should not be killed otherwise." Oxen continued to be mentioned as animals to be slaughtered for guests, and the earliest archaeological excavations in the Ganges Valley at Hastinapur confirm the use of zebu breeds for food (ibid.:39; Allchin and Allchin, 1968:321).

The rise of Buddhism and Jainism in the Ganges Valley in the sixth century B.C. was closely associated with a fundamental challenge to the Brahminical control over animal sacrifice and the redistribution of meat. Buddha condemned animal sacrifice (but did not insist on a pure vegetarian diet). The Jains were more opposed to meat in any form. Nonetheless, during the early part of the Maurya and Sunga periods (300 B.C. to 75 A.D.), Brahmins and royalty continued to eat cattle, along with a wide variety of feral and domesticated animals. The emperor Asoka temporarily made Buddhism an imperial religion, and meat-eating and animal sacrifice were partially repressed. But a resurgence of Brahmanism followed with the founding of the Sunga dynasty in 185–72 B.C., and there are indications that meat-eating flourished among the ruling and priestly castes throughout the period from 75 to 350 A.D. On the basis of a passage in the Caraka Samhita, Prakash (1961:141) includes cows in the list of animals eaten in these times.

Despite the prohibition on ox flesh in the Brhadaranyaka Upanishad (6.3.13), allusions to cow-killing and the eating of cow flesh occur in the Vedic, Buddhist, and classical Sanskrit texts for the period 600 B.C. to 200 A.D. According to A. N. Bose, these inconsistencies raise the suspicion that orthodox Hindu interpolations against eating beef were made in later periods, and this is definitely the case for the thirteen chapters devoted to the greatness of the cow which occur in the Anushasanaparva (Bose, 1961: fn. 1, 113). In the Satapatha Brahmana, Yajnavalkya is fond of tender beef (III.1.2–21); the meaning of the word for guest, *goghna*, is "one for whom a cow is killed"; cows are slaughtered at the reception of a guest, and at the worship of manes and at marriage feasts. Butchers are familiar figures in the Buddhist texts; and there were special slaughterhouses where cows were sometimes slaughtered. Concludes Bose (1961:109): "It rather appears that beef was the commonest flesh consumed."

For the ensuing Gupta period, 300 A.D. to 750 A.D., Prakash writes:

Side by side with vegeterian diet, meat diet was also in vogue. Meat and fish formed part of the daily diet of the royal families. Flesh of various animals was served to Brahmanas at Sraddhas. The Kurma Purana goes to the extent of saying that one who does not take flesh in a Sraddha is born again and again as an animal. (1961:175–176; cf. Mitra, 1881:29)

Buddhism and Jainism were revitalization movements challenging the Vedic and Hindu stratification systems. In response, Hinduism co-opted the Buddhist and Jainist doctrine of *ahimsa*, the sacredness of life. As explained by Rajendra Mitra (1881:34–35)

The Brahmanas had to contend against Buddhism which emphatically and so successfully denounced all sacrifices. . . . they found the doctrine of respect for animal life too strong and too popular to be overcome, and therefore gradually and imperceptibly adopted it in such a manner as to make it appear part of their Sastra [laws]. They gave prominence to such passages as preached benevolence and mercy for all animated creation, and so removed to the background the sacrificial ordinances as to put them out of sight.

To sum up: the development of strong beef-eating taboos involved the conversion of ruling and priestly classes and castes from sacrificers and redistributors of meat to protectors of the cow and its male traction progeny.

But why did this conversion occur where and when it did? As in the case of the pig in the Middle East, the underlying reason for this change was the intensification of production, the rise in population density, and the shift to new modes of production. Population in the Ganges Valley at 1,000 B.C. was scanty and spread out in small villages (Davis, 1951:24). During Vedic times, cattle were the principal means of wealth, and they were used extensively—as many as twenty-four oxen were harnessed to a single plow (*Cambridge History of India*, 1:135–37). By 300 B.C. there were vast irrigation works, great cities, and a population estimated between 50 and 100 million people (Spengler, 1971; Davis, 1951; Nath, 1929). Although it is frequently asserted that this population did not increase thereafter until the arrival of the British, the evidence for the base line is shaky, and no firm conclusions are warranted. Spengler (1971:38) says "it is probable that population grew between 300 A.D. and Akbar's time [1550]." It is clear, however, that part of the total of 255 million recorded in the first census of 1871 must have been added between 300 B.C. and the arrival of the British. With the increase in population, and in the number of towns and cities, India became subject to increasingly severe droughts and famines, due in part at least to deforestation and settlement of marginal lands. The Ganges Valley is a classic case of environmental depletions created by the intensification of production:

A definite stage in the spread and intensification of famine was the destruction of the primeval forests, the great natural reservoirs of rain which "kept the fruit of the summer's rain till winter, while the lighter winter rains were treasured there in turn till the June monsoon came again." The [Hindu] Epics narrate the working of extensive schemes of colonization and deforestation which in course of their progress extended the rigour, recurrence, and area of scarcity to make it a calamity of the first magnitude. (Bose, 1961:131)

Bose summarizes a description of a twelve-year drought in the Mahabharata as follows:

Lakes, wells and springs were dried up. . . . Sacrifices were in abeyance. Agriculture and cattle-rearing were given up. Markets and shops were abandoned. Stakes for binding sacrificial animals disappeared. Festivals died out. Everywhere heaps of bones were seen and cries of creatures heard. The cities were depopulated, hamlets burnt down. People fled from fear of one another or of robbers, weapons, and kings. Places of worship were deserted. The aged were turned out of their houses. Kine, goats, sheep, and buffaloes fought and died in large numbers. The Brahmanas died without protection. Herbs and plants withered. The earth looked like trees in a crematorium. In that dreadful age when righteousness was at an end, men . . . began to eat one another.

Just as in Mesopotamia and Egypt, an animal whose flesh was previously consumed became too costly to be used as food as a result of fundamental changes in the ecosystem and the mode of production. Its flesh therefore became the focus of a series of ritual restrictions. But here the resemblances cease; the pig becomes an abomination; the cow an object of veneration.

The attempt to explain this specific difference is the crunch that alternative strategies cannot withstand. The explanation is this: cost-benefits of the pig involve only its utility as meat. When that meat became ecologically too expensive, the whole pig becomes an abomination because it was useless—worse than useless, a danger in its entirety. But when beef in India became too expensive ecologically, the animal in its entirety did not lose its value. On the contrary, the slaughter and beef-eating taboos actually reflect the indispensability of cattle as a source of traction under conditions of high preindustrial population densities and rainfall agriculture. Hence the cow became holy rather than dirty in order to protect its vital function as the mother of the bullock. As Mohandas K. Gandhi once explained: "Not only did she give milk but she also made agriculture possible."

To complete the specification of why it was cattle and not some other animal that became the venerated object of an antislaughter cult, one has to examine the relative cost-benefits of the available domestic species. Indian cattle are primarily small, nondairy traction breeds selected for their ability to pull plows at low cost. Inputs are kept low by maintaining bullocks (and cows) on short rations, garbage, and leaves throughout most of the year. At plowing time the bullocks are fed supplements and rapidly recuperate from their normal state of semistarvation. During the dry season in the Gangetic plain, when *nighttime* temperatures often remain above 40 degrees Celsius, the Indian breeds show remarkable resistance to heat stress. Except in deep mud, cattle outperform all other available plow species. Buffalo lack the versatility of cattle, and in modern India buffalo are used primarily for specialized dairy production rather than as plow animals except in humid rice-growing regions. Buffalo are extremely costly to maintain during the dry seasons and are vulnerable to droughts, because like pigs they must cool themselves with external moisture, preferably by wallowing. Horses and donkeys are also less versatile, have poor drought resistance, and have lower traction efficiencies than cattle. Camels of course are heat-tolerant, but pound for pound in comparison with a zebu bullock, they cost far more to manage and maintain.

The structural Marxist claim that cultural materialists cannot specify the causality determining structural and superstructural features represents a commitment to an unproductive principle: the principle of "it can't be done." Obviously such specifications cannot be done as long as plausible lines of research into infrastructural processes are barred by the dogma that structure dominates infrastructure.

"A Beef with Sahlins"*

A CHARACTERISTIC reaction to plausible infrastructural explanations of food taboos is for critics to turn away from the solution of the solved puzzle (for which no nomothetic solution was previously offered) to a fresh example of apparently irrational and uneconomic food preferences. This makes cultural materialists lunge about in odd ways from one challenge to another. The new puzzles are set up like hurdles over which we must leap in order to satisfy a grandstand full of one-legged judges whose sole function seems to be the creation of more obstacles. The latest such challenge involves contemporary preferences for beef among Americans, and the corresponding taboo on dog meat and horse meat. I turn to the consideration of these final instances not to offer solutions but to demonstrate that the pontifications of the structural Marxists against infrastructural causality are aimed at closing off known productive boulevards of research in order to keep open a known unproductive back alley.

Taking his inspiration from Lévi-Strauss (see p. 188), Sahlins (1976:171) writes that what is valuable and edible in the American diet "is in no way justifiable by biological, ecological or economic advantage." On the contrary, the structural model of a meal determines biological, ecological, and economic advantage:

The exploitation of the American environment, the mode of relation to the landscape depends on the model of a meal that includes a central meat element with peripheral support of carbohydrates and vegetables.

The reason meat occupies this central place goes back to the "Indo-European identification of cattle . . . with virility." Hence "the indispensability . . . of steak as the epitome of virile meats."

Hence also a corresponding structure of agricultural production of food grains, and in turn a specific articulation to world markets—all of which would change overnight if we ate dogs. (Ibid.:171)

I cannot embark upon a full-scale rebuttal of Sahlins's attribution of the U.S. beef-eating complex to whimsical Indo-European identifica-

*Courtesy of Eric Ross.

tions of cattle with virility. But the history of the cattle complex in India suffices to show the failure of Sahlins's explanation. If all it takes to worship steak is Indo-European ancestry, then why is the *absence* of steak the mark of a proper meal in India?

Like Alland, Sahlins overlooks some elementary historical facts. Beef has not always been the preferred meat in the U.S.A. During most of the nineteenth century, more pork than beef was consumed, and ham rather than steak enjoyed the status of honorific meat. It was not until the invention of the refrigerated railroad car in the 1870s that beef acquired an honorific status superior to that of ham. This reversal climaxed a long demographic, technological, economic, and environmental process. Pork remained ascendant as long as population remained sparse, extensive forests were available, the Corn Belt was close to the East Coast, and beef had to be salted rather than consumed fresh. When the railroads began to cross the Great Plains, it became possible for mass-production meatpackers in Chicago to deliver cheap range-fed refrigerated beef to the Boston and New York markets. Beef acquired its preferential status because it was the principal target of a new capital-intensive agribusiness method for mass-producing fresh meat. Capital invested in beef exceeded capital invested in pork, not because cattle were a symbol of virility, but because pigs couldn't eat the free grass available on the Western rangelands. Steak acquired its special honorific status because it epitomizes the attempt to mass-produce meat that was tender and chewable as well as fresh. Moreover, the premium value placed on tenderness was not merely an arbitrary preference, but one based on the prevalence of missing and rotted teeth in the mouths of the urban consumers (Harris and Ross, 1978).

As for the taboo on dogs, Sahlins proposes that nothing but the whimsical feeling that "dogs are like people" prevents Americans from eating them. But the reason Americans feel that way about dogs surely is related to the practical disadvantages of a dog-meat industry. Dogs are animals bred to provide companionship and security. Why raise dogs for meat when one has cattle, sheep, hogs, and poultry, all of which gain weight best on pulses and grains, while dogs gain weight best by eating meat (National Research Council, 1975). Dogs, like people, are generally eaten in cultures that lack cheap alternative sources of meat from large domesticated ruminants and omnivores.

Finally, there is the question of why horse meat is taboo in the U.S.A. Here the distinction between etics and emics is once again crucial. It is true that American horse lovers protest advertised sales of horse meat by American supermarkets. The horse, after all, is reared today primarily for sport and for its qualities as a pet rather than for traction or transport. Nonetheless, Sahlins is mistaken about the etics of horse-meat consumption. Being a large animal, when it is no longer serviceable as a pet, horses are seldom merely sent to a final resting place. Rather, they are slaughtered or dismembered and find their way back into the food chain as canned food for cats and dogs. Sahlins himself emphasizes this fact, for it seems to make the horse-flesh taboo even more exotic: "There is even an enormous industry for raising horses as food for dogs" (ibid.).

What Sahlins overlooks in his eagerness to dematerialize the United States economy, however, is that people as well as pets eat pet food—people who are treated like dogs: old, ill, and desperately poor people. One should know something about how much of the pet-food industry (which incidentally does not raise horses for meat but merely uses old horses raised for other purposes) is actually supported by the human quest for cheap animal protein.

Similarly, Sahlins does not "honor" (his word, see above) American culture by perpetuating the myth that all Americans eat steak or other meat or even want to eat steak or other meat with every meal. One may "honor" a culture by accepting its mystifications, but in so doing, one does not honor the science of history. Despite the efforts of the beef industry to encourage beef eating, per capita consumption of beef in the United States has probably peaked. As the petrochemical inputs of U.S. agribusiness become more expensive due to intensification, depletion, and pollution, more and more meatless meals lie over the horizon. This is scarcely the appropriate moment to be telling people that the only reason they want to eat meat is because meat is good to think. The reason for the recent high per capita consumption of meat in the United States is that people have not been eating meat but cheap petrochemicals. What people should be told is that the high per capita levels of animal protein consumption to which we have become accustomed can no longer be sustained as a result of the depletion and skyrocketing costs of petrochemicals.

I shall consider another example of Sahlins's careless and purely negative approach to the question of food preferences in the final chapter of this book. There we shall see the extent to which the obscurantism inherent in structuralism and structural Marxism has emerged as Sahlins's dominant strategic commitment. In the meantime, I think I have said enough on this subject to show that structural Marxism, like structuralism, is not so much an attempt to penetrate beneath the surface of social life as an attempt to float above it.

Chapter Nine

Psychological and Cognitive Idealism

ALTHOUGH STRUCTURALISM has found a home in many North American universities, the favorite American idealist strategies follow a different tradition. American cultural idealism tends to be strongly committed to an empiricist epistemology. It is deeply concerned with operationalizing its methods and rigorously testing its theories. American cultural idealists are often faultlessly "scientific" in all matters but one: their subordination of the study of etic structure and infrastructure to the study of emic and mental superstructure.

In this chapter I shall deal with two major types of currently active cultural idealist strategies. The practitioners of the first identify themselves under the labels "psychological anthropology" or "culture and personality." This strategy addresses the question of how people acquire the normal and/or deviant mental and emotional complexes typical of different sociocultural systems. It is also concerned with the problem of universal psychological constituents of the human personality.

The second type of cultural idealist strategy is concerned primarily with the narrower cognitive aspects of mental and emic superstructure. In many ways it constitutes an empirical, nondialectical analogue of structuralism. Its practitioners identify themselves under such labels as "cognitive anthropology," "ethnoscience," "formal analysis" and "symbolic anthropology."

All empirical varieties of emic, mental, and personality studies, insofar as they are purely descriptive or merely posit functional relationships, are in principle compatible with cultural materialism. Indeed, to the extent that cognitive and personality studies illuminate the pervasive effects of infrastructural conditioning on human thought and behavior, they can be of great theoretical and practical interests to cultural materialists. An adversary situation exists between cultural materialism and cognitivist and psychological strategies only when cognitivists and psychological anthropologists claim that the mental, emic, and personality aspects of sociocultural systems determine the etic and behavioral aspects, or when they claim that cultural materialism cannot explain the causes of mental and emic sociocultural differences and similarities. A further source of controversy exists when cognitivists and psychological anthropologists attempt to limit the definition of culture to mental and emic superstructure and to limit the scope of anthropology, ethnology, or ethnography to the study of culture defined in the idealist image.

Psychological Anthropology

ONE POPULAR set of psychologistic theories of sociocultural causality sets out from the assumption that each society has a national character, a modal personality, or some other definite range of personality types. Provided that proper empirical procedures are employed to measure and define a group's personality complex, I find nothing objectionable in such an assumption. I accept the proposition that the emic and mental aspects of human cultures differ cross-culturally; therefore I am necessarily also committed to the position that personalities differ cross-culturally. For what is personality if not a summing up of an individual's mental propensities for thought, feeling, and behavior expressed in a psychologistic vocabulary (for example, "aggressive," "passive," "anxious," "extroverted," and so forth)? And since emic and mental culture is a summing up of a group's propensities for thought, feeling, and behavior, there must be a correspondence between emic and mental culture and the group's personality type.

Strategic conflict between psychological anthropologists and cultural materialists arises when psychological anthropologists fail to implicate the etic infrastructure in the causal chain responsible for personality complexes, or when they go further and propose that structural and infrastructural changes are predetermined by the existence of a particular modal or basic personality type or national character: as, for example, if one asserts that the Germans are predetermined to have dictatorships because they have authoritarian personalities; or Americans are predetermined to be technologically superior to the rest of the world because they have a spirit of inquiry and a high need for achievement.

Cultural materialists hold that personality configurations are the product of infrastructural conditions, and that while there is feedback between such configurations and infrastructure, the infrastructure is probabilistically dominant.

To make personality the dominant factor or even to assign it equal weight is to abandon the quest for nomothetic causal theories of sociocultural evolution. This happens because like all idealists, those who believe in the primacy of psychological configurations must either trace a particular configuration back through a unique sequence of antecedent configurations until the historical chain is lost in antiquity, or must concede that differences in group personality configurations are unpredictable.

The Mutability of National Character

HOW FAST can the personality configuration of a culture change? How much can a given personality configuration advance, retard, or deflect the evolution of infrastructure? As in the case of the superstructure in general, the personality configuration of the moment obviously must be taken into account in making predictions about the direction and rate of change. The crux of the cultural materialist position, however, is that in principle, radical infrastructural and structural changes can lead to complete reversals of personality configurations in a very short time.

This position contradicts the view advanced by pioneer figures in psychological anthropology that personality configurations are the stable, enduring core of social life. Ruth Benedict (1934), for example, stressed the peaceful, noncompetitive, and even-tempered disposition of the Pueblo Indians, disregarding the fact that in the sixteenth and seventeenth centuries the same Pueblo Indians had fought a series of bloody messianic wars during which they had massacred the Spanish priests and set fire to their churches. When the Jews in Nazi Germany failed to organize an effective resistance against their own genocide, psychologists depicted them as having lost the capacity for forceful struggle. In a single generation, however, Jewish refugees created a militaristic state defended by one of the world's most formidable small armies. During World War II, psychological anthropologists depicted the Japanese as pathologically obedient. But postwar generations of Japanese college youth proved even more rebellious than their U.S. counterparts. During the 1960s every major Japanese campus was the scene of pitched battle between thousands of students and police officers. In addition, large numbers of Japanese youth abandoned traditional Japanese clothing, etiquette, music, and family life in favor of Western models, in open contempt for parental authority (Krauss, Rohlen, and Steinhoff, 1978).

Abram Kardiner once depicted the Afro-American male as a psychologically damaged individual whose aggressive impulses were turned inward, giving rise to feelings of worthlessness and inadequacy. In their effort to please members of the superordinate white groups, blacks allegedly exaggerated their own shortcomings by accepting the self-image of a slow-witted, affable, shuffling "Sambo." The black power movement broke the Sambo stereotype. Haughtily self-confident black leaders fought the Sambo image in the courts and in the streets, as well as in the nursery (Hannerz, 1970).

Weston La Barre (1966) called the Aymara of Bolivia "morose, cruel, vindictive, sullen, hateful, and treacherous" on the basis of his analysis of Aymara folktales. Every Aymara tale collected by La Barre turned out to be concerned with conflict over food, deceitfulness, chicanery, violence, busybody informers, murderers, and sorcerers. La Barre recognized that the temperament of the Aymara reflected a historic process of sustained deprivation and exploitation at the hands of both Indian and Spanish ruling classes.

If the Aymara, as evidenced in their folktales (and indeed throughout the rest of their culture), are apprehensive, crafty, suspicious, violent, treacherous, and hostile, one important reason for this may be that such a character structure is an understandable response to their having lived for perhaps as long as a millennium under rigidly hierarchic and absolutist economic, military, and religious controls. (La Barre, 1966:143)

La Barre neglected to point out, however, that since infrastructure and structure determined Aymara personality in the past, one must conclude that they are probably determining it in the present.

Freudian Strategies

THE STRONGEST claims for the priority of psychological causation arise from Freudian and neo-Freudian principles aimed at understanding pan-human psychodynamic processes. These principles, like the structuralist principle of universal mental dialectical tendencies, can at best account for the uniformities and similarities of sociocultural systems. But they cannot account for the differences. At the outset, therefore, one might reasonably claim that Freudian psychodynamic strategies are less adequate than strategies that intend to explain both differences and similarities. I do not wish to rest my case on this point alone, however, since there are grave doubts as to whether or not the Freudians have a proper handle on the causes of the uniformities.

Freudian theoretical principles postulate a universal tendency for human beings to mature through oral, anal, and genital stages and to develop Oedipal strivings which are resolved by males and females in psychodynamically different ways. Mature "genital" males resolve their oedipal strivings by manifesting masculine dominance of females, and mature "genital" females resolve their oedipal strivings by accepting a passive role and by compensating for not having a penis by having babies. Psychodynamic patterns that resemble oedipal strivings in the minimal sense of sexually charged hostility between older generation males and their sons or nephews are indeed very widespread (Roheim, 1950; A. Parsons, 1964; Foster, 1972; Barnouw, 1973). It is therefore tempting to suppose that oedipal strivings, castration complex of males, penis envy of girls, and a broad variety of such aggressive male-dominated activities as competitive sports, male initiation rites, and warfare are all manifestations of universal psychodynamic processes. In the words of Maurice Walsh and Barbara Scandalis (1975):

As an outgrowth of the psychoanalytic approach to an understanding of social motivation and behavior it is our hypothesis that primitive male initiation rites and modern organized warfare are equivalent behavior patterns [136]. . . . [Both] have a common single motivating force—Oedipal rivalry [138]. . . . Psychoanalytic research demonstrates that the Oedipal rivalry alone of all possible causes adequately explains. . . institutionalized situations where sons are murdered by an "enemy" through manipulation by the father generation [148–149]. . . . The aggression of the sons and the father is thus unconsciously transferred to the "enemy" men and to the women and children who are raped and destroyed as proxies for the repressed aggressive and sexual desires [150]. . . .

From a cultural materialist perspective, the causal arrows in this theory are pointing backwards. All of the conditions for creating castration fears and penis envy, aggressive males and passive females, are present in the male supremacy complex—in the male monopoly over weapons, in the training of males for bravery in combat, and in the training of females to accept roles as rewarders of masculine virtues; and in patrilineality, polygyny, bride price, and many other male-centered institutions. Wherever the objective of child rearing is to produce aggressive, "masculine," dominant men and passive, "feminine" women, there will develop something like a castration fear between males in adjacent generations who feel insecure about their manliness, and something like penis envy among women, who will be brainwashed into exaggerating the power and significance of the male genitalia. All of this leads to the conclusion that war is not caused by the Oedipus complex; rather, the Oedipus complex is caused by war, which in turn is caused by specific infrastructural conditions (see p. 90) and not by something innate in human nature (Divale and Harris, 1976).

The cultural materialist alternative is preferable to the Freudian alternative because we know that the alleged manifestations of the Oedipus complex are extremely variable. Not all societies have intense puberty rituals; in some societies men are less aggressive; and not all societies have developed warfare to the same degree. Indeed, in order to cope with the variability of the psychodynamic end product of the Freudian constants, psychological anthropologists were inevitably obliged to pay attention to the institutional structures that impinge on infants and children during socialization. Hence there arose the neo-Freudian interest in culture-specific child-training practices such as sphincter and bladder control; suppression or encouragement of masturbation; nursing and weaning schedules; and infant-mother sleeping arrangements. Calling these practices "primary institutions," Abram Kardiner hypothesized that they were linked to a set of "secondary institutions" consisting of religion and mythology through the "projection" of unconscious fantasies formed during childhood. Labeling childhood training institutions "primary," however, could not for long obscure the fact that they were not at all primary. The real primary institutions had to be those which determined the childhood training institutions. But what were these? Kardiner himself threw up his hands:

Psychology can cast no light whatsoever without the aid of history on how these primary institutions took their final forms. So far as we know, no satisfactory explanations have ever been made of primary institutions. (Kardiner, 1939:471)

Later, John Whiting (1969) rescued the psychodynamic approach from this know-nothing stance by grounding one set of childhood training institutions in specific infrastructural conditions. Whiting and his coworkers proposed that intense male puberty rituals were produced by a causal chain starting with protein deficiency. This leads to prolonged nursing, postpartum sex taboo, polygyny, exclusive mother-child sleeping arrangements, male child training by women, cross-sex identification by male children, and finally the need for severe male initiation as a means of strengthening masculine identity in societies in which men dominate political life. (I shall give more extended treatment to Whiting's theory in the next chapter.) Robert Levine (1973) has generalized this approach and explicitly elevated ecology, economy, and social structure to the status of "primary" institutions that determine child-rearing practices (also still called "primary"). This of course renders culture and personality studies completely compatible with the cultural materialist principle of infrastructural determinism, although neither Whiting nor Levine has yet to discuss the larger strategic implications of their reversal of the Freudian causal arrow.

The central weakness of the Freudian notions of psychodynamic universals is precisely the same as the weakness lying at the heart of sociobiology and structuralism. In each case, universal components of human nature are said to account for a remarkably variable set of institutions. And in each case uniformity has to be translated into diversity by intervening variables. In sociobiology, diversity arises from the switching effect of ecological conditions; in structuralism, from the contingencies of history; and in Freudian culture and personality, from the conditioning institutions of childhood. In cultural materialistic perspective, the problem of the intervening variables looms larger than that of the alleged universals. In order to explain why the constant yields such variable results, the causes of variation necessarily become the focus of research. And once these causes have been grounded in the infrastructure, the heuristic value of the constant becomes increasingly dubious. Finally, the constant loses all strategic value as more and more puzzles involving both similarities and differences find their solution in the similarities and differences of the etic and behavioral infrastructure.

Cognitivism

I TURN NOW to the more narrow form of American cultural idealism, cognitivism. According to Stephen Tyler (1969:3), the aim of cognitive anthropology is to "understand the organizing principles underlying behavior."

In essence, cognitive anthropology seeks to answer two questions: What material phenomena are significant for the people of some culture; and how do they organize these phenomena [in their minds].

For Marshal Durbin (1973:470), the key concept of cognitive anthropology is rules.

Culture is best seen as a set of control mechanisms—plans, recipes, rules, instructions, which are the principal bases for the specificity of behavior and an essential condition for governing it.

Ward Goodenough (quoted in Black, 1973:522), one of the pioneer figures in the development of modern cultural idealist strategies in the United States, defines culture as follows:

A society's culture consists of whatever it is one has to know or believe in order to operate in a manner acceptable to its members. . . . [It is] the end product of learning . . . not things, people, behavior or emotions, but the organization of these things . . . that people have in their minds, their models for perceiving, relating and otherwise interpreting them.

Cognitivism thus is a strategy for describing in the most effective and emically authentic fashion the rules or other mental programs that allegedly account for behavior. Cognitivists do not attempt to explain the existence of these rules themselves. Instead, they take the entire emic sector as a given. Then, using the detailed knowledge of emics expressed as semantic components, taxonomic structures, systems of beliefs, systems of rules, or "plans for behavior," cognitivism attempts to account for the entire etic sector of sociocultural life.

The "accounting for" in this procedure cannot be given any single meaning. For some cognitivists, "accounting for" means prediction of behavior stream events (Kay, 1970; Geoghegan, 1969). However, for other cognitivists, knowledge of emic rules is not a way of getting at what people will actually do. Rather, "accounting for" means merely appropriately anticipating what they will do.

> . . . an ethnography should be a theory of cultural behavior in a particular society, the adequacy of which is to be evaluated by the ability of a stranger to the culture . . . to use the ethnography's statements as instructions for appropriately anticipating the scenes of the society. I say "appropriately antici-pate" rather than "predict" because failure of an ethnographic statement to predict correctly does not necessarily imply predictive inadequacy as long as the members of the described society are as surprised by the failure as is the ethnographer. (Frake, 1964:112)

Cognitivists who reject or ignore the centrality of predictive adequacy in scientific descriptions rest their case on an analogy with linguistics. The goal of linguistics is to state the finite set of rules by which infinite numbers of grammatical sentences can be generated. Most linguists, however, do not hope to be able to predict what people will say at any given moment in time. This accepted relationship between grammar and etic speech acts leads many cognitivists to feel satisfied with a restricted meaning of "accounting for." They believe that the behavior stream is virtually synonymous with chance or chaos. In the words of Ward Goodenough (1964:39):

> The great problem for a science of man is how to get from the objective world of materiality, with its infinite variability, to the subjective world of form as it exists in what, for lack of a better term, we must call the minds of our fellow man. . . . Structural linguistics has, I think, made us conscious at last of their nature, and has gone on to convert this consciousness into a systematic method.

Etic and behavioral culture, for cognitivists such as Goodenough, is composed of the incomprehensible flickering shadows on the walls of Plato's cave. Comprehensible or regular forms or structures consist of the permanent ideas underlying (or accounting for) the epiphenomenal events of history. In Oswald Werner's (1973:288) words:

Behavior is ephemeral. It depends on (1) cultural knowledge . . . (2) prior tangible products of behavior (props) and (3) probably other factors (e.g. the state of the actor, such as his sobriety, tiredness, or drunkenness). Some additional factors affecting behavior (4) are surely chance.

Behavior Is Not More Ephemeral Than Thought

I SHALL EXAMINE the claim that cognitivists can predict the "grammaticality" of an etic performance in another section. But let me point out some consequences of the conviction that behavior stream events (verbal or nonverbal) are essentially unpredictable. In terms of Maxwell's criterion (p.25), such a conviction ought to be fatal to the prospects of cognitive strategies in comparison with other strategies not sharing that conviction. In order to have a rational reason for preferring a strategic option of such restricted compass, one would want some kind of proof that prediction of behavior stream events cannot be achieved. It is inconceivable, however, how such a proof could be offered without tentatively adopting a research strategy such as cultural materialism, which intends to explore the limits of probabilistic predictions about behavior stream events. Beyond this logical flaw, the accumulated evidence of archaeology, history, and ethnography all point toward the nonephemeral, recurrent nature of behavior stream events. Werner is not totally oblivious of these recurrences, but he masks them in point 2 above as "prior tangible products of behavior," as if such "props" as houses, fields of grain, pots of food, weapons of war, pyramids, temples, villages, factories, cities, and so forth did not themselves furnish proof that behavior was in fact not incomprehensible, unpredictable, or wholly or even largely "ephemeral"! Even in the domain of etic speech acts, one can point to enough instances of utterances that recur in determined contexts to warrant the assumption that the semantic content as well as the grammaticality of speech acts is predictable ("Good morning"!). The conviction that speech acts are essentially unpredictable arises from the historic failure of linguists to study actual speech in etic contexts. This failure in turn rests on the platonic idealist distinction between *langue*, the realm of pure form, and *parole*, the realm of imperfect material representation. The attempt to impose this stunted strategy upon the study of whole sociocultural systems has contributed significantly to the current upwelling of obscurantist and antiscientific treatments of vital social issues (see below).

Convergence of Cognitivism and Structuralism

MANY COGNITIVE anthropologists in the United States accept a neopositivist and modified empiricist definition of science. Within the framework of ethnoscience and formal analysis, anthropologists have pioneered in the development of methodologically sophisticated emic data-gathering techniques and have urged the adoption of sound criteria of testability. In fact, some of the harshest criticisms directed against Lévi-Strauss and structuralism have been launched by tough-minded cognitivists. As Oswald Werner (1973:299), speaking on behalf of a proposed computer-facilitated investigation of "huge lexical semantic fields," has put it:

If the task of science is to show the nature of the postulated structure, then Lévi-Strauss has succeeded only insofar as the dialectic structure (a:b::c:d) is adequate. At best these oppositions are elements of still larger, implicit, and more complex structures. At worst they are empty because they are not testable. There is very little structure in Lévi-Strauss' structuralism.

The difference between structuralism and cognitivism is most extreme in the matter of informant feedback. While a few cognitivists seem to be able to dispense with informants (e.g. Lounsburry, 1965), the hallmark of cognitivism in the United States has been a highly operationalized concern with the elicitation of uncontaminated native categories from native informants during repeated, intensive, and highly structured interviews. Nonetheless, I view structuralism and cognitivism as convergent strategies nourished by the same underlying currents of cultural idealism.

There is a growing tendency among cognitivists to join with structuralists in describing their ultimate goals as the discovery of universal mental principles. Werner (1973:290, 293), for example, diagrams the final output of both structuralism and cognitivism as the "nature of man (or man's mind)" as shown by "universal principles of culture" and Brent Berlin and Paul Kay's (1969) demonstration of the alleged evolution of a universal color taxonomy is frequently cited as the supreme accomplishment of ethnoscience. Moreoever, the search for universal mental structures is also an important trend in American linguistics, and hence, to the extent that cognitivists are enthralled by linguistic models, convergence toward the goals of French structuralism is virtually assured:

> More than ever before both fields [anthropology and linguistics] have turned toward a search for universals. . . . The overall goal of both fields at the present time is to understand the way in which man processes information from his surrounding environment (Durbin, 1973:468)

This achievement, when it occurs, will leave cognitivism along with structuralism without any principle for explaining the divergent as well as convergent trajectories of sociocultural evolution. Finding out about how people process information from their environment is a respectable endeavor. But it cannot be the central concern of a science of culture. It will not tell us, for example, why the message we get is sometimes a love song while on other occasions it is the smell of burning flesh. In cognitivism, as in the sterile dialectic of structuralism, the more things change, the more they remain the same.

Predicting Behavior from a Knowledge of Rules

I TURN NOW to those cognitivists for whom "accounting for" means predicting etic behavior on the basis of a knowledge of emic rules. While some degree of predictability obviously can be achieved from a knowledge of emic rules, the strategic emphasis upon rules runs counter to cultural materialist assumptions about the dependent nature of the entire mental and emic sector. The ultimate objective of cultural materialism is to predict the emic and mental aspects of culture from a knowledge of etic infrastructural processes. The causal priority of etic behavioral over mental sectors makes it unlikely—even when we are dealing with systems in an entirely synchronic frame—that predictability can best be achieved by concentrating on emic and mental components. Even if one has a perfect knowledge of all the rules that one must know to act like a native—that is, even if one has been brought up as a native, a privilege all human beings enjoy with respect to at least one culture—predictions based on a knowledge of those rules alone cannot in principle predict the great bulk of behavior stream events. On the other hand, in principle, the great bulk of rules can be predicted from a sufficiently detailed knowledge of behavior stream events—especially, of course, those involving the etic infrastructure.

Five propositions underlie this claim: (1) etic outputs require etic inputs; (2) emic rules are ambiguous; (3) for every emic rule there is an alternative; (4) authorities never go unchallenged; (5) rules are not forever.*

Etic Outputs Require Etic Inputs

PAUL KAY has attempted to demonstrate the predictive efficacy of a knowledge of rules on the basis of an example involving postmarital residence. Kay claims that etic behavior will correspond to rules if the rules are stated in terms of contingencies and alternatives. Predictions about residence patterns, for example, should take the form: "reside post-maritally with the husband's matri-sib if that sib (a) is localized (i.e., is in possession of territory), and (b) owns uncultivated land." But Kay (1970:28) admits that "to predict distributions of actual residence patterns on an aggregate scale, we have to furnish as input to the postulated cognitive model the joint distribution of matri-sib membership, matri-sib localization, wealth in land and so on, for the entire population." Kay also points out that William Geoghegan's (1969) method for predicting the distribution of residence types among the Samal of the Philippines requires inputs on the distribution of age, sex, marital status, and other census data. But Kay fails to make clear that the inputs for these predictions must be etic inputs. What Geoghegan's method generates is not a native model but an incomplete etic census. Without accurate statistical inputs (numbers of children, adults, males, females, households, and so forth), there can be no accurate statistical output (number of different residence types). Rules cannot a census make.

It follows from this fact that a single cognitive model can generate a variety of etic outputs depending on the etic inputs. The point has been clarified by Roger Keesing (1974:82): "The same conceptual principles might yield densely clustered villages or scattered home-steads, depending on the water sources, terrain, arable land, demogra-

*The following discussion clarifies and amplifies Harris, 1975.

phy and the peaceful or headhunting predilections of the neighboring tribes."

Cultural materialists do not deny that under certain circumstances reliable predictions about behavior can be made from a knowledge of etic conditions and emic rules. Allen Johnson (1974), for example, has shown that knowledge of how Brazilian peasants classify their soils and crops combined with the observer's knowledge of soils and crops can be used to predict how much land will be devoted to a particular crop. It remains an open question, however, whether knowledge of emic rules is always essential for making such predictions. In principle, a thorough understanding of the etic infrastructural, structural, and superstructural components of peasant communities ought to lead to predictions concerning land use as well as to the emic rules by which etically appropriate choices of inputs are made.

To repeat: the objective of cultural materialism is to predict both ideas and behavior from a knowledge of behavior. This remains an unfinished but, in principle, not an impossible task. The same cannot be said of idealist proposals to replace etic rules with emic rules and to predict both ideas and behavior from the latter. This is clearly impossible in principle.

Ambiguity of Emic Rules

IS IT TRUE that mental and emic culture can be reduced to a finite set of emic rules in conformity with linguistic models? Cultural materialism is opposed to this view of human mental life. No aspect of a sociocultural system can be properly understood in a closed synchronic frame, since human mental life is in constant flux and does not constitute a closed system. To view the rules of a culture as a closed finite set cannot lead to an understanding of what people are actually thinking when they make up their minds to do something.

One symptom of the openness of emic systems is the presence of ambiguous and vague meanings in the lexical items from which emic rules are constructed. In order for emic systems to close in on themselves, they would have to consist of rules that every native speaker understood at the lexical level to mean the same thing. A considerable body of evidence, however, indicates that many lexical items are understood differently by members of the same speech community.

I first became involved with this problem during my studies of race relations in Brazil. In the state of Bahia, one frequently hears people being characterized as *moreno* or *mulato*. Since color or skin tone in Brazil is a salient marker for distinguishing one person from another, it seemed reasonable to suppose that *moreno* and *mulato* designated skin-tone differences (as well as differences in hair form and lip and nose shape). "Who is darker, a *moreno* or a *mulato?*" is a perfectly meaningful question to Bahians. They respond to it with conviction and without hesitation. Yet when it was put to the residents of a small fishing village, it produced an evenly divided set of opinions as to which was the darker type (Harris and Kottak, 1963). Later I tried to define the dimensions of the cognitive field of Brazilian "racial" types by showing informants standardized drawings of men and women whose facial features were systematically varied. A deck of seventy-two such drawings elicited over three hundred "racial" types from a hundred informants. The term most frequently used was *moreno*, but it was used in such a way as to defy definition by means of the features depicted on the drawings (skin tone, hair form, lip shape, nose shape). The entire semantic field of racial types in northeastern Brazil is filled with ambiguities; these ambiguities are not artifacts of the eliciting procedures. Rather, they reflect the fact that northeastern Brazil lacks sharply defined racial groups or racial castes that play distinctive roles in the allocation of resources (Harris, 1970).

The possibility that other semantic fields are structured in an ambiguous fashion has not been systematically explored by anthropologists. Notable exceptions are Terrance Hays's (1974) study of plant taxonomies in New Guinea, and Richard Pollnac's (1975) study of color terminologies in Buganda. John Roberts (1951, 1961) found extensive behavioral and ideological variation on an individual and household basis among the Navajo and Zuni, while Stephen Fjellman (1972) has shown that kinship terminology is far from uniform in one African culture. This is also true of American kinship terminology. Americans do not agree on the difference between first and second cousins, and first and second cousins once or twice removed, nor do they agree on what to call father's second wife, or wife's brother's wife's brother. Ethnographers either ignore the problem of semantic diversity or try to dismiss it as "noise" or as methodological artifact. The reason for this is that most contemporary ethnographic research is conducted under the auspices of idealist strategies which assume that shared values and beliefs not only define a culture but account for its existence (see below). A more reasonable assumption is that people have diverse and ambiguous beliefs and values. Yet few ethnographers have found it expedient to search out and quantify the actual extent of cognitive ambiguity and diversity (Pelto and Pelto, 1975).

The more complex the semantic construct, the greater the likelihood that it will be understood in the abstract, or applied in the concrete instance, differently by different people (or even differently by the same person at different times). In the perspective of cultural materialism, cognitive disagreement cannot be less frequent or analytically less significant than behavioral disagreement or conflict. Even in the most intimate domestic groups, people constantly misunderstand simple messages. Given the complexity of roles and the pervasiveness of hierarchical privileges, it is folly to assume that people always can or always want to understand each other (see pp. 43ff).

For Every Emic Rule There Is an Alternative

COGNITIVISTS are of course aware that rules are frequently broken. But they hope to subsume all instances of broken rules under yet another finite set of rules: rules for breaking rules. This was the response to my criticism of Ward Goodenough's (1965) concept of a "duty scale" among the people who live on the Island of Truk in Micronesia. According to the rules of this duty scale, fathers should (1) crouch or crawl if a married daughter is seated; (2) avoid initiating action in her presence; (3) avoid speaking harshly to her; (4) honor any request; and (5) never assault her "regardless of provocation." But Goodenough saw at least one father breaking all five rules. The reason for this, Goodenough explained, was that "her petulant behavior had been getting on her kinsmen's nerves for some time." She had indulged in "an early morning tirade against her husband, whom she suspected of having just come from an amorous visit to her lineage sister next door." It was therefore "poetic justice" from the Truk Islander's point of view for the woman's father to hit her: "A good hard jolt was just what she deserved" (ibid.:11–12). I claimed that the incident constituted a breakdown in Goodenough's ability to predict behavior from a knowledge of rules. Paul Kay (1970:20), however, says that it is nothing of the sort:

Goodenough has uncovered a Trukese cultural rule which is formally analogous to the American cultural rule prohibiting homicide except in self defense.

. . . The moral of Goodenough's story is precisely that cultures, seen as cognitive systems, are extremely complex, and that cultural rules characteristically contain *except* and *unless* clauses.

Kay (1970:22) proposes that such rules for breaking rules refer to "one set of narrowly defined occasions." But the comparison with American rules prohibiting homicide seems infelicitous, since it is impossible to define a narrow set of conditions that are the "except" and "unless" clauses for self-defense. For example, natives of the United States would presumably regard it as inappropriate for a man who shoots and kills an unarmed eight-year-old boy to invoke the rule of self-defense. Yet suppose the man involved is a police officer, and the child is tall for his age; suppose also that the encounter takes place on a street in a high-crime area and the boy is accompanied by an adult who makes a menacing gesture. In this actual instance no consensus could be reached that the act was culturally "inappropriate."

What cognitive anthropologists in general fail to realize is that the rule for breaking a rule is also subject to a rule for breaking rules, and that the conditions defining occasions as appropriate for one rule rather than another are expressed by means of inherently ambiguous vernacular categories. Thus the rules elicited to explain, justify, or predict behavior contain an irreducible residue of interpretation, judgment, and uncertainty. I claim that this constitutes grounds for the inference that the set of rules for breaking rules is infinite. To every emic behavioral condition there can always be added another emic condition calling for the reinterpretation of the previous judgment that a given response was appropriate.

As an example, consider the research carried out by V. K. Kochar (1976) and his associates on the sociocultural causes of hookworm infection in West Bengal. Kochar begins with the salient Hindu rule that fecal contact is polluting and the paradoxical etic fact that hookworm, transmissible only through fecal contact, is endemic. All informants prefer to defecate away from the presence of human fecal remains. Yet investigation showed that 75 percent of all stools were deposited within three feet of recognizable traces of previous stools. The ethnographer elicited six rules that might lead to the breaking of the rule against fecal contact: (1) a spot must be found not too far from the house; (2) the spot must provide protection against being seen by others; (3) it must offer an opportunity to see others approaching; (4) it must be near a source of water for washing; (5) it must be upwind of unpleasant odors; (6) it must not be in a field with growing crops. Each of these rules is in turn subject to a considerable amount of individual interpretation and uncertainty. Old people defecate closer to the house and hence are subject to more frequent reinfection from their own stools. Perhaps there is a rule that old people need not walk as far or be as well hidden as others. If so, does this rule have equal saliency among old men and old women, is it equally applicable in sickness and in health, in rain or shine, in caste and class, and so on?

The openness and irreducible ambiguity of the conditions for rules and for the rules for breaking rules can lead to only one conclusion: people have a rule for everything they do. No matter how deviant or unexpected the act, a psychologically intact human being can always appeal to some set of rules someone else will recognize as legitimate, although perhaps as misinterpreted or misapplied.

Note that I refrain from saying that every act is therefore *caused* by a rule. Old people do not break the fecal contact rule more often because they have a rule permitting them to stay closer to the house; rather, they break the rule more often because they are old and feeble.

A further consequence of the fact that every act has a rule is that an ethnographer's knowledge of the set of emic rules will expand in proportion to knowledge gained about the set of known acts. But the set of known acts need not expand in proportion to knowledge of rules. Unless alternative acts are observed, alternative rules probably won't be elicited. This is especially true of the rules for breaking rules. It is difficult to know the rules for breaking the rules of homicide, pollution, cow worship (see p. 38ff), marital fidelity, or mother love until acts of murder, defilement, cow slaughter, adultery, and infanticide are observed and the actors are questioned concerning their motives. Thus a purely emic approach to sociocultural systems not only guarantees that some behavior will be unpredictable but also makes it easier for most of the rules for breaking rules to go unnoticed.

Since we intuitively know that there is a rule for everything, we are easily misled into believing that rules govern or cause behavior. But the principle that rules govern or cause behavior is no more credible than the proposition that the earth is flat. Rules facilitate, motivate, and organize our behavior; they do not govern or cause it. The causes of behavior are to be found in the material conditions of social life. The conclusion to be drawn from the abundance of "unless" and "except" clauses is not that people behave in order to conform to rules, but they select or create rules appropriate for their behavior.

There Are No Unchallenged Authorities

IF EVERY ACT has a rule, the cognitivists' ability to predict when natives will acknowledge a performance as "grammatical" must also be questioned. If every act has a rule, then every act will be deemed appropriate by at least one actor and possibly many more. What determines how many actors will acknowledge a particular act as appropriate?

The "cultural grammarians" are not unaware of the possible existence of disagreements concerning the interpretation of conditions for the rules for breaking rules. Indeed, Goodenough (1970:99) admits that "no two persons in Truk have identical standards for what they regard as Trukese culture, and the amount of variance they accept in one another's behavior differs from one subject matter to another and from one kind of situation to another."

Nonetheless, despite the fact that the culture of a group is "necessarily somewhat different for every one of the group's members," Goodenough (1970:102) insists that an ethnographer can formulate "a set of standards that, taken as a guide for acting and interpreting the acts of others, leads to behavior the community's members perceive as in accord with their expectations of one another—behavior they accept as being properly Trukese, country Irish, or whatever."

Goodenough's (1970:100–101) solution to the problem of ambiguity and diversity depends on the identification of individuals whom he calls "authorities."

In any community . . . there are some people who are regarded as having greater knowledge of what the standards for the group are supposed to be. They are called upon to pronounce what the standards are in disputes about them [the standards]. Thus, for some subjects at least, there are acknowledged authorities whose judgments regarding the agreed-upon standards and whose pronouncements as to whether something is right or wrong are accepted by others in the group. . . . People want such authorities. Ethnographers concerned to describe a group's culture, in the sense in which I am using the term, make a regular practice of seeking out recognized local authorities and experts in order to use them as their principal sources of information. . . . Even in ordinary matters, one does not use a five-year-old as a reliable informant about adult activities.

What Goodenough fails to realize in granting to authorities the ability to decide right or wrong is that general behavioral conformity to such decisions is in no way proof of general consensus. People obey rules endorsed by authorities, not necessarily because they are obedient to rules but because they are obedient to authorities. The question of conformity to authoritative or "authentic" rules thus leads directly to the consideration of the distribution of power within a population. For people are generally obedient to authorities who have power—who have control over energy and material forces of coercion. Thus the prediction of the degree of conformity or consensus with rules, even in the minimal sense of acknowledging competence, requires an analysis of etic behavioral conditions. To neglect the fact that there are weak as well as strong authorities and that there are different levels, ranges, qualities, and intensities of emic consensus is to caricature and obfuscate the nature of human social life. Ideological-moral consensus is neither the precondition nor the normal mode of human social existence. Rather, such consensus is always an illusion fostered by those who are "authorities" or who work for them.

Goodenough's caveat that "even in ordinary matters, one does not use a five-year-old as a reliable informant about adult activities" illustrates the irrelevance of the grammars of rules as predictors of behavior. For regardless of what parental "authorities" may think ought to happen in their domestic life, what their children do to them as much as what they do to their children determines what both children and adults finally end up actually doing. This can be illustrated by data from the study of "ordinary matters" in the life of four New York families as described in Chapter 2. It seems a reasonable assumption that when people ask each other to do something, they have in mind some general rule that entitles them to make the request. Whatever these rules are, the members of families more often than not give them variant interpretation or oppose them by rules for breaking rules, for noncompliances far outnumber compliances (Dehavenon, 1977). The rate of compliance is therefore unpredictable from any native authority's (i.e., parent's) knowledge of the rules of family life. I doubt that any model for predicting behavior based on the assumption that behavior is determined by shared cognitive orientations can advance our understanding of how families manage to function as social groups. This is a crucial test of the relevance of emics to behavior, because domestic groups are widely believed to be the model for homogeneous small-scale societies in which shared cognitive orientations predominate over the specialized cognitive orientations characteristic of more complex social groups.

Rules Are Not Forever

THE CRUX of the conflict between cognitivism and cultural materialism is not the question of whether human behavior is to some degree rule-governed. The central question is where *both* the rules and the behavior come from. Unless a strategy can analyze the diachronic causal processes responsible for the emergence of observed patterns of thought and behavior, it cannot be said to have achieved a high level of predictability with respect to either thought or behavior. For the most perfect description of the rules of sociocultural life derived from one generation of informants may prove to be utterly irrelevant for predicting the behavior of the next generation of informants. Cognitivism, in other words, derives its credibility as a major research strategy from an implicit assumption that sociocultural systems change very slowly or not at all. As soon as one asks how long a particular grammar of culture can go on "accounting for" the behavior of a particular population, cognitivists must lapse into silence. For cognitivism is totally devoid of causal theories that can account for sociocultural differences.

The Struggle for "Culture"

ACCORDING TO Ward Goodenough (1969:330): "Culture consists of an inventory of precepts and concepts—of ideational forms—and a set of principles for ordering them." As a consequence of the influence of cognitivism and other idealist strategies, a whole generation of anthropologists has been reared to accept this definition of the central concept of the human sciences—a definition which implies that the etic and behavioral components of sociocultural systems are to be studied by an as-yet-unborn discipline. Some anthropologists even seem to believe that "culture" always excluded behavior. Philip Bock (1968:-17), for example, states that Edward Tylor's definition of culture—the first ever made by a professional anthropologist—contains an "emphasis upon ideas and ideals." But this is not accurate.

Tylor (1871:1) wrote that culture is a "complex whole which includes knowledge, belief, art, law, morals, custom and any other capabilities and habits acquired by man as a member of society." To which he added: "Culture is a subject apt for the study of laws of human thought and action." Moreover, like most modern anthropologists, Tylor regarded material objects as an essential part of culture. In fact Tylor devoted the bulk of his *Anthropology,* the first textbook to bear that title, to technology, subsistence, and material items. If Tylor wanted future anthropologists to view his beloved hand shuttles, crossbows, blowguns, drills, screws, water wheels, and other instruments, tools, and weapons merely as ideas and symbols or rules and instructions, he never said so. Material culture was the key to anthropology's successful institutionalization in museums of natural history and science and to the corresponding absence of sociology departments from such institutions. Clark Wissler (1923) elaborated his universal cultural patterns while curator of the American Museum of Natural History. For him, culture consisted of three main divisions: "material traits," "social activities" and "ideas." Concern with material culture also reflects a century of collaboration between ethnologists studying cultures in the present and anthropological archaeologists studying cultures in the past.

Alfred Kroeber, more than any other prominent theoretician of the first half of the twentieth century, helped to make culture the central concept of anthropology. Although Kroeber, like most students of Franz Boas, was opposed to materialist strategies, his earliest definitions of culture followed Tylor's. In 1948, in his standard-setting textbook *(Anthropology),* culture was not yet a realm of pure idea.

The mass of learned and transmitted motor reactions, habits, techniques, ideas, and values—and the behavior they induce—is what constitutes *culture.* (Kroeber, 1948:8)

But several convergent trends soon induced Kroeber to modify this view.

Enter Talcott Parsons

THE DOMINANT STRATEGY among American sociologists at midcentury was structural-functionalism. Its chief architect was Talcott Parsons. Structural-functionalism emphasized the causal saliency of rules, values, and expectations in the maintenance of society. According to Parsons (1967), societies have four systems: (a) expectations of role-performance; (b) organization of role-units into collectivities; (c) patterning of rights and obligations; and (d) commitments to values (Parsons, 1967). The last of these corresponds to what Parsons means by culture, elsewhere described by him as "standards of selective orientation and ordering" (Parsons, 1951:327). As the founder of the Department of Social Relations at Harvard, Parsons's influence spread into "numerous subcenters with highly institutionalized training provisions for postgraduate students" (Shils, 1970:796). Harvard's Department of Social Relations aimed at "integrating the theories of social structure, culture, and personality" (ibid.:795). The anthropologist Clyde Kluckhohn, one of the department's co-founders, upheld the interest in culture. But Kluckhohn accepted from the outset the purely emic and idealist definition of culture that was part of Parsons's scheme. Parsons's influence on anthropology was facilitated by the close intellectual and personal relationship between Kluckhohn and Kroeber, who soon produced the influential book *Culture: A Critical Review of Concepts and Definitions*. One can only conclude that it was Parsons's influence through Kluckhohn that led Kroeber to begin to modify the definition he had proposed in 1948. Kroeber continued to hold that culture consisted of "patterns of behavior," but he and Kluckhohn now added that the "essential core" of culture was "ideas . . . and . . . values":

patterns, explicit and implicit, of and for behavior acquired and transmitted by symbols, constituting the distinctive achievement of human groups, including their embodiments in artifacts; the essential core of culture consists of traditional (i.e., historically derived and selected) ideas and especially their attached values; culture systems may, on the one hand, be considered a product of action, on the other as conditioning elements of further action. (Kroeber and Kluckhohn, 1952:181)

In 1958, however, Kroeber moved completely over to accommodate Parsons's scheme. He and Parsons now co-authored a concordat in which they observed that "Comte and Spencer, and Weber and Durkheim spoke of society as meaning essentially the same thing that Tylor meant by culture." The time had come, however, to end "this condensed concept of culture-and-society because . . . we believe that knowledge and interests have become sufficiently differentiated so that further distinctions need to be made and stabilized in the routine usage of the relevant professional groups." The reigning theoreticians of sociology and anthropology then exorcised the last devils of behavior from the culture concept:

We suggest that it is useful to define the concept culture for most usages more narrowly than has been generally the case in the American anthropological tradition, restricting its reference to transmitted and created content and patterns of values, ideas, and other symbolic-meaningful systems as factors in the shaping of human behavior and the artifacts produced through behavior. (Kroeber and Parsons, 1958:583)

Note that what had been "patterns . . . of and for behavior" in 1952 was now "patterns of values, ideas, and other symbolic-meaningful systems." Behavior that in 1948 was induced by learning "motor reactions, habits, techniques" now was shaped exclusively by "values, ideas and other symbolic-meaningful systems." This "definition" in fact is much more than a definition. It is an encapsulated statement of the research strategy of cultural idealism, since it explicitly gives research priority to the principle that ideas determine behavior. Additional paradigmatic consequences were spelled out, intended to reconcile cultural anthropology with other aspects of Parsons's scheme. Thus the cultural idea-system was to be restricted to what I have called the emic superstructure. This was to be the main focus of cultural anthropology. Sociology, on the other hand, was to concentrate on Parsons's "social system," by which was meant "the specifically relational system of interaction among individuals and collectivities" (ibid.). This corresponds to what I have called the emics of domestic and political organization.

The essence of Parsons's brand of cultural idealism has been perpetuated by a small but influential number of Harvard-trained anthropologists, including, most prominently, Clifford Geertz (who brought anthropology to the Institute for Advanced Studies at Princeton) and David Schneider (who developed the Department of Anthropology at the University of Chicago into a major center for the study of structural and superstructural emics). For Schneider, whom Parsons (1970:859) identifies as "my old student and friend," behavior is "quite irrelevant to the question of whether there is or is not a cultural unit, a cultural concept, a cultural entity" (Schneider, 1968:7). Culture, following Parsons, consists in the "system of symbols and meanings embedded in the normative system but which is a quite distinct aspect of it . . ." (Schneider, 1972:38). For Geertz to study culture is to study a semiotic field. Culture is to be interpreted as one interprets an "assemblage of texts" through a process of "thick description" (Geertz, 1972; cf. Keesing, 1974:79). Schneider and Geertz both reject the reductionist formalisms attempted by ethnoscientists and structuralists, but their commitment to cultural idealist principles is no less intense.

The Role of Linguistics

ACCEPTANCE of Kroeber and Parsons's dematerialized concept of culture was facilitated on both sides of the Atlantic by the strategic thrust of structural and generative linguistics. As linguistic models gained in prestige, they were taken as exemplars by both structuralists and cognitivists in search of noncausal and nonpredictive but formalistic schemes for describing mental and emic phenomena.

As we have seen, formal analysis of phonological and phonemic systems by structural linguists directly influenced Lévi-Strauss's concept of hidden contrastive structures. At the same time, structural linguistics provided the model for the cognitivist system of componential analysis, by which the contrastive elements in such domains as kinship terminology, botanical classifications, and color categories were elicited from informants (Z. Harris, 1951; Goodenough, 1968:-186).

In the United States, Noam Chomsky's (1964) attack on B. F. Skinner's behaviorist approach to human verbal behavior was instrumental in encouraging cultural idealists to get inside people's heads as a respectable form of scientific activity. But as I pointed out in Chapter 1, there was no behaviorist tradition in cultural anthropology to attack as there was in psychology. Hence, all that Chomsky's prestige guaranteed the science of dematerialized culture was that the behavior stream would be neglected even more than it had been during the first half of the century. Chomsky's concept of "deep structure" was also completely convergent with and directly supportive of the tendency to view culture as a set of rules or a code for generating behavior judged appropriate by natives possessing "competence" in the culture (cf. Hymes, 1968). Thus linguistics provided the perfect justification for a science of culture that would be formally elegant, but nonpredictive, noncausal, and divorced from the conflicts and contingencies of etic behavior.

The Influence of Durkheim

ONE MORE CONVERGENT thrust toward the dematerializations of the structuralists, cognitivists, and other modern varieties of cultural idealism remains to be identified. Despite the fact that Schneider and Geertz both reject the reductionist linguistic formalisms attempted by the ethnoscientists and French structuralists, Parsonian idealism and linguistically inspired cognitivism do have common roots. As Keesing (1974:79–80) states, Geertz's "thick description" implies "no ethnoscience optimism that the cultural code can be formalized as a grammar, no Lévi-Straussian glibness at decoding. . . ." But the key concepts of the Parsonians and structuralists have a common point of departure in the strikingly idealist viewpoints of Emile Durkheim.

Durkheim was responsible for the attempt to develop a "scientific," state-supported system of morality based on *collective conscience* and *organic solidarity* (cf. Turner, 1977). Durkheim became the dominant figure in French sociology following the electoral success of the misnomered Radical party, a centrist liberal party whose political philosophy was known as solidarism. Leon Bourgeois (!), the leading solidarist and premier of France from 1895 to 1896, regarded Durkheim's work as proof that Marxist class conflict could be avoided. In Durkheim's analysis, class struggle was a temporary pathology, and organic solidarity, not revolution, was the predictable outcome of industrialization. For Durkheim, as I pointed out in Chapter 7, "social facts" are expressions of the collective "conscience" or "consciousness" and this conscience/consciousness is the essence of all that is technically social— a combination of superorganic consciousness and moral imperative:

In short, social life is nothing but the moral milieu that surrounds the individual . . . or to be more accurate, it is the sum of the moral milieus that surround the individual. By calling them moral, we mean to say that they are made up of ideas. (quoted in Turner, 1974)

Durkheim's book *The Rules of the Sociological Method* contains a consistent epistemology of sociocultural phenomena in which collective moral ideas exterior to the individual are assumed to determine thought and actual behavior. As we have seen, minus the binary oppositions and dialectical flimflam, Durkheim expounding on the collective conscience/collective consciousness is Lévi-Strauss expounding on hidden structures (p. 167).

Now Durkheim's collective conscience/collective consciousness not only inspired Lévi-Strauss but it also was the direct inspiration for Parsons's definitions of the social and cultural as pure idea (Parsons, 1951). It also clearly anticipates, minus the notion of code, the cognitivists' notion of culture as a set of rules—the "moral milieu."

Durkheim's influence can be traced further in the subsequent elaboration of the notion of organic solidarity. Distinguishing his position with respect to Marx and Weber on the issue of the nature of modern societies, Parsons writes: "The principal point of reference for a different view in my case has been the work of Durkheim, notably his conception of organic solidarity" (1970:855). Organic solidarity is a covert but persuasive theme in the work of Lévi-Strauss. It was Durkheim's student Marcel Mauss, who inspired Lévi-Strauss's analysis of marriage systems as reciprocal exchanges and both Parsons and Lévi-Strauss repeat Durkheim's response to Marx in stressing consensus and solidarity over dis-sensus and conflict as the salient object of sociocultural inquiry.

Finally, there is the curious detail that even in Lévi-Strauss's adoption of elements of linguistics, setting structuralists off from such Parsonians as Schneider and Geertz, the influence of Durkheim can still be felt. Lévi-Strauss's ideas of hidden structure come from Ferdinand de Saussure's distinction between *langue* and *parole*. And what De Saussure was trying to do was nothing less than to apply Durkheim's concept of social fact in a linguistic context—that is, to separate the reality of the collective conscience that lies behind specific utterances from the unreality of the utterances themselves (Hymes, 1968:355).

The Ideological Significance of Culture as Pure Idea

THE IDEALIST expropriation of culture is not a matter of whim or taste, but a recurrent product of persistent ideological and political conditions.

Idealist cultural anthropology fulfills the conservative bias inherent in institutionalized social science. The fact that individual anthropologists may engage in left-liberal or radical politics while their professional activities are yoked to a grammarian's paradigm does not alter the politico-ideological thrust of their mentalistic definition of culture. (What this paradox confirms is the lack of theory in the practice of contemporary radical and left-liberal politics.) It does not alleviate the massive ideological occlusion associated with solidarist, structuralist, and grammarian principles. While the American grammarians belong to an intellectual tradition unrelated in a narrowly conventional historical sense to Talcott Parsons or to Durkheim, all modern varieties of cultural idealism are convergent and functionally equivalent expressions of the same conservative restrictions. Like the Parsonians, the grammarians and ethnoscientists accept the system as given and seek to account for its stability. This bias protects them from the obligation of predicting or retrodicting the evolution of sociocultural differences and similarities. Indeed, because of the epistemological clarity of the linguistic model, the grammarians go even further than the Parsonians in avoiding contact with etic behavioral events. They not only renounce prediction, but they relieve themselves of having to say what is happening in the present. Again, like the Parsonians, the grammarians offer a consensus theory of social structure. The linguistic paradigm both in French structuralism and American cognitivism reaffirms Durkheim's collective conscience. Organic solidarity is reborn in the homogeneous mental field possessing deep structures that allegedly organize the consensus of "competent natives" and Goodenough's "authorities." All sociocultural phenomena are to be "accounted for" in terms of this consensus; lack of consensus and incompetent natives are epiphenomenal.

Never has there been a strategy less suited to the study of conflict and political process. The subjects prohibited to "modern cultural anthropology" are the guts of contemporary life. No amount of knowledge of "competent natives' " rules and codes can "account for" phenomena such as poverty; underdevelopment; imperialism; the population explosion; minorities; ethnic and class conflict; exploitation, taxation, private property; pollution and degradation of the environment; the military-industrial complex; political repression; crime; urban blight; unemployment; or war. These phenomena, like everything else that is important to human beings, are the consequence of intersecting and contradictory vectors of belief, will, and power. They cannot be scientifically understood as manifestations of codes or rules.

In the light of the foregoing analysis, the choice of structuralism, cognitivism, or any of their variants as a research strategy carries with it the implication that one does not believe it is possible to have an anthropology that is capable of explaining both divergent and convergent, emic and etic, sociocultural phenomena in causal terms. I do not see how such a choice can be scientifically justified without first making an effort to achieve what is said to be unachievable.

Chapter Ten

Eclecticism

I HAVE FOUND most of my colleagues think it unscientific to make an explicit commitment to one or another research strategy. They listen attentively to the claims and counterclaims of each strategic option, but they refuse to acknowledge a need for adopting one strategy to the exclusion of the rest. Does not science oblige researchers to keep an open mind? In the human sciences this seems like an especially good idea. With so many extreme positions being advocated at once, isn't it likely that they all have something worthwhile to offer? It scarcely seems possible that only one out of the lot could have a decisive advantage over all the others. Isn't it obvious that prudent scientists will not follow any particular strategy but rather will reserve the right to pick and choose among the whole spectrum of epistemological and theoretical principles according to whatever seems to work best for the particular problem they happen to be working on?

Those who believe that prudence and common sense demand that one must avoid a commitment to any particular research strategy fail to realize that such a belief constitutes a commitment to a definite research strategy—the strategy of eclecticism. This strategy scarcely qualifies as prudent or scientifically sensible. By picking and choosing epistemological and theoretical principles to suit the convenience of each puzzle, eclecticism guarantees that its solutions will remain unrelated to each other by any coherent set of principles. Hence eclecticism cannot lead to the production of a corpus of theories satisfying the criteria of parsimony and coherence. Rather, eclecticism is a prescription for perpetual scientific disaster: middle-range theories, contradictory theories, and unparsimonious theories without end.

Definition of Eclecticism

SOCIOLOGIST Arthur Stinchcombe (1968:4–6) identifies his "point of view" as "deliberately eclectic." This means:

I have a firm conviction that some things are to be explained one way and some another . . . If one approach does not work . . . the theorist should try another.

According to Stinchcombe, social scientists must be adept at all kinds of approaches so that they will "never be at a loss for alternative explanations."

In a similar vein, anthropologist Jack Goody (1973:208) remarks:

If some see anthropology as the sociology of other cultures, and if others insist upon an evolutionary or developmental approach, there should be no questions of engaging in one of these and rejecting everything else. The approach like the technique, depends upon the question you ask and the material you're dealing with.

I will discuss the consequences of Goody's eclecticism later on in this chapter.

Elman Service's (1969:406) "Down with prime-movers!" is eclecticism in a more aggressive mood:

Could technology be *sometimes* a determiner of evolutionary changes in certain other aspects of culture? Yes. Could competition or conflict among individuals be *sometimes* . . . ? Yes. Could competition or conflict among societies be *sometimes* . . . ? Yes. Could consciously formed social and political schemes and plans be *sometimes* . . . ? Yes. (Ibid.:1969:407–408)

Cultural materialists would also answer all of these questions in the affirmative. Obviously all sectors of sociocultural systems may *some-*

times be determinant. Hence such questions are hopelessly vague. Why ask first and foremost if technology, competition, or political schemes are *sometimes* determiners of evolutionary changes? Science does not set out from a concern with what *sometimes* happens; science sets out from a concern with what *generally* happens. Cultural materialism asserts that infrastructure *generally* determines structure and super-structure. Eclecticism consists of the refusal to state what generally determines what. Therefore it cannot organize the collection of data around the task of testing what can generally be expected to account for sociocultural differences and similarities. Inadvertently, it organizes the collection of data around the task of testing what can least be expected to account for sociocultural differences and similarities.

The hallmark of eclecticism is not that it regards all strategic options as *equally* probable or all sectors of sociocultural systems as *equally* determinative under all conditions. Such assertions are entirely too definite, too "dogmatic" for the eclectic strategy. To be eclectic is to be strategically agnostic in no definable manner. It is to grant only that all strategic options *might* be equally probable. But it is to deny that there is sufficient reason to justify anyone's belief that they actually are equally probable. Similarly, to follow an eclectic strategy is to grant that all sectors of sociocultural systems *might* be equally determinative, but it is not to insist that they actually are equally determinative.

Versatility Is Not Eclecticism

MANY ANTHROPOLOGISTS resent criticisms of eclecticism because they incorrectly equate eclecticism with the freedom to indulge in a wide variety of research interests. What is wrong with being interested in music, mythology, the dance, back scratchers, and sand painting as well as in the modes of production and reproduction? Nothing. Eclec-tics cannot be faulted for their wide-ranging curiosity, and the defini-tion of eclecticism has nothing whatsoever to do with this issue. Cul-tural materialism no less than eclecticism embraces everyday as well as exotic phenomena, seeks the solution of mental, behavioral, emic, etic, infrastructural, structural, and superstructural, diachronic and syn-chronic puzzles. The point at issue is not the range of problems consid-ered by eclectics, but the range of the principles they employ to solve them.

Nor is eclecticism to be confused with methodological versatility.

The choice of methodology is an issue that is entirely separate from the choice of epistemological or theoretical principles. Methodologies are the means one employs to test hypotheses and theories. Cultural materialism places no restrictions on methodological techniques as long as they conform to the need for public and replicable operations in conformity with the general epistemological principles of the scientific way of knowing. Cultural materialists no less than eclectics insist that different theories should be tested by different methodologies. Cultural materialists no less than eclectics rely on emic, etic, participant and nonparticipant, qualitative, quantitative, single-culture, cross-cultural, archival, archaeological, biological, ecological, demographic, and linguistic methods, depending on the nature of the specific theory under consideration. Eclecticism cannot be distinguished from cultural materialism by the kinds of methodologies used to test theories, but by the kind of principles used to construct the theories to be tested.

Consequences of Eclecticism

ECLECTICISM RESULTS IN theories that do not link up with or interpenetrate each other and that are often mutually exclusive. Eclecticism produces this result not because its practitioners operate without hypotheses but because they operate with too many. Eclecticism is not mere narrow, Baconian inductionism. One can advocate the importance of the interplay between theory—even macro theory—and the collection of "facts," and still practice eclecticism. Thus eclectics are often interested in producing theories of relatively broad scope. But it is no more reasonable to suppose that such theories will be mutually compatible and interpenetrating than it is to suppose that research conducted in a pure inductionist vein will lead to powerful hypotheses.

Eclectics are not disturbed by the jumble of isolated and contradictory theories hitherto produced under eclectic auspices. They believe that with the passage of time and the accumulation of more data, a more unified vision will emerge. If this does not happen, then one can conclude that the chaotic condition of theory is faithful to the disorderly nature of human phenomena. To this I would respond: first, the more time that is given (and the more resources), the less likely it becomes that a synthesis will ever be made out of the eclectic corpus; and second, the fragmentation and inconsistency does not reflect the nature of sociocultural phenomena but rather the absence of principles capable of directing research efforts consistently along lines that could conceivably produce a coherent corpus of interpenetrating theories.

Holocultural Chaos

TO ILLUSTRATE what I mean by the fragmentation and inconsistency of eclecticism, let us turn to Raoul Naroll's (1973) summary of theories that have been tested statistically against cross-cultural samples. Naroll calls such theories "holocultural theories," since they are intended as generalizations about all cultures (or all known cultures of a certain type).

Naroll's eclecticism is more or less explicit. For example, in discussing the option of explaining human behavior in terms of genes, climate, diet, pathology, roles, values, social relationships or "psychogenic" factors, he states:

It seems clear to me that each of these modes of explanation is sometimes important; conscientious behavioral scientists seeking to explain culture cannot a priori rule out any one of them. (Ibid.:348)

Naroll sets out to defend the holocultural method by listing "all the holocultural theories I could find" (ibid.:310). The resulting corpus, consisting of 152 studies, covers a broad variety of topics Naroll classifies as follows:

Kinship
"Main sequence" kinship theory
Structural analysis of kinship systems
Kin avoidances
Inheritance
Marriage
Divorce
Origin myths

Cultural Evolution
Weak to strong
Generalists to specialists
Simple organizations to complex organizations
Rural to urban

Wealth sharing to wealth hoarding
Consensual leadership to authoritative leadership
Responsible elite to eploitative elite
Vengeance war to political war

Life-styles and Cultural Evolution
Art styles
Games and riddles
Song and dance styles
Theology
Need-for-achievement orientation
Deference patterns
Other traits

Child Rearing and Adult Behavior
Cultural maintenance systems and child training
Child training and personality traits
Child training and projective systems
Child training and physiology

Social Setting and Antisocial Behavior
Alcoholism
Crime
Internal war
Frustration and aggression
Suicide
Witchcraft accusations

For each of the theories, Naroll evaluates the validity of the sampling procedures and of the other logical and statistical methods employed, a task he is superbly qualified to carry out. I don't want to question the validity of holocultural studies as a method for testing theories—I have long urged that they be so employed. Rather I intend to question the value of the corpus of theories upon which Naroll lavishes so much effort. My contention is that despite the empirical soundness of the theories treated by Naroll, the entire set diminishes rather than enhances our understanding of sociocultural causality.

The first thing that one notices about these studies (or at least Naroll's approach to them) is that they are not based upon any shared understanding of the universal structure of sociocultural systems. The labels under which they appear are obviously not coordinated with infrastructural, structural, or superstructural components, nor with mental/behavioral or emic/etic distinctions. Second, it is apparent that the studies have not been carried out with any shared commitment to both diachronic and synchronic correlations and causal processes. If such a commitment existed, it would not be possible to carry out kinship, child rearing and adult behavior, or social setting and antisocial behavior studies apart from the two categories of theories labeled "evolutionary"—cultural evolution and life-styles and cultural evolution. Whatever the specific theories may be under the "nonevolutionary" rubrics, they cannot be very powerful theories, since they evidently fail to control for conditions that are subject to evolutionary change. Let us examine some of the specific theories falling into this category.

Alcoholism

ACCORDING to Naroll (ibid.:345), holocultural studies prove that

high insobriety ratings are more likely to be found at lower levels of social development, as reflected in one or more of the following: foraging economy, nomadic settlements, small settlements, little political ramification (hierarchies) and little social stratification.

Six holocultural studies are cited in support of this theory, but I can offer absolute guarantees that the theory obfuscates the fundamental causal chain that has led to alcoholism in modern populations. The production of potent alcoholic beverages on a large scale depends upon the domestication of plants and the development of fermentation and distilling technologies by sedentary village and state-level societies. Thus the theory cannot apply to foraging, nomadic, and unstratified societies prior to the evolution of the state or prior to the contact with state-level (colonial) systems. The reason that societies "at lower levels of social development" now show high rates of alcoholism cannot be understood apart from the stresses created by contact with the societies providing them with alcohol. This applies to all the native peoples of the United States and Canada, none of whom possessed inebriating alcoholic beverages prior to the European invasion.

Crime and Internal War

NAROLL believes that Bacon, Child, and Barry (1963) have proved that theft and personal assault are "more frequent where opportunity for the young boy to identify himself with his father was limited or absent altogether" (Naroll, 1973:346). Naroll evaluates this study as one having a high degree of validity judged from a technical point of view (see chart, ibid.:322). Yet the theory that crime is caused by the absence of fathers is fundamentally misleading. Obviously there are other factors in crime that are not implicated in the theory—such factors as class, ethnic, and racial conflicts, glaring wealth differences, unemployment, urban decay, and so forth. To be sure, the theory does not state that absence of fathers is the only cause of theft and assault. But it is the special weakness of eclecticism to suppose that there is no way short of actually carrying out additional tests involving these factors to judge whether other factors are more or less important than absence of father. I contend that without such a preliminary sense of research priorities, not only will minor or peripheral factors constantly be put forward as if they were major or central, but the entire body of theory will be disjointed and riddled with logical contradictions. This is borne out by Naroll's discussion of internal war—which follows immediately after the discussion of crime. According to Naroll, in primitive societies, "strong internal conflict such as feuding . . . stems from the presence of localized groups of related males who support one another in conflict situations" (ibid.:346). Now these "fraternal interest groups" include fathers and sons. Hence this theory manifestly contradicts the previous one, which in effect attributes a high incidence of violent assaults to the absence of fathers. Present fathers in one case and absent fathers in the other; both lead to violent assaults. The theory that absent fathers leads to belligerent sons might be improved by adding the proviso "except in band and village societies." But many other provisos are needed. The effect of father's absence upon juvenile assault rates is modified by whether residence is urban or rural, whether we are talking about capitalist or socialist economies; by whether there are superordinate or subordinate classes, castes, and ethnic statuses; and so forth. In other words, the theory that crime is caused by absent fathers is a middle-range theory which can be saved from falsification only by drastically restricting its range of applicability. Such a theory explains neither crime and violence nor relationships between fathers and sons.

Puberty Rites

ECLECTIC THEORIES also suffer from their tendency to accept crucial sets of causal variables as givens in order to facilitate the study of the effects of less important variables. For example, John Whiting's (1969) theory of the causes of severe male puberty rites, which also appears in Naroll's list, illustrates how this practice tends to fragment one's knowledge of causal processes. (Naroll lacks confidence in Whiting's theory, but on methodological grounds not related to the point I wish to make.)

Severe male puberty rites are characterized by circumcision or other mutilations, prolonged seclusion, beatings, and trials of courage and stamina. As I mentioned in the previous chapter (p. 264), Whiting shows that such rites are correlated with a number of variables: (1) protein scarcity; (2) nursing of infants for more than a year; (3) postpartum taboo on sex for more than a year; (4) polygyny; (5) domestic sleeping arrangements in which mother and child sleep together and father sleeps elsewhere; (6) women in control of children during early childhood; and (7) patrilocality. Charles Harrington and John Whiting (1972:492) give this explanation of the links in Whiting's theory:

Low protein availability and the risk of Kwashiorkor were correlated with an extended post-partum sex taboo to allow mother time to nurse the infant through the critical stage before becoming pregnant again. The post-partum sex taboo was significantly correlated with the institution of polygyny, providing alternate sexual outlets to the male. Polygyny in turn is associated with mother-child households, child training by women, resultant cross-sex identity, and *where patrilocality is also present,* with initiation rites to resolve the conflict and properly inculcate male identity. [Italics added]

These relationships can be diagrammed as follows:

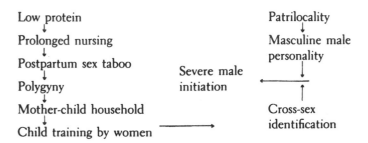

Whiting's scheme implicates infrastructural variables—production of protein—in the explanation of all variables except patrilocality. But what causes patrilocality? Moreover, Whiting's scheme makes severe male initiations intelligible only as a result of a postulated complex psychodynamic process, a "sex identity conflict." A more parsimonious theory of broader scope and wider applicability can easily be constructed by relating patrilocality to infrastructure, by making psychological processes dependent on material conditions, and by adding causal variables arbitrarily neglected by Whiting

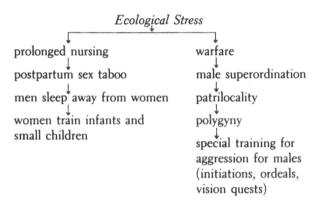

Ecological Stress

prolonged nursing ↓ postpartum sex taboo ↓ men sleep away from women ↓ women train infants and small children

warfare ↓ male superordination ↓ patrilocality ↓ polygyny ↓ special training for aggression for males (initiations, ordeals, vision quests)

In this model, severe initiation rites for boys are viewed as consistent with male superordination and the needs of fraternal interest groups involved in intensive warfare. Unlike Whiting, I see no structural conflict in the fact that women train infants and small children. Such a conflict would exist only if women did not treat little boys and girls differently—which seems unlikely—or if women trained boys to be submissive—even more unlikely. The model predicts that the severity of the rites is governed by the severity of warfare involving fraternal interest groups, and that if there is intensive warfare men will frequently sleep away from women and children regardless of whether there is prolonged nursing or a postpartum sex taboo. Also the model indicates why men are not subject to the postpartum sex taboo—sex being the reward for aggressive masculinity, as explained in Chapter 4.

To sum up: under eclectic auspices it is possible to continue to construct theories of middle scope and middle applicability indefinitely without linking one theory to another. The eclectic strategy is therefore an excellent source of proliferating research tasks, but it is a highly inefficient way to study the causes of sociocultural differences and similarities.

The Limited Good of the Image of Limited Good

THE MARK of an incoherent corpus of theories is the existence side by side of contradictory theories in the work of a single researcher. A classic case occurs in the work of George Foster. According to Foster (1967), the peasants of Tzintzuntzan, a village in the Tarascan region of Mexico, are the victims of an emic and mental complex which he calls the "Image of Limited Good." This *image* consists of a set of values, attitudes, and beliefs to the effect that life must always be a dreary struggle, that very few people can achieve "success" and that those who achieve success do so at the expense of other people:

By Image of Limited Good, I mean that . . . Tzintzuntzenos see their social, economic, and natural universes—their total environment—as one in which all desired things in life such as land, other forms of wealth, health, friendship, love, manliness, honor, respect, power, influence, security, and safety *exist in absolute quantities insufficient to fill even minimal needs of villagers. . . .* Consequently . . . *it follows that an individual or a family can improve its position only at the expense of others. . . .* Hence . . . any significant improvement is perceived . . . as a threat to *all* individuals and families. (Ibid.:123–124)

Foster's study is concerned in its entirety with showing how this cognitive orientation expresses itself in every domain of village life. Speaking like a cultural idealist, Foster declares:

The first, and basic argument advanced in these pages, from which the other arguments follow, is that all normative group behavior—the culture of every society—is a function of a particular *understanding* of the conditions that delimit and determine life, a correlate of certain implicit *assumptions,* of which the average person is totally unaware. In Tzintzuntzan (and in other peasant societies) this "particular understanding" can be described by the Image of Limited Good. (Ibid.:350; italics added)

Continuing in the same idealist strategic vein, Foster claims that if the changes that are going on in Mexico are going to lead to a "better and happier life for Tzintzuntzenos," instead of to "social unrest," then the first thing that must be gotten rid of is the *image:*

Hence in listing the fundamental factors which hold back the village, and which must be solved if the first of our two alternative futures [better and happier life] is to be achieved, we must put at or near the top increasingly outdated assumptions about conditions that govern life. (Ibid.)

This conviction, however, does not prevent Foster on the very same page from assuring us that the *image* is *not* "the major factor holding back Tzintzuntzan and other peasant villages" (ibid.). Speaking now as a materialist, he goes on to declare that the "villager's inherent economic potential, its natural resources, its geographical location, the national and international demand for its present and its potential products, and its population growth . . . is the key factor" (ibid.:351; italics added). If that is the case, why then has Foster devoted the entire book to the study of the *image?* Why has he not studied the "inherent economic potential," "geographical location," the national and international markets, and so forth?

Noting that it is the *image* and not the infrastructure Foster discusses, James Acheson (1972) takes Foster to task for exaggerating the superstructural and emic variables in underdevelopment. Acheson shows on the basis of his own research in another Tarascan community that when economic opportunities are present in the infrastructure, the image does not prevent people from taking advantage of them. (Actually, Foster himself unwittingly shows that the people of Tzintzuntzan were so little constrained by the image that they were readily gulled into a series of disastrous business ventures promulgated by irresponsible development experts (see Harris, 1980). Defending himself, Foster says he holds with Acheson "that the primary reasons that most individuals do not act to raise per capita income is that no opportunities exist" (Foster, 1974:55).

But in the very next paragraph, Foster once again contradicts himself:

Acheson's understanding of the economic motivation, however, is unnecessarily limiting. He fails to recognize that the bare presence of economic opportunity alone is not what counts. It is the *perception* of this opportunity, the *recognition* of its possibilities on the part of the entrepreneur, his basic ability, and the absence of sociocultural and personality factors sufficiently strong to dissuade him from action that converts the potential of the situation into an actuality. (Ibid.:55–56)

Foster then sends forth the familiar eclectic battle cry against simplistic, monistic determinism. We shall never formulate development theory from "simplistic economic explanations alone, but from careful, cautious, broadly based analyses of all the economic, political, historical, social and psychological factors that are at play in modern Mexico" (ibid.:57). Unfortunately, Acheson doesn't tell Foster that no one can study all the economic, political, historical, social and psychological factors at play in modern Mexico! Instead, he says that

what we need is not pious reminders that the problem is difficult and complicated, but, rather, specific studies attempting to pinpoint the exact set of "socio/cultural," "personality/infrastructure" factors affecting development in specific locales. (Acheson, 1974:61)

No. That is not what we need either. What we need is a coherent research strategy.

Who Needs the Image?

THE STRATEGIC alternative in development studies that Acheson implicitly pursued but failed to express is this: let us persist in the examination of the etic variables, infrastructure first, structure second, seeking the fullest possible understanding of economic growth *and* its concomitant emic features in relation to these variables. Let us postpone the conclusion that any specific emic or superstructural factors are vital for an understanding of the variance in economic growth until a serious attempt has been made to account for that variance in terms of etic and behavioral infrastructural and structural factors, and until it has been shown that the emic and mental aspects of the situation cannot be explained in terms of these same factors. It so happens that Foster's *image* of the limited good is unnecessary for an explanation of the level of economic growth in Tzintzuntzan. Foster himself inadvertently admits this when he states that the image of limited good is not a crippling false consciousness but a rather realistic appraisal of the facts of life in a society where economic success or failure is determined by forces beyond one's control or comprehension:

For the underlying, fundamental truth is that in an economy like Tzintzuntzan's, hard work and thrift are moral qualities of only the slightest functional value. Because of the limitations on land and technology, additional hard work does not produce a significant increment in income. It is pointless to talk of thrift in a subsistence economy, because usually there is no surplus with which to be thrifty. Foresight, with careful planning for the future, is also a virtue of dubious value in a world in which the best laid plans must rest on a foundation of chance and capriciousness. (Foster, 1967:150).

It follows from this that one ought to study the etic and behavioral infrastructural and structural conditions limiting the development of Mexico's peasantry. For example, a national system of class relations clearly has a great deal to do with the subordinate status of the people who live in villages like Tzintzuntzan. And there is an international system of political and economic relationships that subordinates Mexico's economy to the material interests of the developed industrial nations. Foster's attempt to focus attention on emic and mental factors in the underdevelopment equation therefore constitutes a diversion of research effort away from the factors most likely to account for the observed variance in economic welfare. Where material benefits clearly outweigh material costs, peasants in the aggregate are as likely as anyone else to perceive their own advantage correctly, regardless of the extant system of values and attitudes—provided, of course, that their perceptions are not subject to continued manipulation by classes or factions that benefit from the status quo.

The Poverty of "Culture"

OSCAR LEWIS'S concept of the "culture of poverty" is an exact analogue of Foster's "image of limited good," developed under the same eclectic auspices, but applied to urban rather than rural poverty. Lewis, like Foster and the structural Marxists, wants his materialism and his idealism too. Indeed, he describes himself as an "eclectic materialist":

My theoretical position in anthropology has a good deal in common with Harris's cultural materialism. My major disagreement with Harris is that there is very little room for the *human element* in his system of environmental and techno-economic determinism. I think of myself rather as an eclectic materialist. (Lewis, 1970:viii; italics added)

What Lewis means by "human" in this context is paying attention to the mental and emic aspects of social life. But cultural materialism, as I have said repeatedly, does not neglect these aspects of social life; it merely seeks to demystify their causes. So-called humanists might argue that by following an eclectic strategy Lewis arrives at an explanation of poverty that is more "human" because it is fragmented, unparsimonious, and illogical. But there is nothing especially *humane* about Lewis's explanation of urban poverty, since like Foster's explanation of peasant poverty, it leads to the conclusion that the poor are partially if not wholly to blame for their plight. This kind of rhetoric obscures the basic issue. Regardless of who is more "humane" or "human," Lewis's eclectic materialism does not lead to a coherent explanation of poverty.

According to Lewis, the culture of poverty is both a self-perpetuating set of values governing behavior and "an adaptation and reaction of the poor to their marginal position in a class-stratified, highly individuated capitalist society" (Lewis, 1966a:21). The self-perpetuating nature of poverty allegedly arises from the enculturation experience of children born into pauperized families:

By the time slum children are six or seven they have usually absorbed the basic attitudes and values of their subculture. Thereafter they are psychologically unready to take full advantage of changing conditions or improving opportunities that may develop in their lifetime.

Like Foster, Lewis pictures the poor as fearful, suspicious, and apathetic toward the major institutions of the larger society; they have "a strong present-time orientation with relatively little disposition to defer gratification and plan for the future," coupled with a "sense of resignation and fatalism." Lewis carefully hedges his estimate of the self-reinforcing power of ideology. He says that only 20 percent of the urban poor actually have the culture of poverty, implying that 80 percent fall into the category of those whose poverty results from etic conditions rather than from emic heritage or "design" for poverty living. Although Lewis does not explain why only 20 percent of the poor are victims of their own values, there is no doubt that he enhanced the popular appeal of his theory by this apparently sensible balancing of emic and etic factors. Isn't it plain common sense that to some extent at least the poor are unable to take advantage of real opportunities because their values prevent them from doing so? Doesn't cultural materialism admit that there is a feedback between emics and etics? Couldn't the 20 percent be a measure of the variance for which the material conditions are unable to account? Not at all. Obviously in the United States children of the poor tend to be poor. But Lewis is well aware of the fact that abject poverty is not found in all varieties of contemporary state societies. (Norway and Sweden, for example, simply do not have a poverty class.) If the "traits" Lewis attributes to the "culture of poverty" are not universals, then the first requisite of a theory of abject poverty is to identify the conditions under which abject poverty occurs.

Lewis himself links the culture of poverty with capitalism (see above), but he fails to analyze the etic factors within certain capitalist societies that guarantee the existence of a mercilessly pauperized class. Thus Lewis avoids the otherwise inescapable conclusion that not 80 percent but 100 percent of the extreme forms of poverty in the United States is due to the etic aspects of capitalism in the United States. None of the victims of the culture of poverty are victims of a self-replicating design for living because every aspect of that design for living is determined by the etic infrastructure and structure of U.S. capitalism. The poor are not victims of their own values; rather, they are victims, as Anthony Leeds has put it,

of certain kinds of labor markets which are structured by the condition of national technology, available capital resources, enterprise location, training institutions, relation to foreign and internal markets, balance-of-trade relations, and the nature of the profit system of capitalist societies. The forms and characteristics of the labor market can be predicted from states of these variables, and with that prediction also the states and rates of un- and underemployment can be reasonably predicted. These are not independent traits of some supposed culture, but characteristics or indices of certain kinds of total economic systems. . . . (Leeds, 1970:246)

I hasten to point out that by rejecting in its entirety Lewis's explanation of poverty, I am not denying that there is feedback between the emic and etic components of capitalist societies. Certainly aspects of Lewis's culture of poverty help to explain why the pauperized stratum in the United States is unable to organize itself into an effective political force. The ignorance, demoralization, fatalism, suspicion, ill-health, and fears of the poverty class help to perpetuate the dismal plight not only of the poor but of the working class as well. They do so by lowering the capacity of the victims to fight back effectively and thereby make the overall system more secure despite its glaring inequalities. But responsibility for the system as a whole cannot be prorated equally among the superordinate and subordinate classes. The values of the culture of poverty, like all cognitive patterns, arise in response to definite material conditions. The poor cannot control these conditions precisely because they are poor. These conditions in turn will persist as long as the systemic basis for a poverty class persists.

I do not intend to deny the possibility that the poor can play a role in the development of a political-economic system with no poverty class. Nor do I intend to deny that values have a vital role to play if the poor are to be mobilized effectively on behalf of radically transforming the poverty-producing labor market and poverty-producing profit system. The point Lewis fails to make—and his analysis obscures—is that the values appropriate for mobilizing the poor in a struggle against the systemic causes of poverty are quite different from the values that help individuals escape from the poverty class. To change the system the appropriate values are not those that lead to individual upward mobility but those that question the legitimacy of the concentration of wealth and power in super-rich families and corporate empires— values about political action on behalf of a more equitable distribution of wealth and economic opportunity.

Thus both system-maintaining and system-transforming values must be considered in the feedback between infrastructure and superstructure. Lewis concerned himself only with the system-maintaining values and incorrectly attributed the etics of poverty to the emics of the poor.

Cultural materialism differs from eclecticism in that it views both kinds of values as dependent variables, as manifestations of etic conditions. The cultural materialist approach to poverty is concerned with both system-maintaining and system-transforming material conditions and with the dependent system-maintaining and system-transforming superstructures that arise in relation to the infrastructural conditions. Material pauperization and exploitation breed not only apathy but also anger and revolutionary zeal. The latter in turn incite material and ideological counterattacks by the superordinate classes. In predicting the outcome of this complex process, cultural materialism has no magic formula to offer. It merely insists that sociocultural transformations in general are likely to be determined by the material conditions of the infrastructure and of the other etic components. Predictions about the transformation of a specific society thus require careful scrutiny of the specific infrastructure as the first line of research. Lewis's first line of research in approaching the problem of poverty was not the infrastructure; rather, it was the emics of the poverty class. The confusion and incomprehension resulting from such a strategy cannot be mitigated by calling oneself a materialist—much less by calling oneself an eclectic materialist!

Quitting Early

FROM THE CULTURAL materialist viewpoint, the chief vice of eclecticism is that it discourages researchers who encounter the least bit of difficulty from persisting in the attempt to identify plausible infrastructural determinants. The most irritating examples of eclectic retreats from materialism are those which follow hard on the heels of partial success with an infrastructural theory. "Yes, this devilish infrastructural theory is a success," the researcher says. "But fear not, I am no devil worshiper. The fact that an infrastructural component was dominant here, does not mean that infrastructure is dominant everywhere."

Jack Goody's explanation of differences between Eurasian and sub-Saharan African states is a case in point. Goody wants to know why in general the ruling male elites of African states married exogamously, paid bride price, and did not devolve property upon their daughters, whereas the ruling male elites of Eurasian states married endogamously, did not pay bride price, and devolved property upon their daughters in the form of dowry. As outlined in Chapter 4, Goody's (1976) explanation relates these differences to the intensity of Eurasian and African agriculture. The absence of the plow in Africa south of the Sahara (except for Ethiopia) blocked the development of an elite whose power derived from control over land and agricultural labor. Without the plow, population density remained low and land remained relatively abundant. "If there is a plentiful supply of land no man need bend his knee to a lord simply in order to get a living." The power of the African elites derived from taxes on trade, and obligatory gifts from traders rather than on rent or taxes on agricultural production. "One man's holdings was much like another's." Therefore the chief's sisters could marry commoners, since "the living standards of the family groups that exploited the land were little affected by the transmission [inheritance] of the means of production." (Goody neglects to add that chiefs obtained political advantages by marrying women from a large number of villages and that they benefited economically from the heavy bride price paid for their sisters and daughters.) In Eurasia, on the other hand, where population density was higher, land more valuable, and access to it more restricted, the elite's daughters could not marry commoners without losing their privileged way of life.

To maintain the socio-economic standing of his sons and daughters, a man had to provide them both with part of his property. . . . In the case of the girl, her position enabled her to acquire a husband who would in the well-worn phrase, "maintain her in the standard of life to which she was accustomed" . . . through the medium of the dower. (Ibid.:109)

As Goody also points out, dowry frequently constitutes a conjugal fund administered jointly by husband and wife. Since joint conjugal funds would be difficult to administer if husbands had plural wives, the trend toward monogamy in the Eurasian feudal states may also be linked to the increasing importance of landed wealth and the intensification of plow agriculture.

The defects in Goody's theory arise from his fear of the materialist devil and his consequent reluctance to explore the infrastructural conditions responsible for state formation on a global basis. His infrastructural theory accounts for the specific features of African states, but it stands apart from and contradicts other infrastructural theories of state formation. It cannot, for example, be reconciled with theories of state formation applicable to the New World. There were neither plows nor plow animals in Mesoamerica and the Andes, yet elite marriages were conspicuously endogamous, and there was no dowry. To understand why Aztec and Inca domestic and political hierarchies were more rigid than those of West Africa, Goody would have to probe more deeply into the whole demo-techno-econo-environmental conjunction and not just into the presence or absence of the plow. Technology has little significance apart from the other infrastructural components. One might at least expect some reference to the difference between plows in rainfall and irrigation contexts. Goody also disregards the fact that although the plow was used throughout Eurasia, the range of political economic differences within Eurasian polities was at least as great as the range represented by the contrast between medieval Europe and West Africa. He also treats the problem of dowry in a fragmented fashion. This institution cannot be understood merely as a mechanism of property devolution. Men pay dowry on behalf of daughters, not on behalf of sons; almost everywhere in Eurasian peasant societies the woman's share of family property is inferior to that of her brothers and usually consists of movable wealth rather than land. It is therefore incorrect to say that dowry is a form of pre-mortem inheritance; in many instances it is a form of female pre-mortem disinheritance, functioning not to devolve landed property but to consolidate its control among the senior male heirs. Goody's theory represents a limited exploration of the infrastructural processes. Pursued further, it might plausibly account for these additional quandaries. But Goody thinks that it would be counterproductive to continue to adhere to a "vulgar materialist" perspective.

In seeing systems of kinship as being related to the economic and political differences between states in Africa and Eurasia, I am not of course denying the existence of other important differences that cannot be explained in this way. Nor am I trying to assign a universal preeminence to (or determination by) economic or material factors, though their role, "in the last instance," I take as given (a statement I find neither very surprising nor very illuminating). . . . One does not have to be a "vulgar materialist" to understand that hunters and gatherers do not have centralized systems of government. Except at this level, there is unlikely to be a one-to-one relationship between economy and polity. . . . We need to search for the other relevant factors, which may certainly include religious and ideological ones. . . . In some cases the causal chain or arc takes one direction; in other cases a different one. (Ibid.:118–119)

Why abandon a research strategy just as it begins to make sense out of a whole series of previously unsolved riddles? True enough, Goody's exploration of the possibilities of "vulgar materialism" is flawed. But in comparison with earlier attempts to explain African political systems, his contribution is outstanding. Goody's mentors, Meyer Fortes and E. E. Evans-Pritchard (1940), both noted for their opposition to materialist principles, had left the field in total chaos. Fortes and Evans-Pritchard held that in Africa there was no relationship between higher population density and state formation. (Unlike Goody, Fortes and Evans-Pritchard were even unwilling to grant "that hunters and gatherers do not have centralized systems of government.") Goody's interest in the significance of the absence of the plow in Africa took shape during his attempt to rebut Robert Stevenson's (1968) critique of

Fortes and Evans-Pritchard. Goody (1973:206) insisted that Stevenson's defense of a population density/state formation hypothesis in Africa was wrong*; but unlike his mentors, he felt obliged to say why Africa was different from Eurasia. His answer, as we have seen, was couched in materialist terms: because of the absence of the plow, African state formation centered on control over trade rather than on the agricultural surplus made available by intensive agriculture. This line of inquiry turned out to be richly rewarding; by following it, Goody reached his interesting but incomplete explanation of the difference between Eurasian and African systems of marriage, inheritance, and class structure. Why, then, does Goody end his book by insisting on the need to search for the "other relevant factors" of religion and ideology? Why does he not end his book by suggesting that greater attention be paid to infrastructural conditions as the source of these "other relevant factors." The answer to these queries is not that Goody has made a serious attempt to probe the remaining puzzles from an infrastructural point of view and found them wanting, but that he is committed to an eclectic strategy. Here are his reasons for why "we need to search for other relevant factors, which may certainly include religious and ideological ones":

In some circumstances the latter may not be merely contributory but "dominant." For example, certain written codes which I find to be consistent with or even expressions of, diverging devolution [inheritance], may be extended to other very different types of society by process of imperial conquest or religious conversion. It is precisely this way that Christian (European), Muslim and Buddhist codes have reached into areas that might otherwise have re-

*Fortes claimed that the Tallensi of northern Ghana were acephalous and yet had a higher population density than most African states. Stevenson protested that the Tallensi were not acephalous but were in fact part of the Mamprusi kingdom. Goody rejoined that the Tallensi were not part of the Mamprusi kingdom when first contacted by the British in the late nineteenth century. However, he admitted that the Tallensi were refugees driven into the Tong Hills and compacted there as a result of the brigandage and slave raiding carried out by members of both the Mamprusi and Mossi states prior to the arrival of the British. The presence of superordinate lineages identified with the Mossi further enhances the possibility that the Tallensi were at one time under more direct control of the states surrounding them (Hart, n.d.). Hence despite Goody's acerbic charges, the basic thrust of Stevenson's criticism remains unchallengeable. In order to understand the high population density of the Tallensi, one must view them not as an isolated acephalous society, as Fortes had proposed, but as a society closely dependent on the state systems surrounding them in pre-European times.

tained features we have associated with the separation of male and female property. (Goody, 1976:119)

How valid a reason is this for downgrading infrastructural conditions in favor of religious and ideological factors as strategic determinants of domestic organization? Obviously no one denies that Islam, Buddhism, and Christianity prescribe different patterns of marriage and the family. But if one wants to know how determinative religious and ideological factors have been in such matters as polygyny, sex roles, and inheritance, merely invoking religious tradition is a cop-out. To begin with, there is the question of why Christianity, Islam, or Buddhism achieved their particular geographic distributions. All the major world religions were spread primarily by means of imperial conquests —conquests that can only be understood in relationship to the struggle for control over material resources and human labor power. Then there is the question of the enormous variation in the etic practice of these religions, not to mention the perpetual attempts to interpret and reinterpret doctrines, all of which contribute to the rise and fall of thousands of sects, movements, and cults adapted to local "infrastructural conditions." Religion and ideology cannot be said to explain anything about domestic organization unless a systematic effort has been made to show that the actual etic practices were not determined by structural or infrastructural conditions. Quitting early precludes eclectics from making the necessary systematic effort.

Boasian Eclecticism

ECLECTICISM was the dominant research strategy in the United States during the first half of this century. Under the pervasive influence of Franz Boas, American anthropologists devoted themselves to the collection of field data over a broad range of topics roughly corresponding to Wissler's scheme of universal categories. All aspects of social life from subsistence to art were considered equally relevant to the ethnographic enterprise and to the eventual formulation of hoped-for laws of cultural development. In promoting their brand of eclecticism, the Boasians systematically attempted to disprove the Marxian point of view that subsistence, economics, and other material conditions provided the best road to historical understanding. There was no royal road to history, they insisted. They mislabeled Marxian materialism as a monistic or single-factor approach (ignoring the multifactor nature of infrastructure) and proclaimed the impossibility of explaining anything so complex as human phenomena by means of a "simplistic" single-factor theory. Simplistic, monistic materialism could never account for the vast number of historically specific irrational and quixotic aspects of sociocultural life. "We do not see how art styles, the form of ritual or the special forms of religious belief could possibly be derived from economic forces," wrote Boas (1948:256). Boas was confident that no one would ever be able to formulate a general law capable of dealing with the relationship between economics and political organization: "We have simple industries and complex organization," and "diverse industries and complex organization" (ibid.:266). Ditto for environmental factors: "It is fruitless to try to explain culture in geographical terms" (ibid.). Ditto for domestic organization: "There is no evidence that density of population, stability of location, or economic status is necessarily connected with a particular system of relationship and of behavior connected with it" (Boas, 1938:680).

Boas's rejection of infrastructural determinism was not intended merely to put an end to theories implicating material conditions. Rather, it was intended to show the futility of trying to understand culture by means of a restricted set of theoretical principles. In setting out to do field research, Boas believed that the ethnographer ought to leave behind all preconceived notions of causality. The facts from the various sectors of sociocultural life must be given an opportunity to speak for themselves. So little did the facts speak for themselves however, that after forty years of research among the Kwakiutl, Boas was unable to provide a coherent summary of Kwakiutl social life. The ethnography of the Kwakiutl had to be distilled posthumously by Boas's students (Codere, 1966; Rohner, 1969).

Among the Boasians, the most intrepid critic of infrastructural interpretations of history was Robert Lowie (1920). Ranging over the entire ethnographic literature, Lowie cited example upon example of traits and institutions that appeared to be inexplicable from a materialist viewpoint: class stratification and irrational destruction of property among the hunting-gathering Nootka; private land holdings among the hunting-gathering Algonkians, Veddas, and Queensland aborigines; warfare among the Crow and other Plains Indians for the prestige that came from acts of bravado; rejection of milk by the Chinese for aesthetic reasons; failure of the Shilluk, Zulu, and other African peoples to use their cattle for meat except on festive occasions; greater attention paid by such peoples to twisting the horns of their cattle into "grotesque shapes" than to their economic utility; pigs tabooed in Egypt; pigs in Melanesia used for social prestige "without noticeably adding to mass subsistence"; horses not milked in Europe; old men scorned among the Lapps but revered among the Chukchee, even though both cultures depend on herding reindeer for their subsistence. Lowie "quit early" on a grand scale. Fifty years later we are beginning to see how much he missed and how misleading his eclecticism often turns out to be. Much of the work of cultural materialism has been carried out as a rejoinder to Lowie's premature conclusions.

Yet as an eclectic Lowie was convinced that causal relationships of a limited sort could be found among the different sectors of sociocultural systems. He viewed ethnology as a "wholly objective discipline" searching for "epistemologically purified" causality and finding it in the "demonstration of functional relationships." But that is not all. Despite his vehement rejection of economic determinism as a strategy, Lowie actually believed the economic factors were the most important source of functional and causal relationships. In his last major publication he "pointed out the potency of economic forces, not in abstract, which is hardly necessary nowadays, but by suggesting that certain specific changes in economic life have led to specific modifications in social life, even affecting sentimental attitudes" (1948:v). Without using the precise phrase, Lowie, as much as Goody, could pay lip service to the "final instance" of new-wave Marxists:

As the eminent French scholar Henri Sée has remarked, it is difficult "to unravel the tangle of causes and effects in history"; but in the infinite sea of historical events economic determinism has helped to furnish us with a guiding thread which keeps us from being lost. (Ibid.:24)

So we see that by structural Marxist standards, even Robert Lowie could pass as a Marxist.

The Eclecticism of Chairman Mao

LITTLE COULD the Boasians have surmised that their eclectic qualifications of the role of infrastructure in history would one day be touted as the unique intellectual contribution of Karl Marx and Mao Tse-tung.

As I stated during the discussion of structural Marxism (p. 229), eclecticism carried out in the name of Marx remains eclecticism. The degeneration of Marxism into eclecticism cannot be prevented by uttering secular pieties on behalf of the principle that infrastructure is determinative in the "final instance." As in the case of Lowie and Jack Goody, non-Marxists as well as Marxists can invoke the principle that infrastructure is the guiding thread or final instance. Marxists who adhere to the same "final instance" of infrastructural determinism have a political and ideological stake in insisting that it is an important principle: it is frequently their sole link to the Marxist pantheon. In practice, however, the final instance often makes as little difference for the conduct of Marxist research and the corpus of Marxist theories as it does for the research and theories of such frankly bourgeois eclectics as George Foster who deny it outright.

A dramatic example of the convergence of Marxist eclecticism and bourgeois eclecticism is to be found in the work of Mao Tse-tung and his followers. Like Franz Boas, George Foster, and Oscar Lewis, and structural Marxists, the Maoists insist that any part of the sociocultural system may achieve causal dominance. They reject the extreme voluntarism that arises from too great an emphasis on superstructural factors, but at the same time they reject the "mechanical" determinism that arises from too great a stress on etics and infrastructure. For example, in his essay "On Contradiction," Mao indicated that dialectical contradictions at every level of organization had to be given equal weight:

Some people think that this is not true of certain contradictions. For instance, in the contradiction between productive forces and the relations of production, the productive forces are the principal aspect; in the contradiction between theory and practice, practice is the principal aspect; in the contradiction between the economic base and the superstructure, the economic base is the principal aspect; and there is no change in their respective positions. This is a mechanical materialist conception, not the dialectical materialist conception. (Mao, 1966:58)

According to Andrew Walder (1977:158), Mao's great contribution to social theory is that the economic basis of human society must be transformed simultaneously with the superstructure:

Mao has consistently asserted that ideological and superstructural change cannot be sustained without an underlying change in the relations of production—and, simultaneously, that changes in the relations of production cannot be sustained without attitudinal and superstructural change. For Mao, there exists a reciprocal relationship between the two, indicating a Marxian conception of society as a densely interrelated, "organic" structure, with social factors scarcely separable.

Walder's elaboration of this Marxian "organic" conception of society deserves our careful attention:

The economic base no more *causally* determines human consciousness than human consciousness *causally* determines the economic base. Instead, a dense *structure* exists, with a change in any one of the aspects of the structure necessitating a shift in the relations of all the aspects and patterns, even changing the nature of the structure as a whole. An insensitivity to the difficulties inherent in Marx's use of concepts and definitions leads to an interpretation of Marx that sees causation between separate social factors if, perhaps, with some secondary, vestigal reaction—rather than mutual "inneraction" between the densely interrelated aspects of a single conceptual structure. This first interpretation accounts for the economic determinism of orthodox Marxism. . . . (Walder, 1977:132)

Walder is correct when he insists that Maoism does not add up to voluntarism. For it to do so, Mao would have had to stress the causal priority of superstructure over infrastructure, and of emics over etics. But Walder seems unaware of the fact that the "organic" position lying between cultural materialism and cultural idealism has long been preempted by some of the bitterest enemies of the Chinese Revolution.

The notion that all the parts of sociocultural systems are equally determinative of each other is a prescription for theoretical chaos as much for Marxists as for anyone else. There is as little room in the social sciences for the idea that all parts of sociocultural organisms "inneract" equally, as there is room in physiology for the belief that all parts of a plant or animal are equally vital for the maintenance of life functions. Applied to the human body, eclectic "inneraction" licenses the surgeon to cut off a hand as readily as a barber would shave a beard. Applied to China, eclecticism produced equally bizarre results.

With Mao's death, the common ground shared by Maoism, structural Marxism, and bourgeois eclecticism ceased to be something that only vulgar materialists and Soviet propagandists could recognize. The Chinese themselves, at the highest levels, now condemn the idea that superstructure is as important as infrastructure for the success of their revolution, although they have sloughed the responsibility for this error from Mao himself to his wife and the other members of the scapegoat "gang of four." As stated in the *Peking Review:*

It is obviously wrong to maintain the view that continuing the revolution under the dictatorship of the proletariat is confined only to the superstructure. . . . The productive forces are the most active and revolutionary factors: whether they are developed or not determines what the relations of production will be.

The reaction of the superstructure on the economic base finds expression basically in either promoting or holding back the development of the latter. To judge whether those things in the superstructure (politics and the Party's leadership included) promote or hold back social development, we have to take into consideration whether they promote or hold back the development of the social productive forces and whether they help resolve the contradictions between the productive forces and the relations of production. The superstructure cannot bypass the mode of production and play a decisive role in directly pushing society forward.

Only when the productive forces develop and the relations of production move forward can society advance in a decisive manner. Whether the leading role of the superstructure is good or bad hinges on whether it conforms to the laws governing economic activities and promotes the development of the productive forces. (Wu Chiang, 1978:6)

The Chinese people may have paid dearly for Mao's eclecticism. Believing that superstructure was as important as infrastructure for the birth of a communist society, Mao sent his scientists into the fields to learn manual skills. He substituted propaganda and self-criticism for material rewards as a means of increasing productivity. He squandered resources and labor power by inviting the masses to opt for political agitation as an alternative to technological advance. But according to China's new leaders, the hoped-for birth of "communist man" in the form of a selfless revolutionary mass has not yet taken place. The New leaders accept the fact that to complete the transformation of China, the transformation of the etic and behavioral infrastructure must take precedence over the waving of Little Red Books and the chanting of anti-Confucian ditties. Thus, post-Mao political ideology has backed off rapidly from the eclecticism that lay behind the futile cultural revolutions of the 1960s in the West as well as in China. Perhaps the fad of Marxist eclecticism is about to end in Eurocommunist circles as well. But it remains to be seen whether the new leaders of China will have the courage to give due consideration to Marx and Wittfogel's warnings concerning the influence of China's immense hydraulic infrastructure on the future structure of the state's managerial bureaucracy (Fried, 1978a).

Chapter Eleven
Obscurantism

OBSCURANTISM is a research strategy whose aim is to subvert the possibility of achieving a science of human social life. Obscurantists deny the applicability of scientific research principles to the study of divergent and convergent sociocultural phenomena. Their aim orientation is to increase rather than decrease the semblance of disorder in the sociocultural realm and to cast doubt on all existing scientific theories without providing plausible scientific alternatives.

All nonscientific strategies are not necessarily obscurantist. As I said earlier, there are domains of experience, knowledge of which cannot be achieved by scientific research. The ecstatic knowledge of mystics and saints, the visions and hallucinations of drug users and schizophrenics, and the aesthetic insights of artists, poets, and musicians are certainly not obscurantist merely because they are not based on scientific research principles. The issue of obscurantism arises only when knowledge obtained through nonscientific means is deliberately used to cast doubt on the authenticity of scientific knowledge within the domains suitable for scientific inquiry. To be obscurantist, in other words, a research strategy must be antiscientific rather than merely nonscientific.

On the popular level, obscurantism has acquired many of the features of a social movement. Standards, inclinations, and attitudes associated with a large number of convergent nonscientific interests implicitly or explicitly deny the feasibility or utility of a science of social life. Obscurantism is an important component in the emics of astrology, witchcraft, messianism, hippiedom, fundamentalism, cults of personality, nationalism, ethnocentrism, and a hundred other contemporary modes of thought that exalt knowledge gained by inspiration, revelation, intuition, faith, or incantation as against knowledge obtained in conformity with scientific research principles. Philosophers and social scientists are implicated both as leaders and as followers in the popular success of these celebrations of nonscientific knowledge, and in the strong antiscientific components they contain.

Phenomenological Obscurantism

ONE OF THE most fecund sources of contemporary obscurantist attitudes in the social sciences is phenomenology, the neo-Kantian philosophy founded by Edmund Husserl. Like other neo-Kantians, especially Heinrich Rickert, Wilhelm Windelband, and Wilhelm Dilthey, Husserl sought to draw a sharp line between the physical and social sciences (between the *Naturwissenschaften* and the *Geisteswissenschaften* or *Kulturwissenschaften*—i.e., between the natural sciences and the sciences of the human mind or culture). Husserl proposed that ordinary natural science cannot be applied to sociocultural life because social acts involve a property not present in other sectors of the universe—namely, the property of meaning. According to Husserl, meaning can only be understood subjectively. Hence to understand social acts, one must understand what they mean as a subjective, "lived experience." By assuming that the subjective experiences of others are similar to one's own, observers can draw analogies between their own intentions and goals and those of other actors and in this way begin to explain social life. Husserl's philosophy, transmitted through the writings of Alfred Schutz (1967), form the foundation for the cognitivist obscurantist strategies known as ethnomethodology and symbolic interactionism.

At the beginning of this century anthropology had already come under the influence of the neo-Kantian movement. Generations of Boasian fieldworkers accepted the phenomenological demarcation of the human sciences and saw their primary mission to be that of finding out how natives think. In an attenuated form, therefore, the emic bias of phenomenology has always been an integral part of idealist strategies. Phenomenology is also perfectly continuous with the Durkheim-Parsons-Weber notion of social action and with the main currents of cognitive idealism as discussed in Chapter 9. Phenomenologists agree with Talcott Parsons that social action and emic goals are indissoluble:

As Parsons has emphasized, the very notion of an action requires the idea of the actor's end or purpose. That is, for an action to be perceived, purpose and meaning must be perceived. Thus a change in the perceived meaning or purpose entails a change in the action that is perceived. (Wilson, 1970:67, fn.)

Phenomenologists deny the possibility that etic behavior stream actions are worth studying independently of the actor's meaning or purpose:

... social actions are *meaningful* actions, that is, ... they must be studied and explained in terms of their situations and their meanings to the actors themselves. (Jack Douglas, 1970:4)

Thus, phenomenology shares a common starting point with other idealist and emic approaches. But it relentlessly drives toward sectarian conclusions many idealists are not prepared to accept. Combining their commitment to the "lived experience" with an attack on positivism, phenomenologists reject the possibility of separating observers from the observed. Observation is itself to be approached as a lived experience in which the subjective meanings of both observer and participant are constantly "reflected" on. Moreover, the participant observer can never find the truth of the lived experience, apart from the consensus about such things found in the community in which the observer participates. Truths are always relative and social.

Truth is never a feature of the sensations of a discrete individual; it is always to be recognized in the knowledge of members of communities. (Silverman, 1975:75) Truths are always recognized with (as) the system of intelligibility of a community. Truths are always for and within a community. . . . (Ibid.: 77)

At first reading, this assertion about the social nature of truth appears to be quite reasonable and innocuous. Who would deny that truths are always established in conformity with socially specified rules of accountability and significance? Science itself is clearly nothing but a "system of intelligibility of a community." But in the strategy of phenomenology the social nature of truth has profoundly obscurantist implications. Since phenomenology equates social action with the emics of mental and behavioral phenomena, thereby denying the knowability of etic behavioral and mental events, the insistence on the social nature of truth reduces to the proposition that sociocultural theories are true only to the extent that they are reflections of the "system of intelligibility" of the people being studied. This differs from and is antagonistic to the cultural materialist strategy for coping with the social nature of scientific theory. Cultural materialism grants that scientific truth is a social product, but it denies that the corpus of scientific theory necessarily differs from culture to culture. The community that establishes the authenticity of scientific theories is not a community of participants in any given culture, but rather the transcultural community of scientific observers. For this community, as for the communities in the phenomenologist's formula, emic truths must be viewed relativistically, altering with each culture's system of intelligibility. But for this community the realm of sociocultural truths is not exhausted by emics; there are also etic truths, and these do not alter in conformity with each culture's system of intelligibility. Rather, they alter only in conformity with the agreed-upon data collection and theory-testing procedures of the community of scientific observers.

Thus phenomenology, like other varieties of cultural idealism, conflicts with cultural materialism because phenomenologists deal only with emic phenomena. But the conflict goes deeper and is less amenable to solution than in the case of cognitivism, since the phenomenologists insist that the etic behavior stream is unreal or completely subordinate to the reality of each culture's system of knowing.

Inherent in this approach is a capacity for boundless confusion and deception about the nature of human social problems. Whereas other idealist strategies merely ignore or misrepresent the causes of poverty, sexism, and other central dilemmas of human social life, phenomenological idealism denies that such causes exist.

By reducing and confining all sociocultural events to the motivations and plans of immediate experience and communal consensus, phenomenology eventually even leads to the denial of the existence of sociocultural systems and of the universal components of such systems (such as infrastructure, structure or superstructure). For many phenomenologists, such things as ruling classes, imperialist powers, capitalism, or socialism also have no existence apart from the communities of participant observers who happen to believe in them. Processes such as evolution, adaptation and exploitation are also unreal. Phenomenologists dismiss such entities and processes as "reifications." The only social reality worth talking about is the everyday lived experience in which individuals encounter one another and interact in terms of arbitrary symbols and conventional meanings. The task of social "science" is to penetrate and explicate these symbols and meanings, nothing more.

The Phenomenology of Don Juan

CARLOS CASTANEDA's widely read books about the alleged lived experience of Don Juan, a Yaqui Indian shaman, exemplify the obscurantist consequences of phenomenology. At the University of California in Los Angeles, Castaneda studied under the ethnomethodologist Harold Garfinkel, in turn a student of Alfred Schutz—mentioned above. (Garfinkel [1967], who was on Castaneda's dissertation committee at the University of California at Los Angeles, is famous for experiments designed to prove that the essence of social reality consists of conventional meanings attached to everyday activities by communal consensus. The experiments consisted of having students board buses and decline to pay the fare, or having them go home and sit at the dinner table and refuse to pass the salt.) Inspired by his phenomenological mentors, Castaneda resolved to do fieldwork that would involve him in the symbols and conventional meanings of a lived experience entirely different from that of Western social reality.

The Yaqui Indians provided Castaneda with a suitably exotic context for studying the "separate reality" of another culture, especially as he singled out and sought to penetrate and participate in the the most exotic aspect of this culture—the activities and thoughts of the community of Yaqui sorcerers and shamans. To a certain point, therefore, Castaneda's phenomenological journey merely qualifies as a typical cultural idealist study of the mental superstructure. An exclusive preoccupation with mental and emic superstructure adds up to an ineffectual, stunted, and scientifically undesirable strategy, but it does not necessarily add up to an obscurantist strategy. The obscurantism of Castaneda's approach arises from his presentation of the emic reality associated with shamanic consciousness as a challenge to the legitimacy of the epistemological principles upon which science is based.

Castaneda reports that Yaqui shamans believe they can fly through the air, change into animals, kill an adversary by sorcery, and see through opaque objects. None of this is news. Many anthropologists have provided vivid accounts of shamanistic exploits without becoming national celebrities and without being accused of obscurantism. Castaneda's account differs from the others because he tells his story from the "inside," deliberately letting the emics and his own subjective feelings dominate the narrative. The aim of the narrative is to get the reader to participate in the shaman's system of intelligibility and thereby to demonstrate that reality is the creature of social consensus. If we can be persuaded to participate in the shamanic consensus, we will believe that shamans can fly. (Just as we will believe drug-induced hallucinations when they are happening to us.)

The influence of Garfinkel's phenomenology is apparent in the little-read technical addenda to Castaneda's first book, *The Teachings of Don Juan.* Castaneda here portrays his apprenticeship to Don Juan as a search for the validating consensus that converts the nonordinary component element of his experiences from illusion to reality. (In other words, if two people have the same fantasy, it is no longer a fantasy.) Since these nonordinary component elements were not subject to ordinary consensus, their "perceived realness" would have been only an illusion if he had been incapable of obtaining agreement on their existence. For Castaneda, the "special consensus" came from the sorcerer himself:

In Don Juan's teachings, special consensus meant tacit or implicit agreement on the component elements of non-ordinary reality.... This special consensus was not in any way fraudulent or spurious, such as the one two persons might give each other in describing the component elements of their individual dreams. The special consensus Don Juan supplied was systematic.... With the acquisition of the systematic consensus the actions and the elements perceived in non-ordinary reality became consensually real.... (1969:232)

Eventually, through a process by which Don Juan put Castaneda into the proper state of mind, hundred-foot gnats and man-sized butterflies ceased to be illusions. They became instead another reality—another ordinary reality—for "the classifications 'ordinary' and 'non-ordinary' [became] meaningless for me":

there was another separate but no longer unordinary realm of reality, the "reality of special consensus." (Ibid.:250)

To expose the flaw in Castaneda's phenomenological exercise, I should like to compare the expository technique of the Don Juan books with that of an even more compelling phenomenological account rendered in another medium; that of the classic Japanese movie *Rashomon*. In this movie the viewer witnesses four different versions of the "same" scene. The principal actors are a man, his wife, a stranger, and an onlooker hidden in the bushes. Each of the actors narrates a different version of the lived experience, and each version appears on the screen as the lived reality. Manly heroism in one version is abject cowardice in another; chastity in one is carnal heat in another; magnanimity in one is brutality in another; and so on. Each narrative unfolds as a graphic, vivid reality, and the audience is left on its own to decide which version, if any, actually represents the event—or indeed, if there ever was an "event" to begin with.

For a cultural materialist there are only two possible solutions of *Rashomon*'s contradictions and ambiguities: one of the versions is etically correct and the others are false; or they are all etically false. For the phenomenologist there is a third solution: all versions are equally true. This third possibility arises because in the phenomenological strategy, there is no way to distinguish etic from emic events. If the participants are not lying, then what they saw within their system of intelligibility must be accepted as true.

The very fact that *Rashomon* (or Don Juan) can be presented as a problem of multiple truths, however, proves that the problem of which version, if any, is true can be solved. In order to convince the audience that truth is relative to consensus, the film maker actually obtains a consensus concerning the truth of what the camera sees during each version. The camera shows vividly and unequivocally that there is a seduction, a rape, a murder, a duel, and so forth. These events are the analogues of etic events in the strategy of cultural materialism. Since it is possible to obtain a consensus about what happened in each episode, even though each version contradicts the others, one must conclude that a film maker could have filmed the actual event and achieved the same kind of consensus. Such a film would not constitute the whole truth, but it would provide us with a sound basis for deciding which one of the other versions was most nearly correct or whether they were all equally false. Except by trickery or incompetence, a camera could never show them all to be equally true.

Of course I am aware that a filmed version of an event involves selective viewing, and that interpretations of pictures, like interpretations of lived scenes, are influenced by a person's total perceptual and cognitive framework. Yet one does not need to obtain the total and absolute truth about a scene in order to refute the obscurantist claim that contradictory versions of scenes may all be equally true. The fallacy involved here is a variant of the search for empirical certainty discussed in Chapter 1. It does not follow from our inability to obtain absolutely certain knowledge that all knowledge is equally uncertain. By using recording devices under explicitly operationalized conditions, the community of scientific observers can get closer to what happened etically even though they may never get to the absolute final truth. Cultural materialism is committed to getting closer and closer to this etic reality: phenomenology is committed to getting further and further away from it.

Again: "What Does It Matter?"

NO ONE CAN object to Castaneda's artful presentation of the different reality of shamanic consensus. Unfortunately, however, his attempt to get closer to the emics of the shamanic world is shackled to a mischievous attempt to mystify what was happening while he was cultivating the shamanic consciousness. In fact, there is so little about the etic who, what, when, where of Castaneda's experiences in his books that substantial doubts arise as to whether or not Don Juan exists —doubts which Castaneda has never taken the trouble to dispel (*Time*, 1973; Harris, 1974:246ff; Beals, 1978; *New West*, January 29, 1979). Internal inconsistencies in the chronologies of the earlier and later volumes, the absence of a Yaqui vocabulary, the close parallel between Castaneda's visionary experiences and those reported in other works on shamanism, testimony of his ex-wife, friends, and colleagues, and Castaneda's failure to defend himself against the accusation that he deceived his Ph.D. committee at UCLA, make it very unlikely that Castaneda was ever an apprentice to Don Juan (De Mille, 1976). This is not to assert that Castaneda's knowledge of shamanism in a more general sense is defective, nor that his vivid descriptions of shamanic consciousness are without redeeming value. Castaneda probably has much first hand as well as literary knowledge of shamanic practices, and he has communicated that knowledge in a uniquely effective manner. The only problem is that without the etic context, we do not know whose system of intelligibility is represented. We cannot rule out the possibility that Castaneda never interviewed any Yaqui Indian shaman, and that the apparent authenticity of his shamanic experiences derive entirely from his own shamanic gifts and literary and imaginative powers.

Since Castaneda shows no interest in defending himself against this speculation, many of his admirers have been obliged to consider the question of whether it matters to them if the Don Juan stories are fact or fiction. Professor David Silverman (1975:xi), lecturing in the Department of Sociology at UCLA, had no problem disposing of this issue: "It does not matter to me in the least whether any or all of the 'events' reported by Castaneda ever 'took place,' " just as it does not matter to Lévi-Strauss if his "book on myths is itself a kind of myth" (p. 169). Lévi-Strauss rationalizes his indifference to fact or fiction on the basis of his conviction that his own mind works the same as any Indian's mind; Silverman rationalizes his indifference on the ground that any phenomenological account is interesting in its own right. Castaneda's books are a phenomenological account or a "text." Since truth is always relative to a system of intelligibility, there is always an "invented" imaginative, or fictional component in such "texts." "What text is not a construction?" asks Silverman.

Going one step further, the novelist and literary critic Ronald Sukenick sees everything that happens as a story or a story of a story, and so forth. And stories are "neither true nor false, only persuasive or unreal." This has been the great revelation inspired equally by Zen, the Book of the Dead, witch lore, Sufism, various Eastern disciplines, Western mystical tradition, Jungian speculations, Wilhelm Reich, and Carlos Castaneda:

All versions of "reality" are of the nature of fiction. There's your story and my story, there's the journalist's story and the historian's story, there's the philosopher's story and the scientist's story. . . . Our common world is only a description . . . reality is imagined. . . ." (Sukenick, 1976:113)

This invitation to intellectual suicide returns us full circle to the epistemological anarchism of Paul Feyerabend (another one of Castaneda's admirers). The rebuttal of Sukenick, like the rebuttal of Feyarabend (see p. 22), comes in two parts, intellectual and moral. Let me attend to the intellectual part first. Does Sukenick seriously believe that all versions of reality are fictions? If so, then he believes his version of reality is a fiction. Since he believes that everything he says is a fiction including what he says about reality, only a fool would believe such a man about anything.

More astonishing than the intellectual obscurantism of phenomenology is its moral opacity. Morality is the acceptance of principled responsibility for the way in which one's actions or lack of actions affect the well-being of other members of the human species. The absolute precondition for any kind of moral judgment is our ability to identify who did what to whom when, where, and how. The doctrine that all fact is fiction and that all fiction is fact is a morally depraved doctrine. It is a doctrine that conflates the attacked with the attacker; the tortured with the torturer; and the killed with the killer. It is true that at Dachau there was the SS's story; and the prisoners' story; and that at Mylai, there was Calley's story and there was the kneeling mother's story; and that at Kent State there was the guardsmen's story and the story of the students shot in the back, five hundred feet away. Only a moral cretin would wish to maintain that all these stories could be equally true.

Obscurantism as Radicalism

A STRATEGY that obliterates the distinction between what happened in history or what is happening now and what people think or say happened in history or is happening now can only serve the interests of classes and nations that have the most to hide concerning their etic performances. Yet phenomenological relativism satisfies many of its enthusiasts primarily because they regard it as a radicalizing and liberating point of view. During the 1960s the California phenomenologists even thought of themselves as members of a sociological "underground" (Jack Douglas, 1970:32 fn. 39). They saw phenomenology as a radical movement because it challenges positivism's claim to "God's truth." Phenomenology reduces the stance of the establishment's scientific "absolutist" objectivity to a mere arbitrary subjective experience among other arbitrary subjective experiences. It destroys the myth of value-free science by exposing the value-laden presuppositions of social scientists and their unauthorized questionnaires and surveys. It liberates the observed from the types, rubrics, and categories into which the bogus technocrats heartlessly seek to cram everybody but themselves. Hence phenomenology appeals to many anthropologists who are dissatisfied with the status quo, and who identify with the aspirations of oppressed minorities, the young, and the third world. The phenomenological stance represents for them a means of attacking the inequities of corporate industrialism and the technocratic establishment. Rational, disciplined, empirical, objective knowledge symbolizes the enemy. Science is a capitalist machine which must be smashed in order to restore knowledge to the service of humanity (Paul and Rabinow, 1976).

This Luddite impulse is well exemplified in the apocalyptic writings of the anthropologist Kurt Wolff (1972:113). According to Wolff, "The great inventions of science and technology have induced us to use them . . . for controlling, manipulating, exploiting ourselves and everything else." Therefore anthropologists ought to join the "largely instinctive effort . . . of young-men-and-women-hippie-flower-children's confrontations of war by 'love' " . . . "and the other chief group of critics of our society—the militant blacks and representatives of the Third World" (ibid.:115). According to Wolff:

These two groups constitute . . . the main hope for us of entering history, of realizing in knowledge, rather than in primitive innocence of it, worth, mana, power, grace, *pneuma.* (Ibid.:115)

Wolff's article displays a strong sense of mission, but an even better sense of fantasy:

This alliance [hippies, blacks, third-world critics, and radical anthropologists], that is to say, *we,* we constitute the vanguard of history and must diffuse the worth we remember, so that others, too, remember their own, lest all that they, all that we, are left with be violence.

Wolff admits that his vanguard, *we,* may not exactly know who it is, what it is doing, or what it wants to do. But this does not shake his conviction that it is both radical and anthropological. Ignorance somehow seems to portend a redemption to be acquired through knowledge at some future date. Although Wolff admits that he does not know how to resolve current political problems, he claims his analysis "is prepolitical to the extent and in the sense that 'the maximal suspension of received notions' is the precondition of knowing what we must do—

whatever this may be." And so on to the manifesto that will set us free: "Men of critical mind and good will, we everywhere, must unite, for we realize that we may very well have 'nothing to lose' but our lives" (ibid.: 115). Wolff sees ranks of flower children, blacks, Cubans, Chinese, American Indians, and radical anthropologists marching through the cities, arm and arm into the future. No matter that there are others who see nothing but empty streets.

By encouraging the belief that the subjective experience of shamanism, witchcraft, and transcendental meditation are just as valid and "true" as the objective truths of social science, many conservative presuppositions about social life are indeed cast into doubt. But the belief that the resulting state of intellectual anarchy and paralysis of sociocultural theory can make a significant contribution to the organization of political movements capable of radically transforming etic structures and infrastructures is the ultimate fantasy of exhausted, bewildered, and put-upon people. The creation of a purely emic social science and the glorification of subjectivity is indeed a harbinger of change—but scarcely the kind of change that the radical anthropologist flower children want to bring about. Rather, it presages and is actually being accompanied by a fragmentation of radical political power, deepening isolation, alienation, retreatism, strengthening of the apparatus of police-military control and of the military-industrial complex, and increased danger of foreign adventures leading to nuclear confrontation.

Blowing Out the Candle

HAVING REACHED the conclusion that a *completely* objective social science is impossible, radicals find themselves hard put to justify their own identities as social scientists. If anthropologists are not objective scientists pursuing the truth wherever it may be found, then what are they? According to an increasing number of third-world critics the answer is that they are agents of Euro-American capitalism and colonialism. The involvement of U.S. anthropologists in various government-sponsored anticommunist and antisocialist research projects (cf. Wolf and Jorgensen, 1970; Horowitz, 1967; Berreman et al., 1968; Gough, 1973) and the protests against anthropological findings by third-world peoples themselves (cf. Magubane, 1971; Cooper, 1973; Deloria, 1969; Willis, 1972), leave no doubt as to the direct or indirect complicity of many anthropologists in the exploitative and repressive aspects of capitalism and Western colonialism. For the antipositivist, phenomenologically inclined radicals, therefore, the choice seems to be very limited indeed: either one is an oppressor, exploiter, or spy—"part of the problem"—or one is a partisan in the struggle for liberation, a "part of the solution."

For when numbers of subordinated societies begin to identify the anthropologist per se as one of their oppressors rather than as one of their liberators, as an exploiter rather than an enlightener, as a spy rather than a scientist, and as part of the problem rather than part of the solution, anthropologists as individuals should consider undertaking a visionary quest of their own that might lead them to their own personal revitalizations. (Clemmer, 1972:244)

In effect, what some anthropologist radicals are proposing is this: be partisan and identify with the people one studies, in the absence of, or even in defiance of, an objective scientific justification of the choice one has made. Counterculture enthusiasts such as Kurt Wolff would even have us believe that anthropologists can improve the prospects for global peace and harmony by making nonobjective "instinctual" commitments—as if less conflict will result as soon as more people discover how to be properly militant in the pursuit of narrow ethnic and nationalistic self-images.

But the choice is not quite so restricted. It is true that *complete* objectivity is a will-o'-the-wisp. There will never be a perfect solution to the *Rashomon* problem, nor will a state of pure political neutrality ever be attained by those who carry out research on human subjects. It is shamefully true that social science for the most part has favored the interests of capitalists and imperialists at the expense of peasants and minorities. But I do not hold that the conservative consequences of scientific research result from the fact that anthropologists tried too much to be objective. The solution to the *Rashomon* problem, and to the problem of political-ideological bias, is not to abandon one's attempt to be scientific but to attempt to overcome subjective limitations by being more scientific. The phenomenological obscurantists would have us believe that no objectivity is better than a little objectivity. They blow out the candle and praise the dark.

Reflexive Obscurantism

IT IS FAR easier to say what is wrong with narrow-minded versions of positivism and empiricism than to propose a workable alternative. Robert Scholte (1972:435), for example, holds that positivistic "scientism" can never "hope to be entirely value-free and transcultural" and that its "naive, uncritical application may either simply hide ideological presuppositions or unwittingly generate reactionary political consequences." True enough. But what is the alternative? For Scholte, it is something called "reflexive and critical" anthropology. What does this mean?

This would mean that every procedural step in the constitution of anthropological knowledge is accompanied by radical reflection and epistemological exposition. (Ibid.:441)

Nice-sounding words these, but useless for defining and evaluating any particular research strategy. The more Scholte insists on being reflexive, the more murky his "reflexions." Anthropological studies, he insists, should be "radically contextual, immanently dialectical, genuinely comparative . . . emphatically motivated . . . normative . . . evaluative . . . liberating" (ibid.:437). Like the phenomenologists, Scholte believes that

Man, in contrast to all other phenomena in the universe, can be done justice to only by surrender and catch—or invention— . . . rather than by customary varieties of describing, defining, or reducing to instances of generalization (Wolff, quoted in Scholte, 1972:438).

Yet Scholte recoils from the prospect of a completely phenomenological and relativist picture of the world. Reflection and critique, he warns, should not constitute the whole of anthropology:

Whatever the paradigmatic limitations of anthropological activity may be, they still provide us with important ethnographic information and significant ethnological generalizations. . . . In sum, a reflexive and critical stance is a necessary though not a sufficient condition for an encompassing anthropology. (Ibid.:443)

Since the objectivity of scientism is anathema to Scholte, it soon becomes apparent that he has nothing objective or even definite to say about how reflections and critiques carried out by different anthropologists operating with conflicting strategic principles are to be evaluated. All he knows is that we ought to have humane, emancipatory principles and standards, though he hasn't yet figured out what this means:

Still, the process of comparative differentiation and discrimination does not itself suggest any compelling criteria for critical judgment. If these are to be found at all, I would advocate that we seek them in the normative and emancipatory interests of anthropological praxis, that is the degree to which anthropological activity violates or sustains pertinent "life-preserving" values and in the extent to which it inhibits or realizes human freedom. I am painfully aware of the fact that this is more easily said than done. *I also admit that I have not as yet arrived at any satisfactory substantive definitions for these crucially important interests.* (Ibid.:446, italics added)

Lest it be imagined that I have vindictively lifted this admission out of context, permit me to quote again, from the concluding paragraph of the same article:

In what would the normative interest of a self-reflexive and critical anthropology lie? . . . as I have said, I have no satisfactory reply. (Ibid.:449)

Scholte is convinced that we ought to pay heed to the principles of a self-reflexive and critical anthropology—even though he himself doesn't know what they are.

Praxis as Obscurantism

HAVING COMMITTED themselves to the total destruction of the positivist bourgeois science truth machine, obscurantists obviously cannot avail themselves of scientific standards and principles to define the reflexive, critical, dialectical, and radical activities which they would like anthropologists to engage in. They cannot admit that the reflexive and critical discipline they seek might be science itself, the bourgeois truth machine, redesigned to work better rather than smashed to pieces to work not at all. On the other hand, they are loath to admit that their political, ethical, and aesthetic partisanship rests purely on self-interest or worse, that it is merely a matter of irrational preference. Obscurantism arises here in its most deadly form from the attempt to hedge all of these options in the name of the dialectical mix called "praxis." In Stanley Diamond's (1972:426) words:

> Clearly, the study of man can reconstitute itself only in the struggle against the civilized objectification of men, in their own society and elsewhere. Anthropologists who recognize this may now decide to turn to the arena in which the generality of men, notably peasants and primitives, the conventional "objects" of study are now re-creating themselves as subjects in the revolutionary dramas of our time. In accordance with their competence, these anthropologists are likely to declare themselves partisans in the movements for (1) national liberation . . . and (2) . . . socialism. . . . If fieldwork remains possible for them, it will not be in the pursuit of their careers, but independently as amateurs, in order to learn, not to "examine," in dynamic and possibly revolutionary circumstances.

I regard this as an obscurantist program because it ignores the fact that "national liberation" and "socialism" must be objectified—i.e., defined scientifically as a presupposition of rational commitment. Given a sufficiently unobjectified series of definitions, agreement to struggle for freedom and equality can be found not only among the oppressed peasants and primitives but among their oppressors as well. It is obscurantism to gloss over the fact that national liberation does not necessarily lead to socialism and that socialism does not necessarily lead to national liberation. Furthermore, it is obscurantism to pretend that revolutionary dramas always have two—and only two—sides: namely, the liberators and the oppressors. This point is especially relevant in Diamond's case because of his well-known partisanship in support of the attempt by the Ibo people (the dominant ethnic faction in the secessionist state of Biafra) to secede from Nigeria. According to Diamond (1970:25-26), the Ibos were the "victims" of Nigeria's "Northern establishment," while the Nigerian federal government was the "aggressor." The Christian Ibos were genuinely interested in establishing a Nigerian national identity; but the Moslem-dominated north latched on to the concept of Nigerian unity only in order to destroy the Ibo, gaining thereby an "illusory strength."

So it is the Ibos, now the pariahs of Nigeria, who are helping others to construct the fiction of their own national identity. But the aggressor's sense of unity is almost always a fiction; it is the victim who learns the real name of the game. The federal government attacked the Ibos, those premature Nigerian unitarians, in the name of unity and so generated an illusory strength —the strength of the aggressor who resents the faith that was invented by the victim and imposed on the others.

I do not question Diamond's right as an anthropologist to make statements of this sort. (I made similar pronouncements [Harris, 1972] on behalf of FRELIMO as a result of my fieldwork in the former Portuguese colony of Mozambique.) What I question is the right to make such statements in the name of dialectical praxis rather than in the name of objective truth. When misrepresentations of fact and errors of theory are being used to promote a particular political cause, anthropologists possessing more objective knowledge and better theories not only have the right but the strongest obligation to make their viewpoint known. But for anthropologists to take sides in this manner presupposes a very careful *objectification* of the issues (which means objectification of the people involved in the issues). Anything less than a total effort to assess the etic relationships and to separate them from the political-ideological emics constitutes a betrayal of one's professional colleagues, no matter how much it may count as loyalty elsewhere.

Before the outbreak of the Biafran war, Diamond found himself embroiled in a controversy with several Nigerians over his interpretation of treason trials that had taken place in western Nigeria. His adversaries accused him among other things of "chiseling at truth to fit it into prefabricated molds . . . ingenious attempt to falsify history . . . unreliability as an objective scholar . . . lacking . . . an understanding of what truth is" (Anekwe, 1967); ". . . damnable ignorance of the true state of affairs . . . unscrupulous political hireling . . . professor of untruth . . . unworthy of his claim as an anthropologist" (Anyians, 1967), and so forth. Diamond (1967:55) replied that the attacks were "notable for their misinterpretations, irrelevancies, distortion and inaccuracies." It never occurred to me to doubt that Diamond had indeed sincerely attempted to present a conventionally "objective" view of the history of those trials. But Diamond himself, by proposing that the truths of scientific anthropology are negated in praxis—"in the knowledge—and in the actions—of men" (1972:426), definitely goes out of his way to shake one's convictions about the value of trying to be objective about such things. It requires an act of intellectual masochism for one to believe in the objectivity of scholars who refuse to defend objectivity. It is Diamond himself and not Anekwe or Anyians who has lately come to tell us that "the issue of truth . . . transcends the presentation of facts . . ." (1972:413). And it is Diamond himself and not his critics who repeats the refrain of this chapter: "any attempt at ethnology, has in short, to be a fiction, a constitution of reality" (ibid.). Now it is possible to reconcile both of these statements with the logico-empirical meaning of scientific objectivity. Truth *does* transcend the presentation of facts in the sense that facts collected under the auspices of some paradigms have greater theory value than facts collected under other auspices. And ethnology must be "a constitution of reality" in the sense that theories are abstract models that emphasize generalities at the expense of particularities. But I have no intention of entering such a defense on behalf of people who refuse to acknowledge that the search for objectively valid knowledge under the auspices of a scientific epistemology is the only possible way to avoid relativistic anarchy on the one hand, or ethnocentrism, nationalism, or something worse on the other (cf. Kaplan, 1974, 1975).

"Business on the Scale of History"

OBSCURANTISM IS actually a more common strategic commitment than this chapter seems to suggest. Powerful obscurantist currents flow through many of the alternative strategies discussed in the previous chapters. The attacks on positivism launched by dialectical materialists, structuralists, and structural Marxists converge with those launched by phenomenologists. They contribute as much to a broad-based rejection of the possibility of a science of culture as do the outspoken advocates of epistemological anarchy, total relativism, and unanalyzed praxis.

Of course, I do not mean to say that every rejection of a principle or theory congenial to cultural materialism counts as the advocacy of obscurantism. Rather, it is the general nature of the arguments advanced, especially their overwhelming negativity, that places many new-wave Marxists and structuralists in the obscurantist camp. Let me illustrate this contention with some concluding remarks about the stance adopted by Marshall Sahlins toward cultural materialism.

Sahlins (1978) equates the "overall view" of cultural materialism with the bourgeois ethnocentric notion that "culture is business on the scale of history." He bases this equation on the fact that cultural materialism finds explanations for sociocultural phenomena in the relative costs and benefits of alternative activities. Sahlins's *idée fixe* is that costs and benefits are the same as "profit" and "loss" and that they therefore are applicable only to cultures that economize in conformity with the formal categories of capitalism. This is consistent with Sahlins's advocacy of the substantivist position in the substantivist-formalist debate, as discussed in Chapter 8. However, as I have already indicated (p. 236), the epistemological position of cultural materialism corresponds to neither side in that debate. The costs and benefits of cultural materialism are the etic behavioral costs and etic behavioral benefits of alternative innovations in reference to the bio-psychological constants proposed on page 63. Although the precise quantitative operationalization of these costs and benefits presents a great challenge, rough approximations can easily be obtained in terms of such measures as rising or declining death rates, calorie and protein intake, incidence of disease, ratio of labor input to output, other energetic balances, amount of infanticide, casualties in war, and many other etic and behavioral indices. These etic costs and benefits clearly constitute categories distinct from price market econometric notions of profit and loss measured in monetary terms. They are relevant to a much broader set of concerns—namely, the more or less efficacious solution of infrastructural problems experienced by all human beings and all cultures. If a mere concern with efficacious solutions to the problems of production and reproduction is sufficient to characterize cultural materialists as bourgeois formalists, then Sahlins must also tar Marx and Engels with the same brush. Indeed, anyone who has a lively concern with the basic material conditions of human welfare emerges from Sahlins's analysis as a proponent of the "western business mentality."* This is a distinction that businessmen east or west scarcely deserve.

"To Get Some Meat"

SAHLINS DOES not stop at fantasizing the ideological implications of a science of culture rooted in the analysis of material costs and benefits. He also misrepresents the manner in which cultural material-

---

*Paul and Rabinow (1976) also contend that an orientation toward practical mundane costs and benefits is "bourgeois rationalism." They prefer to be impractical and irrational.

ism actually applies optimizing principles to the explanation of specific puzzles. From Sahlins's account, one would suppose that cultural materialism treats the costs and benefits of alternative innovations as if they were timeless options open to any society at any moment in its history But the corpus of cultural materialist theory is evolutionistic. Particular sequences of intensifications and depletions are viewed as long-term involuntary processes, and specific optimizing alternatives are viewed as actionable only in a definite portion of that process.

Neglect of the evolutionary context of cultural materialist theories leads Sahlins to misrepresent the cultural materialist explanation of Aztec cannibalism (first proposed in Harner, 1977). According to Sahlins, the point of my version of this theory (Harris, 1977a) is that in effect the Aztec ate people "to get some meat." What Sahlins omits is that both Harner and I insist that cannibalism was widely practiced in Mesoamerica before the Aztecs arrived in the Valley of Mexico, and that as part of the small-scale ritual sacrifice of prisoners of war it was probably almost universal among chiefdoms in both hemispheres. We contend further that as states developed, they usually reduced or eliminated human sacrifice, substituting animal for human victims, and that they invariably gave up the practice of eating prisoners of war. Our explanation for this trend is that it was part of the general tendency for successful expansionist states to adopt ecumenical religions. As discussed earlier (p. 109), these religions enhanced the ability of the state to incorporate defeated populations into the victor's political economy as peasants, serfs, or slaves. However, in the Aztec case, and as far as we know, only in the Aztec case, the state itself took over the earlier human sacrifice and cannibalism complex and made it the main focus of its ecclesiastical rituals. As the Aztecs became more powerful they did not stop eating their enemies; instead, they ate more and more of them. At least 20,000 captives were immolated in four days at the dedication of the main Aztec temple in 1487, and by the beginning of the sixteenth century at least 15,000 to 20,000 people were being eaten per year in Tenochtitlán, the Aztec capital (Harner, 1977:119). Since the skulls of the victims in Tenochtitlán were placed on display racks after the brains were taken out and eaten, it was possible for the members of Hernando Cortés's expedition to make a precise count of one category of victims. They found that the rack contained 136,000 heads, but they were unable to count another group of victims whose heads were added to two tall towers made entirely of crania and jaw-bones (ibid.:122).

The scale of this complex bears no resemblance to any other cannibal complex before or since. The Aztec are a unique case, and they therefore demand a unique explanation. Sahlins, however, tries to lump the Aztec complex with instances of small-scale pre-state ritual cannibalism in Oceania and elsewhere. He distorts the problem from one of explaining Aztec cannibalism in particular to one of explaining cannibalism in general. What has to be explained is not why the Aztecs became cannibals but why they remained cannibals.

Why, then, were the Aztecs unique? According to Harner, that the Aztec did not give up cannibalism because the faunal resources of the Valley of Mexico had become uniquely depleted. As a result of millennia of intensification and population growth the Central Mexican highlands were stripped of domesticable herbivores, swine and feral birds, fish, and ungulates in numbers sufficient to supply significant amounts of animal protein per capita per year (Sanders, Santley, and Parsons). The few available domesticated species, birds and dogs, could not be raised in sufficient quantities to make up for the absence of cattle, sheep, goats, horses, pigs, guinea pigs, llamas, or alpacas. All other populous ancient states, including the Inca of Peru, possessed a variety of domesticated herbivores that were intensively exploited either for meat or for some other form of animal proteins, such as milk or cheese.

This is not the place for a lengthy discussion of the biochemical and physiological advantages associated with animal versus plant sources of protein. It is sufficient to note that animal sources of protein in the form of milk or meat are universally valued over plant sources of protein and are everywhere given a central place in ecclesiastical redistributions, honorific feasts, and upper-class commissaries. (Hindu India, the world center of vegetarian ideologies, is one of the world's largest consumers of milk and milk products.) The reason for this is that proteins are essential not only for normal body function but for recuperation from infections and wounds. To make proteins, the human body needs twenty different kinds of amino acids. It can synthesize all but eight or nine of them, the so-called essential amino acids. To obtain these essential components from plants, one must eat large amounts of carefully balanced combinations of plant foods at the same meal. Meat, eggs, and other animal proteins however, provide the essential amino acids in balance even when eaten in small quantities. The world-wide preference for animal protein therefore reflects an adaptive cultural and nutritional strategy. Any population that did not seek to maximize its animal protein intake relative to that of neighboring populations would soon find itself physically smaller, less healthy, and less capable of recuperating from the trauma of disease and the wounds of combat (cf. Scrimshaw, 1977).

The theory advanced by Michael Harner and me is that the uniquely severe depletion of animal protein resources made it uniquely difficult for the Aztec ruling class to prohibit the consumption of human flesh and to refrain from using it as a reward for loyalty and bravery on the battlefield. It was of greater advantage to the ruling class to sacrifice, redistribute, and eat prisoners of war than to use them as serfs or slaves.* Cannibalism therefore remained for the Aztecs an irresistible sacrament, and their state-sponsored ecclesiastical system tipped over to favor an increase rather than a decrease in the ritual butchering of captives and the redistribution of human flesh. The Aztec ruling class, unlike any government before or since, found itself waging war more and more not to expand territory but to increase the flow of edible captives. All of this bears little resemblance to the economistic fable concocted by Sahlins in which the Aztecs go to war to "get some meat" because it is cheaper for them to cook people than to eat beans. The critical optimized costs and benefits are those associated not only with the choice between two sources of protein but also with the choice between alternate modes of justifying ruling-class hegemony in a severely depleted habitat at a definite moment in an evolutionary process.

Sahlin's Aztec Arcadia

THE ABOVE theory is based on the contention that the Valley of Mexico was a uniquely depleted habitat. Sahlins, however, not only rejects this contention, but makes the claim that the Valley of Mexico was a veritable protein paradise. He claims that "of all the peoples in the hemisphere who practiced intensive agriculture, the Aztecs probably had the greatest natural protein resources." Hidden in this state-

---

*It is true, as Sahlins points out, that the Aztec sometimes fattened up their prisoners before eating them, but that scarcely means that they were engaging in some final mismangement of resources—they had to provide food only for the fattening, not for the rearing, of their victims. It is also true that the "trunks" of the victims were fed to animals in the zoo. But no one knows if the flesh was still on the bones; nor is the feeding of carnivores at the zoo at odds with the other amusements of the Aztec ruling class.

ment about greatest *natural* resources is the indisputable fact that the Aztecs had the least *domesticated* protein resources among the ancient states of either hemisphere. That is the crucial point, for it is an established archaeological, ecological, and plain common-sense fact that hunting and nonmaritime fishing cannot be sustained at high levels in the immediate vicinity of densely urbanized populations. Even village-level societies with densities below two or three persons per square mile require large reserve areas in order to sustain per capita animal protein intake at modest levels (say, 30 grams, or less than half of the current U.S. ration). In this perspective, Sahlin's contention that the 1,500,000 people who lived in the Valley of Mexico could have gotten an ample supply of meat from hunting is worth about as much as the suggestion that New York City could get its meat from deer captured in the Catskills.

W. Sanders, R. Santley, and J. Parsons have studied the archaeological evidence for overkill and depletion in the Valley of Mexico for the period 1500 B.C. to 1500 A.D. They estimate that at the beginning of this period deer meat contributed 13.5 percent of the calories in the diet. In Aztec times, "overkill had become so acute" that only 0.1 percent of calories could come from deer meat. They estimate that "total meat from all wild sources could not have exceeded 0.3 percent of the annual requirement [of calories]." This works out to 0.6 grams of protein per capita per day.*

The idea that the lakes in the Valley of Mexico could have supplied significant amounts of fish protein per capita per year is no less incorrect. These lakes in precontact times were in large part swamps averaging less than three feet deep; at the lower elevations in the chain the water was too salty to drink, and during the dry season the surface area shrank considerably due to evaporation. The lakes bloomed with algae out of which the Aztecs made their famous "scum cakes." These algae blooms themselves contradict the possibility that fish were abundant in the same water. According to Charles Gibson (1964:340), in the early seventeenth century, the two most productive lakes were yielding over a million fish, none larger than nine inches and most smaller. Tripling this number for the early sixteenth century, one arrives at a total of the equivalent of two herrings per capita per year or about 0.12 grams of protein per day per capita.

*At 2,000 calories per capita; at 2 calories per gram of lean meat; and at 20 percent protein per gram of lean meat.

Next come the waterfowl. Sahlins says there were "millions of ducks." Gibson (ibid.:343) estimates that about 1 million ducks were taken annually in the eighteenth century. Since these were hunted with guns when the population of the Valley of Mexico was much smaller than in Aztec times, there is no reason to adjust Gibson's total upwards. That gives every Aztec something less than three-quarters of a duck per year. If we allow a generous two kilos undressed weight per duck, this yields about 1.0 grams of protein per capita per day.

But the real worth of the Aztec arcadia we are told lay in its invertebrates. The place was "teeming" with small "wildlife," writes Sahlins—with "bugs, grubs, and small red worms." And Sahlins again accuses me of bourgeois ethnocentrism for my failure to realize that such *animalitos* taste good to non-Westerners. Taste, however, is not in dispute; rather, it is the ability to recurrently harvest small, patchy, and trophically subordinate invertebrates on a scale sufficient to provide a dense urbanized population with significant amounts of animal protein. It is one thing to relish piquant morsels of witchety grubs and snails as a supplement to meat and fish; it is quite another to make such fare one's primary source of animal flesh. Ordinarily people let the fish and the birds eat the worms, and then they eat the birds and the fish. The only sensible conclusion to be drawn from the fact that Aztecs ate more worms than anything else is that they had eaten up most of the birds and the fish, and having eaten up most of the birds and fish, they ate people as well. Sahlins thinks this shows that the Aztecs were an affluent society. This conclusion honors his concept of culture, but it dishonors the relentless efforts people have always had to make to satisfy nutritional needs.

To further establish the point that the Aztec actually inhabited an environment rich in natural sources of protein, Sahlins declares "there was no shortage of meat in the markets described by the Spanish," neglecting to add that Cortés was convinced that much of it was human meat. (If they can't eat scum cakes, let them eat people.) In places like Calcutta one also finds that for those who can afford it there is no shortage of anything. If one adds up all possible sources, exclusive of human flesh it is difficult to see how the Aztecs could have gotten more than two or three grams of animal flesh per capita per year, or about half of the current animal protein ration in India (Nair and Vaidyanathan, 1978).*

---

*If we assume that they got as much protein from the bugs and worms as they did from the ducks, then the total is as follows:

Against Sahlins's ducks, bugs, and scum cakes there is hard evidence from the chroniclers concerning devastating crop failures and famines. Between 1500 and 1519, the year of the arrival of Cortés, there were either famines or near famines in 1501, 1505, 1507, and 1515. The worst recorded famine occurred in the fifteenth century. It lasted from 1451 to 1456 and was followed by an intense period of warfare and prisoner sacrifice. Harner estimates that famines occurred on the average every three or four years. No scholar has ever questioned the reports of Aztec famines. Their occurrence discredits Sahlins's notions about the abundance of wildlife.

Positivist Cant

FROM THE ARDOR with which Sahlins argues for abundance on the bases of the evidence for scarcity, one might suppose that he wishes to promote his own explanation of the Aztec puzzle. But Sahlins has no alternative explanation. The sole purpose of his unremittingly negative critique is to prove that Aztec "culture is meaningful in its own right," a proposition to which one cannot object but which has no bearing on the question of whether or not Aztec cannibalism can be explained by cultural materialist theories.

According to Sahlins, the fascinated contemplation of the richness of human sacrifice as the Aztec priests and their victims understood it alone defines the anthropologist's proper task. Indeed, Sahlins warns that if we persist in trying to learn something about the etic and behavioral conditions that create butcher priests skilled at yanking the hearts out of living people, "we shall have to give up all anthropology." Why this should be so eludes me. I rather think it more likely that we shall have to give up anthropology once the idea gets around that Sahlins's constriction of anthropology to the emic and mental aspects of Aztec sacrifice exemplifies the true anthropological calling. No one can doubt that "culture is meaningful in its own right," but many will doubt Sahlins's authorization for telling us what it meant to be dragged up the pyramid by the hair—even if it was "magical hair," as he

$$\frac{\text{meat}}{0.6} + \frac{\text{fish}}{0.12} + \frac{\text{ducks}}{1.0} + \frac{\text{"animalitos"}}{1.0} = 2.7 \text{ grams.}$$

Of course, this does not take into account the seasonality of many of these creatures, nor does it take into account the sharp differences in consumption privileges among the Aztec's social classes.

proposes in a footnote—to be bent back spread-eagled and cut open. Sahlins claims it mattered to the victims whose screams ended five hundred years ago that they were part of a sacrament and not just part of a meal. "It is positivist cant," writes Sahlins, to impose Western categories such as cannibalism on these high holy rites. It wasn't cannibalism, he continues, it was the "highest form of communion"—as if communion is not also a Western concept and as if labeling human sacrifice "communion" transubstantiates obsidian knives and human meat into things we can't recognize as being sharp and nutritious respectively. We should certainly try to understand why people think they behave the way they do, but we cannot stop at that understanding. It is imperative that we reserve the right not to believe their explanations. Most of all we must reserve the right not to believe ruling-class explanations. A ruling class that says it is eating some people out of concern for the welfare of all is not telling the whole story. An anthropology that can do no more than make that viewpoint seem plausible serves neither science nor morality. Aztec cannibalism was the highest form of communion for the eaters but not for the eaten. For the eaten, it was not only cannibalism but the highest form of exploitation. (Even the bourgeoisie refrains from dining on its workers.) If it be positivist cant to describe human relationships in such terms, long live positivism. If it be anthropology to struggle against the mystification of the causes of inequality and exploitation, long live anthropology.

The Name of the Game

ONE TEMPTING answer to Pontius Pilate's "What is truth?" has always been that truth is whatever people can be persuaded to believe. If we stop to ponder the further question "What persuades people to believe?" sooner or later some impatient soul will answer "Power." The ability to make people believe is rooted in the ability to make people conform. Do we not hold that truth is constantly being created and re-created out of struggle? A recurrent resolution of obscurantism therefore does not lie in the power of argument but in guns, prisons, and torture. If the truth cannot be found, it is often imposed.

According to the "Marxist" socialists Barry Hindiss and Paul Q. Hirst (1975:179), who believe that "nothing which has happened or has existed in Asia or elsewhere" can ever establish the legitimacy of concepts such as the Asiatic mode of production, historical truth is useless for praxis.

Marxism, as a theoretical and a political practice, gains nothing from its association with historical writing and historical research. The study of history is not only scientifically but also politically valueless. (Ibid.:312)

What matters is the present, not as an objective product of history but as "current situation," the object of political struggle:

History renders unrecognizable that which is the primary object of Marxist theoretical and political practice. It dislocates that necessary connection between theoretical analysis and politics which is the very core of Marxism. (ibid.:313)

These are ominous words. If we capitulate to obscurantism in the name of political clarity, we capitulate to the brutalized visions of truth that exist in the minds of those sadistic few who know best how to persuade people to believe that fact is fiction and fiction is fact. Until such time as anthropologists reacquire some respect for scientific objectivity, and demonstrate that respect by distinguishing between behavior and thought, between emics and etics, between empirical and nonempirical statements, between subjective and objective points of view, between fact and fiction, and between theory and practice—until they stop indulging in rhetoric designed to inflame all parochial prejudices, justify any political whim, and mystify every material relationship, the name of *their* game will be the name of a new age of ignorance and oppression.

To assert as Alvin Gouldner (1970:103) does, that "objectivity is the compensation men offer themselves when their capacity to love has been crippled," is to deny that truth can be both the object and means of expressing love. To erect a barrier between truth and love is to wantonly degrade and limit human nature. There are many, but not enough, for whom objectivity is the path that leads to both.

Bibliography

Aberle, D.F., A.K. Cohen, A.K. Davis, M.J. Levy, Jr., and F.X. Sutton
1950 "The Functional Prerequisites of a Society." *Ethics* 60: 100–111.
Abruzzi, William
1979 "Flux Among the Mbuti Pygmies of the Ituri Forest: An Ecological Interpretation." In Eric Ross, ed., *Behind the Myths of Culture.* New York: Academic Press, in press.
Acheson, J.M.
1972 "Accounting Concepts and Economic Opportunities in a Tarascan Village: Emic and Etic Views." *Human Organization* 31: 83–92.
1974 "Reply to George Foster." *American Anthropologist* 76: 57–62.
Ackerman, Charles
1964 "Structure and Statistics: The Purum Case." *American Anthropologist* 66: 53–65.
1965 "Structure and Process: The Purum Case." *American Anthropologist* 67: 83–91.
Adams, R.G.W.
1977 *The Origins of Maya Civilization.* Albuquerque: University of New Mexico Press.
Alexander, Richard
1974 "Evolution of Social Behavior." *Annual Review of Ecological Systems* 5: 325–383.
1976 "Evolution, Human Behavior, and Determinism." *Philosophy of Science Association—Proceedings of the Biennial Meetings* 2: 3–21.
Alland, Alexander
1975 "Adaptation." *Annual Review of Anthropology* 4: 59–73.
Allchin, Bridget, and Raymond Allchin
1968 *The Birth of Indian Civilization.* Baltimore: Penguin.
Allchin, F.R.
1964 "Early Domestic Animals in India and Pakistan." In P. Ucko and

I wish to express profound thanks to Brian Ferguson for his indefatigable labors on behalf of this part of the book.

G. Dimbleby, eds., *The Domestication and Exploitation of Plants and Animals.* Chicago: Aldine, pp. 317–321.

Anderson, J.
1973 "Ecological Anthropology and Anthropological Ecology." In J. Honigmann, ed., *Handbook of Social and Cultural Anthropology.* Chicago: Rand McNally, pp. 179–240.

Anekwe, Simon Obi
1967 "The Tragedy of Professor Diamond." In Stanley Diamond, ed., *Nigeria: Model of a Colonial Failure.* New York: American Committee on Africa, pp. 47–52.

Angel, J. Lawrence
1975 "Paleoecology, Paleodemography and Health." In S. Polgar, ed., *Population, Ecology and Social Evolution.* The Hague: Mouton, pp. 167–190.

Anyiam, Chief F.U.
1967 "Does Stanley Diamond Exist?" In Stanley Diamond, ed., *Nigeria: Model of a Colonial Failure.* New York: American Committee on Africa, pp. 52–54.

Armelagos, George, and Alan McArdle
1975 "Population, Disease and Evolution." *American Antiquity* 40 (pt. 2): 1–10.

Armstrong, Louise
1978 *Kiss Daddy Goodnight.* New York: Hawthorn.

Ayer, Alfred
1959 *Logical Positivism.* Glencoe, Ill.: Free Press.

Azzi, Corry
1974 "More on India's Sacred Cattle." *Current Anthropology* 15: 317–321.

Bacon, Francis
1875 *The Works of Francis Bacon,* Vol. IV. J. Spedding, R. Ellis, and D. Heath, eds. London: Longmans & Company.

Bacon, M., J. Child, and I. Barry
1963 "A Cross-Cultural Study of Correlates of Crime." *Journal of Abnormal and Social Psychology* 66: 241–300.

Barnouw, Victor
1973 *Culture and Personality.* Homewood, Ill.: Dorsey Press.

Beals, Ralph
1978 "Sonoran Fantasy or Coming of Age?" *American Anthropologist* 80: 355–362.

Bekoff, Marc, ed.
1978 *Coyotes: Biology, Behavior, and Management.* New York: Academic Press.

Benedict, Ruth
1934 *Patterns of Culture.* New York: Houghton Mifflin.

Bennet, J.W.
1967 "On the Cultural Ecology of Indian Cattle." *Current Anthropology* 3: 251–252.
Berger, Allen
1976 "Structural and Eclectic Revisions of Marxist Strategy: A Cultural Materialist Critique." *Current Anthropology* 17: 290–304.
Berlin, Brent, and Paul Kay
1969 *Basic Color Terms: Their Universality and Evolution.* Berkeley: University of California Press.
Berreman, Gerald, G. Gjessing, and K. Gough
1968 "Social Responsibilities Symposium." *Current Anthropology* 9: 391–407.
Bertalanffy, L. von
1955 "An Essay on the Relativity of Categories." *Philosophy of Science* 22: 243–263.
Bicchieri, M.G., ed.
1972 *Hunters and Gatherers Today.* New York: Holt, Rinehart and Winston.
Birdsell, Joseph
1968 "Some Predictions for the Pleistocene Based on the Equilibrium Systems among Recent Hunter-gatherers." In R. Lee and I. DeVore, eds., *Man the Hunter.* Chicago: Aldine, pp. 229–249.
Black, Mary
1973 "Belief Systems." In J. Honigmann, ed., *Handbook of Social and Cultural Anthropology.* Chicago: Rand McNally, pp. 509–577.
Bloch, Maurice, ed.
1975 *Marxist Analysis and Social Anthropology.* London: Malaby Press.
Boas, Franz
1932 *Bella Bella Tales.* Memoir of the American Folklore Society 25.
1948 *Race, Language and Culture.* New York: Macmillan.
Boas, Franz, ed.
1938 *General Anthropology.* New York: Heath.
Bock, Phillip
1969 *Modern Cultural Anthropology: An Introduction.* New York: Knopf.
Bose, A.N.
1961 *Social and Rural Economy of Northern India, 600 B.C.–200 A.D.* Calcutta: Firma K.L. Mukhopadhyay.
Bridgeman, Percival
1927 *The Logic of Modern Physics.* New York: Macmillan.
Brown, Paula
1978 "New Guinea: Ecology, Society, and Cuture." *Annual Review of Anthropology* 7: 263–291.

Buchbinder, Georgeda
in press *Nutrition and Population Dynamics: A Case Study from the New Guinea Highlands.* Queens, N.Y.: Spectrum.
Bulmer, Ralph
1967 "Why Is a Cassowary Not a Bird?" *Man* 2: 5–25
Butzer, Karl
1976 *Early Hydraulic Civilization in Egypt: A Study in Cultural Ecology.* Chicago: University of Chicago Press.
Cahalane, Victor
1947 *Mammals of North America.* New York: Macmillan.
Calaby, J.H.
1971 "Man, Fauna and Climate in Aboriginal Australia." In D.J. Mulvaney and J. Golson, eds., *Aboriginal Man and Environment in Australia.* Canberra: Australian National University Press, pp. 80–93.
Cambridge History of India
1923–1927 Cambridge University Press: Cambridge.
Campbell, Donald
1974 "Natural Selection as an Epistemological Model." In Raoul Naroll and R. Cohen, eds., *A Handbook of Method in Cultural Anthropology.* New York: Columbia University Press, pp. 51–85.
Carneiro, Robert
1970 "A Theory of the Origin of the State." *Science* 169: 733–738.
Carneiro, Robert, and D. Hilse
1966 "On Determining the Probable Rate of Population Growth during the Neolithic." *American Anthropologist* 68: 177–181.
Castaneda, C.
1969 *The Teachings of Don Juan: A Yaqui Way of Knowledge.* New York: Ballantine.
Casteel, Richard
1972 "Two Static Maximum Population Density Models for Hunter-Gatherers: A First Approximation." *World Archaeology.* 4(1): 19–40.
Chomsky, Noam
1964 (1959) "Review of B. F. Skinner, *Verbal Behavior.*" In J.A. Fodor and J.J. Katz, eds., *The Structure of Language: Readings in the Philosophy of Language.* Englewood Cliffs, N.J.: Prentice-Hall, pp. 547–578.
Clemmer, Richard O.
1972 "Truth, Duty and the Revitalization of Anthropologists: A New Perspective on Culture Change and Resistance." In Dell Hymes, ed., *Reinventing Anthropology.* New York: Random House, pp. 213–247.

Coale, Ansley
1974 "The History of the Human Population." *Scientific American* 231(3): 41–51.
Codere, Helen, ed.
1966 *Kwakiutl Ethnography.* Chicago: University of Chicago Press.
Coe, Michael
1968 *America's First Civilization: Discovering the Olmec.* New York: American Heritage.
Cohen, Mark
1977 *The Food Crisis in Prehistory: Overpopulation and the Origins of Agriculture.* New Haven: Yale University Press.
Cohen, Myron
1976 *House United, House Divided: The Chinese Family in Taiwan.* New York: Columbia University Press.
Cohen, Yehudi
1978 "The Disappearance of the Incest Taboo." *Human Nature* 1(7): 72–78.
Comte, Auguste
1830–1842 *Cours de Philosophie Positive.* Paris: Bachelier.
Cook, Scott
1966 "The Obsolete 'Anti-Market' Mentality: A Critique of the Substantive Approach to Economic Anthropology." *American Anthropologist* 68: 323–345.
1974 "Economic Anthropology: Problems in Theory, Method and Analysis." In J. Honigmann, ed., *Handbook of Social and Cultural Anthropology.* Chicago: Rand McNally, pp. 795–860.
Cooper, Eugene
1973 "An Interview with Chinese Anthropologists." *Current Anthropology* 14: 480–482.
Cunningham, Frank
1973 *Objectivity in Social Science.* Toronto: University of Toronto Press.
Dally, Herman
1971 "A Marxian Malthusian View of Poverty and Development." *Population Studies* 25: 25–38.
Dalton, George
1960 "A Note of Clarification on Economic Surpluses." *American Anthropologist* 62: 483–490.
1963 "Economic Surplus, Once Again." *American Anthropologist* 65: 389–394.
1972 "Peasantries in Anthropology and History." *Current Anthropology* 13: 385–416.
1974 "How Exactly Are Peasants Exploited?" *American Anthropologist* 76: 553–561.

Dandekar, V.M.
1969 "Cow Dung Models." *Economic and Political Weekly* (Bombay), August 2: 1267–1271.
Davis, Kingsley
1951 *The Population of India and Pakistan.* Princeton, N.J.: Princeton University Press.
Dehavenon, Anna Lou
1977 *Rank-Ordered Behavior in Four Urban Families: A Comparative Video-analysis of Patterns of Superordination in Two Black and White Families.* Ph.D. dissertation, Columbia University.
Dehavenon, Anna Lou, and Harris, M.
n.d. "Hierarchical Behavior in Domestic Groups: A Videotape Analysis."
Deloria, Vine
1969 *Custer Died for Your Sins.* London: Collier-Macmillan.
DeMille, Richard
1976 *Castaneda's Journey.* Santa Barbara, Calif.: Capra.
Dentan, Robert
1968 *The Semai: A Non-Violent People of Malaya.* New York: Holt, Rinehart and Winston.
Despres, Leo
1975 "Ethnicity and Resource Competition in Guyanese Society." In Leo Despres, ed., *Ethnicity and Resource Competition in Plural Societies.* The Hague: Mouton, pp. 87–118.
Devereux, George
1967 "A Typological Study of Abortion in 350 Primitive, Ancient, and Pre-Industrial Societies." In H. Rosen, ed., *Abortion in America.* Boston: Beacon Press, pp. 95–152.
Diamond, Stanley
1967 *Nigeria: Model of a Colonial Failure.* New York: American Committee on Africa.
1970 "Reflections on the African Revolution: The Point of the Biafran Case." *Journal of Asian and African Studies* 5: 16–27.
1972 "Anthropology in Question." In Dell Hymes, ed., *Reinventing Anthropology.* New York: Random House, pp. 401–429.
Diamond, Stanley, B. Scholte, and B. Wolf
1975 "Anti-Kaplan: Defining the Marxist Tradition." *American Anthropologist* 77: 870–875.
Dickeman, Mildred
1975a "Demographic Consequences of Infanticide in Man." *Annual Review of Ecology and Systematics* 6: 100–137.
1975b "Female Infanticide and Hypergyny: A Neglected Relationship." Paper presented at the meeting of the American Anthropological Association, San Francisco.
1979 "Female Infanticide and the Reproductive Strategies of Stratified

Human Societies: A Preliminary Model." In Napoleon Chagnon and William Irons, eds., *Sociobiology and Human Social Organizations*. North Scituate, Mass.: Duxbury, in press.

Diener, Paul, and E. Robkin
1978 "Ecology, Evolution, and the Search for Cultural Origins: The Question of Islamic Pig Prohibition." *Current Anthropology* 19: 493–540.

Divale, W.
1975 "An Explanation for Matrilocal Residence." In Dana Raphael, ed., *Being Female: Reproduction, Power, and Change*. The Hague: Mouton, pp. 99–108.

Divale, W., and M. Harris
1976 "Population, Warfare, and the Male Supremacist Complex." *American Anthropologist* 78: 521–538

Divale, W., M. Harris, and D. William
1978 "On the Measure of Statistics: A Reply to Hirschfeld et al." *American Anthropologist* 80: 379–386.

Donald, Leland, and D.H. Mitchell
1975 "Some Correlations of Local Group Rank among the Southern Kwakiutl." *Ethnology* 14: 325–346.

Douglas, Jack, ed.
1970 *Understanding Everyday Life: Toward the Reconstruction of Sociological Knowledge*. Chicago: Aldine

Douglas, Mary
1966 *Purity and Danger: An Analysis of Concepts of Pollution and Taboo*. New York: Praeger.
1967 "The Meaning of Myth." In Edmund Leach, ed., *The Structural Study of Myth and Totemism*. ASA Monograph No. 5. London: Tavistock, pp. 46–69.
1972 "Deciphering a Meal." *Daedalus* 101: 61–82.

Ducos, P.
1968 *L'Origine des Animaux Domestiques en Palestine*. Bordeaux: Imprimeries Delmas.
1969 "Methodology and Results of the Study of the Earliest Domesticated Animals in the Near East (Palestine)." In P. Ucko and G. Dimbleby, eds., *The Domestication and Exploitation of Plants and Animals*. Chicago: Aldine, pp. 265–276.

Dumond, Don E.
1975 "The Limitation of Human Population: A Natural History." *Science* 187: 713–720.

Durbin, Marshall
1973 "Cognitive Anthropology." In John Honigmann, ed., *Handbook of Social and Cultural Anthropology*. Chicago: Rand McNally, pp. 447–478.

Durkheim, Emile
1915 *The Elementary Forms of the Religious Life,* J.W. Swain, trans. London: Allen & Unwin.
1962 (1895) *Rules of Sociological Method.* Glencoe, Ill.: Free Press.
Dyson-Hudson, Rada, and N. Dyson-Hudson
1969 "Subsistence Herding in Uganda." *Scientific American* 220(2): 76–89.
Eberhard, Mary Jane
1975 "The Evolution of Social Behavior by Kin Selection." *The Quarterly Review of Biology* 50: 1–33.
Edwardes, Michael
1967 *British India 1772–1947.* London: Sidgwick and Jackson.
Ember, Carol
1978 "Myths about Hunter-Gatherers." *Ethnology* 17: 439–448.
Engels, Frederick
1959 (1890) "Letter to Joseph Bloch." In *Basic Writings on Politics and Philosophy: Karl Marx and Frederick Engels,* Lewis Feuer, ed. Garden City, N.Y.: Anchor Books, pp. 397–400.
1972 (1878) *Herr Eugen Dühring's Revolution in Science (Anti-Dühring).* New York: International Publishers.
1972 (1884) *The Origin of the Family, Private Property, and the State.* New York: International Publishers.
Epstein, H.
1971 *The Origin of the Domestic Animals of Africa,* 2 vols. New York: Africana Publishing Corporation.
Ferguson, Brian
n.d. "War on the Northwest Coast." Unpublished paper.
Feyerabend, Paul
1963 "Explanations, Predictions, Theories." In F. Baumrin, ed., *Philosophy of Science: The Delaware Seminar,* Vol. 2. New York: Interscience, pp. 3–39.
1970 "Problems of Empiricism, Part II." In R. Colodny, ed., *Nature and Function of Scientific Theories.* Pittsburgh: University of Pittsburgh Press, pp. 275–353.
1975 *Against Method.* Atlantic Highlands, N.J.: Humanities.
Firth, Raymond
1975 "The Skeptical Anthropologist? Social Anthropology and Marxist Views on Society." In Maurice Bloch, ed., *Marxist Analyses and Social Anthropology.* London: Malaby Press, pp. 29–60.
Fisher, Lawrence, and O. Werner
1978 "Explaining Explanation: Tension in American Anthropology." *Journal of Anthropological Research* 34: 194–218.
Fjellman, Stephen
1972 *The Organization of Diversity: Akamba Kinship Terminology.* Unpublished Ph.D. dissertation, Stanford University.

Flannery, Kent
1973 "The Origins of Agriculture." *Annual Review of Anthropology* 2: 270–310.
Fortes, Meyer, and E.E. Evans Pritchard, eds.
1940 *African Political Systems.* London: Oxford University Press.
Foster, George
1967 *Tzintzuntzan: Mexican Peasants in a Changing World.* Boston: Little, Brown.
1972 "The Anatomy of Envy: A Study in Symbolic Behavior." *Current Anthropology* 13: 165–202.
1974 "Limited Good or Limited Goods: Observations on Acheson." *American Anthropologist* 76: 53–57.
Frake, Charles
1964 "A Structural Description of Subanum 'Religious Behavior.'" In W. Goodenough, ed., *Explorations in Cultural Anthropology.* New York: McGraw-Hill, pp. 111–129.
Frank, Gunder
1970 "On Dalton's 'Theoretical Issues in Economic Anthropology.'" *Current Anthropology* 11: 67–71.
Franke, Richard W.
1974 "Miracle Seeds and Shattered Dreams." *Natural History* 83(1): 10 ff.
Fried, Morton H.
1967 *The Evolution of Political Society: An Essay in Political Anthropology.* New York: Random House.
1978a "Reconsiderations: Oriental Despotism." *Human Nature* 1(12): 90–93f.
1978b "The State, the Chicken and the Egg; or What Came First?" In R. Cohen and E. Service, eds., *Origins of the State.* Philadelphia: Institute for the Study of Human Issues, pp. 35–47.
Friedman, Jonathan
1974a "Marxism, Structuralism and Vulgar Materialism." *Man* 9: 444–469.
1974b "The Place of Fetishism and the Problem of Materialist Interpretation." *Critique of Anthropology* 1: 26–62.
1975 "Tribes, States and Transformations." In Maurice Bloch, ed., *Marxist Analyses and Social Anthropology.* London: Malaby Press, pp. 161–202.
Frisch, Rose
1975 "Critical Weights, A Critical Body Composition, Menarche and the Maintenance of Menstrual Cycles." In E. Watts, F. Johnston, and G. Lasker, eds., *Biosocial Interrelations in Population Adaptation.* The Hague: Mouton, pp. 309–318.
1978 "Reply to Trussel." *Science* 200: 1509–1513.

Frisch, Rose, and J. McArthur
1974 "Menstrual Cycles: Fatness as a Determinant of Minimum Weight for Height Necessary for Their Maintenance or Onset." *Science* 185: 949–951.

Gamst, Frederick
1975 "Rethinking Leach's Structural Analysis of Color and Instructional Categories in Traffic Control Signals." *American Ethnologist* 2: 271–296.

Garfinkel, Harold
1967 *Studies in Ethnomethodology.* Englewood Cliffs, N.J.: Prentice-Hall.

Geertz, Clifford
1963 *Agricultural Involution: The Process of Ecological Change in Indonesia.* Berkeley: University of California Press.
1972 "Deep Play: Notes on the Balinese Cockfight." *Daedalus* 101(1): 1–37.

Gelb, Ignaz
1972 "From Freedom to Slavery." In D.O. Edzard, ed., *18th Rencontre Assyriologique Internationale—Munich.* Bayerischen: Akademic Der Wissensdaffen.
1973 "Prisoners of War in Early Mesopotamia." *Journal of Near Eastern Studies* 32: 70–98.

Geoghegan, William
1969 "Decision Making and Residence on Tagtabon Island." Wekey Paper 17. Language Behavior Research Laboratory. University of California, Berkeley.

Geoghegan, William, and Paul Kay
1964 "More Structure and Statistics: A Critique of C. Ackerman's Analysis of the Purum." *American Anthropologist* 66: 1351–1355.

Gibbons, E.
1964 *Stalking the Blue-Eyed Scallop.* New York: McKay.

Gibson, Charles
1964 *The Aztecs Under Spanish Rule.* Stanford: Stanford University Press.

Gifford, James
1974 "Recent Thoughts Concerning the Interpretation of Maya Prehistory." In Norman Hammond, ed., *Mesoamerican Archaeology: New Approaches.* Austin: University of Texas Press, pp. 77–98.

Godelier, Maurice
1974 "On the Definition of a Social Formation: The Example of the Incas." In *Critique of Anthropology,* London Alternative Anthropology Group. London: L.S.E. Printing Services, pp. 63–72.
1975 "Modes of Production, Kinship, and Demographic Structures." In

Maurice Bloch, ed., *Marxist Analyses and Social Anthropology.*
London: Malaby Press, pp. 3–27.

1977 *Perspectives in Marxist Anthropology.* New York: Cambridge University Press.

Goldstein, Melvyn

1978 "Pahari and Tibetan Polyandry Revisited." *Ethnology* 17: 325–338.

Goodenough, Ward

1964 "Cultural Anthropology and Linguistics." In Dell Hymes, ed., *Language in Culture and Society.* New York: Harper & Row, pp. 36–39.

1965 "Rethinking Status and Role: Toward a General Model of Cultural Organization of Social Relations." In M. Banton, ed., *The Relevance of Models for Social Anthropology.* New York: Praeger, pp. 1–22.

1968 "Componential Analysis." *Encyclopedia of the Social Sciences,* Vol. 3, pp. 186–192.

1969 "Frontiers of Cultural Anthropology: Social Organization." *Proceedings of the American Philosophical Society* 113: 329–335.

1970 *Description and Comparison in Cultural Anthropology.* Chicago: Aldine.

Goody, Jack

1973 "British Functionalism." In R. Naroll and F. Naroll, eds., *Main Currents in Cultural Anthropology.* New York: Appleton-Century-Crofts, pp. 185–215.

1976 *Production and Reproduction.* New York: Cambridge University Press.

Gough, Kathleen

1973 (1968) "World Revolution and the Science of Man." In *To See Ourselves: Anthropology and Modern Social Issues,* gen. ed. T. Weaver. Glenview, Ill.: Scott, Foresman, pp. 156–165.

Gouldner, Alvin

1970 *The Coming Crisis of Western Sociology.* New York: Basic Books.

Gramby, Richard

1977 "Deerskin and Hunting Territories: Competition for a Scarce Resource in the Northeast Woodlands." *American Antiquity* 42: 601–605.

Greengo, Robert

1952 "Shellfish Foods of California Indians." *Kroeber Anthropological Society Papers* 7: 63–114.

Grigg, D.B.

1974 *The Agricultural System of the World: An Evolutionary Approach.* Cambridge: Cambridge University Press.

Gross, Daniel

1975 "Protein Capture and Cultural Development in the Amazon Basin." *American Anthropologist* 77: 526–549.

Hall, Eugene
1946 *Mammals of Nevada.* Berkeley and Los Angeles: University of California Press.
Hall, Eugene, and Keith Kelson
1959 *The Mammals of North America.* New York: Ronald Press.
Hamilton, W.D.
1964 "The Genetical Evolution of Social Behavior." *Journal of Theoretical Biology* 7: 1–52.
Hammond, Norman, ed.
1978 *Social Process in Maya Prehistory.* New York: Academic Press.
Hannerz, Ulf
1970 "What Ghetto Males Are Like: Another Look." In N.E. Whitten and J.F. Szwed, eds., *Afro-American Anthropology: Contemporary Perspectives.* New York: Free Press, pp. 313–328.
Harner, Michael
1970 "Population Pressure and the Social Evolution of Agriculturalists." *Southwestern Journal of Anthropology* 26: 67–86.
1977 "The Ecological Basis for Aztec Sacrifice." *American Ethnologist* 4: 117–135.
1978 "Reply to Ortiz de Montellano." Paper read at the New York Academy of Science, November 27, 1978.
Harrington, Charles, and J. Whiting
1972 "Socialization Process and Personality." In Francis Hsu, ed., *Psychological Anthropology.* Cambridge, Mass.: Schenkman, pp. 469–507.
Harris, Marvin
1959 "The Economy Has No Surplus?" *American Anthropologist* 61: 189–199.
1964a *Patterns of Race in the Americas.* New York: Walker.
1964b *The Nature of Cultural Things.* New York: Random House.
1966 "The Cultural Ecology of India's Sacred Cattle." *Current Anthropology* 7: 51–59.
1968 *The Rise of Anthropological Theory.* New York: T. Y. Crowell.
1970 "Referential Ambiguity in the Calculus of Brazilian Racial Identity." *Southwestern Journal of Anthropology* 26(1): 1–14.
1971a "Comments on Alan Heston's 'An Approach to the Sacred Cow of India.' " *Current Anthropology* 12: 199–201.
1971b *Culture, Man and Nature: Introduction to General Anthropology.* New York: T. Y. Crowell.
1972 "Portugal's Contribution to the Underdevelopment of Africa and Brazil." In Ronald Chilcote, ed., *Protest and Resistance in Angola and Brazil.* Berkeley: University of California Press, pp. 209–223.
1974a "Reply to Corry Azzi." *Current Anthropology* 15: 323.
1974b *Cows, Pigs, Wars and Witches: The Riddles of Culture.* New York: Random House.

1975 "Why a Perfect Knowledge of All the Rules That One Must Know in Order to Act Like a Native Cannot Lead to a Knowledge of How Natives Act." *Journal of Anthropological Research* 30: 242–251.
1976 "Lévi-Strauss et La Palourde." *L'Homme* 16: 5–22.
1977a *Cannibals and Kings: The Origins of Cultures.* New York: Random House.
1977b "Bovine Sex and Species Ratios in India." Paper read at American Anthropological Association meetings in Houston.
1979 "Reply to Sahlins." *New York Review of Books,* in press.
1980 *Culture, People, Nature,* 3rd ed. New York: Harper & Row.

Harris, Marvin, and Conrad Kottak
1963 "The Structural Significance of Brazilian Racial Categories." *Sociologia* 25: 203–208 (São Paulo).

Harris, Marvin, and Eric Ross
1978 "The Origins of the U.S. Preference for Beef." *Psychology Today,* October: 88–94.

Harris, Zellig
1951 *Methods in Structural Linguistics.* Chicago: University of Chicago Press.

Harrison, Peter D., and B.L. Tunner, eds.
1978 *Pre-Historic Maya Agriculture.* Albuquerque: University of New Mexico Press.

Hart, Keith
n.d. "The Economic Basis of Tallensi Social History in the Early Twentieth Century." Unpublished paper.

Hassan, Ferki
1973 "On Mechanisms of Population Growth During the Neolithic." *Current Anthropology* 14: 535–542.

Hays, Terrance
1974 *Mauna: Exploration in Ndumba Ethnobotany.* Unpublished Ph.D. dissertation, University of Washington, Seattle.

Hempel, Carl
1965 *Philosophy of Natural Science.* Englewood Cliffs, N.J.: Prentice-Hall.

Heston, Alan
1971 "An Approach to the Sacred Cow of India." *Current Anthropology* 12: 191–210.

Hewitt de Alcantara, Cynthia
1976 *Modernizing Mexican Agriculture.* Geneva: United Nations Research Institute for Social Development.

Hickerson, H.
1965 "The Virginia Deer and Inter-Tribal Buffer Zones in the Upper Missippippi Valley." In A. Leeds and A.P. Vayda, eds., *Man, Culture, and Animals: The Role of Animals in Human Ecological*

Adjustments. Washington, D.C.: American Association for the Advancement of Science, pp. 43–66.

Hindess, Barry, and P.Q. Hirst
1975   *Pre-Capitalist Modes of Production.* London: Routledge & Kegan Paul.

Hoffer, Carol
1975   "Bundu: Political Implications of Female Solidarity in a Secret Society." In Dana Raphael, ed., *Being Female: Reproduction, Power, and Change.* The Hague: Mouton, pp. 155–164.

Holton, Gerald
1973   *Thematic Origins of Scientific Thought: Kepler to Einstein.* Cambridge: Harvard University Press.

Horowitz, Irving, ed.
1967   *The Rise and Fall of Project Camelot.* Cambridge, Mass.: M.I.T. Press.

Hull, David
1973   *Darwin and His Critics.* Cambridge: Harvard University Press.

Hume, David
1955 (1748)   *An Inquiry Concerning Human Understanding.* New York: Liberal Arts Press.

1975 (1739)   *Treatise of Human Nature.* Oxford: Clarendon Press.

Hunt, Robert, and Eva Hunt
1976   "Canal Irrigation and Local Social Organization." *Current Anthropology* 17: 389–411.

Hymes, Dell
1968   "Linguistics: The Field." *Encyclopedia of the Social Sciences* 9: 351–371.

Itani, J., and A. Nishimura
1973   "The Study of Infrahuman Culture in Japan: A Review." In E.W. Menzel, ed., *Precultural Primate Behavior.* Basel: S. Karger, pp. 26–50.

Johnson, Allen
1974   "Ethnoecology and Planting Practices in a Swidden Agricultural System." *American Ethnologist* 1: 87–101.

Johnson, M.E., and H.J. Snook
1967   *Seashore Animals of the Pacific Coast.* New York: Dover.

Kahn, Joel
1975   "Economic Scale and the Cycle of Petty Commodity Production on West Sumatra." In Maurice Bloch, ed., *Marxist Analysis and Social Anthropology.* London: Malaby Press, pp. 137–158.

Kaplan, David
1974   "The Anthropology of Authenticity: Everyone His Own Anthropologist." *American Anthropologist* 76: 824–839.

1975   "The Idea of Social Science and Its Enemies: A Rejoinder." *American Anthropologist* 77: 876–880.
Kardiner, Abram, ed.
1939   *The Individual and His Society.* New York: Columbia University Press.
Kasakoff, Alice
1974   "Lévi-Strauss' Idea of the Social Unconscious: The Problem of Elementary and Complex Structures in Gitskan Marriage Choice." In Ino Rossi, ed., *The Unconscious in Culture: The Structuralism of Claude Lévi-Strauss in Perspective.* New York: E.P. Dutton, pp. 143–169.
Kay, Paul
1970   "Some Theoretical Implications of Ethnographic Semantics." *Bulletin of the American Anthropological Association* 3 (no.3, pt. 2): 19–31.
Keesing, R.M.
1972   "Paradigm Lost: The New Ethnography and the New Linguistics." *Southwestern Journal of Anthropology* 28: 299–332.
1974   "Theories of Culture." *Annual Review of Anthropology* 3: 73–98.
Kochar, V.K.
1976   "Human Factors in the Regulation of Parasitic Infections." In F. Grollig and H. Haley, eds., *Medical Anthropology.* The Hague: Mouton, pp. 287–312.
Kolata, Gina
1974   "!Kung Hunter-Gatherers: Feminism, Diet and Birth Control." *Science* 185: 932–934.
Korn, Francis
1973   *Elementary Structures Reconsidered: Lévi-Strauss on Kinship.* Berkeley: University of California Press.
Krader, Lawrence
1972 ed.   *The Ethnological Notebooks of Karl Marx.* Assen, Netherlands: Van Gorcum and Company.
1973a   "Karl Marx as Ethnologist." *Transactions of the New York Academy of Sciences* 35: 304–313.
1973b   "The Works of Marx and Engels in Ethnology Compared." *International Review of Social History* 18: 223–275.
Krauss, Ellis, T.P. Rohlen, and P. Steinhoff
1978   "Conflict in Postwar Japan." *Itema* 32: 21–26.
Kroeber, Alfred
1948   *Anthropology.* New York: Harcourt Brace Jovanovich.
Kroeber, Alfred, and H. Driver
1932   "Quantitative Expression of Cultural Relationships." *University of California Publications in Archaeology and Ethnology* 29: 252–423.

Kroeber, Alfred, and C. Kluckholn
1952   *Culture: A Critical Review of Concepts and Definition.* Papers of the Peabody Museum of American Archaeology and Ethnology, vol. 47. Cambridge: Harvard University Press..

Kroeber, Alfred, and T. Parsons
1958   "The Concept of Culture and of Social Systems." *American Sociological Review* 23: 582–583.

Kuhn, Thomas
1970   *The Structure of Scientific Revolutions,* 2nd ed Chicago: University of Chicago Press.
1977   "Second Thoughts on Paradigms." In Frederick Suppe, ed., *The Structure of Scientific Theories,* 2nd ed. Urbana: University of Illinois Press, pp. 459–481.

LaBarre, Weston
1966   "The Aymara: History and World View." *Journal of American Folklore* 79: 130–144.

Lakatos, I.
1970   "Falsification and the Methodology of Scientific Research Programmes." In I. Lakatos and A. Musgrave, eds., *Criticism and the Growth of Knowledge.* Cambridge: Cambridge University Press, pp. 91–195.

Lathrap, Donald
1973   "The 'Hunting' Economies of the Tropical Forest Zone of South America: An Attempt at Historical Perspective." In Daniel Gross, ed., *Peoples and Cultures of Native South America.* New York: Natural History Press, pp. 83–95.

Laudan, Larry
1977   *Progress and Its Problems: Towards a Theory of Scientific Growth.* Berkeley: University of California Press.

Leach, Edmund R.
1970   *Lévi-Strauss.* London: Fontana/Collins.

Leacock, Eleanor
1972   "Introduction" to F. Engels, *Origins of the Family, Private Property and the State.* New York: International Publishers, pp. 7–67.
1978   "Women's Status in Egalitarian Society: Implications for Social Evolution." *Current Anthropology* 19: 247–275.

Lee, Richard, and Irwin DeVore, eds.
1968   *Man the Hunter.* Chicago: Aldine.
1976   *Kalahari Hunter-Gatherers: Studies of the Kung San and Their Neighbors.* Cambridge: Harvard University Press.

Leeds, Anthony
1970   "The Culture of Poverty: Conceptual, Logical and Empirical Problems, with Perspectives from Brazil and Peru." In E. Leacock, ed.,

The Culture of Poverty: A Critique. New York: Simon & Schuster, pp. 226–284.

Legros, Dominique
1979 "Chance, Necessity, and Mode of Production: A Marxist Critique of Cultural Evolutionism." In James Silverberg, ed., *Mode of Production.* New York: Queens College Press.

Lenin, V.I.
1972 *Materialism and Empirio-Criticism: Critical Comments on a Reactionary Philosophy.* New York: International Publishers.

LeVine, Robert
1973 *Culture, Behavior and Personality,* Chicago: Aldine.

Lévi-Strauss, Claude
1963 *Structural Anthropology.* New York: Doubleday.
1966 *The Savage Mind.* Chicago: University of Chicago Press.
1969a *The Raw and the Cooked.* New York: Harper & Row.
1969b *The Elementary Structures of Kinship.* rev. ed. J.H. Bell, trans., J.R. von Sturmer and Rodney Needham, eds. Boston: Beacon Press.
1971 *L'Homme Nu.* Paris: Plan.
1972 "Structuralism and Ecology." Gildersleeve Lecture delivered March 28, 1972, at Barnard College, New York, New York. (Reprinted in Andrew Weiss, ed., *Readings in Anthropology 75/76.* Guilford, Conn.: Dushkin, pp. 226–233.)
1976 "Structuralisme et Empirisme." *L'Homme* 16: 23–39.

Lewis, Oscar
1966a "The Culture of Poverty." *Scientific American* 215(4): 19–25.
1966b *La Vida.* New York: Random House.
1970 *Anthropological Essays.* New York: Random House.

Lindenbaum, Shirley
1979 *Kuru Sorcery.* Palo Alto, Calif.: Mayfield.

Lomax, Alan, et al.
1968 *Folk Song Style and Culture.* American Association for the Advancement of Science Publication 88.

Lomax, Alan, and C. Arensberg
1977 "A Worldwide Evolutionary Classification of Cultures by Subsistence Systems." *Current Anthropology* 18: 659–708.

Lounsburry, F.
1965 "Another View of Trobiand Kinship Categories." *American Anthropologist* 67 (pt. 2): 142–185.

Lowie, Robert
1920 *Primitive Society.* New York: Boni and Liveright.
1948 *Social Organization.* New York: Holt, Rinehart and Winston.

Luzetak, Louis
1954 "The Socio-Religious Significance of a New Guinea Pig Festival."
    Anthropological Quarterly 2: 59–80, 102–128.
MacNeish, Richard·
1978 *The Science of Archaeology?* Belmont, Calif.: Duxbury Press.
Magee, Bryan
1973 *Karl Popper.* New York: Viking Press.
Magubane, B.
1971 "A Critical Look at Indices Used in the Study of Social Change in
    Colonial Africa." *Current Anthropology* 12: 419–466.
Mamdani, Mahmood
1973 *The Myth of Population Control, Family Caste and and Class in an
    Indian Village.* New York: Monthly Review Press.
Mao Tse-tung
1966 *Four Essays on Philosophy.* Peking: Foreign Language Press.
Maquet, Jacques
1974 "Isomorphism and Symbolism as 'Explanations' in the Analysis of
    Myths." In Ino Rossi, ed., *The Unconscious in Culture: The Struc-
    turalism of Claude Lévi-Strauss in Perspective.* New York: Dutton,
    pp. 123–133.
Marshall, John
1931 *Mohenjo-daro and the Indus Civilization,* 3 vols. London.
Marx, Karl
1970 (1859) *A Contribution of the Critique of Political-Economy.* New·
    York: International Publishers.
1971 (1846) "Letter to P.V. Annenkov." In *The Poverty of Philosophy.*
    New York: International Publishers, pp. 179–194.
1971 (1847) *The Poverty of Philosophy.* New York: International Publish-
    ers.
1973 (1857/58) *Grundrisse: Foundations of the Critique of Political
    Economy.* Martin Nicolaus, trans. New York: Vintage.
1975 (1867) *Capital: A Critique of Political Economy,* Vol. I. New York:
    International Publishers.
1976 (1845) "Theses on Feuerbach." In *Collected Works of Marx and
    Engels,* Vol. 5 New York: International Publishers, pp. 3–5.
Marx, Karl, and Frederick Engels
1959 (1848) *The Communist Manifesto.* In L. Feuer, ed., *Marx and
    Engels: Basic Writings on Politics and Philosophy.* Garden City,
    N.Y.: Doubleday, pp. 1–41.
1976 (1846) *The German Ideology.* In *Collected Works of Marx and
    Engels,* Vol. 5. New York: International Publishers, pp. 19–92.
Maxwell, Nicholas
1974a "The Rationality of Scientific Discovery. Part I: The Traditional
    Rationality Problem." *Philosophy of Science* 41: 123–153.

1974b "The Rationality of Scientific Discovery. Part II: An Aim Oriented Theory of Scientific Discovery." *Philosophy of Science* 41: 247–295.

McDonald, David
1977 "Food Taboos: A Primitive Environmental Protection Agency (South America)." *Anthropos* 72: 734–748.

Meek, Ronald
1971 *Marx and Engels on the Population Bomb.* Berkeley: Ramparts Press.

Meggitt, Mervyn
1977 *Blood Is Their Argument: Warfare Among the Mae Enga Tribesmen of the New Guinea Highlands.* Palo Alto: Mayfield Publishing.

Mencher, Joan
1966 "Kerala and Madras: A Comparative Study of Ecology and Social Structure." *Ethnology* 5: 135–171.

Minge-Kalman, Wanda
1978 "The Evolution of Commodity Reproduction: The Rise of the Cost of Children in Western Industrial Societies." *Comparative Studies in Society and History,* in press.

Mitchell, William
1973 "The Hydraulic Hypothesis: A Reappraisal." *Current Anthropology* 4: 532–534.

Mitra, Rajendra
1881 *The Indo-Aryans.* Calcutta: W. Newman and Company. Volume 1, Chapter 6, as reprinted by Swami Bhumananda, Calcutta, 1967.

Montagu, Ashley
1976 *The Nature of Human Aggression.* New York: Oxford University Press.

Morgan, Lewis Henry
1877 *Ancient Society.* New York: Holt, Rinehart and Winston.

Morren, George
1974 *Settlement Strategies and Hunting in a New Guinea Society.* Ph.D. dissertation, Columbia University.

Morris, P.
1952 *A Field Guide to Shells of the Pacific Coast and Hawaii.* Boston: Houghton Mifflin.

Mount, Lawrence
1968 *The Climatic Physiology of the Pig.* London: Edward Arnold.

Murdock, George
1949 *Social Structure.* New York: Macmillan.
1959 *Africa: Its Peoples and Their Cultural History.* New York: McGraw-Hill.

1967 *Ethnographic Atlas.* Pittsburgh: University of Pittsburgh Press.
Murphy, R.F.
1971 *The Dialectics of Social Life.* New York: Basic Books.
Nag, Moni, B. White, and R. Peet
1978 "An Anthropological Approach to the Study of the Value of Children in Java and Nepal." *Current Anthropology* 19: 293–306.
Nair, N.N., and A. Vaidyanathan
1978 "Interstate Differences in Milk Consumption in India." Trivandrum: Center for Development Studies Working Paper 62.
Namboodripad, E.
1967 *Kerela: Yesterday, Today and Tomorrow.* Calcutta: National Book Agency.
Naroll, Raoul
1973 "Introduction," in R. Naroll and F. Naroll, eds. *Main Currents in Anthropology.* New York: Appleton-Century-Crofts, pp. 1–23.
Nash, Manning
1967 "Book Review of 'Primitive and Peasant Economic Systems.' " *Current Anthropology* 8: 244–250.
Nath, Pran
1929 *A Study in the Economic Condition of Ancient India.* London: Royal Asiatic Society.
National Research Council
1975 *Agricultural Production Efficiency.* Washington, D.C.: National Academy of Sciences.
Needham, Rodney
1971 *Rethinking Kinship and Marriage.* London: Tavistock.
Newcomer, Peter
1977 "Toward a Scientific Treatment of 'Exploitation': A Critique of Dalton." *American Anthropologist* 79: 115–119.
Newcomer, Peter, and H. Rubenstein
1975 "Peasant Exploitation: A Reply to Dalton." *American Anthropologist* 77: 337–338.
Odend'hal, Stuart
1972 "Energetics of Indian Cattle in Their Environment." *Human Ecology* 1(1): 3–32.
Odum, H.
1971 *Environment, Power and Society.* New York: Wiley.
O'Laughlin, B.
1975 "Marxist Approaches in Anthropology." *Annual Review of Anthropology* 4: 341–370.
Olson, Gerald W.
1978 "Effects of Activities of the Ancient Maya upon Some of the Soils in Central America." Paper read at meeting of the Society for American Archaeology in Tuscon, Arizona.

Olson, Ronald
1955 "Notes on the Bella Bella Kwakiutl." *Anthropological Records* 14. University of California Press, pp. 319–348.
Ortiz de Montellano, B.R.
1978 "Aztec Cannibalism: An Ecological Necessity?" *Science* 200: 611–617.
Parsons, Anne
1964 "Is the Oedipus Complex Universal?" *The Psychoanalytic Study of Society* 3: 278–328.
Parsons, Talcott
1951 *The Social System.* Glencoe, Ill.: Free Press.
1967 "Sociological Theory." *Encyclopaedia Britannica* 20: 799–802.
1970 "On Building Social System Theory: A Personal History." *Daedalus* 99: 826–881.
Paul, Robert, and P. Rabinow
1976 "Bourgeois Rationalism Revived." *Dialectic Anthropology* 1: 121–134.
Pearson, Harry
1957 "The Economy Has No Surplus: Critique of a Theory of Development." In K. Polanyi, H. Pearson, and C. Arensberg, eds., *Trade and Market in the Early Empires.* New York: Free Press, pp. 1–36.
Pearson, Karl
1937 (1892) *The Grammar of Science.* London: J.M. Dent & Sons.
Pelto, P., and Pelto, G.
1975 "Intra-cultural Diversity: Some Theoretical Issues." *American Ethnologist* 2: 1–18.
Piggott, Stuart
1965 *Ancient Europe.* Edin Curgle: University Press.
1975 *The Druids.* New York: Praeger.
Pike, K.L.
1967 *Language in Relation to a Unified Theory of the Structure of Human Behavior,* 2nd ed. The Hague: Mouton.
Pillai, A.K. Balakrishna
1975 *The Culture of Social Stratification: The Economics, Politics, and Rituals of Marriage—A Case Study of the Nayars.* Ph.D. dissertation, Columbia University.
Polanyi, Karl
1944 *The Great Transformation.* New York: Holt, Rinehart and Winston.
Polgar, Steven, et. al.
1972 "Population History and Population Policies from an Anthropological Perspective." *Current Anthropology* 13: 202–215.
Pollnac, Richard
1975 "Intracultural Variations in the Structure of the Subjective Color Lexicon in Buganda." *American Ethnologist* 2: 89–109.

Popper, Karl
1959   *The Logic of Scientific Discovery.* New York: Basic Books.
1964   *The Poverty of Historicism.* New York: Harper & Row.
1965   *Conjectures and Refutations: The Growth of Scientific Knowledge.* New York: Basic Books.
Prakash, Om
1961   *Food and Drinks in Ancient India: From Earliest Times to C. 1200 A.D.* Delhi: Munshi Ram Monohar Lal.
Pyke, G.H., Pullman and E.L. Charnov
1977 · "Optimal Foraging: A Selective Review of Theory and Tests." *Quarterly Review of Biology* 52: 137–154.
Raj, K.N.
1969   "Investment in Livestock in Agrarian Economies: An Analysis of Some Issues Concerning 'Sacred Cows' and 'Surplus Cattle.'" *Indian Economic Review* 4: 1–33.
1971   "India's Sacred Cattle: Theories and Empirical Findings." *Economic and Political Weekly* 6 (March 27): 717–722.
Rao, C.H.H.
1970   "India's 'Surplus' Cattle." *Economic and Political Weekly* 5 (October 3): 1649–1651.
Rappaport, Roy
1967   *Pigs for the Ancestors.* New Haven: Yale University Press.
Renfrew, Colin
1973   *Before Civilization.* New York: Knopf.
Roberts, John
1951   "Three Navaho Households: A Comparative Study in Small Group Culture." Papers of the Peabody Museum of American Archaeology and Ethnology, vol. 40, no. 3. Cambridge: Harvard University Press.
Roberts, John
1961   "The Zuni." In F. Kluckholn and F. Strodtbeck, eds., *Variations in Value Orientations.* Evanston, Ill.: Row, Peterson, pp. 281–316.
Rodman, Hyman
1971   *Lower-Class Families: The Culture of Poverty in Negro Trinidad.* New York: Oxford University Press.
Roheim, Geza
1950   *Psychoanalysis and Anthropology.* New York: International Universities Press.
Rohner, Ronald, ed.
1969   *The Ethnography of Franz Boas.* Chicago: University of Chicago Press.
Roosevelt, Anna
1977   *Subsistence and Demography in the Prehistory of Panama.* Ph.D. dissertation, Columbia University.

Rosaldo, M.Z., and L. Lamphere, eds.
1974 *Women, Culture and Society.* Stanford: Stanford University Press.
Ross, Eric
1978 "Food Taboos, Diet and Hunting Strategy: The Adaptation to Animals in Amazon Cultural Ecology." *Current Anthropology* 19: 1–36.
in press "Reply to Lizot." *Current Anthropology.*
Rossi, Ino
1974a "Structuralism as Scientific Method." In Ino Rossi, ed. *The Unconscious in Culture: The Structuralism of Claude Lévi-Strauss in Perspective.* New York: Dutton, pp. 60–106.
1974b "Structure and History in *The Elementary Structures of Kinship.*" In Ino Rossi, ed., *The Unconscious in Culture: The Structuralism of Claude Lévi-Strauss in Perspective.* New York: Dutton, pp. 107–122.
Ruyle, Eugene
1973 "Slavery, Surplus and Stratification on the Northwest Coast: The Ethnoenergetics of an Incipient Stratification System." *Current Anthropology* 14: 603–631.
1975 "Mode of Production and Mode of Exploitation: The Mechanical and the Dialectical." *Dialectical Anthropology* 1: 7–23.
Rus, John
1978 "Bossism and the Civil-Religious Hierarchies of Highland Chiapas." Paper read at the meetings of the American Anthropological Association, Los Angeles, California.
Sahlins, Marshall
1960 "Political Power and the Economy in Primitive Society." In G. Dole and R. Carneiro, eds., *Essays in the Science of Culture In Honor of Leslie White.* New York: T. Y. Crowell, pp. 390–415.
1972 *Stone Age Economics.* Chicago: Aldine.
1973 "Economic Anthropology and Anthropological Economics." In Morton Fried, ed., *Explorations in Anthropology.* New York: T. Y. Crowell, pp. 274–288.
1976 *Culture and Practical Reason.* Chicago: University of Chicago Press.
1978 "Culture as Protein and Profit." *New York Review of Books,* November 23: 45–53.
Sanday, Peggy
1973 "Toward a Theory of the Status of Women." *American Anthropologist* 75: 1682–1700.
Sanders, William T.
1972 "Population, Agricultural History, and Societal Evolution in Mesoamerica." In B. Spooner, ed., *Population Growth: Anthropological Implications.* Cambridge, Mass.: M.I.T. Press, pp. 101–153.

Sanders, William, R. Santley, and J. Parsons
1979 *The Basin of Mexico: The Cultural Ecology of a Civilization*. New
      York: Academic Press.
Schneider, David
1968 *American Kinship: A Cultural Account*. Englewood Cliffs, N.J.:
      Prentice-Hall.
1972 ·"What Is Kinship All About?" In P. Reining, ed., *Kinship Studies
      in the Morgan Centennial Year*. Washington, D.C.: Washington
      Anthropological Society, pp. 32–63.
Schneider, David, and Kathleen Gough, eds.
1961 *Matrilineal Kinship*. Berkeley: University of California Press.
Schneider, Harold
1957 "The Subsistence Cattle Among the Pakot and in East Africa."
      American Anthropologist 59: 278–300.
Scholte, Bob
1972 "Toward a Reflexive and Critical Anthropology." In Dell Hymes,
      ed., *Reinventing Anthropology*. New York: Random House, pp.
      430–457.
Schutz, Alfred
1967 *The Phenomenology of the Social World*. Evanston, Ill.: Northwest-
      ern University Press.
Scrimshaw, Nevin
1977 "Through a Glass Darkly: Discerning the Practical Implications of
      Human Dietary Protein-Energy Relationships." *Nutritional Re-
      views* 35: 321–337.
Seigel, Jerrold
1978 *Marx's Fate*. Princeton, N.J.: Princeton University Press.
Selsam, Howard, and Harry Martel
1963 *Reader in Marxist Philosophy*. New York: International Publishers.
Service, Elman
1969 "The Prime-Mover of Cultural Evolution." *Southwestern Journal of
      Anthropology* 24: 396–409.
1978 "Classical and Modern Theories of the Origin of Government." In
      R. Cohen and E. Service, eds., *Origins of the State*. Philadelphia:
      Institute for the Study of Human Issues, pp. 21–34.
Shankman, Paul
1969 "Le Rôti et le Bouilli: Lévi-Strauss' Theory of Cannibalism." *Ameri-
      can Anthropologist* 71: 54–69.
Shils, Edward
1970 "Tradition, Ecology and Institution in the History of Sociology."
      Daedelus 99: 760–825.
Silverman, David
1975 *Reading Castaneda: A Prologue to the Social Sciences*. London:
      Routledge & Kegan Paul.

Sipes, Richard
1973 "War, Sports, and Aggression: An Empirical Test of Two Rival Theories." *American Anthropologist* 75: 64–86.
Skinner, Burrhus F.
1957 *Verbal Behavior.* New York: Appleton-Century-Crofts.
Smith, William R.
1956 *The Religion of the Semites.* New York: Meridian Books.
Spengler, Joseph
1971 *Indian Economic Thought: A Preface to Its History.* Durham, N.C.: Duke University Press.
Steveson, Robert
1968 *Population and Political Systems in Tropical Africa.* New York: Columbia University Press.
Steward, Julian
1938 *Basin-Plateau Aboriginal Socio-Political Groups.* Bureau of American Ethnology Bulletin 120.
Stinchcombe, Arthur
1968 *Constructing Social Theories.* New York: Harcourt Brace Jovanovich.
Storie, S., and J. Gould
1973 *Bella Bella Stories Told by the People of Bella Bella.* British Columbia Advisory Committee Project, 1968–1969. Victoria, B.C.: Indian Advisory Committee.
Sturtevant, William
1964 "Studies in Ethnoscience." *American Anthropologist* 66 (pt. 2): 99–131.
Sukenick, Ronald
1976 "Upward and Juanward: The Possible Dream." In Daniel Noel, ed., *Seeing Castaneda: Reactions to the "Don Juan" Writings of Carlos Castaneda.* New York: Putnam, pp. 110–120.
Suppe, Frederick, ed.
1977 *The Structure of Scientific Theories,* 2nd ed. Urbana: University of Illinois Press.
Thomas, David H.
1972 "A Computer Simulation Model of Great Basin Shoshonean Subsistence and Settlement Patterns." In David L. Clarke, ed., *Models in Archaeology.* London: Methuen and Company, pp. 671–704.
Thomas, L.L., and J. Kronenfeld and D. Kronenfeld
1976 "Asdiwal Crumbles: A Critique of Lévi-Strauss on Myth Analysis." *American Ethnologist* 3: 147–174.
Tiger, Lionel
1970 *Men in Groups.* New York: Vintage.
Time Magazine
1976 "Don Juan and the Sorcerer's Apprentice." In Daniel Noel, ed., *Seeing Castaneda.* New York: Capricorn, pp. 93–109.

Trigger, Bruce
1978 "Iroquois Matriliny." *Pennsylvania Archaeologist* 48: 55–65.
Trussel, James
1978 "Menarche and Fatness: Re-examination of the Critical Body Composition Hypothesis." *Science* 200: 1506–1509.
Turner, Brian
1974 "An Unknown Durkheimian Text." Unpublished manuscript.
1977 *The Social Origins of Academic Sociology: Durkheim.* Ph.D. dissertation, Columbia University.
Tyler, S.
1969 *Cognitive Anthropology* (Introduction). New York: Holt, Rinehart and Winston.
Tylor, E.B.
1871 *Primitive Culture: Researches into the Development of Mythology, Philosophy, Religion, Language, Art and Custom.* London: J. Murray.
Van Ginneken, J.K.
1974 "Prolonged Breastfeeding as a Birth-Spacing Method." *Studies in Family Planning* 5: 201–208.
Vayda, A., A. Leeds, and D. Smith
1961 "The Place of Pigs in Melanesian Subsistance." In Viola Garfield, ed., *Proceedings of the American Ethnological Society.* Seattle: University of Washington.
Wagley, Charles
1963 *An Introduction to Brazil.* New York: Columbia University Press.
Walder, Andrew
1977 "Marxism, Maoism and Social Change." *Modern China* 3:125–160.
Wallerstein, Emanuel
1974 *The Modern World-System.* New York: Academic Press.
Walsh, Maurice, and B. Scandalis
1975 "Institutionalized Forms of Intergenerational Male Aggression." In M. Nettleship, R. Dalegivens, and A. Nettleship, eds., *War, Its Causes and Correlates.* The Hague: Mouton, pp. 135–155.
Wasserstrom, Robert
1978 "Religious Service in Zinacantan." Paper read at the 1978 meetings of the American Anthropological Association, Los Angeles, California.
Webb, Malcom
1975 "The Flag Follows Trade: An Essay on the Necessary Integration of Military and Commercial Factors in State Formation." In Jeremy Sabloff and C.C. Lamberg Karlovsky, eds., *Ancient Civilization and Trade.* Albuquerque: University of New Mexico Press, pp. 155–209.
Webster, David
1975 "Warfare and the Evolution of the State." *American Antiquity* 40: 464–470.

Werner, Oswald
1973 "Structural Anthropology." In R. Naroll and F. Naroll, eds. *Main Currents in Anthropology.* New York: Appleton-Century-Crofts, pp. 281–307.
White, Benjamin
1976 "The Economic Importance of Children in a Javanese Village." In Moni Nag, ed., *Population and Social Organization.* The Hague: Mouton, pp. 127–146.
White, Douglas
1973 "Mathematical Anthropology." In John Honigmann, ed., *Handbook of Social and Cultural Anthropology.* Chicago: Rand McNally, pp. 369–446.
Whiting, John
1969 "Effects of Climate on Certain Cultural Practices." In A.P. Vayda, ed., *Environment and Cultural Behavior.* Garden City, N.Y.: Natural History Press, pp. 416–455.
Whorf, Benjamin
1956 *Language, Thought, and Reality.* New York: Wiley.
Whyte, R.D.
1961 "Evolution of Land Use in South-Western Asia." In L.D. Stamp, ed., *A History of Land Use in Arid Regions.* UNESCO Arid Zone Research 17:14.
Wilder, William
1971 "Purum Descent Groups: Some Vagaries of Method." In Rodney Needham, ed., *Rethinking Kinship and Marriage.* London: Tavistock, pp. 203–218.
Wilkinson, Richard
1973 *Poverty and Progress: An Ecological Perspective on Economic Development.* New York: Praeger.
Willer, David, and Judith Willer
1973 *Systematic Empiricism: Critique of a Pseudoscience.* Englewood Cliffs, N.J.: Prentice-Hall.
Willis, William
1972 "Skeletons in the Anthropological Closet." In Dell Hymes, ed., *Reinventing Anthropology.* New York: Random House, pp. 121–152.
Wilson, E.O.
1975 *Sociobiology: The New Synthesis.* Cambridge: Harvard University Press.
1977 "Biology and the Social Sciences" *Daedalus* 106 (4): 127–140.
Wilson, E.O., and Marvin Harris
1978 "The Envelope and the Twig." *The Sciences* 18: 10–15, 27.
Wilson, Thomas
1970 "Normative and Interpretive Paradigms in Sociology." In Jack Douglas, ed., *Understanding Everyday Life.* Chicago: Aldine, pp. 57–79.

Winterhalder, Bruce
  1977   *Foraging Strategy Alternatives of the Boreal Forest Cree: An Evaluation of Theories and Models from Evolutionary Ecology.* Ph.D dissertation, Cornell University.
Wissler, Clark
  1923   *Man and Culture.* New York: T.Y. Crowell.
  1926   *The Relation of Nature to Man in Aboriginal America.* New York: Oxford University Press.
Wittfogel, Karl
  1957   *Oriental Despotism: A Comparative Study of Total Power.* New Haven: Yale University Press.
  1972   "The Hydraulic Approach to Pre-Spanish Mesoamerica." In Richard MacNeish, ed., *Chronology and Irrigation. The Prehistory of the Tehuacan Valley,* Vol. IV. Andover: Robert S. Peabody Foundation; and Austin: University of Texas Press.
Wolf, Eric R.
  1972   "American Anthropologists and American Society." In Dell Hymes, ed., *Reinventing Anthropology.* New York: Random House, pp. 251–263.
Wolf, Eric, and Joseph Jorgenson
  1970   "Anthropologists on the Warpath." *New York Review of Books,* November 19: 26–35.
Wolff, Kurt H.
  1972   "This Is the Time for Radical Anthropology." In Dell Hymes, ed., *Reinventing Anthropology.* New York: Random House, pp. 99–115.
Wu Chiang
  1978   "The Tasks of Continuing the Revolution Under the Dictatorship of the Proletariat." *Peking Review* 3: 5–9.
Zohary, Daniel, and M. Hopf
  1973   "Domestication of Pulses in the Old World." *Science* 182: 887–894.

Index